studysync

Student Edition
American Literature Volume 2

UNITS 4–6

studysync

studysync.com

Copyright © BookheadEd Learning, LLC
All Rights Reserved.

Send all inquiries to:
BookheadEd Learning, LLC
610 Daniel Young Drive
Sonoma, CA 95476

No part of this publication may be reproduced or transmitted in any form, by any means, electronic or mechanical, including photocopy, recording, or utilized by any information storage or retrieval system, without written permission from BookheadEd Learning, LLC.

ISBN 978-1-97-016274-5

1 2 3 4 5 6 LWI 24 23 22 21 20

A

Contents

VOLUME 2

Our Lives, Our Fortunes
How do ideologies affect our lives?

UNIT 4

xi

Life, Liberty, and the Pursuit of Happiness
How do our goals inform our actions?

UNIT 5

169

We Hold These Truths
How do stories capture change?

UNIT 6

329

Please note that excerpts and passages in the StudySync® library and this workbook are intended as touchstones to generate interest in an author's work. The excerpts and passages do not substitute for the reading of entire texts, and StudySync® strongly recommends that students seek out and purchase the whole literary or informational work in order to experience it as the author intended. Links to online resellers are available in our digital library. In addition, complete works may be ordered through an authorized reseller by filling out and returning to StudySync® the order form enclosed in this workbook.

Reading & Writing Companion

Student Guide

Getting Started

Welcome to the StudySync Reading & Writing Companion! In this book, you will find a collection of readings based on the literary focus of the unit you are studying. As you work through the readings, you will be asked to answer questions and perform a variety of tasks designed to help you closely analyze and understand each text selection. Read on for an explanation of each section of this book.

Close Reading and Writing Routine

In each unit, you will read texts and text excerpts that are from or are in some way connected to a particular period of American literature. Each reading encourages a closer look through questions and a short writing assignment.

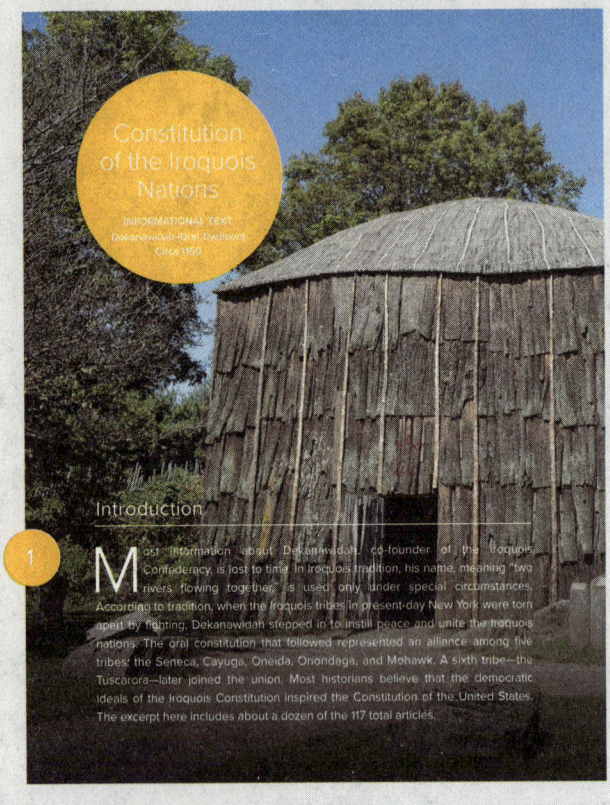

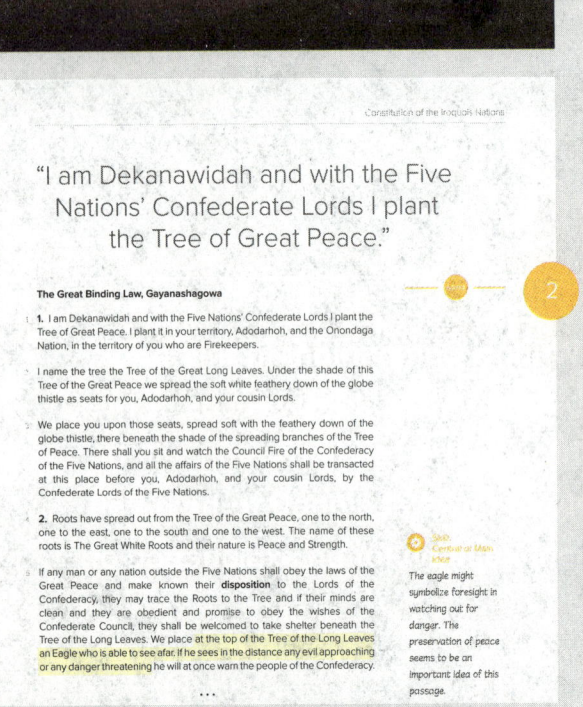

1 Introduction

An Introduction to each text provides historical context for your reading as well as information about the author. You will also learn about the genre of the text and the year in which it was written.

2 Notes

Many times, while working through the activities after each text, you will be asked to **annotate** or **make annotations** about what you are reading. This means that you should highlight or underline words in the text and use the "Notes" column to make comments or jot down any questions you have. You may also want to note any unfamiliar vocabulary words here.

You will also see sample student annotations to go along with the Skill lesson for that text.

Reading & Writing Companion

3 First Read

During your first reading of each selection, you should just try to get a general idea of the content and message of the reading. Don't worry if there are parts you don't understand or words that are unfamiliar to you. You'll have an opportunity later to dive deeper into the text.

4 Think Questions

These questions will ask you to start thinking critically about the text, asking specific questions about its purpose, and making connections to your prior knowledge and reading experiences. To answer these questions, you should go back to the text and draw upon specific evidence to support your responses. You will also begin to explore some of the more challenging vocabulary words in the selection.

5 Skills

Each Skill includes two parts: Checklist and Your Turn. In the Checklist, you will learn the process for analyzing the text. The model student annotations in the text provide examples of how you might make your own notes following the instructions in the Checklist. In the Your Turn, you will use those same instructions to practice the skill.

Reading & Writing Companion

vii

Close Read & Skills Focus

After you have completed the First Read, you will be asked to go back and read the text more closely and critically. Before you begin your Close Read, you should read through the Skills Focus to get an idea of the concepts you will want to focus on during your second reading. You should work through the Skills Focus by making annotations, highlighting important concepts, and writing notes or questions in the "Notes" column. Depending on instructions from your teacher, you may need to respond online or use a separate piece of paper to start expanding on your thoughts and ideas.

Write

Your study of each selection will end with a writing assignment. For this assignment, you should use your notes, annotations, personal ideas, and answers to both the Think and the Skills Focus questions. Be sure to read the prompt carefully and address each part of it in your writing.

Extended Writing Project and Grammar

This is your opportunity to use genre characteristics and craft to compose meaningful, longer written works exploring the theme of each unit. You will draw information from your readings, research, and own life experiences to complete the assignment.

1 Writing Project

After you have read all of the unit text selections, you will move on to a writing project. Each project will guide you through the process of writing your essay. Student models will provide guidance and help you organize your thoughts. One unit ends with an **Extended Oral Project,** which will give you an opportunity to develop your oral language and communication skills.

2 Writing Process Steps

There are four steps in the writing process: Plan, Draft, Revise, and Edit and Publish. During each step, you will form and shape your writing project, and each lesson's peer review will give you the chance to receive feedback from your peers and teacher.

3 Writing Skills

Each Skill lesson focuses on a specific strategy or technique that you will use during your writing project. Each lesson presents a process for applying the skill to your own work and gives you the opportunity to practice it to improve your writing.

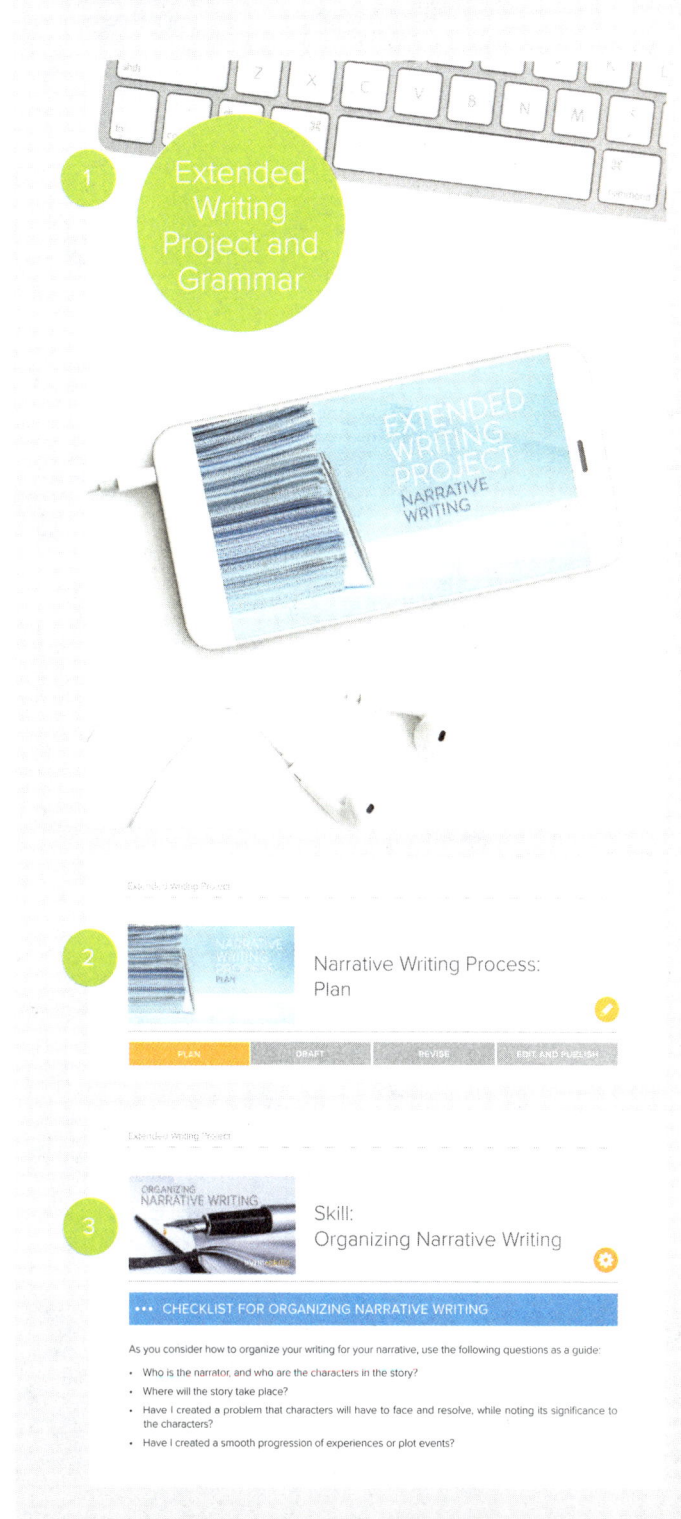

studysync

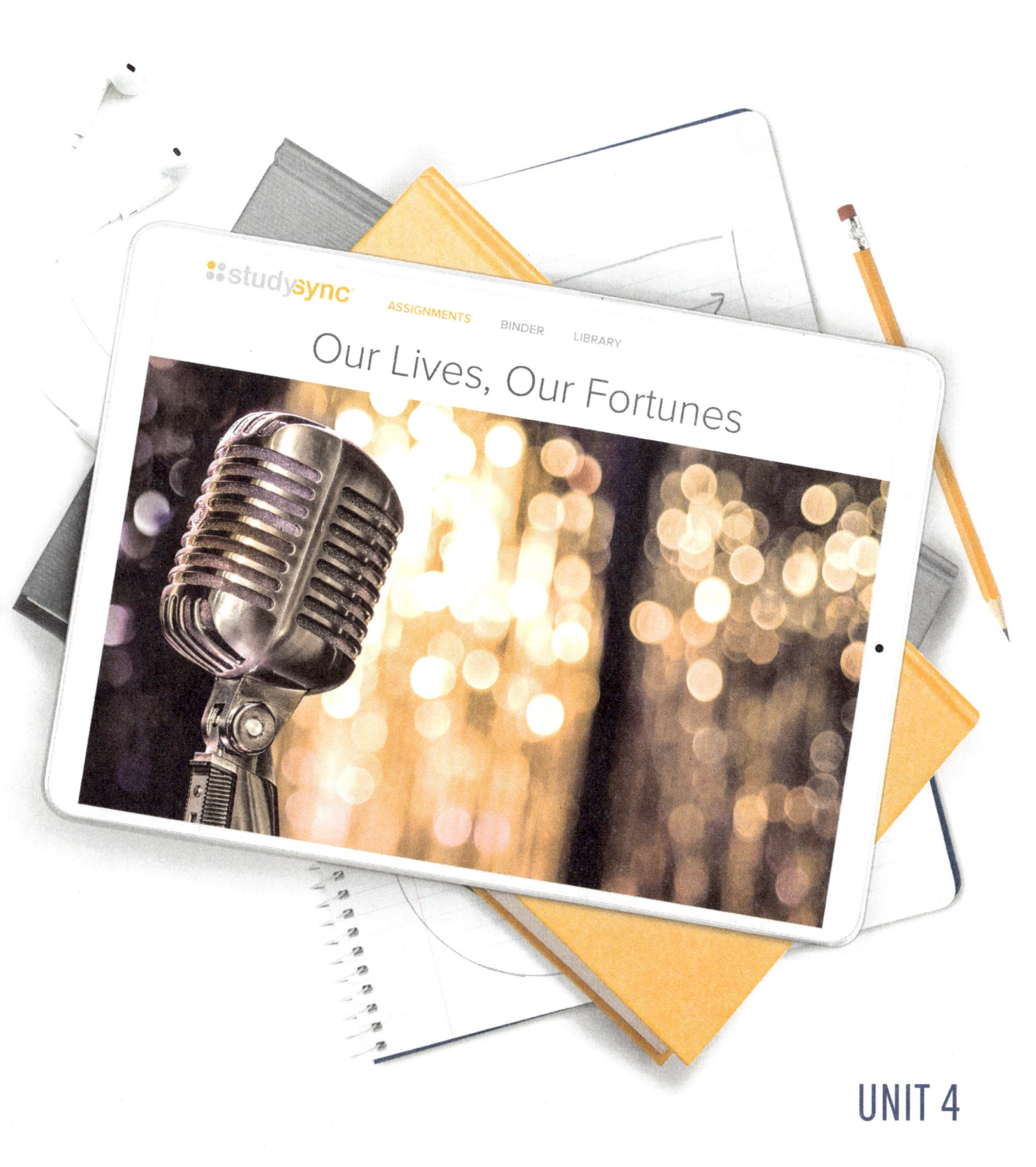

Our Lives, Our Fortunes

UNIT 4

Our Lives, Our Fortunes

How do ideologies affect our lives?

Literary Focus: **AMERICAN MODERNISM AND THE HARLEM RENAISSANCE**

Texts

Paired Readings

1	Literary Focus: **AMERICAN MODERNISM**	
6	The Yellow Wallpaper FICTION Charlotte Perkins Gilman	
29	The Story of an Hour FICTION Kate Chopin	
39	"These Wild Young People" by One of Them ARGUMENTATIVE TEXT John F. Carter Jr.	
46	The Great Gatsby FICTION F. Scott Fitzgerald	
55	A Farewell to Arms FICTION Ernest Hemingway	
60	A Rose for Emily FICTION William Faulkner	
70	Literary Focus: **THE HARLEM RENAISSANCE**	
78	Literary Seminar: Alain Locke and the Harlem Renaissance	
84	In Our Neighborhood FICTION Alice Dunbar-Nelson	
92	The Old Cabin POETRY Paul Laurence Dunbar	
96	The Negro Speaks of Rivers POETRY Langston Hughes	
99	The Color of an Awkward Conversation Talk Back Text INFORMATIONAL TEXT Chimamanda Ngozi Adichie	
103	How It Feels to Be Colored Me INFORMATIONAL TEXT Zora Neale Hurston	
116	Invisible Man FICTION Ralph Ellison	

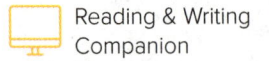

Extended Writing Project and Grammar

125   Research Writing Process: Plan

Planning Research
Evaluating Sources
Research and Notetaking

143   Research Writing Process: Draft

Critiquing Research
Paraphrasing
Sources and Citations
Print and Graphic Features

158   Research Writing Process: Revise

Using a Style Guide
Grammar: Contested Usage
Grammar: Hyphens

166   Research Writing Process: Edit and Publish

Talk Back Texts are works from a later period that engage with the themes and tropes of the unit's literary focus. Demonstrating that literature is always in conversation, these texts provide dynamic new perspectives to complement the unit's more traditional chronology.

Unit 4: Our Lives, Our Fortunes
How do ideologies affect our lives?

CHIMAMANDA NGOZI ADICHIE

Chimamanda Ngozi Adichie (b. 1977) grew up in Nigeria and studied medicine at the University of Nigeria before leaving for the United States to study communications and political science in Philadelphia at Drexel University. She later completed a master's degree from Johns Hopkins University and received a master of arts in African Studies from Yale University. Her novel *Americanah* (2013) was selected as one of "The 10 Best Books of 2013," and won the National Book Critics Circle Award for Fiction. She was awarded a MacArthur Fellowship in 2008.

JOHN F. CARTER JR.

John Franklin Carter Jr. (1897–1967) grew up in Fall River, Massachusetts, and attended Yale University. A prolific writer, Carter wrote everything from detective novels to presidential speeches. Carter also wrote a twelve-year syndicated column entitled "We, the People," under the pseudonym Jay Franklin, in which he predicted the then-unexpected victory of Harry S Truman in the 1948 presidential election.

KATE CHOPIN

A popular short story writer, Kate Chopin (1850–1904) sparked controversy with the publication of her novel *The Awakening* in 1899. Though it was consistent with much of her previous work that probed the inner lives of strong, independent female characters, the novel scandalized audiences with its frank depiction of female sexuality. Married at age twenty, Chopin moved from St. Louis, Missouri, to Louisiana, where most of her stories are set. She began to write only after being widowed at the age of thirty-one.

PAUL LAURENCE DUNBAR

Born the son of freed slaves from Kentucky, Paul Laurence Dunbar (1872–1906) published his first poem before he graduated from high school. Dunbar briefly worked as an editor for the *Dayton Tattler*, a newspaper published by classmate Orville Wright. Unable to afford law school and rejected by newspapers because of the color of his skin, Dunbar became an elevator operator. He wrote in his spare time, self-published the collection *Oak and Ivy*, published poems and essays in newspapers nationwide, and eventually achieved international acclaim.

ALICE DUNBAR-NELSON

Activist and author Alice Dunbar-Nelson (1875–1936) was born in New Orleans, Louisiana, and began her schoolteacher career after graduating Straight University in 1892. Three years later, she published her first collection of short stories and poems, *Violets and Other Tales*. She later became politically active and helped organize for the women's suffrage movement. In 1918 she worked for the Women's Committee of the Council of Defense, and in 1924 she campaigned for the Dyer Anti-Lynching Bill. She died in Philadelphia at the age of sixty.

RALPH ELLISON

Ralph Waldo Ellison (1914–1994) is best known for his novel *Invisible Man*, which won the National Book Award. He was born in Oklahoma City, Oklahoma, attended the Tuskegee Institute in Alabama, and then moved to New York City. There, he lived at a YMCA on 135th Street in Harlem and met Langston Hughes and Richard Wright. He was not drafted into World War II but did enlist in the United States Merchant Marine. Later, he made money writing book reviews but focused on writing *Invisible Man*. He died of pancreatic cancer at the age of eighty-one.

WILLIAM FAULKNER

Nobel Prize–winning author, screenwriter, and two-time winner of the Pulitzer Prize, William Faulkner (1897–1962) was born in Mississippi. He never graduated from high school, but due to his World War I service, he was able to attend the University of Mississippi. Faulkner published his first novel in 1927 to mixed reviews. His next two novels were poorly received, and his publisher dropped him. Penniless, Faulkner began what would become his fourth novel, *The Sound and the Fury*. His short story "A Rose for Emily" was published the next year.

F. SCOTT FITZGERALD

Author of *This Side of Paradise* and *The Great Gatsby*, F. Scott Fitzgerald (1896–1940) was raised mostly in upstate New York. While attending Princeton University, Fitzgerald was placed on academic probation; he dropped out and joined the army and was commissioned as a second lieutenant just before World War I ended. While stationed at Camp Sheridan in Alabama, he met his future wife, Zelda Sayre, beginning a dramatic courtship that took them from New York City, Paris, and the French Riviera into the salons of the artistic expatriate community.

CHARLOTTE PERKINS GILMAN

After giving birth to her first child, Charlotte Perkins Gilman (1860–1935) documented her depression in her diary. Her doctor prescribed the Rest Cure, which included having her child with her all the time, limiting "intellectual life" to two hours a day, and never writing again. Gilman's anxiety and depression and the prescribed cure inspired her short story "The Yellow Wallpaper." Her depression lifted when she divorced her husband and moved to California. She became involved in the feminist and women's suffrage movements and lectured across the country.

ERNEST HEMINGWAY

During World War I, eighteen-year-old American Ernest Hemingway (1899–1961) was posted to the Italian front as an ambulance driver. After suffering an injury during the war, Hemingway made his way to Paris, where he befriended a group of American expatriate authors and artists. Under their influence, Hemingway developed what have become some of the most celebrated novels and short stories in American fiction. In his 1929 novel *A Farewell to Arms*, Hemingway drew from his wartime experiences as a young man.

LANGSTON HUGHES

When his parents divorced and his father fled to Mexico, Langston Hughes (1902–1967) lived with his grandmother in Lawrence, Kansas, while his mother traveled to find work. Of that time, Hughes noted in his 1940 autobiography *The Big Sea*, "I began to believe in nothing but books and the wonderful world in books—where if people suffered, they suffered in beautiful language, not in monosyllables, as we did in Kansas." Hughes attended Columbia University and sailed around West Africa before becoming a leader of the Harlem Renaissance.

ZORA NEALE HURSTON

When Zora Neale Hurston (1891–1960) was growing up in the all-black town of Eatonville, Florida, she only encountered white people when they passed through the town on their way to or from Orlando. Hurston studied anthropology at Howard, Barnard, and Columbia before dedicating herself to literature. These educational experiences later informed her writing on race and identity. Referencing her time at Barnard, she wrote, "I feel most colored when I am thrown against a sharp white background."

LITERARY FOCUS: American Modernism

Introduction

This informational text provides readers with cultural and historical information about the time period that gave rise to American Modernism. American Modernism was a literary movement that sought to rebel against the values of the Romantic and Victorian eras. Writers such as Ezra Pound, William Faulkner, Gertrude Stein, and F. Scott Fitzgerald were part of a generation of creative minds that were wearied by the violence and horror of World War I. Their disillusionment led them to experiment with new forms and themes in their work, leading to classics such as *The Great Gatsby* and *As I Lay Dying*. Discover how the volatility of the time period led to innovative writing techniques that came to define American Modernism.

Literary Focus: American Modernism

"The Great War had shattered people's perceptions of the world."

1   When you were a small child, you probably thought your parents knew everything and could do anything. When you became a teenager, however, things changed. Suddenly, adults didn't seem so brilliant and amazing. They may have even seemed stubborn and foolish. Even worse is the realization when you become an adult that the certainty you once thought all adults naturally possessed is suddenly nowhere to be found. These rude awakenings capture the feelings of Modernism (1914–1945), a movement of writers and artists who realized that traditional artistic conventions had little to offer when it came to finding meaning in a world suddenly and violently thrust into modernity after global war.

After the Great War

American airforce personnel loading shells into the back of a lorry, circa 1917.

2   On June 28, 1914, a Bosnian Serb named Gavrilo Princip shot and killed Archduke Franz Ferdinand, heir presumptive of the Austrian-Hungarian Empire. There had been tensions and smaller conflicts for years, and the

Literary Focus: American Modernism

assassination set off a chain of war declarations as nations pledged to support their allies or oppose their enemies. Thus began a war of unprecedented scale: a World War. When America entered the Great War, or, as we now call it, **World War I**, in 1917, they found a new type of warfare. Machine guns, mustard gas, tanks, airplanes, submarines, and other advancements changed the way wars were fought. Young soldiers who grew up hearing tales of glory instead found chaos and brutality. The Great War showed that the world was not as beautiful and polite as the Romantics and Victorians had claimed. Soldiers, women, young people, and others were disillusioned with traditional values, and a growing artistic movement spoke to the desire to rebel against tradition: Modernism.

3   Many works that are considered examples of early Modernism come from Europe, but the movement quickly spread to America thanks in large part to the **Lost Generation**. The term, usually credited to writer Gertrude Stein, often signifies a group of American writers who lived in Europe after the war. This included Stein herself, Ernest Hemingway, F. Scott Fitzgerald, Ezra Pound, T. S. Eliot, and many others.

Ernest Hemingway Returning from Spain
Ernest Hemingway, noted writer, pictured aboard the S.S. Normandie, on arrival in New York City, May 18th. He returned from Spain where he spent ten weeks reporting the war.

4   Many of these **expatriates** flocked to Paris. Here, they wrote and painted and composed. Their work was popular both in Europe and in America. Ironically, some of the most influential works of American literature were being written outside of America.

Breaking Boundaries

5. Modernism did not just break national boundaries. Modernist writers looked for ways to break other conventions. They experimented with different styles and forms, like nontraditional plot lines, fragmented reality, and an absence of third-person omniscient narration. In Europe, Virginia Woolf, James Joyce, and Dorothy Richardson leveraged a technique called stream of consciousness. American author William Faulkner used this technique in his books *The Sound and the Fury* and *As I Lay Dying*. Stream of consciousness is a type of first-person narration. It seeks to mimic the actual flow of our thoughts, which are usually not so organized and grammatically accurate as literature tends to be.

6. Traditionally, earlier literature reflected the common belief that the poor and struggling had done something to deserve their hardships. Modernists challenged this concept of moral order and broke conventions, often by being critical of religion and society and writing about flawed and inadequate protagonists. This is not to say that their writing was always realistic. Modernists rebelled against realism because they believed its themes and settings were too limited.

7. Like all major movements Modernism had smaller sub-movements. **Imagism** is perhaps the best-known sub-movement within Modernist poetry. Prominent Modernist Ezra Pound was a leader of Imagism and promoted the form. In contrast to previous styles of poetry, Imagism offers little guidance to the reader. Instead, an Imagist seeks to present an image and leave the interpretation to the reader. The speaker of the poem is kept unobtrusive and adjectives are used sparingly. Imagist poems are generally in free verse but use a steady rhythm, which helps to distinguish them from regular prose.

8. **Major Concepts**
   - **Irony**—Many people today use *ironic* to say something is coincidental, curious, or even comical. Its actual meaning is "unexpected." A villainous character who becomes the hero of a story, for example, would be ironic. Since so much of Modernism was about subverting literary and social norms, **irony** became a major feature of the movement.

   - **Rejection of Tradition**—Modernism often rejected traditional beliefs and ideas. Character traits, plotlines, and even the conventions of grammar would be used in unconventional ways. Experimental styles and forms were favored. One of the problems in defining Modernism is that, by its nature, it seeks to break rules.

   - **Alienation**—Modernist protagonists often have a strong sense of alienation, or isolation from the world. Since Modernism rejects certain aspects of society, it is natural that the character, in turn, feels out of place

Literary Focus: American Modernism

in and rejected by society. This feeling of alienation is powerfully exemplified in the character of Jay Gatsby in F. Scott Fitzgerald's *The Great Gatsby*.

9   **Style and Form**
- American Modernist poetry pushed the boundaries of subject matter, form, and style. Poets found inspiration in a wide variety of sources and sought new ways of capturing individual experiences.

- Modernist fiction writers broke from literary tradition. They flouted conventions of grammar, and omitted standard beginnings, transitions, and endings in order to tell stories that reproduced the complex ways in which people think. Ernest Hemingway's short story, "Out of Season," for example, is a Modernist story that has a non-standard beginning and ending.

- Stream of consciousness, which tries to reflect the chaotic flow of thoughts in a person's mind, is a popular Modernist technique.

10 The Great War had shattered people's perceptions of the world. The old powers in Europe had weakened and America was starting to take its place as a world superpower. New technology and ideas had changed the status quo. Modernism was a new movement for a new world. What are examples of popular art or literature that don't follow the typical rules?

Literary Focus

Read "Literary Focus: American Modernism." After you read, complete the Think Questions below.

THINK QUESTIONS

1. What was the significance of World War I for the Modernist movement? Support your response with evidence from the text.

2. How is stream-of-consciousness similar to first-person point of view, and how is it different? Support your response with evidence from the text.

3. What is unusual about Imagism? Support your response with evidence from the text.

4. Use context clues to determine the meaning of the term **Lost Generation**. Write your best definition, along with the words and phrases that were most helpful in determining the meaning of the term. Then, check an encyclopedia to confirm your understanding.

5. The word **expatriate** likely stems from the Latin *ex-*, meaning "away," and *patria*, or "native country." With this information in mind and using context clues from the text, write your best definition of the word *expatriate* as it is used in this text. Cite any words or phrases that were particularly helpful in coming to your conclusion.

The Yellow Wallpaper

FICTION
Charlotte Perkins Gilman
1892

Introduction

Charlotte Perkins Gilman (1860–1935) was an American author and social reformer. She wrote her best-known short story, "The Yellow Wallpaper," after being ordered by her doctor to take a "rest cure" to recover from depression. The result of three months of desperate boredom, this story was sent by Gilman to her doctor as a critique of the sexism in the medical establishment. "The Yellow Wallpaper" follows a sickly wife who has grown bored while on bed rest in the nursery room of a rambling mansion. With a secret journal as her only distraction, she documents an increasing obsession with the wallpaper

"... these nervous troubles are dreadfully depressing."

1. It is very seldom that mere ordinary people like John and myself secure ancestral halls for the summer.

2. A colonial mansion, a hereditary estate, I would say a haunted house, and reach the height of romantic felicity—but that would be asking too much of fate!

3. Still I will proudly declare that there is something queer about it.

4. Else, why should it be let so cheaply? And why have stood so long untenanted?

Charlotte Perkins Gilman

5. John laughs at me, of course, but one expects that in marriage.

6. John is practical in the extreme. He has no patience with faith, an **intense** horror of superstition, and he scoffs openly at any talk of things not to be felt and seen and put down in figures.

7. John is a physician, and PERHAPS—(I would not say it to a living soul, of course, but this is dead paper and a great relief to my mind)—PERHAPS that is one reason I do not get well faster.

8. You see he does not believe I am sick!

9. And what can one do?

10. If a physician of high standing, and one's own husband, **assures** friends and relatives that there is really nothing the matter with one but temporary nervous depression—a slight hysterical tendency—what is one to do?

11. My brother is also a physician, and also of high standing, and he says the same thing.

12. So I take phosphates or phosphites—whichever it is, and tonics, and journeys, and air, and exercise, and am absolutely forbidden to "work" until I am well again.

13. Personally, I disagree with their ideas.

14. Personally, I believe that congenial work, with excitement and change, would do me good.

15. But what is one to do?

16. I did write for a while in spite of them; but it DOES exhaust me a good deal—having to be so sly about it, or else meet with heavy opposition.

17. I sometimes fancy that in my **condition** if I had less opposition and more society and stimulus—but John says the very worst thing I can do is to think about my condition, and I confess it always makes me feel bad.

18. So I will let it alone and talk about the house.

19. The most beautiful place! It is quite alone, standing well back from the road, quite three miles from the village. It makes me think of English places that you read about, for there are hedges and walls and gates that lock, and lots of separate little houses for the gardeners and people.

20. There is a DELICIOUS garden! I never saw such a garden—large and shady, full of box-bordered paths, and lined with long grape-covered arbors with seats under them.

21. There were greenhouses, too, but they are all broken now.

22. There was some legal trouble, I believe, something about the heirs and coheirs; anyhow, the place has been empty for years.

23. That spoils my ghostliness, I am afraid, but I don't care—there is something strange about the house—I can feel it.

24. I even said so to John one moonlight evening, but he said what I felt was a DRAUGHT, and shut the window.

25. I get unreasonably angry with John sometimes. I'm sure I never used to be so sensitive. I think it is due to this nervous condition.

26. But John says if I feel so, I shall neglect proper self-control; so I take pains to control myself—before him, at least, and that makes me very tired.

27 I don't like our room a bit. I wanted one downstairs that opened on the piazza and had roses all over the window, and such pretty old-fashioned chintz hangings! but John would not hear of it.

28 He said there was only one window and not room for two beds, and no near room for him if he took another.

29 He is very careful and loving, and hardly lets me stir without special direction.

30 I have a schedule prescription for each hour in the day; he takes all care from me, and so I feel basely ungrateful not to value it more.

31 He said we came here solely on my account, that I was to have perfect rest and all the air I could get. "Your exercise depends on your strength, my dear," said he, "and your food somewhat on your appetite; but air you can absorb all the time." So we took the nursery at the top of the house.

32 It is a big, airy room, the whole floor nearly, with windows that look all ways, and air and sunshine galore. It was nursery first and then playroom and gymnasium, I should judge; for the windows are barred for little children, and there are rings and things in the walls.

33 The paint and paper look as if a boys' school had used it. It is stripped off—the paper—in great patches all around the head of my bed, about as far as I can reach, and in a great place on the other side of the room low down. I never saw a worse paper in my life.

34 One of those sprawling flamboyant patterns committing every artistic sin.

35 It is dull enough to confuse the eye in following, pronounced enough to constantly irritate and provoke study, and when you follow the lame uncertain curves for a little distance they suddenly commit suicide—plunge off at outrageous angles, destroy themselves in unheard of contradictions.

36 The color is repellent, almost revolting; a smouldering unclean yellow, strangely faded by the slow-turning sunlight.

37 It is a dull yet lurid orange in some places, a sickly sulphur tint in others.

38 No wonder the children hated it! I should hate it myself if I had to live in this room long. There comes John, and I must put this away,—he hates to have me write a word.

. . .

The Yellow Wallpaper

39 We have been here two weeks, and I haven't felt like writing before, since that first day.

40 I am sitting by the window now, up in this atrocious nursery, and there is nothing to hinder my writing as much as I please, save lack of strength.

41 John is away all day, and even some nights when his cases are serious.

42 I am glad my case is not serious!

43 But these nervous troubles are dreadfully depressing.

44 John does not know how much I really suffer. He knows there is no REASON to suffer, and that satisfies him.

45 Of course it is only nervousness. It does weigh on me so not to do my duty in any way!

46 I meant to be such a help to John, such a real rest and comfort, and here I am a comparative burden already!

47 Nobody would believe what an effort it is to do what little I am able,—to dress and entertain, and order things.

48 It is fortunate Mary is so good with the baby. Such a dear baby!

49 And yet I CANNOT be with him, it makes me so nervous.

50 I suppose John never was nervous in his life. He laughs at me so about this wall-paper!

51 At first he meant to repaper the room, but afterwards he said that I was letting it get the better of me, and that nothing was worse for a nervous patient than to give way to such fancies.

52 He said that after the wall-paper was changed it would be the heavy bedstead, and then the barred windows, and then that gate at the head of the stairs, and so on.

53 "You know the place is doing you good," he said, "and really, dear, I don't care to **renovate** the house just for a three months' rental."

54 "Then do let us go downstairs," I said, "there are such pretty rooms there."

Skill: Connotation and Denotation

The use of the word "fancies" seems to have a negative connotation here. The use of this word in the context suggests that the husband is belittling the wife's requests.

55. Then he took me in his arms and called me a blessed little goose, and said he would go down to the cellar, if I wished, and have it whitewashed into the bargain.

56. But he is right enough about the beds and windows and things.

57. It is an airy and comfortable room as any one need wish, and, of course, I would not be so silly as to make him uncomfortable just for a whim.

58. I'm really getting quite fond of the big room, all but that horrid paper.

59. Out of one window I can see the garden, those mysterious deepshaded arbors, the riotous old-fashioned flowers, and bushes and gnarly trees.

60. Out of another I get a lovely view of the bay and a little private wharf belonging to the estate. There is a beautiful shaded lane that runs down there from the house. I always fancy I see people walking in these numerous paths and arbors, but John has cautioned me not to give way to fancy in the least. He says that with my imaginative power and habit of story-making, a nervous weakness like mine is sure to lead to all manner of excited fancies, and that I ought to use my will and good sense to check the tendency. So I try.

61. I think sometimes that if I were only well enough to write a little it would relieve the press of ideas and rest me.

62. But I find I get pretty tired when I try.

63. It is so discouraging not to have any advice and companionship about my work. When I get really well, John says we will ask Cousin Henry and Julia down for a long visit; but he says he would as soon put fireworks in my pillow-case as to let me have those stimulating people about now.

64. I wish I could get well faster.

65. But I must not think about that. This paper looks to me as if it KNEW what a vicious influence it had!

66. There is a recurrent spot where the pattern lolls like a broken neck and two bulbous eyes stare at you upside down.

67. I get positively angry with the impertinence of it and the everlastingness. Up and down and sideways they crawl, and those absurd, unblinking eyes are everywhere. There is one place where two breadths didn't match, and the eyes go all up and down the line, one a little higher than the other.

The Yellow Wallpaper

68 I never saw so much expression in an inanimate thing before, and we all know how much expression they have! I used to lie awake as a child and get more entertainment and terror out of blank walls and plain furniture than most children could find in a toy store.

69 I remember what a kindly wink the knobs of our big, old bureau used to have, and there was one chair that always seemed like a strong friend.

70 I used to feel that if any of the other things looked too fierce I could always hop into that chair and be safe.

71 The furniture in this room is no worse than inharmonious, however, for we had to bring it all from downstairs. I suppose when this was used as a playroom they had to take the nursery things out, and no wonder! I never saw such ravages as the children have made here.

72 The wall-paper, as I said before, is torn off in spots, and it sticketh closer than a brother—they must have had perseverance as well as hatred.

73 Then the floor is scratched and gouged and splintered, the plaster itself is dug out here and there, and this great heavy bed which is all we found in the room, looks as if it had been through the wars.

74 But I don't mind it a bit—only the paper.

75 There comes John's sister. Such a dear girl as she is, and so careful of me! I must not let her find me writing.

76 She is a perfect and enthusiastic housekeeper, and hopes for no better profession. I verily believe she thinks it is the writing which made me sick!

77 But I can write when she is out, and see her a long way off from these windows.

78 There is one that commands the road, a lovely shaded winding road, and one that just looks off over the country. A lovely country, too, full of great elms and velvet meadows.

79 This wall-paper has a kind of sub-pattern in a different shade, a particularly irritating one, for you can only see it in certain lights, and not clearly then.

80 But in the places where it isn't faded and where the sun is just so—I can see a strange, provoking, formless sort of figure, that seems to skulk about behind that silly and conspicuous front design.

81 There's sister on the stairs!

. . .

82. Well, the Fourth of July is over! The people are gone and I am tired out. John thought it might do me good to see a little company, so we just had mother and Nellie and the children down for a week.

83. Of course I didn't do a thing. Jennie sees to everything now.

84. But it tired me all the same.

85. John says if I don't pick up faster he shall send me to Weir Mitchell in the fall.

86. But I don't want to go there at all. I had a friend who was in his hands once, and she says he is just like John and my brother, only more so!

87. Besides, it is such an undertaking to go so far.

88. I don't feel as if it was worth while to turn my hand over for anything, and I'm getting dreadfully fretful and querulous.

89. I cry at nothing, and cry most of the time.

90. Of course I don't when John is here, or anybody else, but when I am alone.

91. And I am alone a good deal just now. John is kept in town very often by serious cases, and Jennie is good and lets me alone when I want her to.

92. So I walk a little in the garden or down that lovely lane, sit on the porch under the roses, and lie down up here a good deal.

93. I'm getting really fond of the room in spite of the wall-paper. Perhaps BECAUSE of the wall-paper.

94. It dwells in my mind so!

95. I lie here on this great immovable bed—it is nailed down, I believe—and follow that pattern about by the hour. It is as good as gymnastics, I assure you. I start, we'll say, at the bottom, down in the corner over there where it has not been touched, and I determine for the thousandth time that I WILL follow that pointless pattern to some sort of a conclusion.

96. I know a little of the principle of design, and I know this thing was not arranged on any laws of radiation, or alternation, or repetition, or symmetry, or anything else that I ever heard of.

97. It is repeated, of course, by the breadths, but not otherwise.

The Yellow Wallpaper

98 Looked at in one way each breadth stands alone, the bloated curves and flourishes—a kind of "debased Romanesque" with delirium tremens—go waddling up and down in isolated columns of fatuity.

99 But, on the other hand, they connect diagonally, and the sprawling outlines run off in great slanting waves of optic horror, like a lot of wallowing seaweeds in full chase.

100 The whole thing goes horizontally, too, at least it seems so, and I exhaust myself in trying to **distinguish** the order of its going in that direction.

101 They have used a horizontal breadth for a frieze, and that adds wonderfully to the confusion.

102 There is one end of the room where it is almost intact, and there, when the crosslights fade and the low sun shines directly upon it, I can almost fancy radiation after all,—the interminable grotesques seem to form around a common centre and rush off in headlong plunges of equal distraction.

103 It makes me tired to follow it. I will take a nap I guess.

104 I don't know why I should write this.

105 I don't want to.

106 I don't feel able.

107 And I know John would think it absurd. But I MUST say what I feel and think in some way—it is such a relief!

108 But the effort is getting to be greater than the relief.

109 Half the time now I am awfully lazy, and lie down ever so much.

110 John says I musn't lose my strength, and has me take cod liver oil and lots of tonics and things, to say nothing of ale and wine and rare meat.

111 Dear John! He loves me very dearly, and hates to have me sick. I tried to have a real earnest reasonable talk with him the other day, and tell him how I wish he would let me go and make a visit to Cousin Henry and Julia.

112 But he said I wasn't able to go, nor able to stand it after I got there; and I did not make out a very good case for myself, for I was crying before I had finished.

113. It is getting to be a great effort for me to think straight. Just this nervous weakness I suppose.

114. And dear John gathered me up in his arms, and just carried me upstairs and laid me on the bed, and sat by me and read to me till it tired my head.

115. He said I was his darling and his comfort and all he had, and that I must take care of myself for his sake, and keep well.

116. He says no one but myself can help me out of it, that I must use my will and self-control and not let any silly fancies run away with me.

117. There's one comfort, the baby is well and happy, and does not have to occupy this nursery with the horrid wall-paper.

118. If we had not used it, that blessed child would have! What a fortunate escape! Why, I wouldn't have a child of mine, an impressionable little thing, live in such a room for worlds.

119. I never thought of it before, but it is lucky that John kept me here after all, I can stand it so much easier than a baby, you see.

120. Of course I never mention it to them any more—I am too wise,—but I keep watch of it all the same.

121. There are things in that paper that nobody knows but me, or ever will.

122. Behind that outside pattern the dim shapes get clearer every day.

123. It is always the same shape, only very numerous.

124. And it is like a woman stooping down and creeping about behind that pattern. I don't like it a bit. I wonder—I begin to think—I wish John would take me away from here!

125. It is so hard to talk with John about my case, because he is so wise, and because he loves me so.

126. But I tried it last night.

127. It was moonlight. The moon shines in all around just as the sun does.

128. I hate to see it sometimes, it creeps so slowly, and always comes in by one window or another.

129. John was asleep and I hated to waken him, so I kept still and watched the moonlight on that undulating wall-paper till I felt creepy.

130. The faint figure behind seemed to shake the pattern, just as if she wanted to get out.

131. I got up softly and went to feel and see if the paper DID move, and when I came back John was awake.

132. "What is it, little girl?" he said. "Don't go walking about like that—you'll get cold."

133. I though it was a good time to talk, so I told him that I really was not gaining here, and that I wished he would take me away.

134. "Why darling!" said he, "our lease will be up in three weeks, and I can't see how to leave before.

135. "The repairs are not done at home, and I cannot possibly leave town just now. Of course if you were in any danger, I could and would, but you really are better, dear, whether you can see it or not. I am a doctor, dear, and I know. You are gaining flesh and color, your appetite is better, I feel really much easier about you."

136. "I don't weigh a bit more," said I, "nor as much; and my appetite may be better in the evening when you are here, but it is worse in the morning when you are away!"

137. "Bless her little heart!" said he with a big hug, "she shall be as sick as she pleases! But now let's improve the shining hours by going to sleep, and talk about it in the morning!"

138. "And you won't go away?" I asked gloomily.

139. "Why, how can I, dear? It is only three weeks more and then we will take a nice little trip of a few days while Jennie is getting the house ready. Really dear you are better!"

140. "Better in body perhaps—" I began, and stopped short, for he sat up straight and looked at me with such a stern, reproachful look that I could not say another word.

141. "My darling," said he, "I beg of you, for my sake and for our child's sake, as well as for your own, that you will never for one instant let that idea enter your mind! There is nothing so dangerous, so fascinating, to a temperament like

yours. It is a false and foolish fancy. Can you not trust me as a physician when I tell you so?"

142 So of course I said no more on that score, and we went to sleep before long. He thought I was asleep first, but I wasn't, and lay there for hours trying to decide whether that front pattern and the back pattern really did move together or separately.

143 On a pattern like this, by daylight, there is a lack of sequence, a defiance of law, that is a constant irritant to a normal mind.

144 The color is hideous enough, and unreliable enough, and infuriating enough, but the pattern is torturing.

145 You think you have mastered it, but just as you get well underway in following, it turns a back-somersault and there you are. It slaps you in the face, knocks you down, and tramples upon you. It is like a bad dream.

146 The outside pattern is a florid arabesque, reminding one of a fungus. If you can imagine a toadstool in joints, an interminable string of toadstools, budding and sprouting in endless convolutions—why, that is something like it.

147 That is, sometimes!

148 There is one marked peculiarity about this paper, a thing nobody seems to notice but myself, and that is that it changes as the light changes.

149 When the sun shoots in through the east window—I always watch for that first long, straight ray—it changes so quickly that I never can quite believe it.

150 That is why I watch it always.

151 By moonlight—the moon shines in all night when there is a moon—I wouldn't know it was the same paper.

152 At night in any kind of light, in twilight, candle light, lamplight, and worst of all by moonlight, it becomes bars! The outside pattern I mean, and the woman behind it is as plain as can be.

153 I didn't realize for a long time what the thing was that showed behind, that dim sub-pattern, but now I am quite sure it is a woman.

154 By daylight she is subdued, quiet. I fancy it is the pattern that keeps her so still. It is so puzzling. It keeps me quiet by the hour.

155 I lie down ever so much now. John says it is good for me, and to sleep all I can.

156 Indeed he started the habit by making me lie down for an hour after each meal.

157 It is a very bad habit I am convinced, for you see I don't sleep.

158 And that cultivates deceit, for I don't tell them I'm awake—O no!

159 The fact is I am getting a little afraid of John.

160 He seems very queer sometimes, and even Jennie has an inexplicable look.

161 It strikes me occasionally, just as a scientific hypothesis,—that perhaps it is the paper!

162 I have watched John when he did not know I was looking, and come into the room suddenly on the most innocent excuses, and I've caught him several times LOOKING AT THE PAPER! And Jennie too. I caught Jennie with her hand on it once.

163 She didn't know I was in the room, and when I asked her in a quiet, a very quiet voice, with the most restrained manner possible, what she was doing with the paper—she turned around as if she had been caught stealing, and looked quite angry—asked me why I should frighten her so!

164 Then she said that the paper stained everything it touched, that she had found yellow smooches on all my clothes and John's, and she wished we would be more careful!

165 Did not that sound innocent? But I know she was studying that pattern, and I am determined that nobody shall find it out but myself!

...

166 Life is very much more exciting now than it used to be. You see I have something more to expect, to look forward to, to watch. I really do eat better, and am more quiet than I was.

167 John is so pleased to see me improve! He laughed a little the other day, and said I seemed to be flourishing in spite of my wall-paper.

168 I turned it off with a laugh. I had no intention of telling him it was BECAUSE of the wall-paper—he would make fun of me. He might even want to take me away.

169 I don't want to leave now until I have found it out. There is a week more, and I think that will be enough.

. . .

170 I'm feeling ever so much better! I don't sleep much at night, for it is so interesting to watch developments; but I sleep a good deal in the daytime.

171 In the daytime it is tiresome and perplexing.

172 There are always new shoots on the fungus, and new shades of yellow all over it. I cannot keep count of them, though I have tried conscientiously.

173 It is the strangest yellow, that wall-paper! It makes me think of all the yellow things I ever saw—not beautiful ones like buttercups, but old foul, bad yellow things.

174 But there is something else about that paper—the smell! I noticed it the moment we came into the room, but with so much air and sun it was not bad. Now we have had a week of fog and rain, and whether the windows are open or not, the smell is here.

175 It creeps all over the house.

176 I find it hovering in the dining-room, skulking in the parlor, hiding in the hall, lying in wait for me on the stairs.

177 It gets into my hair.

178 Even when I go to ride, if I turn my head suddenly and surprise it—there is that smell!

179 Such a peculiar odor, too! I have spent hours in trying to analyze it, to find what it smelled like.

180 It is not bad—at first, and very gentle, but quite the subtlest, most enduring odor I ever met.

181 In this damp weather it is awful, I wake up in the night and find it hanging over me.

182 It used to disturb me at first. I thought seriously of burning the house—to reach the smell.

183 But now I am used to it. The only thing I can think of that it is like is the COLOR of the paper! A yellow smell.

Skill: Connotation and Denotation

Words like "hovering" and "hiding" that often have a neutral connotation take on a more negative connotation here when paired with words like "creeps" and "skulking." Together these words create a sense of fear.

The Yellow Wallpaper

184   There is a very funny mark on this wall, low down, near the mopboard. A streak that runs round the room. It goes behind every piece of furniture, except the bed, a long, straight, even SMOOCH, as if it had been rubbed over and over.

185   I wonder how it was done and who did it, and what they did it for. Round and round and round—round and round and round—it makes me dizzy!

. . .

186   I really have discovered something at last.

187   Through watching so much at night, when it changes so, I have finally found out.

188   The front pattern DOES move—and no wonder! The woman behind shakes it!

189   Sometimes I think there are a great many women behind, and sometimes only one, and she crawls around fast, and her crawling shakes it all over.

190   Then in the very bright spots she keeps still, and in the very shady spots she just takes hold of the bars and shakes them hard.

191   And she is all the time trying to climb through. But nobody could climb through that pattern—it strangles so; I think that is why it has so many heads.

192   They get through, and then the pattern strangles them off and turns them upside down, and makes their eyes white!

193   If those heads were covered or taken off it would not be half so bad.

. . .

194   I think that woman gets out in the daytime!

195   And I'll tell you why—privately—I've seen her!

196   I can see her out of every one of my windows!

197   It is the same woman, I know, for she is always creeping, and most women do not creep by daylight.

198   I see her on that long road under the trees, creeping along, and when a carriage comes she hides under the blackberry vines.

199 I don't blame her a bit. It must be very humiliating to be caught creeping by daylight!

200 I always lock the door when I creep by daylight. I can't do it at night, for I know John would suspect something at once.

201 And John is so queer now, that I don't want to irritate him. I wish he would take another room! Besides, I don't want anybody to get that woman out at night but myself.

202 I often wonder if I could see her out of all the windows at once.

203 But, turn as fast as I can, I can only see out of one at one time.

204 And though I always see her, she MAY be able to creep faster than I can turn!

205 I have watched her sometimes away off in the open country, creeping as fast as a cloud shadow in a high wind.

. . .

206 If only that top pattern could be gotten off from the under one! I mean to try it, little by little.

207 I have found out another funny thing, but I shan't tell it this time! It does not do to trust people too much.

208 There are only two more days to get this paper off, and I believe John is beginning to notice. I don't like the look in his eyes.

209 And I heard him ask Jennie a lot of professional questions about me. She had a very good report to give.

210 She said I slept a good deal in the daytime.

211 John knows I don't sleep very well at night, for all I'm so quiet!

212 He asked me all sorts of questions, too, and pretended to be very loving and kind.

213 As if I couldn't see through him!

214 Still, I don't wonder he acts so, sleeping under this paper for three months.

215 It only interests me, but I feel sure John and Jennie are secretly affected by it.

. . .

The Yellow Wallpaper

216 Hurrah! This is the last day, but it is enough. John is to stay in town over night, and won't be out until this evening.

217 Jennie wanted to sleep with me—the sly thing! but I told her I should undoubtedly rest better for a night all alone.

218 That was clever, for really I wasn't alone a bit! As soon as it was moonlight and that poor thing began to crawl and shake the pattern, I got up and ran to help her.

219 I pulled and she shook, I shook and she pulled, and before morning we had peeled off yards of that paper.

220 A strip about as high as my head and half around the room.

221 And then when the sun came and that awful pattern began to laugh at me, I declared I would finish it to-day!

222 We go away to-morrow, and they are moving all my furniture down again to leave things as they were before.

223 Jennie looked at the wall in amazement, but I told her merrily that I did it out of pure spite at the vicious thing.

224 She laughed and said she wouldn't mind doing it herself, but I must not get tired.

225 How she betrayed herself that time!

226 But I am here, and no person touches this paper but me—not ALIVE!

227 She tried to get me out of the room—it was too patent! But I said it was so quiet and empty and clean now that I believed I would lie down again and sleep all I could; and not to wake me even for dinner—I would call when I woke.

228 So now she is gone, and the servants are gone, and the things are gone, and there is nothing left but that great bedstead nailed down, with the canvas mattress we found on it.

229 We shall sleep downstairs to-night, and take the boat home to-morrow.

230 I quite enjoy the room, now it is bare again.

231. How those children did tear about here!

232. This bedstead is fairly gnawed!

233. But I must get to work.

234. I have locked the door and thrown the key down into the front path.

235. I don't want to go out, and I don't want to have anybody come in, till John comes.

236. I want to astonish him.

237. I've got a rope up here that even Jennie did not find. If that woman does get out, and tries to get away, I can tie her!

238. But I forgot I could not reach far without anything to stand on!

239. This bed will NOT move!

240. I tried to lift and push it until I was lame, and then I got so angry I bit off a little piece at one corner—but it hurt my teeth.

241. Then I peeled off all the paper I could reach standing on the floor. It sticks horribly and the pattern just enjoys it! All those strangled heads and bulbous eyes and waddling fungus growths just shriek with derision!

242. I am getting angry enough to do something desperate. To jump out of the window would be admirable exercise, but the bars are too strong even to try.

243. Besides I wouldn't do it. Of course not. I know well enough that a step like that is improper and might be misconstrued.

244. I don't like to LOOK out of the windows even—there are so many of those creeping women, and they creep so fast.

245. I wonder if they all come out of that wall-paper as I did?

246. But I am securely fastened now by my well-hidden rope—you don't get ME out in the road there!

247. I suppose I shall have to get back behind the pattern when it comes night, and that is hard!

248. It is so pleasant to be out in this great room and creep around as I please!

249 I don't want to go outside. I won't, even if Jennie asks me to.

250 For outside you have to creep on the ground, and everything is green instead of yellow.

251 But here I can creep smoothly on the floor, and my shoulder just fits in that long smooch around the wall, so I cannot lose my way.

252 Why there's John at the door!

253 It is no use, young man, you can't open it!

254 How he does call and pound!

255 Now he's crying for an axe.

256 It would be a shame to break down that beautiful door!

257 "John dear!" said I in the gentlest voice, "the key is down by the front steps, under a plantain leaf!"

258 That silenced him for a few moments.

259 Then he said—very quietly indeed, "Open the door, my darling!"

260 "I can't," said I. "The key is down by the front door under a plantain leaf!"

261 And then I said it again, several times, very gently and slowly, and said it so often that he had to go and see, and he got it of course, and came in. He stopped short by the door.

262 "What is the matter?" he cried. "For God's sake, what are you doing!"

263 I kept on creeping just the same, but I looked at him over my shoulder.

264 "I've got out at last," said I, "in spite of you and Jane. And I've pulled off most of the paper, so you can't put me back!"

265 Now why should that man have fainted? But he did, and right across my path by the wall, so that I had to creep over him every time!

First Read

Read "The Yellow Wallpaper." After you read, complete the Think Questions below.

THINK QUESTIONS

1. What is John's opinion of his wife? Use examples from the text to support your answer.

2. How does the protagonist's mental state change throughout the story? Answer using examples from the text.

3. How do the descriptions of the wallpaper alter as the story goes on? Use examples from the text in your answer.

4. Use context clues to determine the meaning of the word **condition** as it is used in "The Yellow Wallpaper." Write your definition of *condition* here, and explain how you figured it out. Then look up the word in a dictionary and check your definition.

5. Use context clues to determine the meaning of **distinguish**. Then look up the word in a dictionary, and compare your definition with the official definition. Write the definition of *distinguish* here.

The Yellow Wallpaper

Skill:
Connotation and Denotation

Use the Checklist to analyze Connotation and Denotation in "The Yellow Wallpaper." Refer to the sample student annotations about Connotation and Denotation in the text.

••• CHECKLIST FOR CONNOTATION AND DENOTATION

In order to identify the denotative meanings of words, use the following steps:

- ✓ first, note unfamiliar words and phrases; key words used to describe important characters, events, and ideas; or words that inspire an emotional reaction

- ✓ next, determine and note the denotative meanings of words by consulting a reference material such as a dictionary, glossary, or thesaurus

- ✓ finally, analyze nuances in the meanings of words with similar denotations

To better understand the meaning of words and phrases as they are used in a text, including connotative meanings, use the following questions as a guide:

- ✓ What is the genre or subject of the text? Based on context, what do you think the meaning of the word is intended to be?

- ✓ Is your inference the same as or different from the dictionary definition?

- ✓ Does the word create a positive, negative, or neutral emotion?

- ✓ What synonyms or alternative phrasings help you describe the connotative meaning of the word?

To determine the meaning of words and phrases as they are used in a text, including connotative meanings, use the following questions as a guide:

- ✓ What is the denotative meaning of the word? Is that denotative meaning correct in context?

- ✓ What possible positive, neutral, or negative connotations might the word have, depending on context?

- ✓ What textual details signal a particular connotation for the word?

Skill: Connotation and Denotation

Reread paragraphs 59–70 of "The Yellow Wallpaper." Then, using the Checklist on the previous page, answer the multiple-choice questions below.

YOUR TURN

1. Does the protagonist's description of the gardens in the first sentence provide a positive or negative connotation overall?

    - A. Overall, the description has a positive connotation due to words such as *garden*, *arbors*, and *flowers*.
    - B. Overall, the description has a positive connotation due to words such as *mysterious*, *riotous*, and *gnarly*.
    - C. Overall, the description has a negative connotation due to words such as *garden*, *arbors*, and *flowers*.
    - D. Overall, the description has a negative connotation due to words such as *mysterious*, *riotous*, and *gnarly*.

2. Which word does not have a positive connotation as used in this excerpt of the text?

    - A. entertainment
    - B. wink
    - C. impertinence
    - D. hop

The Yellow Wallpaper

Close Read

Reread "The Yellow Wallpaper." As you reread, complete the Skills Focus questions below. Then use your answers and annotations from the questions to help you complete the Write activity.

SKILLS FOCUS

1. Identify when the narrator first describes the yellow wallpaper. What connotations do the words she uses have, and how do these words reveal her attitude toward the wallpaper?

2. Themes regarding overcoming societal challenges were common during this literary period. What challenge does the narrator overcome? Find evidence of this at the end of the story.

3. Toward the end of the story, the narrator mentions creeping women. Who might they represent? What connection does she have to them? Identify evidence to support your answer.

4. This story examines an ideological clash in the domestic sphere, and the narrator has a strange relationship with her "home" in this story. How does the narrator's temporary home begin to feel more like a prison? Identify evidence from the text to support your answer.

WRITE

LITERARY ANALYSIS: How does the author use connotation to develop the narrator's identity? Make an argument in which you analyze the author's language and explain how a deliberate choice of words shapes the narrator's understanding of herself. Support your response with evidence from the text.

The Story of an Hour

FICTION
Kate Chopin
1894

Introduction

American author Kate Chopin (1850–1904) wrote feminist literature before the genre was even recognized. Her writing is famous for depicting strong, independent women, liberated to a degree that made many in her time uncomfortable. Considered today to be a widely influential work of proto-feminist literature, "The Story of an Hour"—first published in *Vogue* magazine in 1894—is a quintessential Chopin narrative. In this brief, powerful tale, a wife learns that her husband has died suddenly. But her reaction after digesting the news might not be what you'd expect.

The Story of an Hour

"Free! Body and soul free!"

1 Knowing that Mrs. Mallard was afflicted with a heart trouble, great care was taken to break to her as gently as possible the news of her husband's death.

2 It was her sister Josephine who told her, in broken sentences; veiled hints that revealed in half concealing. Her husband's friend Richards was there, too, near her. It was he who had been in the newspaper office when intelligence of the railroad disaster was received, with Brently Mallard's name leading the list of "killed." He had only taken the time to assure himself of its truth by a second telegram, and had hastened to **forestall** any less careful, less tender friend in bearing the sad message.

Kate Chopin

3 She did not hear the story as many women have heard the same, with a paralyzed inability to accept its significance. She wept at once, with sudden, wild abandonment, in her sister's arms. When the storm of grief had spent itself she went away to her room alone. She would have no one follow her.

**Skill:
Story Elements**

Words such as "comfortable," "roomy," and "delicious breath" describe the setting in a positive way. This seems to contrast with the terrible news Mrs. Mallard has received and how she must be feeling.

4 There stood, facing the open window, a comfortable, roomy armchair. Into this she sank, pressed down by a physical exhaustion that haunted her body and seemed to reach into her soul.

5 She could see in the open square before her house the tops of trees that were all aquiver with the new spring life. The delicious breath of rain was in the air. In the street below a peddler was crying his wares. The notes of a distant song which some one was singing reached her faintly, and countless sparrows were twittering in the eaves.

6 There were patches of blue sky showing here and there through the clouds that had met and piled one above the other in the west facing her window.

7 She sat with her head thrown back upon the cushion of the chair, quite motionless, except when a sob came up into her throat and shook her, as a child who has cried itself to sleep continues to sob in its dreams.

8 She was young, with a fair, calm face, whose lines bespoke repression and even a certain strength. But now there was a dull stare in her eyes, whose gaze was fixed away off yonder on one of those patches of blue sky. It was not a glance of reflection, but rather indicated a suspension of intelligent thought.

9 There was something coming to her and she was waiting for it, fearfully. What was it? She did not know; it was too subtle and elusive to name. But she felt it, creeping out of the sky, reaching toward her through the sounds, the scents, the color that filled the air.

10 Now her bosom rose and fell **tumultuously**. She was beginning to recognize this thing that was approaching to possess her, and she was striving to beat it back with her will—as powerless as her two white slender hands would have been.

11 When she abandoned herself a little whispered word escaped her slightly parted lips. She said it over and over under the breath: "free, free, free!" The vacant stare and the look of terror that had followed it went from her eyes. They stayed keen and bright. Her pulses beat fast, and the coursing blood warmed and relaxed every inch of her body.

12 She did not stop to ask if it were or were not a monstrous joy that held her. A clear and exalted perception enabled her to dismiss the suggestion as trivial.

13 She knew that she would weep again when she saw the kind, tender hands folded in death; the face that had never looked save with love upon her, fixed and gray and dead. But she saw beyond that bitter moment a long procession of years to come that would belong to her **absolutely**. And she opened and spread her arms out to them in welcome.

14 There would be no one to live for during those coming years; she would live for herself. There would be no powerful will bending hers in that blind persistence with which men and women believe they have a right to impose a private will upon a fellow-creature. A kind intention or a cruel intention made the act seem no less a crime as she looked upon it in that brief moment of illumination.

15 And yet she had loved him—sometimes. Often she had not. What did it matter! What could love, the unsolved mystery, count for in the face of this possession of self-assertion which she suddenly recognized as the strongest impulse of her being!

Skill: Textual Evidence

The labor Mrs. Mallard put into her marriage shows on her face, which is lined but strong. She is tired from enduring a lack of freedom. The phrase "But now" signals a transition in her state of mind.

The Story of an Hour

Skill: Textual Evidence

Louise Mallard locks herself in her room because she is distraught about her husband's death. When she exits her room, the words "triumph" and "Victory" show that she feels like she endured a battle and that she won the fight.

16   "Free! Body and soul free!" she kept whispering.

17   Josephine was kneeling before the closed door with her lips to the keyhole, imploring for admission. "Louise, open the door! I beg; open the door—you will make yourself ill. What are you doing, Louise? For heaven's sake open the door."

18   "Go away. I am not making myself ill." No; she was drinking in a very **elixir** of life through that open window.

19   Her fancy[1] was running riot along those days ahead of her. Spring days, and summer days, and all sorts of days that would be her own. She breathed a quick prayer that life might be long. It was only yesterday she had thought with a shudder that life might be long.

20   She arose at length and opened the door to her sister's **importunities**. There was a feverish triumph in her eyes, and she carried herself unwittingly like a goddess of Victory. She clasped her sister's waist, and together they descended the stairs. Richards stood waiting for them at the bottom.

21   Some one was opening the front door with a latchkey. It was Brently Mallard who entered, a little travel-stained, composedly carrying his grip-sack and umbrella. He had been far from the scene of the accident, and did not even know there had been one. He stood amazed at Josephine's piercing cry; at Richards' quick motion to screen him from the view of his wife.

22   But Richards was too late.

23   When the doctors came they said she had died of heart disease—of the joy that kills.

---

1. **fancy** the things she was interested in

First Read

Read "The Story of an Hour." After you read, complete the Think Questions below.

THINK QUESTIONS

1. At the beginning of paragraph 9, Mrs. Mallard senses "something coming to her." What is it? What physical effect does it have on her? Cite evidence from the text to support your response.

2. In paragraphs 5 through 9, how do the details about the natural setting outside of Mrs. Mallard's room relate to her emotional state? Point to specific evidence from the text to support your response.

3. At the end of the story, why do the doctors think that Mrs. Mallard died of "the joy that kills"? Do you think their diagnosis is accurate? Cite evidence from the text to support your answer.

4. Use context clues to determine the meaning of the word **elixir**. Then write your best definition of the word here, along with the clues that helped you find it.

5. Use context clues to determine the meaning of the word **absolutely** as it is used in "The Story of an Hour." Write your best definition of *absolutely* here. Then consult a print or online dictionary to confirm its meaning.

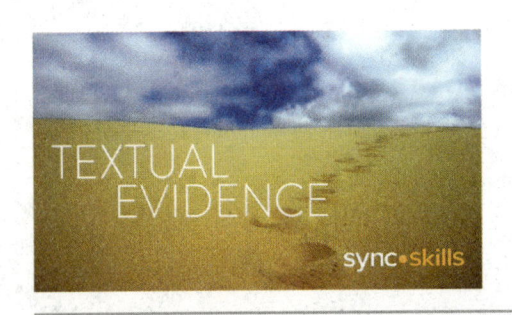

The Story of an Hour

Skill:
Textual Evidence

Use the Checklist to analyze Textual Evidence in "The Story of an Hour." Refer to the sample student annotations about Textual Evidence in the text.

••• CHECKLIST FOR TEXTUAL EVIDENCE

In order to support an analysis by citing evidence that is explicitly stated in the text, do the following:

- ✓ read the text closely and critically
- ✓ identify what the text says explicitly
- ✓ find the most relevant textual evidence that supports your analysis
- ✓ consider why an author explicitly states specific details and information
- ✓ cite the specific words, phrases, sentences, or paragraphs from the text that support your analysis
- ✓ determine where evidence in the text still leaves certain matters uncertain or unresolved

In order to interpret implicit meanings in a text by making inferences, do the following:

- ✓ combine information directly stated in the text with your own knowledge, experiences, and observations
- ✓ cite the specific words, phrases, sentences, or paragraphs from the text that led to and support this inference

In order to cite textual evidence to support an analysis of what the text says explicitly as well as inferences drawn from the text, consider the following questions:

- ✓ Have I read the text closely and critically?
- ✓ What inferences am I making about the text?
- ✓ What textual evidence am I using to support these inferences?
- ✓ Am I quoting the evidence from the text correctly?
- ✓ Does my textual evidence logically relate to my analysis or the inference I am making?
- ✓ Does evidence in the text still leave certain matters unanswered or unresolved? In what ways?

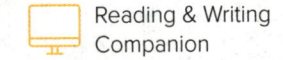

Skill: Textual Evidence

Reread paragraphs 3–7 from "The Story of an Hour." Then, using the Checklist on the previous page, answer the multiple-choice questions below.

YOUR TURN

1. According to the text, Mrs. Mallard's initial response to her husband's death is different from that of other women because—

   ○ A. she weeps immediately.
   ○ B. she wants to grieve alone.
   ○ C. she sobs like a child.
   ○ D. she would rather be outside.

2. In paragraph 5, which pair of words best supports the claim that the scene outside the window is a symbol of renewal?

   ○ A. distant, faintly
   ○ B. twittering, crying
   ○ C. tops, aquiver
   ○ D. open, life

The Story of an Hour

Skill: Story Elements

Use the Checklist to analyze Story Elements in "The Story of an Hour." Refer to the sample student annotations about Story Elements in the text.

• • • CHECKLIST FOR STORY ELEMENTS

In order to identify the impact of the author's choices regarding how to develop and relate elements of a story or drama, note the following:

- ✓ where and when the story takes place, who the main characters are, and the main conflict, or problem, in the plot
- ✓ the order of the action
- ✓ how the characters are introduced and developed
- ✓ the impact that the author's choice of setting has on the characters and their attempt to solve the problem
- ✓ the point of view the author uses, and how this shapes what readers know about the characters in the story

To analyze the impact of the author's choices regarding how to develop and to relate elements of a story or drama, consider the following questions:

- ✓ How do the author's choices affect the story elements? The development of the plot?
- ✓ How does the setting influence the characters?
- ✓ Which elements of the setting impact the plot, in particular the problem the characters face and must solve?
- ✓ Are there any flashbacks or other story elements that have an effect on the development of events in the plot? How does the author's choice of utilizing a flashback affect this development?
- ✓ How does the author introduce and develop characters in the story? Why do you think the author made these choices?

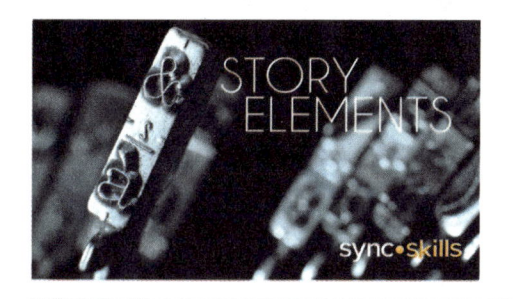

Skill: Story Elements

Reread paragraphs 17–22 from "The Story of an Hour." Then, using the Checklist on the previous page, answer the multiple-choice questions below.

YOUR TURN

1. How does Mrs. Mallard's character develop over the course of the short story?

    - ○ A. Mrs. Mallard begins to recognize that prayer is powerful and that she should begin to pray more so that she can live a long life.
    - ○ B. Mrs. Mallard begins to recognize that she is now a free and independent women who has escaped a confined, unhappy life, and this brings her relief, hope, and excitement.
    - ○ C. Mrs. Mallard begins to recognize that she is an independent women, and this scares her and makes her feel very sad and alone.
    - ○ D. Mrs. Mallard transforms from feeling like an uninteresting, boring women to a goddess who will easily be able to find another husband.

2. How does Mrs. Mallard's character development over the course of the short story impact the story's outcome?

    - ○ A. Mrs. Mallard's shift from feeling trapped to feeling free is snatched from her at the very end of the story, causing her death because her newfound joy is taken from her.
    - ○ B. Mrs. Mallard shifts from feeling trapped to feeling enraged when she finds out her husband is alive, and her anger causes her death.
    - ○ C. Mrs. Mallard's shift from feeling trapped to feeling free is snatched from her at the very end of the story, and it causes her death because she is overjoyed that her husband is alive.
    - ○ D. Mrs. Mallard shifts from feeling very sad about her husband's death to feeling comforted and relieved that he is alive.

The Story of an Hour

Close Read

Reread "The Story of an Hour." As you reread, complete the Skills Focus questions below. Then use your answers and annotations from the questions to help you complete the Write activity.

SKILLS FOCUS

1. Identify details in the beginning of the story that describe how other characters perceive Mrs. Mallard, and explain how this characterization helps develop the plot.

2. Paragraphs 4–6 describe aspects of the setting that Mrs. Mallard observes through her window. Highlight the descriptive phrases about the setting that show what Mrs. Mallard sees and explain how these details influence the plot.

3. In paragraphs 9—11, identify textual evidence that shows Mrs. Mallard's reaction to Mr. Mallard's death once she is alone. Then make an inference about how Mrs. Mallard thinks her husband's death will affect her life, and explain how the textual evidence supports that inference.

4. Reread paragraph 14, and use context clues to determine the meaning of the word **impose**. Highlight the clues that help you determine the word's meaning, and annotate with your best definition of the word.

5. What bearing does the ideology of independence have on Mrs. Mallard's feelings and actions? How much does she value independence?

WRITE

LITERARY ANALYSIS: How does the author use story elements such as setting, character development, or theme to develop the plot of "The Story of an Hour"? In your response, evaluate at least two of the story elements used by the author and how they shape the plot. Use evidence from the text to support your analysis.

"These Wild Young People" by One of Them

ARGUMENTATIVE TEXT
John F. Carter Jr.
1920

Introduction

Written in the first year of the Roaring Twenties, this essay by John F. Carter Jr. (1897–1967) examines the stark generational gap that emerged in the years following World War I. The "war to end all wars" left the nations of the world shell-shocked, and one of the young adults of the "wild" generation had a few things to say to those "oldsters" who expected the young to play by the old rules. Carter was well known for his syndicated column, "We, the People," published from 1936 to 1948, during which time he also worked for President Franklin Delano Roosevelt. He went on to write speeches for President Harry S Truman, with whom he had a contentious relationship. In this article published in *The Atlantic*, Carter rebuts the claims made by two critics of the new generation, Katharine Fullerton Gerould and Mr. Grundy.

"We may be fire, but it was they who made us play with gunpowder."

1 For some months past the pages of our more conservative magazines have been crowded with pessimistic descriptions of the younger generation, as seen by their elders and, no doubt, their betters. Hardly a week goes by that I do not read some indignant treatise depicting our extravagance, the corruption of our manners, the futility of our existence, poured out in stiff, scared, shocked sentences before a **sympathetic** and horrified audience of fathers, mothers, and maiden aunts—but particularly maiden aunts.

2 In the May issue of the *Atlantic Monthly* appeared an article entitled "Polite Society," by a certain Mr. Grundy, the husband of a very old friend of my family. In a kindly manner he

Mentioned our virtues, it is true
But dwelt upon our vices, too.

"Chivalry and Modesty are dead. Modesty died first," quoth he, but expressed the pious hope that all might yet be well if the oldsters would but be content to "wait and see." His article is one of the best-tempered and most gentlemanly of this long series of Jeremiads[1] against 'these wild young people.' It is significant that it should be anonymous. In reading it, I could not help but be drawn to Mr. Grundy personally, but was forced to the conclusion that he, like everyone else who is writing about my generation, has very little idea of what he is talking about. I would not offend him for the world, and if I apostrophize[2] him somewhat brutally in the following paragraphs, it is only because I am talking of him generically; also because his self-styled 'cousin' is present.

3 For Mrs. Katharine Fullerton Gerould has come forward as the latest volunteer prosecuting attorney, in her powerful 'Reflections of a Grundy Cousin' in the August *Atlantic*. She has little or no patience with us. She disposes of all previous explanations of our degeneration in a series of short paragraphs,

---

1. **Jeremiads** long written works in which someone passionately expresses grief about the state of society; the word is an eponym and refers to the Biblical prophet Jeremiah and the Book of Lamentations
2. **apostrophize** to quote a literary work or song in the middle of a speech or essay

then launches into her own explanation: the decay of religion. She treats it as a primary cause, and with considerable effect. But I think she errs in not attempting to analyze the causes for such decay, which would bring her nearer to the **ultimate** truth.

4   A friend of mine has an uncle who, in his youth, was a wild, fast, extravagant young blood. His clothes were the amazement of even his fastest friends. He drank, he swore, he gambled, bringing his misdeeds to a climax by eloping with an heiress, a beautiful Philadelphian seraph[3], fascinated by this glittering Lucifer. Her family disowned her, and they fled to a distant and wild country. He was, in effect, a brilliant, worthless, attractive, and romantic person. Now he is the sedate deacon of a Boston Presbyterian church, very strong on morality in every shape, a terror to the young, with an impeccable business career, and a very dull family circle. Mrs. Gerould must know of similar cases; so why multiply instances? Just think how moral and unentertaining our generation will be when we have emerged from the 'roaring forties'!—and rejoice.

5   There is a story, illustrative of Californian civic pride, about a California funeral. The friends and relatives of the departed were gathered mournfully around the bier, awaiting the arrival of the preacher who was to deliver the funeral oration. They waited and waited and waited, but no preacher appeared. Finally, a messenger-boy arrived with a telegram. It was from the clergyman, and informed them that he had missed his train. The chief mourner rose to the occasion and asked if anyone would like to say a few kind words about the deceased. No one stirred. Finally a long, lanky person got up, cleared his throat, and drawled, "Wa-a-al, if no one else is goin' to speak, I'd like to say a few things about Los Angeles!"

6   I would like to say a few things about my generation.

7   In the first place, I would like to observe that the older generation had certainly pretty well ruined this world before passing it on to us. They give us this Thing, knocked to pieces, leaky, red-hot, threatening to blow up; and then they are surprised that we don't accept it with the same attitude of pretty, decorous enthusiasm with which they received it, 'way back in the eighteen-nineties, nicely painted, smoothly running, practically foolproof. "So simple that a child can run it!" But the child couldn't steer it. He hit every possible telegraph-pole, some of them twice, and ended with a head-on collision for which *we* shall have to pay the fines and damages. Now, with loving pride, they turn over their wreck to us; and, since we are not properly overwhelmed with loving gratitude, shake their heads and sigh, "Dear! dear! We were so much better-mannered than these wild young people. But then we had the

---

3. **seraph** one who is of the six-winged, highest level of angels in the celestial order

advantages of a good, strict, old-fashioned bringing-up!" How intensely *human* these oldsters are, after all, and how fallible! How they always blame us for not following precisely in their eminently correct footsteps!

8   Then again there is the matter of outlook. When these sentimental old world-wreckers were young, the world was such a different place—at least, so I gather from H.G. Wells's picture of the nineties, in *Joan and Peter*[4]. Life for them was bright and pleasant. Like all normal youngsters, they had their little tin-pot ideals, their sweet little visions, their naive enthusiasms, their nice little sets of beliefs. Christianity had emerged from the blow dealt by Darwin[5], emerged rather in the shape of social dogma. Man was a noble and perfectible creature. Women were angels (whom they smugly sweated in their industries and prostituted in their slums). Right was downing might. The nobility and the divine mission of the race were factors that led our fathers to work wholeheartedly for a millennium, which they caught a glimpse of just around the turn of the century. Why, there were Hague Tribunals[6]! International peace was at last **assured**, and according to current reports, never officially denied, the American delegates held out for the use of poison gas in warfare, just as the men of that generation were later to ruin Wilson's great ideal of a league of nations[7], on the ground that such a scheme was an invasion of American rights. But still, everything, masked by ingrained hypocrisy and prudishness, seemed simple, beautiful, inevitable.

9   Now my generation is disillusioned, and, I think, to a certain extent, brutalized, by the cataclysm which *their* complacent folly engendered. The acceleration of life for us has been so great that into the last few years have been crowded the experiences and the ideas of a normal lifetime. We have in our unregenerate youth learned the practicality and the cynicism that is safe only in unregenerate old age. We have been forced to become realists overnight, instead of idealists, as was our birthright. We have seen man at his lowest, woman at her lightest, in the terrible moral chaos of Europe. We have been forced to question, and in many cases to discard, the religion of our fathers. We have seen hideous peculation, greed, anger, hatred, **malice**, and all uncharitableness, unmasked and rampant and unashamed. We have been forced to live in an atmosphere of "to-morrow we die," and so, naturally, we drank and were merry. We have seen the rottenness and shortcomings of all governments, even the best and most stable. We have seen entire social

---

4. **Joan and Peter** a 1918 novel by influential English author H.G. Wells (1866–1946) concerning the situation of English society at the end of World War I
5. **Darwin** Charles Robert Darwin (1809–1882) was a naturalist and author of the 1859 book *On the Origin of Species*, which developed the theory of evolution.
6. **Hague Tribunals** deliberations held at any of the several international courts in Den Haag, Netherlands ("The Hague")
7. **Wilson's great ideal of a league of nations** Initiated by U.S. President Woodrow Wilson (1856–1924), the League of Nations sprang from a peace conference ending World War I as a means for resolving international disputes.

systems overthrown, and our own called in question. In short, we have seen the inherent beastliness of the human race revealed in an infernal apocalypse.

10   It is the older generation who forced us to see all this, which has left us with social and political institutions staggering blind in the fierce white light that, for us, should beat only about the enthroned ideal. And now, through the soft-headed folly of these painfully shocked Grundys, we have that devastating wisdom which is safe only for the burned-out embers of grizzled, cautious old men. We may be fire, but it was they who made us play with gunpowder. And now they are surprised that a great many of us, because they have taken away our apple-cheeked ideals, are seriously considering whether or no *their* game be worth *our* candle.

11   But, in justice to my generation, I think that I must admit that most of us have realized that, whether or no it be worth while, we must all play the game, as long as we are in it. And I think that much of the hectic quality of our life is due to that fact and to that alone. We are faced with staggering problems and are forced to solve them, while the previous incumbents are permitted a graceful and untroubled death. All my friends are working and working hard. Most of the girls I know are working. In one way or another, often unconsciously, the great burden put upon us is being borne, and borne gallantly, by that immodest, unchivalrous set of ne'er-do-wells, so delightfully portrayed by Mr. Grundy and the amazing young Fitzgerald. A keen interest in political and social problems, and a determination to face the facts of life, ugly or beautiful, characterizes us, as it certainly did not characterize our fathers. We won't shut our eyes to the truths we have learned. We have faced so many unpleasant things already,—and faced them pretty well,—that it is natural that we should keep it up.

Zelda Sayre and Francis Scott Fitzgerald arm in arm

12   Now I think that this is the aspect of our generation that annoys the uncritical and deceives the unsuspecting oldsters who are now met in judgment upon us: our devastating and brutal frankness. And this is the quality in which we really differ from our predecessors. We are frank with each other, frank, or pretty nearly so, with our elders, frank in the way we feel toward life and this badly damaged world. It may be a disquieting and misleading habit, but is it a bad one? We find some few things in the world that we like, and a whole lot that we don't, and we are not afraid to say so or to give our reasons. In earlier generations this was not the case. The young men yearned to be glittering generalities, the young women to act like shy, sweet, innocent fawns toward one another. And now, when grown up, they have come to believe that they

actually were figures of pristine excellence, knightly chivalry, adorable modesty, and impeccable propriety. But I really doubt if they were so. Statistics relating to, let us say, the immorality of college students in the eighteen-eighties would not compare favorably with those of the present. However, now, as they look back on it, they see their youth through a mist of muslin, flannels, tennis, bicycles, Tennyson, Browning, and the Blue Danube waltz. The other things, the ugly things that we know about and talk about, must also have been there. But our elders didn't care or didn't dare to consider them, and now they are forgotten. We talk about them unabashed, and not necessarily with Presbyterian disapproval, and so they jump to the conclusion that we are thoroughly bad, and keep pestering us to make us good.

13 The trouble with them is that they can't seem to realize that we are busy, that what pleasure we snatch must be incidental and feverishly hurried. We have to make the most of our time. We actually haven't got so much time for the noble procrastinations of modesty or for the elaborate rigmarole of chivalry, and little patience for the lovely formulas of an ineffective faith. Let them die for a while! They did not seem to serve the world too well in its black hour. If they are inherently good they will come back, vital and untarnished. But just now we have a lot of work, "old time is still a-flying," and we must gather rose-buds while we may.

14 Oh! I know that we are a pretty bad lot, but has not that been true of every **preceding** generation? At least we have the courage to act accordingly. Our music is distinctly barbaric, our girls are distinctly *not* a mixture of arbutus and barbed-wire. We drink when we can and what we can, we gamble, we are extravagant—but we work, and that's about all that we can be expected to do; for, after all, we have just discovered that we are all still very near to the Stone Age. The Grundys shake their heads. They'll *make* us be good. Prohibition is put through to stop our drinking, and hasn't stopped it. Bryan has plans to curtain our philanderings, and he won't do any good. A Draconian[8] code is being hastily formulated at Washington and elsewhere, to prevent us from, by any chance, making any alteration in this present divinely constituted arrangement of things. The oldsters stand dramatically with fingers and toes and noses pressed against the bursting dykes. Let them! They won't do any good. They can shackle us down, and still expect us to repair their blunders, if they wish. But we shall not trouble ourselves very much about them any more. Why should we? What have they done? They have made us work as they never had to work in all their padded lives—but we'll have our cakes and ale for a' that.

---

8. **Draconian** referring to harsh or severe punishment; derived from Draco, legislator of Athens, who instituted strict written codes enforced by law

15 For now we know our way about. We're not babes in the wood, hunting for great, big, red strawberries, and confidently expecting the Robin Redbreasts[9] to cover us up with pretty leaves if we don't find them. We're men and women, long before our time, in the flower of our full-blooded youth. We have brought back into civil life some of the recklessness and ability that we were taught by war. We are also quite fatalistic in our outlook on the tepid perils of tame living. All may yet crash to the ground for aught that we can do about it. Terrible mistakes will be made, but we shall at least make them intelligently and insist, if we are to receive the strictures of the future, on doing pretty much as we choose now.

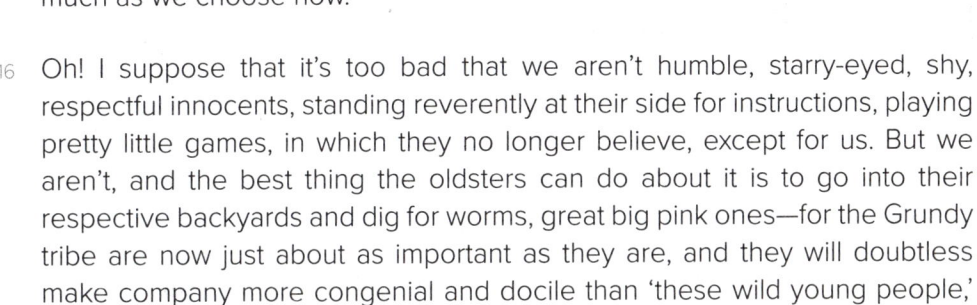

16 Oh! I suppose that it's too bad that we aren't humble, starry-eyed, shy, respectful innocents, standing reverently at their side for instructions, playing pretty little games, in which they no longer believe, except for us. But we aren't, and the best thing the oldsters can do about it is to go into their respective backyards and dig for worms, great big pink ones—for the Grundy tribe are now just about as important as they are, and they will doubtless make company more congenial and docile than 'these wild young people,' the men and women of my generation.

---

9. **Robin Redbreasts** a common and traditional nickname for the robin (Erithacus rubecula), a beloved red-breasted bird known for its song and territorial behavior

WRITE

ARGUMENTATIVE: In this argumentative essay, Carter explains that one of the challenges his generation faces is that it is misunderstood and underappreciated. Write an argumentative essay in which you outline the challenges faced by today's youth. What is the greatest challenge facing today's generation? What can be done to help youth address it? Support your argument with evidence from the texts in previous units, outside resources, or your own experiences.

The Great Gatsby

FICTION
F. Scott Fitzgerald
1925

Introduction

studysync

F. Scott Fitzgerald (1896–1940) was a member of the "Lost Generation" of authors who served in World War I and later wrote about the war and the post-war world. His most famous work, *The Great Gatsby*, is a novel depicting America's extravagant and roaring 1920s. These excerpts explore the relationship between Nick Carraway, the narrator, and Jay Gatsby, a mysterious millionaire whose lavish parties embody the spirit and spectacle that led Fitzgerald to dub the 1920s "The Jazz Age." As Nick delves into the mystery of Gatsby's past, he finds that the legend of Gatsby is as much a tale of one extraordinary man as it is the story of extraordinary times.

"He smiled understandingly—much more than understandingly."

from Chapter 1

1   In my younger and more vulnerable years my father gave me some advice that I've been turning over in my mind ever since.

2   "Whenever you feel like criticizing any one," he told me, "just remember that all the people in this world haven't had the advantages that you've had."

3   He didn't say any more but we've always been unusually communicative in a reserved way, and I understood that he meant a great deal more than that. In consequence I'm **inclined** to reserve all judgments, a habit that has opened up many curious natures to me and also made me the victim of not a few veteran bores. The abnormal mind is quick to detect and attach itself to this quality when it appears in a normal person, and so it came about that in college I was unjustly accused of being a politician, because I was privy to the secret griefs of wild, unknown men. Most of the confidences were unsought—frequently I have **feigned** sleep, preoccupation, or a hostile levity when I realized by some unmistakable sign that an intimate revelation was quivering on the horizon—for the intimate revelations of young men or at least the terms in which they express them are usually plagiaristic and marred by obvious suppressions. Reserving judgments is a matter of infinite hope. I am still a little afraid of missing something if I forget that, as my father snobbishly suggested, and I snobbishly repeat, a sense of the fundamental decencies is parceled out unequally at birth.

4   And, after boasting this way of my tolerance, I come to the admission that it has a limit. Conduct may be founded on the hard rock or the wet marshes but after a certain point I don't care what it's founded on. When I came back from the East last autumn I felt that I wanted the world to be in uniform and at a sort of moral attention forever; I wanted no more riotous excursions with privileged glimpses into the human heart. Only Gatsby, the man who gives his name to this book, was exempt from my reaction—Gatsby who represented everything for which I have an unaffected scorn. If personality is an unbroken series of successful gestures, then there was something gorgeous about him, some heightened sensitivity to the promises of life, as if he were related to one of

Skill: Story Elements

Nick is conflicted and has contradictory ideas. This begins to develop his internal moral struggles. He understands his privilege and has values about how people should conduct themselves. A theme of classism begins to emerge.

those intricate machines that register earthquakes ten thousand miles away. This responsiveness had nothing to do with that flabby impressionability which is dignified under the name of the "creative temperament"—it was an extraordinary gift for hope, a romantic readiness such as I have never found in any other person and which it is not likely I shall ever find again. No—Gatsby turned out all right at the end; it is what preyed on Gatsby, what foul dust floated in the wake of his dreams that temporarily closed out my interest in the **abortive** sorrows and short-winded elations of men.

. . .

from Chapter 3

5   By midnight the hilarity had increased. A celebrated tenor had sung in Italian, and a notorious contralto had sung in jazz, and between the numbers people were doing "stunts" all over the garden, while happy, vacuous bursts of laughter rose toward the summer sky. A pair of stage twins, who turned out to be the girls in yellow, did a baby act in costume, and champagne was served in glasses bigger than finger-bowls. The moon had risen higher, and floating in the Sound was a triangle of silver scales, trembling a little to the stiff, tinny drip of the banjoes on the lawn.

6   I was still with Jordan Baker. We were sitting at a table with a man of about my age and a rowdy little girl, who gave way upon the slightest provocation to uncontrollable laughter. I was enjoying myself now. I had taken two finger-bowls of champagne, and the scene had changed before my eyes into something significant, elemental, and profound.

7   At a lull in the entertainment the man looked at me and smiled.

8   "Your face is familiar," he said, politely. "Weren't you in the Third Division during the war?"

9   "Why, yes. I was in the ninth machine-gun battalion."

10 "I was in the Seventh Infantry until June nineteen-eighteen. I knew I'd seen you somewhere before."

11 We talked for a moment about some wet, gray little villages in France. Evidently he lived in this vicinity, for he told me that he had just bought a hydroplane, and was going to try it out in the morning.

12 "Want to go with me, old sport? Just near the shore along the Sound."

13 "What time?"

14 "Any time that suits you best."

15 It was on the tip of my tongue to ask his name when Jordan looked around and smiled. "Having a gay time now?" she inquired.

16 "Much better." I turned again to my new acquaintance. "This is an unusual party for me. I haven't even seen the host. I live over there—" I waved my hand at the invisible hedge in the distance, "and this man Gatsby sent over his chauffeur with an invitation." For a moment he looked at me as if he failed to understand.

17 "I'm Gatsby," he said suddenly.

18 "What!" I exclaimed. "Oh, I beg your pardon."

19 "I thought you knew, old sport. I'm afraid I'm not a very good host."

20 He smiled understandingly—much more than understandingly. It was one of those rare smiles with a quality of eternal reassurance in it, that you may come across four or five times in life. It faced—or seemed to face—the whole external world for an instant, and then concentrated on you with an irresistible **prejudice** in your favor. It understood you just so far as you wanted to be understood, believed in you as you would like to believe in yourself, and assured you that it had precisely the impression of you that, at your best, you hoped to convey. Precisely at that point it vanished—and I was looking at an elegant young rough-neck, a year or two over thirty, whose elaborate formality of speech just missed being absurd. Some time before he introduced himself I'd got a strong impression that he was picking his words with care.

21 Almost at the moment when Mr. Gatsby identified himself, a butler hurried toward him with the information that Chicago was calling him on the wire. He excused himself with a small bow that included each of us in turn.

22 "If you want anything just ask for it, old sport," he urged me. "Excuse me. I will rejoin you later." When he was gone I turned immediately to Jordan—constrained to assure her of my surprise. I had expected that Mr. Gatsby would be a florid and corpulent person in his middle years. "Who is he?" I demanded. "Do you know?"

23 "He's just a man named Gatsby."

24 "Where is he from, I mean? And what does he do?"

25 "Now you're started on the subject," she answered with a wan smile. "Well, he told me once he was an Oxford[1] man."

26 A dim background started to take shape behind him, but at her next remark it faded away. "However, I don't believe it."

27 "Why not?"

28 "I don't know," she insisted, "I just don't think he went there."

29 Something in her tone reminded me of the other girl's "I think he killed a man," and had the effect of stimulating my curiosity. I would have accepted without question the information that Gatsby sprang from the swamps of Louisiana or from the lower East Side of New York. That was comprehensible. But young men didn't—at least in my provincial inexperience I believed they didn't—drift coolly out of nowhere and buy a palace on Long Island Sound[2].

30 "Anyhow, he gives large parties," said Jordan, changing the subject with an **urbane** distaste for the concrete. "And I like large parties. They're so intimate. At small parties there isn't any privacy."

Excerpted from *The Great Gatsby* by F. Scott Fitzgerald, published by Scribner.

1. **Oxford** the University of Oxford, the oldest university in the English-speaking world, founded in 1096
2. **Long Island Sound** a body of water between Long Island, New York, and the Connecticut shore

First Read

Read *The Great Gatsby*. After you read, complete the Think Questions below.

THINK QUESTIONS

1. What was the advice Nick's father gave him as a youth, and what has been the result of Nick's following this advice? Use details from the text to support your answer.

2. Based on what Nick tells the reader in Chapter 1, what seems to be his attitude toward Gatsby? Provide details from the text that support your response.

3. How did Nick's first impression on meeting Gatsby compare to his prior expectations of the man? Support your answer with textual evidence.

4. Use context and your knowledge of word parts to determine the meaning of the word **feigned** as it is used in paragraph 3. Write your definition of *feign* here and explain the reasoning that led to that definition.

5. Analyze the word **urbane** to provide a possible meaning based on its base word and affix(es). Explain how the context clues in the sentence help you confirm or revise your predicted definition of *urbane*, and explain your process for figuring out its meaning.

The Great Gatsby

Skill:
Story Elements

Use the Checklist to analyze Story Elements in *The Great Gatsby*. Refer to the sample student annotations about Story Elements in the text.

••• CHECKLIST FOR STORY ELEMENTS

In order to identify the impact of the author's choices regarding how to develop and relate elements of a story or drama, note the following:

- ✓ where and when the story takes place, who the main characters are, and the main conflict, or problem, in the plot

- ✓ the order of the action

- ✓ how the characters are introduced and developed

- ✓ the impact that the author's choice of setting has on the characters and their attempt to solve the problem

- ✓ the point of view the author uses, and how this shapes what readers know about the characters in the story

To analyze the impact of the author's choices regarding how to develop and relate elements of a story or drama, consider the following questions:

- ✓ How do the author's choices affect the story elements? The development of the plot?

- ✓ How does the setting influence the characters?

- ✓ Which elements of the setting impact the plot, in particular the problem the characters face and must solve? How does this contribute to the theme?

- ✓ How does the author's choice of utilizing foreshadowing affect the development of the plot or characters?

    - *Foreshadowing* uses words or phrases that hint at something that is going to happen without revealing the story or spoiling the suspense.

- ✓ How does the author introduce and develop characters in the story? Why do you think the author made these choices?

Reading & Writing Companion

Please note that excerpts and passages in the StudySync® library and this workbook are intended as touchstones to generate interest in an author's work. The excerpts and passages do not substitute for the reading of entire texts, and StudySync® strongly recommends that students seek out and purchase the whole literary or informational work in order to experience it as the author intended. Links to online resellers are available in our digital library. In addition, complete works may be ordered through an authorized reseller by filling out and returning to StudySync® the order form enclosed in this workbook.

Skill: Story Elements

Reread paragraphs 6–19 of *The Great Gatsby*. Then, using the Checklist on the previous page, answer the multiple-choice questions below.

YOUR TURN

1. What does the text in paragraphs 6 and 15–17 reveal about Nick's character, and how does this contribute to a theme in the story?

   - A. Nick feels right at home at Gatsby's party and easily connects with the guests, which influences the theme of materialism.
   - B. Nick has insulted Gatsby, which influences the theme of friendship and relationships.
   - C. Nick feels guilty attending a party with grand entertainment and finger-bowls of champagne, which influences the theme that pleasure is a sin.
   - D. Nick feels some discomfort about the way he was invited to the party, which develops the theme about how conflicting values and standards of conduct reveal class division.

2. How does Nick's first encounter with Gatsby foreshadow the development of Gatsby's intriguing character?

   - A. The way in which Gatsby reveals himself to Nick is uncomfortable but also curious, which foreshadows the development of Gatsby's complex, elusive character, as well as Nick's conflicted feelings about him.
   - B. The way in which Gatsby reveals himself to Nick is strange and bizarre, which foreshadows the development of Gatsby's disturbed character, as well as Nick's fear of him.
   - C. The way in which Gatsby reveals himself to Nick is strange but also cordial, which foreshadows the development of Gatsby's dishonest, disturbed character, as well as Nick's conflicted feelings about him.
   - D. The way in which Gatsby reveals himself to Nick is exciting and amusing, which foreshadows the development of Gatsby's outgoing character, as well as Nick's desire to become his good friend.

The Great Gatsby

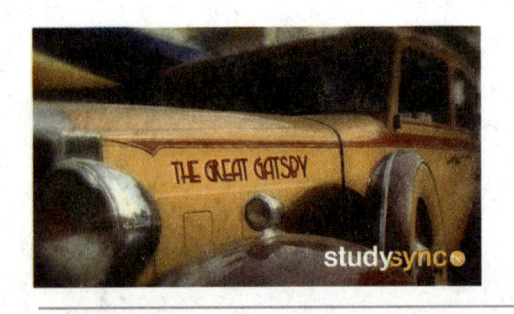

Close Read

Reread *The Great Gatsby*. As you reread, complete the Skills Focus questions below. Then use your answers and annotations from the questions to help you complete the Write activity.

SKILLS FOCUS

1. What is the significance of the advice that Nick's father gives him? What is ironic about it? Identify evidence from the text to support your answer.

2. Identify an instance when Nick experiences a moral dilemma. Determine how Nick's behavior contributes to the dilemma, and then analyze how this moral dilemma demonstrates a theme.

3. Identify a passage that describes the historical context of the novel. How does the setting reveal details about Gatsby?

4. Identify the passage in which Nick describes his encounter with Gatsby. What is his first impression? Identify evidence from the text to support your answer.

5. What does Nick learn about the danger of equating winning with wealth and class? Identify evidence from the text to support your answer.

WRITE

LITERARY ANALYSIS: In the early twentieth century, American writers turned to Modernism as a form of expression. Through their writing, they shared their disillusioned view of the world after World War I. Drawing on the context you gained in reading "'These Wild Young People,' by One of Them," analyze the thoughts, words, and actions of the characters in *The Great Gatsby* and argue how they reflect elements of this literary period. Support your response with evidence from the text.

A Farewell to Arms

FICTION
Ernest Hemingway
1920

Introduction

Known for a life of adventure, American author Ernest Hemingway (1899–1961) based his semi-autobiographical novel *A Farewell to Arms* on his experiences as an ambulance driver in Italy during World War I. The story revolves around the exploits of Lieutenant ("Tenente") Frederic Henry—also an ambulance driver with the Italian Army—and his doomed romance with a British nurse. In this excerpt, Henry engages the drivers under his command in a philosophical debate about war.

A Farewell to Arms

"'Were you there, Tenente, when they wouldn't attack and they shot every tenth man?'"

from Chapter 9

1 "Were you there, Tenente, when they wouldn't attack and they shot every tenth man?"

2 "No."

3 "It is true. They lined them up afterward and took every tenth man. Carabinieri[1] shot them."

4 "Carabinieri," said Passini and spat on the floor. "But those grenadiers[2]; all over six feet. They wouldn't attack."

5 "If everybody would not attack the war would be over," Manera said.

6 "It wasn't that way with the granatieri[3]. They were afraid. The officers all came from such good families."

7 "Some of the officers went alone."

8 "A sergeant shot two officers who would not get out."

9 "Some troops went out."

10 "Those that went out were not lined up when they took the tenth man."

11 "One of those shot by the carabinieri is from my town," Passini said. "He was a big smart tall boy to be in the granatieri. Always in Rome. Always with the girls. Always with the carabinieri." He laughed. "Now they have a guard outside his house with a bayonet and nobody can come to see his mother and father and sisters and his father loses his **civil** rights and cannot even

---

1. **carabinieri** a militarized Italian police force
2. **grenadiers** soldiers who specialize in the use of grenades
3. **granatieri** a mechanized brigade in the Italian armed forces

vote. They are all without law to protect them. Anybody can take their property."

12 "If it wasn't that that happens to their families nobody would go to the attack."

13 "Yes. Alpini would. These V. E. soldiers would. Some bersaglieri[4]."

14 "Bersaglieri have run too. Now they try to forget it."

15 "You should not let us talk this way, Tenente. Evviva l'esercito[5]," Passini said sarcastically.
"I know how you talk," I said. "But as long as you drive the cars and behave—"

16 "—and don't talk so other officers can hear," Manera finished.

17 "I believe we should get the war over," I said. "It would not finish it if one side stopped fighting. It would only be worse if we stopped fighting."

18 "It could not be worse," Passini said respectfully. "There is nothing worse than war."

19 "Defeat is worse."

20 "I do not believe it," Passini said still respectfully. "What is defeat? You go home."

21 "They come after you. They take your home. They take your sisters."

22 "I don't believe it," Passini said. "They can't do that to everybody. Let everybody **defend** his home. Let them keep their sisters in the house."

23 "They hang you. They come and make you be a soldier again. Not in the auto-ambulance, in the **infantry**."

24 "They can't hang every one."

25 "An outside nation can't make you be a soldier," Manera said. "At the first battle you all run."

26 "Like the Tchecos[6]."

---

4. **bersaglieri** members of a light infantry unit in the Italian armed forces
5. **Evviva l'esercito** Italian for "Long live the army"
6. **Tchecos** a person who hails from what is now the Czech Republic

A Farewell to Arms

27 "I think you do not know anything about being conquered and so you think it is not bad."

28 "Tenente," Passini said. "We understand you let us talk. Listen. There is nothing as bad as war. We in the auto-ambulance cannot realize at all how bad it is. When people realize how bad it is they cannot do anything to stop it because they go crazy. There are some people who never realize. There are people who are afraid of their officers. It is with them the war is made."

29 "I know it is bad but we must finish it."

30 "It doesn't finish. There is no finish to a war."

31 "Yes there is."
Passini shook his head.

32 "War is not won by victory. What if we take San Gabriele[7]? What if we take the Carso[8] and Monfalcone[9] and Trieste[10]? Where are we then? Did you see all the far mountains to-day? Do you think we could take all them too? Only if the Austrians stop fighting. One side must stop fighting. Why don't we stop fighting? If they come down into Italy they will get tired and go away. They have their own country. But no, instead there is a war."

33 "You're an **orator**."

34 "We think. We read. We are not peasants. We are mechanics. But even the peasants know better than to believe in a war. Everybody hates this war."

35 "There is a class that controls a country that is stupid and does not realize anything and never can. That is why we have this war."

36 "Also they make money out of it."

37 "Most of them don't," said Passini. "They are too stupid. They do it for nothing. For stupidity."

38 "We must shut up," said Manera. "We talk too much even for the Tenente."

---

7. **San Gabriele** a mountain of high strategic significance in the Italian military struggle against Austria
8. **the Carso** a vast limestone plateau in southwestern modern-day Slovenia and northeastern Italy
9. **Monfalcone** an Italian city on the Adriatic Sea
10. **Trieste** a province in the small strip of land between Slovenia and the Adriatic Sea

39 "He likes it," said Passini. "We will **convert** him."

40 "But now we will shut up," Manera said.

Excerpted from *A Farewell to Arms* by Ernest Hemingway, published by Scribner.

✏️ WRITE

DISCUSSION: Think about how Lieutenant ("Tenente") Frederic Henry's point of view about the war contrasts with the perspective of the other drivers. Discuss these questions: What messages about the ideologies of war do you believe are central to each point of view? What might precipitate a change in Tenente's perspective? Provide examples and evidence from the text to support your ideas. Take notes as answers are suggested, and be prepared to share your group's notes with the rest of the class.

A Rose for Emily

FICTION
William Faulkner
1930

Introduction

Although William Faulkner (1897–1962) spurned fame and said that "the artist is of no importance" compared to the artist's work, he remains one of the most famous and acclaimed prose writers in the history of American literature. A former postmaster who lived most of his life in Oxford, Mississippi, Faulkner often wrote of characters haunted by the past of the fictional Mississippi Yoknapatawpha County—a place not so different from his home region of Lafayette County. Many of Faulkner's most noted works are told from multiple points of view, featuring the reflections, observations, and inner thoughts of a multitude of characters. "A Rose for Emily" was Faulkner's first story published in a national magazine, decades before he won the Pulitzer Prize and the Nobel Prize.

A Rose for Emily

"None of the young men were quite good enough for Miss Emily and such."

Content Advisory: Please be advised that the following text contains mature themes and racial epithets.

I.

1 When Miss Emily Grierson died, our whole town went to her funeral: the men through a sort of respectful affection for a fallen monument, the women mostly out of curiosity to see the inside of her house, which no one save an old man-servant—a combined gardener and cook—had seen in at least ten years.

2 It was a big, squarish frame house that had once been white, decorated with cupolas and spires and scrolled balconies in the heavily lightsome style of the seventies, set on what had once been our most select street. But garages and cotton gins had **encroached** and obliterated even the august names of that neighborhood; only Miss Emily's house was left, lifting its stubborn and coquettish decay above the cotton wagons and the gasoline pumps—an eyesore among eyesores.

3 And now Miss Emily had gone to join the representatives of those august names where they lay in the cedar-bemused cemetery among the ranked and anonymous graves of Union and Confederate soldiers who fell at the battle of Jefferson.

4 Alive, Miss Emily had been a tradition, a duty, and a care; a sort of hereditary obligation upon the town, dating from that day in 1894 when Colonel Sartoris, the mayor—he who fathered the edict that no Negro woman should appear on the streets without an apron—remitted her taxes, the dispensation dating from the death of her father on into perpetuity. Not that Miss Emily would have accepted charity. Colonel Sartoris invented an involved tale to the effect that Miss Emily's father had loaned money to the town, which the town, as a matter of business, preferred this way of repaying. Only a man of Colonel Sartoris'

generation and thought could have invented it, and only a woman could have believed it.

5   When the next generation, with its more modern ideas, became mayors and aldermen, this arrangement created some little dissatisfaction. On the first of the year they mailed her a tax notice. February came, and there was no reply. They wrote her a formal letter, asking her to call at the sheriff's office at her convenience. A week later the mayor wrote her himself, offering to call or to send his car for her, and received in reply a note on paper of an archaic shape, in a thin, flowing calligraphy in faded ink, to the effect that she no longer went out at all. The tax notice was also enclosed, without comment.

6   They called a special meeting of the Board of Aldermen. A deputation waited upon her, knocked at the door through which no visitor had passed since she ceased giving china-painting lessons eight or ten years earlier. They were admitted by the old Negro into a dim hall from which a stairway mounted into still more shadow. It smelled of dust and disuse—a close, dank smell. The Negro led them into the parlor. It was furnished in heavy, leather-covered furniture. When the Negro opened the blinds of one window, they could see that the leather was cracked; and when they sat down, a faint dust rose sluggishly about their thighs, spinning with slow motes in the single sun-ray. On a tarnished gilt easel before the fireplace stood a crayon portrait of Miss Emily's father.

7   They rose when she entered—a small, fat woman in black, with a thin gold chain descending to her waist and vanishing into her belt, leaning on an ebony cane with a tarnished gold head. Her skeleton was small and spare; perhaps that was why what would have been merely plumpness in another was obesity in her. She looked bloated, like a body long submerged in motionless water, and of that pallid hue. Her eyes, lost in the fatty ridges of her face, looked like two small pieces of coal pressed into a lump of dough as they moved from one face to another while the visitors stated their errand.

8   She did not ask them to sit. She just stood in the door and listened quietly until the spokesman came to a stumbling halt. Then they could hear the invisible watch ticking at the end of the gold chain.

9   Her voice was dry and cold. "I have no taxes in Jefferson. Colonel Sartoris explained it to me. Perhaps one of you can gain access to the city records and satisfy yourselves."

10 "But we have. We are the city authorities, Miss Emily. Didn't you get a notice from the sheriff, signed by him?"

11 "I received a paper, yes," Miss Emily said. "Perhaps he considers himself the sheriff . . . I have no taxes in Jefferson."

12 "But there is nothing on the books to show that, you see. We must go by the—"

13 "See Colonel Sartoris. I have no taxes in Jefferson."

14 "But, Miss Emily—"

15 "See Colonel Sartoris." (Colonel Sartoris had been dead almost ten years.) "I have no taxes in Jefferson. Tobe!" The Negro appeared. "Show these gentlemen out."

II.

16 So she vanquished them, horse and foot, just as she had vanquished their fathers thirty years before about the smell.

17 That was two years after her father's death and a short time after her sweetheart—the one we believed would marry her—had deserted her. After her father's death she went out very little; after her sweetheart went away, people hardly saw her at all. A few of the ladies had the temerity to call, but were not received, and the only sign of life about the place was the Negro man—a young man then—going in and out with a market basket.

18 "Just as if a man—any man—could keep a kitchen properly," the ladies said; so they were not surprised when the smell developed. It was another link between the gross, teeming world and the high and mighty Griersons.

19 A neighbor, a woman, complained to the mayor, Judge Stevens, eighty years old.

20 "But what will you have me do about it, madam?" he said.

21 "Why, send her word to stop it," the woman said. "Isn't there a law? "

22 "I'm sure that won't be necessary," Judge Stevens said. "It's probably just a snake or a rat that n----- of hers killed in the yard. I'll speak to him about it."

23 The next day he received two more complaints, one from a man who came in diffident deprecation. "We really must do something about it, Judge. I'd be the last one in the world to bother Miss Emily, but we've got to do something." That night the Board of Aldermen met—three graybeards and one younger man, a member of the rising generation.

24 "It's simple enough," he said. "Send her word to have her place cleaned up. Give her a certain time to do it in, and if she don't . . . "

25 "Dammit, sir," Judge Stevens said, "will you accuse a lady to her face of smelling bad?"

26 So the next night, after midnight, four men crossed Miss Emily's lawn and slunk about the house like burglars, sniffing along the base of the brickwork and at the cellar openings while one of them performed a regular sowing motion with his hand out of a sack slung from his shoulder. They broke open the cellar door and sprinkled lime there, and in all the outbuildings. As they recrossed the lawn, a window that had been dark was lighted and Miss Emily sat in it, the light behind her, and her upright torso motionless as that of an idol. They crept quietly across the lawn and into the shadow of the locusts that lined the street. After a week or two the smell went away.

27 That was when people had begun to feel really sorry for her. People in our town, remembering how old lady Wyatt, her great-aunt, had gone completely crazy at last, believed that the Griersons held themselves a little too high for what they really were. None of the young men were quite good enough for Miss Emily and such. We had long thought of them as a tableau, Miss Emily a slender figure in white in the background, her father a spraddled silhouette in the foreground, his back to her and clutching a horsewhip, the two of them framed by the back-flung front door. So when she got to be thirty and was still single, we were not pleased exactly, but vindicated; even with insanity in the family she wouldn't have turned down all of her chances if they had really materialized.

28 When her father died, it got about that the house was all that was left to her; and in a way, people were glad. At last they could pity Miss Emily. Being left alone, and a pauper, she had become humanized. Now she too would know the old thrill and the old despair of a penny more or less.

29 The day after his death all the ladies prepared to call at the house and offer condolence and aid, as is our custom. Miss Emily met them at the door, dressed as usual and with no trace of grief on her face. She told them that her father was not dead. She did that for three days, with the ministers calling on her, and the doctors, trying to persuade her to let them dispose of the body. Just as they were about to resort to law and force, she broke down, and they buried her father quickly.

30 We did not say she was crazy then. We believed she had to do that. We remembered all the young men her father had driven away, and we knew that with nothing left, she would have to cling to that which had robbed her, as people will.

III.

31. She was sick for a long time. When we saw her again, her hair was cut short, making her look like a girl, with a vague resemblance to those angels in colored church windows—sort of tragic and serene.

32. The town had just let the contracts for paving the sidewalks, and in the summer after her father's death they began the work. The construction company came with n------ and mules and machinery, and a foreman named Homer Barron, a Yankee—a big, dark, ready man, with a big voice and eyes lighter than his face. The little boys would follow in groups to hear him cuss the n------, and the n------ singing in time to the rise and fall of picks. Pretty soon he knew everybody in town. Whenever you heard a lot of laughing anywhere about the square, Homer Barron would be in the center of the group. Presently we began to see him and Miss Emily on Sunday afternoons driving in the yellow-wheeled buggy and the matched team of bays from the livery stable.

33. At first we were glad that Miss Emily would have an interest, because the ladies all said, "Of course a Grierson would not think seriously of a Northerner, a day laborer." But there were still others, older people, who said that even grief could not cause a real lady to forget *noblesse oblige*[1]—without calling it *noblesse oblige*. They just said, "Poor Emily. Her kinsfolk should come to her." She had some kin in Alabama; but years ago her father had fallen out with them over the estate of old lady Wyatt, the crazy woman, and there was no communication between the two families. They had not even been represented at the funeral.

34. And as soon as the old people said, "Poor Emily," the whispering began. "Do you suppose it's really so?" they said to one another. "Of course it is. What else could . . ." This behind their hands; rustling of craned silk and satin behind jalousies closed upon the sun of Sunday afternoon as the thin, swift clop-clop-clop of the matched team passed: "Poor Emily."

35. She carried her head high enough—even when we believed that she was fallen. It was as if she demanded more than ever the recognition of her dignity as the last Grierson; as if it had wanted that touch of earthiness to reaffirm her imperviousness. Like when she bought the rat poison, the arsenic. That was over a year after they had begun to say "Poor Emily," and while the two female cousins were visiting her.

---

1. **noblesse oblige** the implied responsibility of the privileged or wealthy to act with kindness and benevolence

A Rose for Emily

36 "I want some poison," she said to the druggist. She was over thirty then, still a slight woman, though thinner than usual, with cold, haughty black eyes in a face the flesh of which was strained across the temples and about the eyesockets as you imagine a lighthouse-keeper's face ought to look. "I want some poison," she said.

37 "Yes, Miss Emily. What kind? For rats and such? I'd recom—"

38 "I want the best you have. I don't care what kind."

39 The druggist named several. "They'll kill anything up to an elephant. But what you want is—"

40 "Arsenic," Miss Emily said. "Is that a good one?"

41 "Is . . . arsenic? Yes, ma'am. But what you want—"

42 "I want arsenic."

43 The druggist looked down at her. She looked back at him, erect, her face like a strained flag. "Why, of course," the druggist said. "If that's what you want. But the law requires you to tell what you are going to use it for."

44 Miss Emily just stared at him, her head tilted back in order to look him eye for eye, until he looked away and went and got the arsenic and wrapped it up. The Negro delivery boy brought her the package; the druggist didn't come back. When she opened the package at home there was written on the box, under the skull and bones: "For rats."

IV.

45 So the next day we all said, "She will kill herself"; and we said it would be the best thing. When she had first begun to be seen with Homer Barron, we had said, "She will marry him." Then we said, "She will persuade him yet," because Homer himself had remarked—he liked men, and it was known that he drank with the younger men in the Elks' Club—that he was not a marrying man. Later we said, "Poor Emily" behind the jalousies as they passed on Sunday afternoon in the glittering buggy, Miss Emily with her head high and Homer Barron with his hat cocked and a cigar in his teeth, reins and whip in a yellow glove.

46 Then some of the ladies began to say that it was a disgrace to the town and a bad example to the young people. The men did not want to interfere, but at last the ladies forced the Baptist minister—Miss Emily's people were Episcopal—to call upon her. He would never divulge what happened during

that interview, but he refused to go back again. The next Sunday they again drove about the streets, and the following day the minister's wife wrote to Miss Emily's relations in Alabama.

47 So she had blood-kin under her roof again and we sat back to watch **developments**. At first nothing happened. Then we were sure that they were to be married. We learned that Miss Emily had been to the jeweler's and ordered a man's toilet set in silver, with the letters H. B. on each piece. Two days later we learned that she had bought a complete outfit of men's clothing, including a nightshirt, and we said, "They are married." We were really glad. We were glad because the two female cousins were even more Grierson than Miss Emily had ever been.

48 So we were not surprised when Homer Barron—the streets had been finished some time since—was gone. We were a little disappointed that there was not a public blowing-off, but we believed that he had gone on to prepare for Miss Emily's coming, or to give her a chance to get rid of the cousins. (By that time it was a cabal, and we were all Miss Emily's allies to help circumvent the cousins.) Sure enough, after another week they departed. And, as we had expected all along, within three days Homer Barron was back in town. A neighbor saw the Negro man admit him at the kitchen door at dusk one evening.

49 And that was the last we saw of Homer Barron. And of Miss Emily for some time. The Negro man went in and out with the market basket, but the front door remained closed. Now and then we would see her at a window for a moment, as the men did that night when they sprinkled the lime, but for almost six months she did not appear on the streets. Then we knew that this was to be expected too; as if that quality of her father which had thwarted her woman's life so many times had been too virulent and too furious to die.

50 When we next saw Miss Emily, she had grown fat and her hair was turning gray. During the next few years it grew grayer and grayer until it attained an even pepper-and-salt iron-gray, when it ceased turning. Up to the day of her death at seventy-four it was still that **vigorous** iron-gray, like the hair of an active man.

51 From that time on her front door remained closed, save for a period of six or seven years, when she was about forty, during which she gave lessons in china-painting. She fitted up a studio in one of the downstairs rooms, where the daughters and granddaughters of Colonel Sartoris' contemporaries were sent to her with the same regularity and in the same spirit that they were sent to church on Sundays with a twenty-five-cent piece for the collection plate. Meanwhile her taxes had been remitted.

A Rose for Emily

52 Then the newer generation became the backbone and the spirit of the town, and the painting pupils grew up and fell away and did not send their children to her with boxes of color and tedious brushes and pictures cut from the ladies' magazines. The front door closed upon the last one and remained closed for good. When the town got free postal delivery, Miss Emily alone refused to let them fasten the metal numbers above her door and attach a mailbox to it. She would not listen to them.

53 Daily, monthly, yearly we watched the Negro grow grayer and more stooped, going in and out with the market basket. Each December we sent her a tax notice, which would be returned by the post office a week later, unclaimed. Now and then we would see her in one of the downstairs windows—she had evidently shut up the top floor of the house—like the carven torso of an idol in a niche, looking or not looking at us, we could never tell which. Thus she passed from generation to generation—dear, inescapable, **impervious**, tranquil, and perverse.

54 And so she died. Fell ill in the house filled with dust and shadows, with only a doddering Negro man to wait on her. We did not even know she was sick; we had long since given up trying to get any information from the Negro. He talked to no one, probably not even to her, for his voice had grown harsh and rusty, as if from disuse.

55 She died in one of the downstairs rooms, in a heavy walnut bed with a curtain, her gray head propped on a pillow yellow and moldy with age and lack of sunlight.

V.

56 The Negro met the first of the ladies at the front door and let them in, with their hushed, sibilant voices and their quick, curious glances, and then he disappeared. He walked right through the house and out the back and was not seen again.

57 The two female cousins came at once. They held the funeral on the second day, with the town coming to look at Miss Emily beneath a mass of bought flowers, with the crayon face of her father musing profoundly above the bier and the ladies sibilant and macabre; and the very old men—some in their brushed Confederate uniforms—on the porch and the lawn, talking of Miss Emily as if she had been a contemporary of theirs, believing that they had danced with her and courted her perhaps, confusing time with its mathematical progression, as the old do, to whom all the past is not a **diminishing** road but, instead, a huge meadow which no winter ever quite touches, divided from them now by the narrow bottle-neck of the most recent decade of years.

58 Already we knew that there was one room in that region above stairs which no one had seen in forty years, and which would have to be forced. They waited until Miss Emily was decently in the ground before they opened it.

59 The violence of breaking down the door seemed to fill this room with pervading dust. A thin, acrid pall as of the tomb seemed to lie everywhere upon this room decked and furnished as for a bridal: upon the valance curtains of faded rose color, upon the rose-shaded lights, upon the dressing table, upon the delicate array of crystal and the man's toilet things backed with tarnished silver, silver so tarnished that the monogram was obscured. Among them lay a collar and tie, as if they had just been removed, which, lifted, left upon the surface a pale crescent in the dust. Upon a chair hung the suit, carefully folded; beneath it the two mute shoes and the discarded socks.

60 The man himself lay in the bed.

61 For a long while we just stood there, looking down at the profound and fleshless grin. The body had apparently once lain in the attitude of an embrace, but now the long sleep that outlasts love, that conquers even the grimace of love, had cuckolded him. What was left of him, rotted beneath what was left of the nightshirt, had become inextricable from the bed in which he lay; and upon him and upon the pillow beside him lay that even coating of the patient and biding dust.

62 Then we noticed that in the second pillow was the indentation of a head. One of us lifted something from it, and leaning forward, that faint and invisible dust dry and acrid in the nostrils, we saw a long strand of iron-gray hair.

"A Rose for Emily". Copyright 1930 & renewed 1958 by William Faulkner, from COLLECTED STORIES OF WILLIAM FAULKNER by William Faulkner. Used by permission of W.W. Norton & Company, Inc.

WRITE

NARRATIVE: William Faulkner's stories are often told from multiple points of view. "A Rose for Emily" is told from the point of view of unnamed narrators who harbor their own attitudes towards Emily. In a narrative response, rewrite any section of the story from a different point of view: either that of Emily, her father, Tobe, or a character of your own imagination. Be sure to incorporate and modify specific descriptions and dialogue from the text as needed in your alteration of Faulkner's classic story.

LITERARY FOCUS:
The Harlem Renaissance

Introduction

This informational text offers background information about the historical and cultural circumstances that led to the Harlem Renaissance. After the turn of the 20th century, populations were becoming increasingly urban. African Americans living in Northern cities faced widespread discriminatory practices by city landlords, and those living in the South dealt with the racism and injustice of Jim Crow laws. This oppression, along with the North's newfound need for factory workers, led to both the Great Migration and a migration within New York City to the welcoming Harlem area. Partially a response to racist stereotyping and partially to the horror of the first World War, the Harlem Renaissance was an African American-led artistic movement that came to define the 1920s and early '30s and inspired generations of creative minds to come.

Literary Focus: The Harlem Renaissance

"How do artists of the Harlem Renaissance continue to inspire music and culture today?"

1. The Harlem Renaissance was a cultural movement among African Americans in New York City in the 1920s and 1930s. Musicians, writers, and other African American artists were drawn to the Harlem section of Manhattan by plentiful housing. The artistic outpouring lasted until the Great Depression, which forced many Harlem artists to move elsewhere to look for work. The impact of the Harlem Renaissance, however, can still be felt heavily in our culture today.

The Emergence of an African American Community

2. African Americans in New York City began moving to the Harlem area in about 1900. They were eager to move out of the West Side of Manhattan because of the overcrowded apartment buildings and increasing hostility from white neighbors. Harlem had a surplus of apartments, so landlords were eager to welcome African American tenants. When African-American churches began to relocate to Harlem as well, the population of African Americans became solidly established and continued to grow.

3. **Segregation** was widespread in the North as well as the South in the early 1900s. African Americans were banned from many white-owned businesses, including restaurants and hotels. As a result, African Americans started their own businesses to draw on the large number of potential customers in their neighborhood. Among the most successful businesses were nightclubs that featured jazz and blues.

The Great Migration

4. *The Great Migration* is a term that refers to the movement of African Americans from the South to large cities in the North between approximately 1916 and 1940 in its first wave. World War I cut off the flow of European immigrants to the United States. Northern factories were growing and needed more workers. They recruited African Americans from the South to help make up for the shortage of workers. African Americans were eager to leave the South because of Jim Crow laws that led to mistreatment and violence against them. Many were sharecroppers who had difficulty surviving economically, especially when an insect **infestation** decimated the cotton crop during the war. Harlem also attracted black immigrants from the Caribbean, promising greater prosperity and economic opportunity. These movements of people

to large cities were part of a larger trend; in 1920, for the first time in U.S. history, more people lived in urban areas than in rural areas.

An unidentified woman, dressed in a fur-trimmed coat, posing in front of a tree on a Harlem sidewalk, 1920s

A Flowering of the Arts

5   In 1917, playwright Ridgely Torrence's *Three Plays for a Negro Theatre*, often considered among the first major works of the Harlem Renaissance, premiered. The suite of plays featured African-American actors and represented complex characters. The work rejected racial **stereotypes** frequently portrayed in the theater previously. For example, one of the most popular forms of musical entertainment in the late 1800s had been minstrel shows. These shows, featuring white men wearing makeup that made them appear to be African American, consisted of comedy and musical numbers that portrayed African Americans as foolish and simpleminded. In the early 1900s, African American musical performers sought to create their own musical theater that gave a more accurate portrayal of African American life and moved away from stereotypes. Eubie Blake and Noble Sissle wrote a musical called *Shuffle Along* in 1921. It became the first hit Broadway musical written by African Americans.

6   What's more, music attracted people from all races and walks of life to Harlem's nightclubs. This music included the blues, which originated in the Deep South in the late 1800s. The blues grew out of African American spirituals and work songs as well as the music of Africa and folk music. Blues music featured trancelike rhythm and unusual scales and chords.

7   Another musical form, jazz, drew partly from the blues. It, too, was invented by African Americans in the South in the late 1800s. Jazz features **improvisation**, in which the musicians create music as they play rather than reading it from sheets of paper. Bandleaders such as Duke Ellington and performers such as Louis Armstrong created some of the greatest jazz of any era. Jazz was created by African Americans in New Orleans in the late 1800s and represented an integral part of African American culture. It became so popular in the 1920s that the decade is sometimes referred to as the Jazz Age.

Literary Focus: The Harlem Renaissance

8. At the **outset** of the Harlem Renaissance, as African American musicians flocked to Harlem for work in the popular nightclubs, other artists soon followed. African-American artists living in Harlem had the opportunity to be trained and mentored by famous artists and to attend top schools in other parts of New York City. Among the artists who took advantage of these opportunities were painter Aaron Douglas and sculptor Augusta Savage.

9. Rising literacy levels among African Americans in the late 1800s made it possible for African Americans to consider writing as an occupation. Prior to the Civil War, few Southern African Americans could read because it was illegal to give instruction to enslaved persons. The growth of schools in the South for African Americans after the war meant that, when the Great Migration occurred, there was a burgeoning demand for literature and news by and about African Americans. The creation of African-American newspapers and magazines helped meet this need.

10. Among the most important magazines read by people in Harlem were *The Crisis* and *Opportunity: A Journal of Negro Life*. *The Crisis* was published by the National Association for the Advancement of Colored People (NAACP), an organization founded in New York City in 1909. The editor of *The Crisis* was W.E.B. Du Bois, who used the magazine to shed light on the oppression of African Americans and call for increased civil rights. Du Bois, a sociologist, was the leading activist for African Americans during the early 1900s. He appointed Jessie Fauset as literary editor of *The Crisis*. She published works by most of Harlem's leading authors. Another important group of African-American activists, the National Urban League, published *Opportunity*. This journal published, in addition to literature, studies of the difficulties faced by African Americans, including discrimination.

Political Activism Voices of Change

11. At the **outset** of the Harlem Renaissance, Marcus Garvey launched one of the largest mass movements in African American history. Garvey, who had emigrated from Jamaica in 1916, led the Universal Negro Improvement Association. A charismatic speaker, Garvey urged African Americans to become economically strong and suggested that they help form a black-led nation in Africa. He published a newspaper called *Negro World* that ran stories describing achievements of African Americans as well as features about African culture. At its peak his movement had over one million followers. While his ideas could be divisive among members of the Harlem Renaissance movement, his work influenced contemporary political thinking.

12. One of the most widely talented figures in the Harlem Renaissance was James Weldon Johnson. After serving as a **diplomat** to South American countries under President Theodore Roosevelt, Johnson became the first African American to serve as executive secretary of the NAACP. He had

Literary Focus: The Harlem Renaissance

distinguished himself within the organization for his campaign against lynching. As leader of the NAACP, he helped to expand the organization and fight limitations on voting rights in the South. Johnson was also talented in poetry and music. He served as a mentor to young poets and collected their work in important anthologies. He and his brother wrote the song "Lift Every Voice and Sing," sometimes referred to today as the Black National Anthem.

Writer and educator James Weldon Johnson (1871–1938) was one of the founders of the NAACP and served as the group's secretary from 1916 to 1930.

Major Concepts

- **End Stereotypes**—At the time of the Harlem Renaissance, many white people regarded African Americans as not being deserving of equal rights. Negative portrayals of African Americans extended beyond just minstrel shows and could also be found in fiction and motion pictures created by whites. African-American authors worked to **dispel** these images in two ways. First, they portrayed the diversity of African Americans, describing lives in many types of settings. Second, the quality of the literary output of these writers provided strong evidence that they were fully deserving of equal education and equal rights.

- **Protest Oppression**—Harlem writers worked to create a historical record of the injustices endured by African Americans. Lynchings, race riots, and other mob violence were epidemic throughout the period of the Harlem Renaissance. Harlem writers also drew attention to segregation and denials of constitutional rights. Discrimination in all its forms was another important topic.

- **Experiment with Modernism**—The mass slaughter of World War I led many artists to question the traditional beliefs of society. Writers in both Europe and the United States made a break with traditional literary forms and began to experiment. Individuals felt free to explore their own identities and imaginations. Modernist tropes were employed by many Harlem Renaissance writers, such as Jean Toomer's famous engagement with the movement in his novel *Cane* (1923).

- **Preserve Heritage**—Many writers who had migrated from the South wrote important works about their experiences there. They wrote about both the positive aspects of African American communities and the negative experiences of persecution by whites. Another important aspect of preserving heritage was writing about Africa. For example, Countee Cullen explored African themes in some of his finest poetry.

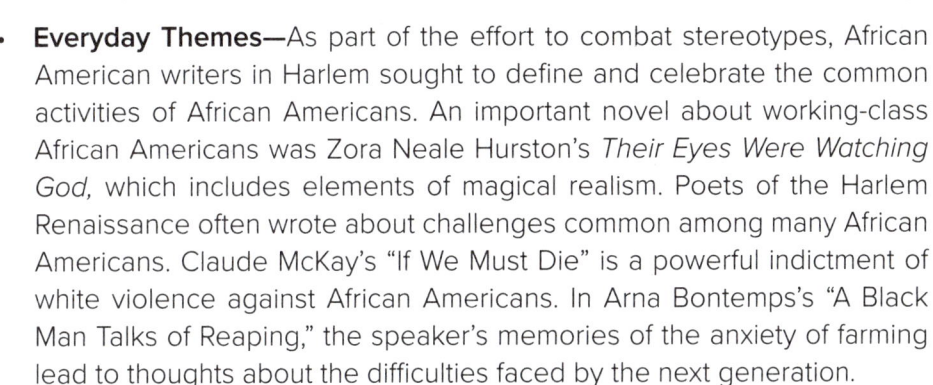

- **Everyday Themes**—As part of the effort to combat stereotypes, African American writers in Harlem sought to define and celebrate the common activities of African Americans. An important novel about working-class African Americans was Zora Neale Hurston's *Their Eyes Were Watching God*, which includes elements of magical realism. Poets of the Harlem Renaissance often wrote about challenges common among many African Americans. Claude McKay's "If We Must Die" is a powerful indictment of white violence against African Americans. In Arna Bontemps's "A Black Man Talks of Reaping," the speaker's memories of the anxiety of farming lead to thoughts about the difficulties faced by the next generation.

Style and Form

Influence of Blues and Jazz

- Jazz and blues strongly influenced the writing style of authors of fiction and poetry during the Harlem Renaissance. It was evident in such literary techniques as rhythm and stream of consciousness, which sometimes mirrored improvised music in style. Such techniques lent a strong Modernist feel to compositions.

- Langston Hughes, one of the leading poets of the twentieth century, spoke about the influence of music on his work. "To me, jazz is a montage of a dream deferred. A great big dream—yet to come—and always *yet*—to become ultimately and finally true." The influence of blues is also evident in Hughes's work. His poem "The Weary Blues" concerns a blues singer and begins,

> Droning a drowsy syncopated tune,
> Rocking back and forth to a mellow croon

Blending the Traditional with the Modern

- Although Harlem Renaissance writers experimented with Modernist forms, there was a strong traditional streak in their work as well. Zora Neale Hurston collected folklore and oral histories from African Americans in the South while she was a college student. Then she moved to Harlem and drew on this research to create satires and other literary forms. Poets, including Countee Cullen and Claude McKay, used traditional forms such as sonnets to frame their Modernist themes.

- Alain Locke, a professor of philosophy at Howard University, urged Harlem artists to draw on African history and subjects in their work. Locke collected

Literary Focus: The Harlem Renaissance

the work of top Harlem writers in *The New Negro*. This anthology showed the diversity of the African-American experience, which was another way of combating the stereotypes that had grown up around portrayals of African Americans in prior decades.

16   The Great Depression is often considered the moment of the Harlem Renaissance's decline, as many African Americans left Harlem in search of jobs elsewhere. The rich artistic output of Harlem's artists would endure, however. Today, a line can be drawn connecting Harlem Renaissance writers and musicians to poets of the Black Arts Movement in the 1960s, such as Amiri Baraka and Nikki Giovanni, and to hip hop artists, like Kendrick Lamar. The Harlem Renaissance was an artistic movement that brought the social, political, and cultural realities of urban African-American life to mainstream culture and remains widely influential today. How do artists of the Harlem Renaissance continue to inspire music and culture today?

Literary Focus

Read "Literary Focus: The Harlem Renaissance." After you read, complete the Think Questions below.

THINK QUESTIONS

1. What caused the Great Migration of African Americans from the South to large Northern cities? Cite textual evidence to support your answer.

2. How did the NAACP play an important role in the Harlem Renaissance?

3. How did Harlem Renaissance writers make a break with the traditions of American literature from previous eras? Support your answer with evidence from the text.

4. The word *stereotype* comes from the Greek *stereos*, meaning "solid" and the Latin *typus*, meaning "image." With this information in mind and using context clues, write your best definition of the word **stereotype** as it used in this text. Cite any words or phrases that were particularly helpful in coming to your conclusion.

5. Use context clues to determine the meaning of the word **improvisation**. Write your best definition here, along with the words and phrases that were most helpful in determining the word's meaning. Then, check a dictionary to confirm your understanding.

LITERARY SEMINAR:
Alain Locke and the Harlem Renaissance

Introduction

In 1916, African Americans began leaving the American South in record numbers, in what would become known as the Great Migration. Most people settled in urban areas, including Harlem, a neighborhood in New York City. In the 1920s, there was an artistic, social, and intellectual movement based in Harlem called the Harlem Renaissance. The Harlem Renaissance was encouraged and chronicled by Alain Locke, whose anthology, *The New Negro: An Interpretation*, showcased talented African American artists and writers. This anthology discussed African American identity, artistic expression, and self determination.

Literary Seminar: Alain Locke and the Harlem Renaissance

". . . Alain Locke who aspired to both capture and catalyze the significance of Harlem's artists."

1. By the turn of the twentieth century, a movement was building. A large contingent of African Americans moved out of the South and into growing communities in the North in conjunction with the Great Migration. Encouraged by job opportunities and seeking a more welcoming place to live, many African Americans came to New York. Over time, an African American community **centered** in the neighborhood of Harlem. The neighborhood swiftly became a vibrant and popular cultural center, the birthplace of a cultural movement known as the Harlem Renaissance.

2. Who was the self-described "midwife" of that movement? He was an academic named Alain Locke who aspired to both capture and catalyze the significance of Harlem's artists.

The New Negro[1] Movement

3. What is now called the "Harlem Renaissance" was referred to at the time as the "Negro Renaissance" or the "New Negro Movement." The "New Negro" was a way contemporary writers, critics, social activists, and intellectuals used to define an African American population less concerned with the artistic

Portrait of Alain Locke by artist Betsy Graves Reyneau.

---

1. **Negro:** common terminology used at the time to refer to an African American person.

Literary Seminar: Alain Locke and the Harlem Renaissance

standards of white and European culture, and more interested in self-expression and a distinctive African American culture.

4 It was the concept of the "New Negro," that Howard University philosopher and professor Alain Locke sought to capture through the creation of an anthology. Alain Locke compiled his anthology, *The New Negro: An Interpretation*, in 1925. It contained artistic and sociological texts from a variety of culturally relevant poets, writers, and researchers, such as Langston Hughes, Zora Neale Hurston, Jean Toomer, Claude McKay, and Countee Cullen. Locke included the art and intellectual ideas of African Americans to document the possibilities and achievements of the African American community and to dispel stereotypes, which he believed art, as opposed to direct political activism, was most equipped to do.

5 He hoped to encourage the movement in its efforts to display the identity and achievements of African Americans and, ultimately, to encourage racial pride. In his anthology, Locke acknowledged the work of W.E.B Du Bois. Locke contended that Du Bois' efforts to create and encourage African American art was for propagandistic purposes, to improve the station of African Americans by educating and motivating an audience to accept racial equality. Locke believed he had distinctly different goals for his anthology, concerned that "propaganda perpetuates the position of group inferiority." Locke and other artists believed that art created by African Americans should be allowed to pursue the goals of art, whether that was for the purpose of individual or group expression.

6 Locke solicited pieces for his anthology that resonated with the themes of self-definition and self-expression of African Americans. Within the anthology, there were different expressions of what that meant. Some artists favored distinguishing themselves entirely from white culture, while others emulated the styles of white artists to gain acceptance or to demonstrate their ability to create art that was equally powerful. One of the successes of the collection is how well it represents some of the important and thoroughly debated ideas of the day.

Style and Self-Definition

7 One tension visible in Locke's anthology is the varied approaches towards writing in dialect. "Dialect poetry" was a popular genre at the time, sometimes written in response or opposition to white plantation tradition literature. Some African American poets, such as Paul Dunbar, wrote poems in dialect, like "The Old Cabin," which often departed a great deal in **tone** and content from the dialect poetry of the plantation tradition. However, with the transition into the 1920's, some authors wanted to move away from the focus on slave narratives and the impact of slavery, including styles like dialect poetry that some artists felt did more to perpetuate stereotypes than celebrate folk culture. Jean Toomer's poems in the collection avoid dialect altogether and

borrow from European styles of poetry, while Zora Neale Hurston's contribution, a short story titled "Spunk," uses dialect to tell the story of an all-African American cast of characters, and plays with the theme of courage. This debate about the use of dialect in writing, which writer Sterling Brown criticized as "an affectation to please a white audience" represented a desire on the part of some African American artists to define their own cultural aesthetic.

The Importance of Heritage

8   Another method of self-expression and racial pride seen in the anthology was an interest in "cultural pluralism," which encouraged an interest in African roots while developing a **unique** African American culture. Locke, in particular, encouraged African Americans to reclaim their African identity and, therefore, a cultural heritage. He was interested in African influences on Caribbean nations and on African Americans and encouraged younger artists to study African culture. In his anthology, he included an essay by W. E. B. Du Bois on the relationship between the "New Negro" movement and events in Africa, including colonialism and struggles for freedom that he believes paralleled the African American plight. Locke chose not to mention Marcus Garvey or his movement, which encouraged African Americans to move to Africa, considering him too controversial a figure and not representative of the "New Negro" he desired to promote.

9   Artists of the time were exploring the idea of an African heritage. Langston Hughes' "The Negro Speaks of Rivers" released prior to the anthology painted the picture of an African-built society, and Africans as a proud and powerful people. Countee Cullen's poem, "Heritage," printed in *The New Negro*, has a more complicated relationship with the concept of African heritage. In it, he repeatedly asks, "What is Africa to me?," highlighting the difficulties of feeling attachment to an African homeland and the culture he has never seen.

Bronze from the Benin kingdom housed in the Ethnological museum in Berlin, Germany. *The New Negro* included an image of a Benin bronze in its pages.

10. Part of defining the "New Negro" was in embracing an African aesthetic and in placing value on African American features and skin color, as can be seen in the images of sculptures included in the pages of *The New Negro*. Striking illustrations, also, by Winold Reiss celebrated a variety of skin colors and facial features using realistic artistic techniques to depict the authors represented in the anthology in a way that had not been popularized visually before.

The Writers and the Audience

11. Although *The New Negro* presented a range of diverse **perspectives** on questions at the heart of African American arts and culture, it was not wholly inclusive of African American perspectives. Some contemporary critics, including a writer named Eric Reader, objected to the makeup of the authors in anthology, citing a lack of poor and working-class African Americans. These perspectives, Reader noted, reflected the majority of African Americans.

12. The writers who made up the collection in *The New Negro*, however, were aware that they were writing for a diverse audience. Alain Locke encouraged the African American artists of this generation to turn their awareness and voice inwards to the black community, rather than trying to prove something to a white audience. Langston Hughes echoed this sentiment in his 1926 essay "The Negro Artist and the Racial Mountain," writing, "We young Negro artists who create now intend to express our individual dark-skinned selves without fear or shame. If white people are pleased, we are glad. If they are not, it doesn't matter."

13. The anthology was popular with a white audience at a time when white audiences were increasingly receptive to African American writing. However, an element of the anthology's success across a white audience can be attributed to the allure and "exoticization" of the African American community and Harlem at the time. Still, the writers included in *The New Negro* became more widely published and better paid.

The Anthology Today

14. One of the most beautiful parts of the Harlem Renaissance was the **complexity** of ideas circulating regarding art, race, and African American identity. Members of the Harlem Renaissance were eager that their art and philosophies were not oversimplified: James Weldon Johnson wrote in his book about the period, *Black Manhattan*, that "Harlem is still in the process of making. It is still new and mixed; so mixed that one may get many different views—which is all right so long as one view is not taken to be the whole picture." Locke's anthology captures some of those many perspectives, allowing modern-day readers to understand that the Harlem Renaissance was a multi-faceted movement encompassing many viewpoints.

Literary Seminar: Alain Locke and the Harlem Renaissance

Read "Literary Seminar: Alain Locke and the Harlem Renaissance." After you read, complete the Think Questions below.

THINK QUESTIONS

1. What criticism did *The New Negro* face in regards to the writers chosen for its publication? Cite specific evidence from the text in your response.

2. What were some challenges that Locke and others faced when creating *The New Negro*? Cite relevant evidence from the text in your response.

3. Why didn't Locke include ideas or writing from political leader and writer Marcus Garvey? Identify and select evidence from the text in your answer.

4. Use context clues to determine the meaning of the word **complexity** as it is used in the text. Write your definition of *complexity* here, along with those words from the text that helped you determine its meaning. Then check a dictionary to confirm your understanding.

5. What is the meaning of the word **tone** as it is used in the text? Write your best definition here, along with a brief explanation of how you arrived at its meaning.

In Our Neighborhood

FICTION
Alice Dunbar-Nelson
1895

Introduction

Alice Dunbar-Nelson (1875–1935) was born in New Orleans to mixed-race parents. Moving easily between genres, she was a journalist, poet, essayist, diarist, and short story writer. As a woman with African American, Caucasian, Native American, and Creole heritage, she wrote elegantly about the complexities of issues such as racism, family, community, gender, ethnicity, and sexuality. "In Our Neighborhood," from Dunbar-Nelson's first book of stories, *Violets and Other Tales,* is a good example of her sure feel for the ironic nuances of a Southern neighborhood.

"The Harts were going to give a party."

1. The Harts were going to give a party. Neither Mrs. Hart, nor the Misses Hart, nor the small and busy Harts who amused themselves and the neighborhood by continually falling in the gutter on special occasions, had mentioned this fact to anyone, but all the interested denizens of that particular square could tell by the unusual air of bustle and activity which pervaded the Hart **domicile**. Lillian, the æsthetic[1], who furnished theme for many spirited discussions, leaned airily out of the window; her auburn (red) tresses carefully done in curl papers. Martha, the practical, flourished the broom and duster with unwonted activity, which the small boys of the neighborhood, peering through the green shutters of the front door, duly reported to their mammas, busily engaged in holding down their respective door-steps by patiently sitting thereon.

2. Pretty soon, the junior Harts,—two in number—began to travel to and fro, soliciting the loan of a "few chairs," "some nice dishes," and such like things, indispensable to every decent, self-respecting party. But to all inquiries as to the use to which these articles were to be put, they only vouchsafed one reply, "Ma told us as we wasn't to tell, just ask for the things, that's all."

3. Mrs. Tuckley the dress-maker, brought her sewing out on the front-steps, and entered a vigorous protest to her next-door neighbor.

4. "Humph," she sniffed, "mighty funny they can't say what's up. Must be something in it. Couldn't get none o' *my* things, and not invite *me*!"

5. "Did she ask you for any?" absent-mindedly inquired Mrs. Luke, shielding her eyes from the sun.

6. "No-o—, but she'd better sense, she knows *me*—she ain't—mercy me, Stella! Just look at that child tumbling in the mud! You, Stella, come here, I say! Look at you now, there—and there—and there?"

7. The luckless Stella having been soundly cuffed, and sent whimpering in the back-yard, Mrs. Tuckley continued, "Yes as I was saying, 'course, taint none o'

---

1. **æsthetic** dated spelling of aesthetic; concerned with beauty or appearance

my business, but I always did wonder how them Harts do keep up. Why, them girls dress just as fine as any lady on the Avenue and that there Lillian wears real diamond ear-rings. 'Pears mighty, mighty funny to me, and Lord the airs they do put on! Holdin' up their heads like nobody's good enough to speak to. I don't like to talk about people, you know, yourself, Mrs. Luke I never speak about anybody, but mark my word, girls that cut up capers like them Hartses' girls never come to any good."

8   Mrs. Luke heaved a deep sigh of appreciation at the wisdom of her neighbor, but before she could reply a re-inforcement in the person of little Mrs. Peters, apron over her head, hands shrivelled and soap-sudsy from washing, appeared.

9   "Did you ever see the like?" she asked in her usual, rapid breathless way. "Why, my Louis says they're putting canvass cloths on the floor, and taking down the bed in the back-room; and putting greenery and such like trash about. Some style about them, eh?"

10 Mrs. Tuckley tossed her head and sniffed contemptuously, Mrs. Luke began to rehearse a time worn tale, how once a carriage had driven up to the Hart house at nine o'clock at night, and a distinguished looking man alighted, went in, stayed about ten minutes and finally drove off with a great clatter. Heads that had shaken ominously over this story before began to shake again, and tongues that had wagged themselves tired with conjectures started now with some brand new ideas and theories. The children of the square, tired of fishing for minnows in the ditches, and making mud-pies in the street, clustered about their mother's skirts receiving occasional slaps, when their attempts at taking part in the conversation became too pronounced.

11 Meanwhile, in the Hart household, all was bustle and preparation. To and fro the members of the house flitted, arranging chairs, putting little touches here and there, washing saucers and glasses, chasing the Hart Juniors about, losing things and calling frantically for each other's assistance to find them. Mama Hart, big, plump and perspiring, puffed here and there like a large, rosy engine, giving impossible orders, and receiving sharp answers to foolish questions. Lillian, the æsthetic, practiced her most graceful poses before the large mirror in the parlor; Martha rushed about, changing the order of the furniture, and Papa Hart, just come in from work, paced the rooms disconsolately, asking for dinner.

12 "Dinner!" screamed Mama Hart, "Dinner, who's got time to fool with dinner this evening? Look in the sideboard and you'll see some bread and ham; eat that and shut up."

13. Eight o'clock finally arrived, and with it, the music and some straggling guests. When the first faint chee-chee of the violin floated out into the murky atmosphere, the smaller portion of the neighborhood went straightway into ecstasies. Boys and girls in all stages of deshabille clustered about the doorsteps and gave vent to audible exclamations of approval or disapprobation concerning the state of affairs behind the green shutters. It was a warm night and the big round moon sailed serenely in a cloudless, blue sky. Mrs. Tuckley had put on a clean calico wrapper, and planted herself with the indomitable Stella on her steps, "to watch the purceedings."

14. The party was a grand success. Even the **intensely** critical small fry dancing on the pavement without to the scraping and fiddling of the string band, had to admit that. So far as they were concerned it was all right, but what shall we say of the guests within? They who glided easily over the canvassed floors, bowed, and scraped and simpered, "just like the big folks on the Avenue," who ate the ice-cream and cake, and drank the sweet, weak Catawba wine amid boisterous healths to Mr. and Mrs. Hart and the Misses Hart; who smirked and perspired and cracked ancient jokes and heart-rending puns during the intervals of the dances, who shall say that they did not enjoy themselves as thoroughly and as fully as those who frequented the wealthier entertainments up-town.

15. Lillian and Martha in gossamer gowns of pink and blue flitted to and fro attending to the wants of their guests. Mrs. Hart, gorgeous in a black satin affair, all folds and lace and drapery, made desperate efforts to appear cool and collected—and failed miserably. Papa Hart spent one half his time standing in front of the mantle, spreading out his coat-tails, and **benignly** smiling upon the young people, while the other half was devoted to initiating the male portion of the guests into the mysteries of "snake killing."

16. Everybody had said that he or she had had a splendid time, and finally, when the last kisses had been kissed, the last good-byes been said, the whole Hart family sat down in the now deserted and disordered rooms, and sighed with relief that the great event was over at last.

17. "Nice crowd, eh?" remarked Papa Hart. He was brimful of joy and second-class whiskey, so no one paid any attention to him.

18. "But did you see how shamefully Maude flirted with Willie Howard?" said Lillian. Martha tossed her head in disdain; Mr. Howard she had always considered her especial property, so Lillian's observation had a rather disturbing effect.

19 "I'm so warm and tired," cried Mama Hart, plaintively, "children how are we going to sleep to-night?"

20 Thereupon the whole family arose to devise ways and means for wooing the drowsy god. As for the Hart Juniors they had long since solved the problem by falling asleep with sticky hands and faces upon a pile of bed-clothing behind the kitchen door.

21 It was late in the next day before the house had begun to resume anything like its former appearance. The little Harts were kept busy all morning returning chairs and dishes, and distributing the remnants of the feast to the vicinity. The ice-cream had melted into a warm custard, and the cakes had a rather worse for wear appearance, but they were appreciated as much as though just from the confectioner. No one was forgotten, even Mrs. Tuckley, busily stitching on a muslin garment on the steps, and unctuously rolling the latest morsel of scandal under her tongue, was obliged to confess that "them Hartses wasn't such bad people after all, just a bit queer at times."

22 About two o'clock, just as Lillian was re-draping the tidies on the stiff, common plush chairs in the parlor, some one pulled the bell violently. The visitor, a rather good-looking young fellow, with a worried **expression** smiled somewhat sarcastically as he heard a sound of scuffling and running within the house.

23 Presently Mrs. Hart opened the door wiping her hand, red and smoking with dish-water, upon her apron. The worried expression deepened on the visitor's face as he addressed the woman with visible embarrassment.

24 "Er—I—I—suppose you are Mrs. Hart?" he inquired awkwardly.

25 "That's my name, sir," replied she with pretentious dignity.

26 "Er—your-er—may I come in madam?"

27 "Certainly," and she opened the door to admit him, and offered a chair.

28 "Your husband is an employee in the Fisher Oil Mills, is he not?"

29 Mrs. Hart straightened herself with pride as she replied in the affirmative. She had always been proud of Mr. Hart's position as foreman of the big oil mills, and was never so happy as when he was expounding to someone in her presence, the difficulties and intricacies of machine-work.

30. "Well you see my dear Mrs. Hart," continued the visitor. "Now pray don't get excited—there has been an accident, and your husband—has—er—been hurt, you know."

31. But for a painful whitening in her usually rosy face, and a quick compression of her lips, the wife made no sign.

32. "What was the accident?" she queried, leaning her elbows on her knees.

33. "Well, you see, I don't understand machinery and the like, but there was something about a wheel out of gear, and a band bursted, or something, anyhow a big wheel flew to pieces, and as he was standing near, he was hit."

34. "Where?"

35. "Well—well, I may as well tell you the truth, madam; a large piece of the wheel struck him on the head—and—he was killed instantly."

36. She did not faint, nor make any outcry, nor tear her hair as he had partly expected, but sat still staring at him, with a sort of helpless, dumb horror shining out her eyes, then with a low moan, bowed her head on her knees and shuddered, just as Lillian came in, curious to know what the handsome stranger had to say to her mother.

37. The poor mutilated body came home at last, and was laid in a stiff, silver-decorated, black coffin in the middle of the sitting-room, which had been made to look as uncomfortable and unnatural as mirrors and furniture shrouded in sheets and mantel and tables divested of ornaments would permit.

38. There was a wake that night to the unconfined joy of the neighbors, who would rather a burial than a wedding. The friends of the family sat about the coffin, and through the house with long pulled faces. Mrs. Tuckley officiated in the kitchen, making coffee and dispensing cheese and crackers to those who were hungry. As the night wore on, and the first restraint disappeared, jokes were cracked, and quiet laughter indulged in, while the young folks congregated in the kitchen, were hilariously happy, until some member of the family would appear, when every face would sober down.

39. The older persons contented themselves with recounting the virtues of the deceased, and telling anecdotes wherein he figured largely. It was astonishing how many intimate friends of his had suddenly come to light. Every other man present had either attended school with him, or was a close companion until he died. Proverbs and tales and witty sayings were palmed off as having emanated from his lips. In fact, the dead man would have been surprised

himself, had he suddenly come to life and discovered what an important, what a modern solomon he had become.

40 The long night dragged on, and the people departed in groups of twos and threes, until when the gray dawn crept slowly over the blackness of night shrouding the electric lights in mists of cloudy blue, and sending cold chills of dampness through the house, but a few of the great crowd remained.

41 The day seemed so gray in **contrast** to the softening influence of the night, the grief which could be hidden then, must now come forth and parade itself before all eyes. There was the funeral to prepare for; the dismal black dresses and bonnets with their long crape veils to don; there were the condolences of sorrowing friends to receive; the floral offerings to be looked at. The little Harts strutted about resplendent in stiff black cravats, and high crape bands about their hats. They were divided between two conflicting emotions—joy at belonging to a family so noteworthy and important, and sorrow at the death. As the time for the funeral approached, and Lillian began to indulge in a series of fainting fits, the latter feeling predominated.

42 Well it was all over at last, the family had returned, and as on two nights previous, sat once more in the deserted and dismantled parlor. Mrs. Tuckley and Mrs. Luke, having rendered all assistance possible, had repaired to their respective front steps to keep count of the number of visitors who returned to condole with the family.

43 "A real nice funeral," remarked the dress-maker at last, "a nice funeral. Everybody took it so hard, and Lillian fainted real beautiful. She's a good girl that Lillian. Poor things, I wonder what they'll do now."

44 Stella, the irrepressible, was busily engaged balancing herself on one toe, *a la* ballet.

45 "Mebbe she's goin' to get married," she volunteered eagerly, "'cos I saw that yeller-haired young man what comes there all the time, wif his arms around her waist, and a tellin' her not to grieve as he'd take care of her. I was a peepin' in the dinin'-room."

46 "How dare you peep at other folks, and pry into people's affairs? I can't imagine where you get your meddlesome ways from. There aint none in *my family*. Next time I catch you at it, I'll spank you good." Then, after a pause, "Well what else did he say?"

WRITE

LITERARY ANALYSIS: This story is built around two central events, a party and a wake. Write an essay analyzing the relationship between the party and the wake. What are the parallels between them? What are the differences? Why do you think the author chose to concentrate on these two events? Be sure to cite specific examples from the text to support your claims.

The Old Cabin

POETRY
Paul Laurence Dunbar
1905

Introduction

Paul Laurence Dunbar (1872–1906) was born and raised in Dayton, Ohio. His mother was a formerly enslaved person who learned how to read to support her son's education. Dunbar published poetry and fiction, as well as song lyrics for Broadway, and was one of the first African American poets to earn nationwide acclaim. As he does in this poem, Dunbar often experimented with writing in regional dialects along with conventional English. Dunbar expressed complicated feelings about writing in dialect. Although this dialect reflected his "natural speech," as he called it, he came to feel that writing in dialect biased white readers to African Americans. In this poem's original printing, "The Old Cabin" is accompanied by a series of black-and-white photographs depicting an African American woman in several scenes of life in slavery.

"I kin see de light a-shinin'"

Note: The text you are about to read contains offensive language. Remember to be mindful of the thoughts and feelings of your peers as you read and discuss this text. If needed, ask your teacher for additional guidance and support.

1. In de dead of night I sometimes,
2. Git to t'inkin' of de pas'[1]
3. An' de days w'en slavery helt me
4. In my mis'ry—ha'd an' fas'.
5. Dough de time was mighty tryin',
6. In dese houahs somehow hit seem
7. Dat a brightah light come slippin'
8. Thoo de kivahs of my dream.

9. An' my min' fu'gits de whuppins
10. Draps de feah o' block an' lash
11. An' flies straight to somep'n' joyful
12. In a secon's lightnin' flash.
13. Den hit seems I see a **vision**
14. Of a dearah long ago
15. Of de childern tumblin' roun' me
16. By my rough ol' cabin do'.

---

1. **Git to t'inkin' of de pas'** Get to thinking about the past

The Old Cabin

17 Talk about yo' go'geous mansions
18 An' yo' big house great an' gran',
19 Des bring up de fines' palace
20 Dat you know in all de lan'.
21 But dey's somep'n' dearah to me,
22 Somep'n' **faihah** to my eyes
23 In dat cabin, less you bring me
24 To yo' mansion in de skies.

25 I kin see de light a-shinin'
26 Thoo de chinks atween de logs,
27 I kin hyeah de way-off **bayin'**
28 Of my mastah's huntin' dogs,
29 An' de neighin' of de hosses
30 Stampin' on de ol' bahn flo',
31 But above dese soun's de laughin'
32 At my deah ol' cabin do'.

33 We would gethah daih at evenin',
34 All my frien's 'ud come erroun'
35 An' hit wan't no time, twell, bless you,

36 You could hyeah de banjo's soun'.
37 You could see de dahkies dancin'
38 Pigeon wing[2] an' heel an' toe—
39 Joyous times I tell you people
40 Roun' dat same ol' cabin do'.

41 But at times my t'oughts gits saddah,
42 Ez I **riccolec'** de folks,
43 An' dey **frolickin'** an' talkin'
44 Wid dey laughin' an dey jokes.
45 An' hit hu'ts me w'en I membahs
46 Dat I'll nevah see no mo'
47 Dem ah faces gethered smilin'
48 Roun' dat po' ol' cabin do'.

2. **pigeon wing** an old-fashioned type of dance

✏️ WRITE

RESEARCH: Poetry written during the Harlem Renaissance incorporated specific themes and references pertaining to African American history and culture. Research this literary focus. Then, write a literary analysis in which you investigate how "The Old Cabin"—written in 1905—prefigures some of the predominant themes and literary characteristics of the poetry of the Harlem Renaissance.

The Negro Speaks of Rivers

POETRY
Langston Hughes
1921

Introduction

One of American literature's most distinguished and innovative writers, Langston Hughes (1902–1967) was a prominent figure of the Harlem Renaissance in the early half of the 20th century. "The Negro Speaks of Rivers" was first published in *The Crisis*, the official magazine of the National Association for the Advancement of Colored People, or NAACP—edited at the time by W. E. B. Du Bois—when Hughes was just 20 years old. The poem remains one of Hughes's most famous. It is a stirring exploration of race and the human past, seen

"My soul has grown deep like the rivers."

1 I've known rivers:
2 I've known rivers **ancient** as the world and older than the
3   flow of human blood in human veins.

4 My soul has grown deep like the rivers.

5 I bathed in the Euphrates[1] when dawns were young.
6 I built my hut near the Congo and it **lulled** me to sleep.
7 I looked upon the Nile and raised the pyramids above it.
8 I heard the singing of the Mississippi when Abe Lincoln
9   went down to New Orleans[2], and I've seen its muddy
10   **bosom** turn all golden in the sunset.

11 I've known rivers:
12 Ancient, **dusky** rivers.

13 My soul has grown deep like the rivers.

American poet and writer Langston Hughes, c. 1945

---

1. **Euphrates** a river that flows from eastern Turkey through Syria and Iraq, bordering what was once Mesopotamia, the birthplace of human civilization
2. **Abe Lincoln / went down to New Orleans** When he was young, Abraham Lincoln twice sailed down the Mississippi River to New Orleans, his first exposure to the magnitude of the slave trade in 19th-century America.

WRITE

POETRY: Langston Hughes composed this poem when he had just graduated from high school, at the age of seventeen, while crossing the Mississippi River by train outside his hometown of St. Louis, Missouri. He was inspired by what he saw and his relationship to the landscape and its history. Think about a view that inspires you. Imagine you are looking out a particular window, at a particular landscape. Now write a poem about what you see and how it influences your sense of self and place. The landscape can be real or imagined but should be one to which you feel a connection. In your poem, mimic Hughes's use of repetition, historical and geographical references, and first-person point of view.

The Color of an Awkward Conversation

INFORMATIONAL TEXT
Chimamanda Ngozi Adichie
2008

Introduction

A bestselling author and winner of the National Book Critics Circle Award for her novel *Americanah*, Chimamanda Ngozi Adichie (b. 1977) has been described by *The New Yorker* as "a keen observer of American attitudes about race." The Nigerian native pursues her unique, humorous perspective on race in America in this essay.

"Still, what is most striking to me are the strange ways in which blackness is talked about."

1 I was annoyed the first time an African American man called me "sister." It was in a Brooklyn store, and I had recently arrived from Nigeria, a country where, thanks to the mosquitoes that kept British colonizers from settling, my skin color did not determine my identity, did not limit my dreams or my confidence. And so, although I grew up reading books about the **baffling** places where black people were treated badly for being black, race remained an exotic abstraction: It was Kunta Kinte[1].

2 Until that day in Brooklyn. To be called "sister" was to be black, and blackness was the very bottom of America's pecking order. I did not want to be black.

3 In college I babysat for a Jewish family, and once I went to pick up first-grader Stephen from his play date's home. The lovely house had an American flag hanging from a colonnade. The mother of Stephen's play date greeted me warmly. Stephen hugged me and went to look for his shoes. His play date ran down the stairs and stopped halfway. "She's black," he said to his mother and stared silently at me before going back upstairs. I laughed stupidly, perhaps to deflate the tension, but I was angry.

4 I was angry that this child did not merely think that black was different but had been taught that black was not a good thing. I was angry that his behavior left Stephen bewildered, and for a long time I half-expected something **similar** to happen in other homes that displayed American flags.

5 "That kid's mother is so ignorant," one friend said. "Ignorant" suggested that an **affluent**, educated American living in a Philadelphia suburb in 1999 did not realize that black people are human beings. "It was just a kid being a kid. It wasn't racist," another said. "Racist" suggested it was no big deal, since neither the child nor his mother had burned a cross in my yard. I called the first friend a Diminisher and the second a Denier and came to discover that both represented how mainstream America talks about blackness.

---

1. **Kunta Kinte** Protagonist of Alex Haley's 1976 novel *Roots: The Saga of an American Family*, Kunta Kinte is captured and transported from Africa into slavery in the American colonies.

6   Diminishers have a subtle intellectual superiority and depend on the word "ignorant." They believe that black people still encounter unpleasantness related to blackness but in **benign** forms and from unhappy people or crazy people or people with good intentions that are bungled in execution. Diminishers think that people can be "ignorant" but not "racist" because these people have black friends, supported the civil rights movements or had abolitionist forebears.

7   Deniers believe that black people stopped encountering unpleasantness related to their blackness when Martin Luther King Jr. died. They are "colorblind" and use expressions like "white, black or purple, we're all the same"—as though race were a biological rather than a social identity. Incidents that black people attribute to blackness are really about other factors, such as having too many children or driving too fast, but if deniers are compelled to accept that an incident was indeed about blackness, they launch into stories of Irish or Native American oppression, as though to deny the legitimacy of one story by generalizing about others. Deniers use "racist" as one would use "dinosaur," to refer to a phenomenon that no longer exists.

8   Although the way that blackness **manifests** itself in America has changed since 1965, the way that it is talked about has not. I have a great and complicated affection for this country—America is like my distant uncle who does not always remember my name but occasionally gives me pocket money—and what I admire most is its ability to create enduring myths. The myth of blackness is this: "Once upon a time, black towns were destroyed, black Americans were massacred and barred from voting, etc. All this happened because of racists. Today, these things no longer happen, and therefore racists no longer exist."

9   The word "racist" should be banned. It is like a sweater wrung completely out of shape; it has lost its usefulness. It makes honest debate impossible, whether about small realities such as little boys who won't say hello to black babysitters or large realities such as who is more likely to get the death penalty. In place of "racist," descriptive, albeit unwieldy, expressions might be used, such as "incidents that negatively affect black people, which, although possibly complicated by class and other factors, would not have occurred if the affected people were not black." Perhaps qualifiers would be added: "These incidents do not implicate all non-black people."

10 There are many stories like mine of Africans discovering blackness in America; of people who are consequently amused, resentful or puzzled by Americans being afraid of them or assuming they play sports or reacting to their intelligence with surprise. Still, what is most striking to me are the strange

The Color of an Awkward Conversation

ways in which blackness is talked about. Ten years after first being called a "sister," I think of Don Cheadle as a talented brother, but I have never stopped being aware of the relative privilege of having had those West African mosquitoes.

Copyright @ 2008 by Chimamanda Ngozi Adichie, used by permission of The Wylie Agency LLC.

✏️ WRITE

PERSONAL ESSAY: Chimamanda Ngozi Adichie has lived in both Nigeria and the United States and continues to split her time between both places, which gives her a unique vantage point from which to write about race. Choose a topic on which you have a unique vantage point, and write a personal essay that describes the topic and how you view it. Why is your perspective unique? How might your experience help others look at the topic in a different light?

How It Feels to Be Colored Me

INFORMATIONAL TEXT
Zora Neale Hurston
1928

Introduction

Zora Neale Hurston (1891–1960) was an African American writer and anthropologist who was one of the leading voices in the Harlem Renaissance. Although Hurston's preacher father sometimes sought to "squinch" her spirit, her mother urged young Zora and her seven siblings to "jump at de sun," and jump she did. Ten years before the publication of her most famous novel, *Their Eyes Were Watching God*, Hurston made her own declaration of independence with the autobiographical essay presented here, "How It Feels to Be Colored Me."

"I remember the very day that I became colored."

Skill: Author's Purpose and Point of View

Hurston explains that when she was a child white people treated her as if she existed for their entertainment. She wants to inform readers that, though African Americans didn't give her money, they gave her a place to belong.

1   I am colored but I offer nothing in the way of extenuating circumstances except the fact that I am the only Negro in the United States whose grandfather on the mother's side was *not* an Indian chief.

2   I remember the very day that I became colored. Up to my thirteenth year I lived in the little Negro town of Eatonville, Florida. It is exclusively a colored town. The only white people I knew passed through the town going to or coming from Orlando. The native whites rode dusty horses, the Northern tourists chugged down the sandy village road in automobiles. The town knew the Southerners and never stopped cane chewing when they passed. But the Northerners were something else again. They were peered at cautiously from behind curtains by the timid. The more venturesome would come out on the porch to watch them go past and got just as much pleasure out of the tourists as the tourists got out of the village.

3   The front porch might seem a daring place for the rest of the town, but it was a gallery seat for me. My favorite place was atop the gatepost. Proscenium box for a born first-nighter. Not only did I enjoy the show, but I didn't mind the actors knowing that I liked it. I usually spoke to them in passing. I'd wave at them and when they returned my salute, I would say something like this: "Howdy-do-well-I-thank-you-where-you-goin'?" Usually automobile or the horse paused at this, and after a queer exchange of compliments, I would probably "go a piece of the way" with them, as we say in farthest Florida. If one of my family happened to come to the front in time to see me, of course negotiations would be rudely broken off. But even so, it is clear that I was the first "welcome-to-our-state" Floridian, and I hope the Miami Chamber of Commerce will please take notice.

4   During this period, white people differed from colored to me only in that they rode through town and never lived there. They liked to hear me "speak pieces" and sing and wanted to see me dance the parse-me-la, and gave me generously of their small silver for doing these things, which seemed strange to me for I wanted to do them so much that I needed **bribing** to stop, only they didn't know it. The colored people gave no dimes. They **deplored** any

joyful tendencies in me, but I was their Zora nevertheless. I belonged to them, to the nearby hotels, to the county—everybody's Zora.

5 But changes came in the family when I was thirteen, and I was sent to school in Jacksonville. I left Eatonville, the town of the oleanders, a Zora. When I disembarked from the river-boat at Jacksonville, she was no more. It seemed that I had suffered a sea change. I was not Zora of Orange County any more, I was now a little colored girl. I found it out in certain ways. In my heart as well as in the mirror, I became a fast brown—warranted not to rub nor run.

6 But I am not tragically colored. There is no great sorrow dammed up in my soul, nor lurking behind my eyes. I do not mind at all. I do not belong to the sobbing school of Negrohood who hold that nature somehow has given them a lowdown dirty deal and whose feelings are all but about it. Even in the helter-skelter[1] skirmish that is my life, I have seen that the world is to the strong regardless of a little pigmentation more or less. No, I do not weep at the world—I am too busy sharpening my oyster knife.

7 Someone is always at my elbow reminding me that I am the granddaughter of slaves. It fails to register **depression** with me. Slavery is sixty years in the past. The operation was successful and the patient is doing well, thank you. The terrible struggle that made me an American out of a potential slave said "On the line!" The Reconstruction said "Get set!" and the generation before said "Go!" I am off to a flying start and I must not halt in the stretch to look behind and weep. Slavery is the price I paid for civilization, and the choice was not with me. It is a bully adventure and worth all that I have paid through my ancestors for it. No one on earth ever had a greater chance for glory. The world to be won and nothing to be lost. It is thrilling to think—to know that for any act of mine, I shall get twice as much praise or twice as much blame. It is quite exciting to hold the center of the national stage, with the spectators not knowing whether to laugh or to weep.

8 The position of my white neighbor is much more difficult. No brown specter pulls up a chair beside me when I sit down to eat. No dark ghost thrusts its leg against mine in bed. The game of keeping what one has is never so exciting as the game of getting.

9 I do not always feel colored. Even now I often achieve the unconscious Zora of Eatonville before the Hegira.[2] I feel most colored when I am thrown against a sharp white background.

---

1. **helter-skelter** in a disorderly or hasty manner
2. **Hegira** the journey of Muhammad and his followers from Mecca to Medina in the 7th century

---

Skill: Figurative Language

This use of hyperbole emphasizes the author's enthusiasm and optimism at this point in her life. Again she uses a stage metaphor, but now she describes herself as being on center stage with the world as her audience.

How It Feels to Be Colored Me

Skill: Central or Main Idea

As an adult, the author is now more aware of her race. She feels like a dark rock, surrounded by white people. She feels her race and how it impacts who she is, but she is still able to be herself.

10 For instance at Barnard.[3] "Beside the waters of the Hudson" I feel my race. Among the thousand white persons, I am a dark rock surged upon, and overswept, but through it all, I remain myself. When covered by the waters, I am; and the ebb but reveals me again.

11 Sometimes it is the other way around. A white person is set down in our midst, but the contrast is just as sharp for me. For instance, when I sit in the drafty basement that is The New World Cabaret with a white person, my color comes. We enter chatting about any little nothing that we have in common and are seated by the jazz waiters. In the abrupt way that jazz orchestras have, this one plunges into a number. It loses no time in **circumlocutions,** but gets right down to business. It constricts the thorax and splits the heart with its tempo and narcotic harmonies. This orchestra grows rambunctious, rears on its hind legs and attacks the tonal veil with primitive fury, rending it, clawing it until it breaks through to the jungle beyond. I follow those heathen—follow them exultingly. I dance wildly inside myself; I yell within, I whoop; I shake my assegai above my head, I hurl it true to the mark *yeeeeooww*! I am in the jungle and living in the jungle way. My face is painted red and yellow and my body is painted blue. My pulse is throbbing like a war drum. I want to slaughter something—give pain, give death to what, I do not know. But the piece ends. The men of the orchestra wipe their lips and rest their fingers. I creep back slowly to the veneer we call civilization with the last tone and find the white friend sitting motionless in his seat, smoking calmly.

12 "Good music they have here," he remarks, drumming the table with his fingertips.

13 Music. The great blobs of purple and red emotion have not touched him. He has only heard what I felt. He is far away and I see him but dimly across the ocean and the continent that have fallen between us. He is so pale with his whiteness then and I am *so* colored.

14 At certain times I have no race, I am *me*. When I set my hat at a certain angle and saunter down Seventh Avenue, Harlem City, feeling as snooty as the lions in front of the Forty-Second Street Library, for instance. So far as my feelings are concerned, Peggy Hopkins Joyce[4] on the Boule Mich with her gorgeous raiment, stately carriage, knees knocking together in a most aristocratic manner, has nothing on me. The cosmic Zora emerges. I belong to no race nor time. I am the eternal feminine with its string of beads.

---

3. **Barnard** a liberal arts college in New York City
4. **Peggy Hopkins Joyce** an American model and actress known for leading a flamboyant, decadent lifestyle

15. I have no separate feeling about being an American citizen and colored. I am merely a fragment of the Great Soul that surges within the boundaries. My country, right or wrong.

16. Sometimes, I feel discriminated against, but it does not make me angry. It merely astonishes me. How *can* any deny themselves the pleasure of my company? It's beyond me.

17. But in the main, I feel like a brown bag of **miscellany** propped against a wall. Against a wall in company with other bags, white, red and yellow. Pour out the contents, and there is discovered a jumble of small things priceless and worthless. A first-water diamond, an empty spool, bits of broken glass, lengths of string, a key to a door long since crumbled away, a rusty knife-blade, old shoes saved for a road that never was and never will be, a nail bent under the weight of things too heavy for any nail, a dried flower or two still a little fragrant. In your hand is the brown bag. On the ground before you is the jumble it held—so much like the jumble in the bags, could they be emptied, that all might be dumped in a single heap and the bags refilled without altering the content of any greatly. A bit of colored glass more or less would not matter. Perhaps that is how the Great Stuffer of Bags filled them in the first place—who knows?

"How It Feels to Be Colored Me" from *I Love Myself When I Am Laughing* by Zora Neale Hurston. Published by The Feminist Press. Used by permission of The Permissions Company, Inc.

How It Feels to Be Colored Me

First Read

Read "How It Feels to Be Colored Me." After you read, complete the Think Questions below.

THINK QUESTIONS

1. How is life in Jacksonville different for Zora than it was in Eatonville? What are the significant changes, and how do they affect her? Cite evidence from the text to support your answer.

2. Why doesn't being the granddaughter of slaves "register depression" in Zora? Summarize Hurston's position on this part of her cultural history, quoting passages from the text to support your response.

3. What does Hurston's anecdote about the New World Cabaret convey to readers? Why does she share this story? Use evidence from the text to support your response.

4. What does the verb **deplored** mean as it appears in the text? Write your best definition of *deplored* here, along with a brief explanation of how you arrived at its meaning.

5. The Latin root *circum* means "around." With this in mind, what context clues helped you determine the meaning of **circumlocutions** as it appears in the text?

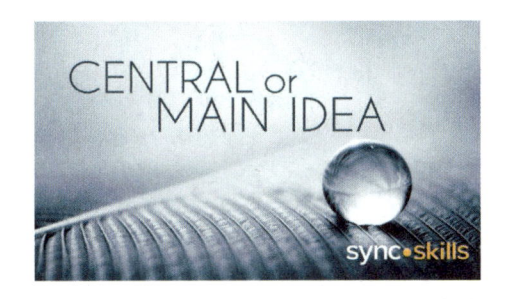

Skill:
Central or Main Idea

Use the Checklist to analyze Central or Main Idea in "How It Feels to Be Colored Me." Refer to the sample student annotation about Central or Main Idea in the text.

••• CHECKLIST FOR CENTRAL OR MAIN IDEA

In order to identify two or more central ideas of a text, note the following:

- ✓ the main idea in each paragraph or group of paragraphs
- ✓ key details in each paragraph or section of text, distinguishing what they have in common
- ✓ whether the details contain information that could indicate more than one main idea in a text
    - a science text, for example, may provide information about a specific environment and also a message on ecological awareness
    - a biography may contain equally important ideas about a person's achievements, influence, and the time period in which the person lives or lived
- ✓ when each central idea emerges
- ✓ ways that the central ideas interact and build on one another

To determine two or more central ideas of a text and analyze their development over the course of the text, including how they interact and build on one another to provide a complex analysis, consider the following questions:

- ✓ What main idea(s) do the details in each paragraphs explain or describe?
- ✓ What central or main ideas do all the paragraphs support?
- ✓ How do the central ideas interact and build on one another? How does that affect when they emerge?
- ✓ How might you provide an objective summary of the text? What details would you include?

How It Feels to Be Colored Me

Skill:
Central or Main Idea

Reread paragraphs 15–17 of "How It Feels to Be Colored Me." Then, using the Checklist on the previous page, answer the multiple-choice questions below.

YOUR TURN

1. This question has two parts. First, answer Part A. Then, answer Part B.

    Part A: What is the main idea of the final paragraph of the essay?

    ○ A. Despite differing appearances on the exterior, all human beings are quite similar on the inside.
    ○ B. The author does not feel threatened by people of other races.
    ○ C. It does not matter what color you are because all human beings are worthy of respect.
    ○ D. There are many random things that make us who we are.

    Part B: Which line from the passage provides the best evidence to your answer in Part A?

    ○ A. "... old shoes saved for a road that never was and never will be, a nail bent under the weight of things too heavy for any nail, a dried flower or two still a little fragrant."
    ○ B. "Against a wall in company with other bags, white, red and yellow."
    ○ C. "Pour out the contents, and there is discovered a jumble of small things priceless and worthless."
    ○ D. "... could they be emptied, that all might be dumped in a single heap and the bags refilled without altering the content of any greatly."

Skill: Figurative Language

Use the Checklist to analyze Figurative Language in "How It Feels to Be Colored Me." Refer to the sample student annotation about Figurative Language in the text.

••• CHECKLIST FOR FIGURATIVE LANGUAGE

In order to determine the meaning of figurative language in context, note the following:

- ✓ words that mean one thing literally and suggest something else
- ✓ figures of speech, including metaphors and similes
- ✓ figures of speech, including hyperbole, or exaggerated statements not meant to be taken literally, such as:
  - a child saying, "I'll be doing this homework until I'm 100!"
  - a claim such as "I'm so hungry I could eat a horse!"

In order to interpret figurative language in context and analyze its role in the text, consider the following questions:

- ✓ Where is there figurative language in the text, and what seems to be the purpose of the author's use of it?
- ✓ Why does the author use a figure of speech rather than literal language?
- ✓ What impact do similes, metaphors, or hyperbole have on your understanding of the text?
- ✓ How does the figurative language develop the message or theme of the text?

Skill: Figurative Language

Reread paragraph 11 of "How It Feels to Be Colored Me." Then, using the Checklist on the previous page, answer the multiple-choice questions below.

YOUR TURN

1. Figurative language such as "rears on its hind legs" and "throbbing like a war drum" suggests what about the author's reaction to the music?

   - A. The figurative language shows that the music makes the author very anxious.
   - B. The figurative language shows that the author very much dislikes the music.
   - C. The figurative language shows that the music brings out something animalistic in the author.
   - D. The figurative language shows that different people have different reactions to music.

2. What is the intended effect of the author's hyperbolic descriptions of her actions while listening to the music?

   - A. They are intended to illustrate the stark contrast between her reaction to the music and that of her white companion.
   - B. They are intended to illustrate the intense personal connection that the author has to jazz music because of where she comes from.
   - C. They are intended to illustrate how negative a reaction the author has to the music.
   - D. They are intended to illustrate for the reader how music plays an important role in the author's adult life.

Skill: Author's Purpose and Point of View

Use the Checklist to analyze Author's Purpose and Point of View in "How It Feels to Be Colored Me." Refer to the sample student annotation about Author's Purpose and Point of View in the text.

CHECKLIST FOR AUTHOR'S PURPOSE AND POINT OF VIEW

In order to identify author's purpose and point of view, note the following:

- ✓ whether the writer is attempting to establish trust by citing his or her experience or education
- ✓ whether the evidence the author provides is convincing and the argument or position is logical
- ✓ what words and phrases the author uses to appeal to the emotions
- ✓ the author's use of rhetoric, or the art of speaking and writing persuasively, such as the use of repetition to drive home a point, as well as allusion and alliteration
- ✓ the author's use of rhetoric to contribute to the power, persuasiveness, or beauty of the text

To determine the author's purpose and point of view, consider the following questions:

- ✓ How does the author try to convince me that he or she has something valid and important for me to read?
- ✓ What words or phrases express emotion or invite an emotional response? How or why are they effective or ineffective?
- ✓ What words and phrases contribute to the power, persuasiveness, or beauty of the text? Is the author's use of rhetoric successful? Why or why not?

Skill: Author's Purpose and Point of View

Reread paragraph 17 of "How It Feels to Be Colored Me." Then, using the Checklist on the previous page, answer the multiple-choice questions below.

YOUR TURN

1. Which of the following sentences **best** describes the purpose the author wants to achieve regarding her audience in this paragraph?

   - A. Hurston wants her audience to recognize that their lives are random and simplistic.
   - B. Hurston wants to show her audience that individual lives are just a random jumble of ideas that mean very little.
   - C. Hurston wants to persuade her audience to see that we're all similar on the inside and that is what matters.
   - D. Hurston wants the audience to share her view that every object in the world is "a fragment of the Great Soul."

2. What point of view is the author imparting in this passage?

   - A. Racism is the result of economic injustice.
   - B. People should share and then redistribute their wealth.
   - C. Race is not an indicator of worth or value.
   - D. People who are alike on the inside get mistreated because of race.

Close Read

Reread "How It Feels to Be Colored Me" and "The Negro Speaks of Rivers." As you reread, complete the Skills Focus questions below. Then use your answers and annotations from the questions to help you complete the Write activity.

SKILLS FOCUS

1. Analyze context, including imagery, to help you determine the nuanced meaning of the word *fast* in paragraph 5. Explain how context clues helped you understand the word's meaning.

2. Highlight an example of how Hurston uses figurative language. Explain how such rhetorical devices affect your reading experience and your understanding the text.

3. Identify an example in which Hurston seems to be encouraging herself to stand strong against the tide of racial difference. What main idea is she communicating to the reader? Analyze how addressing a dual audience deepens the meaning of the text.

4. Find an example of when Hurston feels least confined by perceptions of race as an adult. Analyze how the author's description of herself in this example relates to her purpose and point of view.

5. Hurston's experiences deepened her understanding of the intersection of ideology and identity. How might Hurston's outlook on her identity have been different if she had never left home? Highlight evidence from the text to support your answer.

WRITE

DISCUSSION: The texts "The Negro Speaks of Rivers," "How It Feels to Be Colored Me," and the more contemporary "The Color of an Awkward Conversation" provide insight into the authors' various perspectives about race and society. What are the messages of these texts, and are they expressed effectively? Determine the message of each text and then describe to what extent figurative language strengthens the messages, using relevant evidence from the text.

Invisible Man

FICTION
Ralph Ellison
1952

Introduction

studysync

Winner of the 1953 National Book Award, *Invisible Man* by Ralph Ellison (1914–1994) confronts the social, intellectual, and psychological consequences of living as a black man in America. The unnamed protagonist, who lives rent-free in the forgotten basement of a whites-only apartment on the outskirts of Harlem, tells his life story including his education at Tuskegee, his employment at Liberty Paints in Harlem, and his involvement in a Marxist interracial organization called The Brotherhood. *Invisible Man* is noteworthy not only for its commentary on American race relations but also for its experimental structure, Modernist use of symbolism, stream-of-consciousness narration, and biting satire.

". . . and I might even be said to possess a mind."

From The Prologue

1 I am an invisible man. No, I am not a spook like those who haunted Edgar Allan Poe; nor am I one of your Hollywood-movie **ectoplasms**. I am a man of substance, of flesh and bone, fiber and liquids—and I might even be said to possess a mind. I am invisible, understand, simply because people refuse to see me. Like the bodiless heads you see sometimes in circus sideshows,[1] it is as though I have been surrounded by mirrors of hard, distorting glass. When they approach me they see only my surroundings, themselves, or figments of their imagination—indeed, everything and anything except me.

2 Nor is my invisibility exactly a matter of a bio-chemical accident to my **epidermis**. That invisibility to which I refer occurs because of a peculiar disposition of the eyes of those with whom I come in contact. A matter of the construction of their inner eyes, those eyes with which they look through their physical eyes upon reality. I am not complaining, nor am I protesting either. It is sometimes advantageous to be unseen, although it is most often rather wearing on the nerves. Then too, you're constantly being bumped against by those of poor vision. Or again, you often doubt if you really exist. You wonder whether you aren't simply a phantom in other people's minds. Say, a figure in a nightmare which the sleeper tries with all his strength to destroy. It's when you feel like this that, out of resentment, you begin to bump people back. And, let me confess, you feel that way most of the time. You ache with the need to convince yourself that you do exist in the real world, that you're a part of all the sound and anguish, and you strike out with your fists, you curse and you swear to make them recognize you. And, alas, it's seldom successful.

3 One night I accidentally bumped into a man, and perhaps because of the near darkness he saw me and called me an insulting name. I sprang at him, seized his coat lapels and demanded that he apologize. He was a tall blond man, and as my face came close to his he looked **insolently** out of his blue eyes and cursed me, his breath hot in my face as he struggled. I pulled his chin down sharp upon the crown of my head, butting him as I had seen the

---

1. **sideshow** an old-fashioned traveling circus featuring games and sensationalized attractions

Skill: Textual Evidence

Reading the text closely, it seems that the narrator has become resentful at feeling invisible, causing him to respond with violence in order to be recognized, even though this isn't often effective.

Invisible Man

West Indians do, and I felt his flesh tear and the blood gush out, and I yelled, "Apologize! Apologize!" But he continued to curse and struggle, and I butted him again and again until he went down heavily, on his knees, **profusely** bleeding. I kicked him repeatedly, in a frenzy because he still uttered insults though his lips were frothy with blood. Oh yes, I kicked him! And in my outrage I got out my knife and prepared to slit his throat, right there beneath the lamplight in the deserted street, holding him by the collar with one hand, and opening the knife with my teeth—when it occurred to me that the man had not seen me, actually; that he, as far as he knew, was in the midst of a walking nightmare! And I stopped the blade, slicing the air as I pushed him away, letting him fall back to the street. I stared at him hard as the lights of a car stabbed through the darkness. He lay there, moaning on the asphalt; a man almost killed by a phantom. It unnerved me. I was both disgusted and ashamed. I was like a drunken man myself, wavering about on weakened legs. Then I was amused. Something in this man's thick head had sprung out and beaten him within an inch of his life. I began to laugh at this crazy discovery. Would he have awakened at the point of death? Would Death himself have freed him for wakeful living? But I didn't linger. I ran away into the dark, laughing so hard I feared I might rupture myself. The next day I saw his picture in the Daily News, beneath a caption stating that he had been "mugged." Poor fool, poor blind fool, I thought with sincere compassion, mugged by an invisible man!

4   Most of the time (although I do not choose as I once did to deny the violence of my days by ignoring it) I am not so overtly violent. I remember that I am invisible and walk softly so as not to awaken the sleeping ones. Sometimes it is best not to awaken them; there are few things in the world as dangerous as sleepwalkers. I learned in time though that it is possible to carry on a fight against them without their realizing it. For instance, I have been carrying on a fight with Monopolated Light & Power for some time now. I use their service and pay them nothing at all, and they don't know it. Oh, they suspect that power is being drained off, but they don't know where. All they know is that according to the master meter back there in their power station a hell of a lot of free current is disappearing somewhere into the jungle of Harlem. The joke, of course, is that I don't live in Harlem but in a border area. Several years ago (before I discovered the advantage of being invisible) I went through the routine process of buying service and paying their outrageous rates. But no more. I gave up all that, along with my apartment, and my old way of life: That way based upon the **fallacious** assumption that I, like other men, was visible. Now, aware of my invisibility, I live rent-free in a building rented strictly to whites, in a section of the basement that was shut off and forgotten during the nineteenth century, which I discovered when I was trying to escape in the night from Ras the Destroyer. But that's getting too far ahead of the story, almost to the end, although the end is in the beginning and lies far ahead.

5. The point now is that I found a home—or a hole in the ground, as you will. Now don't jump to the conclusion that because I call my home a "hole" it is damp and cold like a grave; there are cold holes and warm holes. Mine is a warm hole. And remember, a bear retires to his hole for the winter and lives until spring; then he comes strolling out like the Easter chick breaking from its shell. I say all this to assure you that it is incorrect to assume that, because I'm invisible and live in a hole, I am dead. I am neither dead nor in a state of suspended animation. Call me Jack-the-Bear,[2] for I am in a state of hibernation.

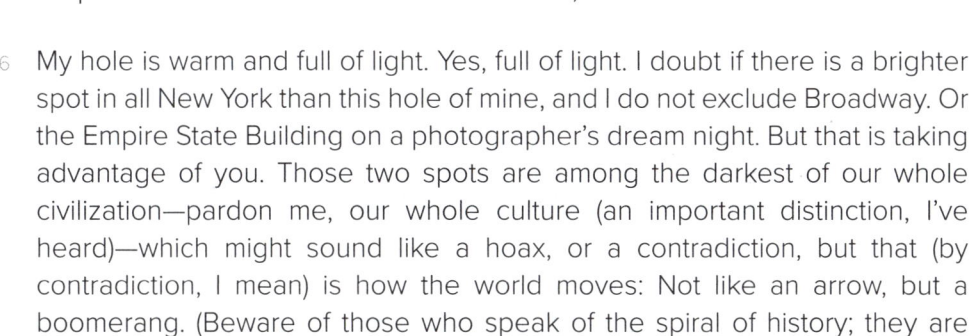

6. My hole is warm and full of light. Yes, full of light. I doubt if there is a brighter spot in all New York than this hole of mine, and I do not exclude Broadway. Or the Empire State Building on a photographer's dream night. But that is taking advantage of you. Those two spots are among the darkest of our whole civilization—pardon me, our whole culture (an important distinction, I've heard)—which might sound like a hoax, or a contradiction, but that (by contradiction, I mean) is how the world moves: Not like an arrow, but a boomerang. (Beware of those who speak of the spiral of history; they are preparing a boomerang. Keep a steel helmet handy.)

7. I know; I have been boomeranged across my head so much that I now can see the darkness of lightness. And I love light. Perhaps you'll think it strange that an invisible man should need light, desire light, love light. But maybe it is exactly because I am invisible. Light confirms my reality, gives birth to my form.

Excerpted from *Invisible Man* by Ralph Ellison, published by Vintage International.

2. **Jack-the-Bear** a trickster figure from Southern folk stories of anthropomorphized animals

Invisible Man

First Read

Read *Invisible Man*. After you read, complete the Think Questions below.

THINK QUESTIONS

1. According to the narrator, what are some advantages of invisibility? Cite specific evidence from the text to support your answer.

2. What does the protagonist mean when he says he wants to "bump people back," and why? Cite evidence from the text in support of your answer.

3. Where does the narrator live and how does he describe his living space? Point to evidence from the text to support your answer.

4. Use context clues to determine the meaning of the word **epidermis** as it is used in *Invisible Man*, and write your best definition of the word here. Describe which clues led you to your answer.

5. Use context clues to determine the meaning of the word **fallacious** as it is used in *Invisible Man*. Write your definition of *fallacious* here and explain how you figured out its meaning.

Skill:
Textual Evidence

Use the Checklist to analyze Textual Evidence in *Invisible Man*. Refer to the sample student annotations about Textual Evidence in the text.

••• CHECKLIST FOR TEXTUAL EVIDENCE

In order to support an analysis by citing evidence that is explicitly stated in the text, do the following:

- ✓ read the text closely and critically
- ✓ identify what the text says explicitly
- ✓ find the most relevant textual evidence that supports your analysis
- ✓ consider why an author explicitly states specific details and information
- ✓ cite the specific words, phrases, sentences, or paragraphs from the text that support your analysis
- ✓ determine where evidence in the text still leaves certain matters uncertain or unresolved

In order to interpret implicit meanings in a text by making inferences, do the following:

- ✓ combine information directly stated in the text with your own knowledge, experiences, and observations
- ✓ cite the specific words, phrases, sentences, or paragraphs from the text that led to and support this inference

In order to cite textual evidence to support an analysis of what the text says explicitly as well as inferences drawn from the text, consider the following questions:

- ✓ Have I read the text closely and critically?
- ✓ What inferences am I making about the text?
- ✓ What textual evidence am I using to support these inferences?
- ✓ Am I quoting the evidence from the text correctly?
- ✓ Does my textual evidence logically relate to my analysis or the inference I am making?
- ✓ Does evidence in the text still leave certain matters unanswered or unresolved? In what ways?

Invisible Man

Skill: Textual Evidence

Reread paragraph 4 of *Invisible Man*. Then, using the Checklist on the previous page, answer the multiple-choice questions below.

YOUR TURN

1. This question has two parts. First, answer Part A. Then, answer Part B.

    Part A: Identify an inference based on evidence from the passage.

    - A. The sleeping ones, or sleepwalkers, are the white people who refuse to see him.
    - B. The narrator does not like where he lives.
    - C. The narrator used to work for Monopolated Light & Power.
    - D. The narrator thinks that he pays too much for electricity.

    Part B: Which sentence supports your answer to the question in Part A?

    - A. "All they know is that according to the master meter back there in their power station a hell of a lot of free current is disappearing somewhere into the jungle of Harlem."
    - B. "Now, aware of my invisibility, I live rent-free in a building rented strictly to whites, in a section of the basement that was shut off and forgotten during the nineteenth century . . . "
    - C. "But no more. I gave up all that, along with my apartment, and my old way of life: That way based upon the **fallacious** assumption that I, like other men, was visible."
    - D. "But that's getting too far ahead of the story, almost to the end, although the end is in the beginning and lies far ahead."

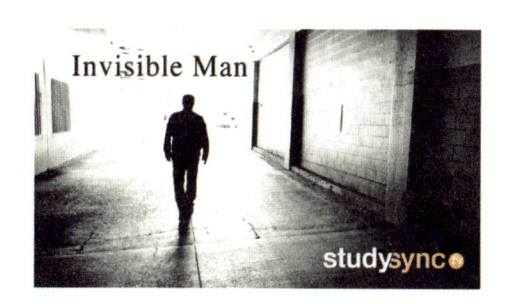

Close Read

Reread *Invisible Man*. As you reread, complete the Skills Focus questions below. Then use your answers and annotations from the questions to help you complete the Write activity.

SKILLS FOCUS

1. Identify evidence that demonstrates the ways the protagonist is invisible. Explain how the evidence from the text you've chosen addresses your reasoning.

2. Reread paragraph 3 and use context clues to determine the meaning of the word **insolent**. Highlight the clues that help you determine the word's meaning, and annotate with your best definition of the word.

3. Explain how ideologies, either the narrator's or others', affect the narrator's life. Identify evidence from the text to support your response.

WRITE

LITERARY ANALYSIS: In the excerpt from *Invisible Man*, the narrator reflects on his identity in a world that does not see him. In a written response, analyze the narrator's representation of his invisibility and make an argument about how that invisibility profoundly impacts the narrator's interactions with others. Support your response with evidence from the text.

Extended Writing Project and Grammar

EXTENDED WRITING PROJECT
RESEARCH WRITING

Research Writing Process: Plan

| PLAN | DRAFT | REVISE | EDIT AND PUBLISH |

The Harlem Renaissance was a period when African American art and culture began to flourish in mainstream American culture. Poets, musicians, artists, and writers sought to define and explore the African American experience on African American terms. What emerged was a proliferation of work that examined the influence of slavery on the lives of black Americans, brought attention to African American folklore, introduced a context in which to describe black urban life in the North, addressed the impacts of discrimination, and celebrated African American culture at large. By bringing these issues into the American cultural mainstream, the Harlem Renaissance also laid the groundwork for the burgeoning civil rights movement of the 1940s and 1950s.

WRITING PROMPT

What role do art and culture have in bringing awareness to social issues?

Choose one to two artists or writers, not included in this unit, from the Harlem Renaissance whom you would like to research. For example, you might research a writer who was born in the South but moved to a Northern city, such as Richard Wright. You might choose to focus on the early life of writer Claude McKay, the career of Paul Robeson, or the success of Ma Rainey. Research your chosen topic, and formulate a position on how your subjects' work contributed to gaining greater visibility for African Americans in mainstream culture, how the work impacted society, or how your subjects' life experiences impacted their work. Then, write an informative research essay, using textual evidence and source material to support your ideas. Be sure your informative research paper includes the following:

- an introduction
- supporting details from at least three credible sources
- a clear text structure
- a conclusion
- a works cited page

Writing to Sources

As you gather ideas and information from sources, be sure to:

- use evidence from multiple sources, and
- avoid overly relying on one source.

Introduction to Informative Research Writing

Research writing, a type of informative writing, examines a topic and conveys ideas by citing and analyzing information from credible sources. Good research papers use textual evidence, including facts, statistics, examples, and details from reliable sources, to provide information about a topic and to support the analysis of complex ideas. Research helps writers not only to discover and confirm facts but also to draw new conclusions about a topic. The characteristics of research writing include:

- an introduction with a clear thesis statement
- relevant facts, supporting details, and quotations from credible sources
- analysis of the details to explain how they support the thesis
- a clear and logical text structure
- a formal style
- a conclusion that wraps up your ideas
- a works cited page

In addition to these characteristics, writers also carefully narrow the focus of their research by generating research questions and developing a research plan. The research process requires patience as you evaluate the validity and usefulness of sources related to your topic. Researchers develop the skills of locating sources and assessing their appropriateness over time.

As you continue with this Extended Writing Project, you'll receive more instruction and practice in crafting each of the characteristics of informative research writing to create your own research paper.

Extended Writing Project and Grammar

Before you get started on your own informative research paper, read this research paper that one student, Daniela, wrote in response to the writing prompt. As you read the Model, highlight and annotate the features of informative research writing that Daniela included in her essay.

STUDENT MODEL

Post-Reconstruction Blues:

How Gertrude "Ma" Rainey Sang Black Rural Southerners into Popular American Culture

1   Legendary blues vocalist and Harlem Renaissance artist Gertrude "Ma" Rainey, known as the "Mother of Blues," introduced blues music to a mainstream audience, transforming the genre and expanding opportunities for African American artists. Through lyrical depictions of black Southern life and the complex experiences of African American women, Rainey's music increased the visibility of a people silenced in popular culture. While less well-known today, Rainey left a legacy that continues to influence musicians and broaden our knowledge of life for African Americans in the post-Reconstruction era.

2   Ma Rainey was born Gertrude Malissa Nix Pridgett on April 26, 1886, in Columbus, Georgia. Rainey possessed a musical talent from a young age and performed in public for the first time at age 14 at the Springer Opera House in Columbus. Soon after, she found her calling singing on tour in vaudeville and African American minstrel shows. For more than thirty years, Rainey performed in troupes, such as F.S. Wolcott's Rabbit Foot Minstrels and Tolliver's Circus and Musical Extravaganza.

Vaudeville: Ma Rainey's Early Career

3   Ma Rainey used vaudeville and minstrel shows as a platform to showcase her talent and share her life experiences. Originating from minstrel shows, vaudeville became popular at the turn of the century and featured unrelated acts such as singing, dancing, comedy, acrobatics, and magic. While no video recordings of Ma Rainey exist, the memory of her vibrant performances has been passed down through written reviews. According to critic Mary L. Bogumil in *Understanding August Wilson*, Rainey wore "flamboyant" jewelry and costumes and performed in front of a backdrop that featured a

large gramophone design, "which gave the appearance of Ma emerging right from the speaker, issuing from and manifesting the music itself" (qtd. in Timmel). Such extravagant details exemplify the sensational nature of vaudeville shows. Rainey's bold and brilliant stage persona was magnetic. She forced the audience, who were often men, to listen to what she had to say.

4   The variety show format of vaudeville allowed performers to communicate larger themes to the audience. For example, PBS's *American Masters* says of immigrant performers, "Their acts were a form of assimilation, in which they could become active parts of popular culture through representations of their heritage" ("Vaudeville: About Vaudeville"). In other words, immigrant performers used the highly adaptable and entertaining structure of vaudeville to disseminate information about where they came from. Ma Rainey was not an immigrant. However, as an African American woman, she belonged to a class of citizens who were underrepresented, misunderstood, and discriminated against. Like the immigrants, she used the modes of performance available to her to subvert boundaries and bring the experiences of Southern African American women into the mainstream ("Vaudeville: About Vaudeville"). That Ma Rainey was also the first woman to include blues music in her act only further illustrates her ability to use this mode of performance to break barriers and convey an important message (Orr).

The Blues: Ma Rainey's Medium

5   The blues played a central part in Rainey's performances. Originating in the South at the turn of the century, blues emerged from such African musical traditions as field hollers, work songs, spirituals, and country string ballads ("What Is the Blues?"). Most blues songs follow a 12-bar structure with an AAB verse pattern where "the first and second lines are repeated, and the third line is a response to them—often with a twist" ("Understanding the 12-Bar Blues"). Blues music tends to explore melancholy topics, such as sadness, desire, and longing. While many of Rainey's songs had a melancholy tone, her music also served to empower women by approaching topics most women could not discuss freely.

6   Ma Rainey's audience easily connected to her songs because her lyrics discussed aspects of everyday life for black rural Southerners as well as her personal experiences. According to William Barlow in *Looking Up at Down*, Rainey's lyrics captured "the southern landscape of African Americans in the Post-Reconstruction era" through "simple, straightforward stories" (qtd. in Biography.com Editors). For example, in 1923, Rainey recorded her own rendition of the traditional boll weevil song, titled "Bo Weavil Blues." In the first verse, she sang, "Bo-weavil, don't sing them blues no more / Bo-weavil's here, bo-weavil's everywhere you'll go." A boll weevil is a type of beetle that feeds on cotton plants. Because boll weevils infested cotton crops in the United States in the 1920s, this lyric reflected rural Southern life at the time. Rainey established a call-and-response structure between the first and second verses as she sang, "I'm a lone bo-weavil, been out a great long time / I'm gonna sing these blues to ease the bo-weavil's lonesome mind." Here, she expanded the boll weevil reference to her personal life. Although there were boll weevils "everywhere you'll go," she still felt "lonesome." Boll weevils represented all the men, or potential romantic partners, available to her.

7   Ma Rainey's candid discussion of love was unique to blues artists of her time. She was lonely but also embraced her independence ("I don't want no man to put sugar in my tea."). Rainey's rejection of a male partner was radical, for women in this time period were expected to build their lives around being married and having a family. In *Blues Legacies* and *Black Feminism*, Angela Davis pointed out that "black women of that era were acknowledging and addressing issues central to contemporary feminist discourse" (Davis 28). Black female blues artists like Ma Rainey were ahead of

their time in terms of asserting their agency. Rainey's performance of this song introduced the idea of liberated black women into the mainstream. Rainey added complexity to this with a twist in the third verse:

> I went downtown and bought me a hat
> I brought it back home, I laid it on the shelf
> Looked at my bed, I'm getting tired of sleeping by myself (Rainey)

8   Ma Rainey used straightforward phrases to explain how she tried to compensate for her loneliness by purchasing a hat, but it did not help. The expression "tired of sleeping" emphasized her internal conflict. Sleep is the solution for tiredness, just as a relationship should have been the solution for her loneliness. Yet, Rainey preferred her independence. In only twelve lines, she referenced a regional metaphor, discussed the relatable concept of loneliness, and expressed her personal struggles balancing love and freedom.

Ma Rainey and the Mainstream Music Industry

9   Rainey's vocals had a deep and unembellished tone expressing raw emotion that resonated with a wide range of audiences. "The gravelly timbre of her . . . raspy, deep voice" (Orr) as well as her "moaning style" (Timmel) entranced listeners. Her flashy visual representation attracted the attention of the audience. Her measured and gripping delivery kept them waiting for more. Ma Rainey was one of the first professional female blues artists to make a phonograph record. During the Great Migration, blues music spread from the South into other regions of the nation.

THE GREAT MIGRATION
The Migration of African Americans from the American South (1910 - 1970)

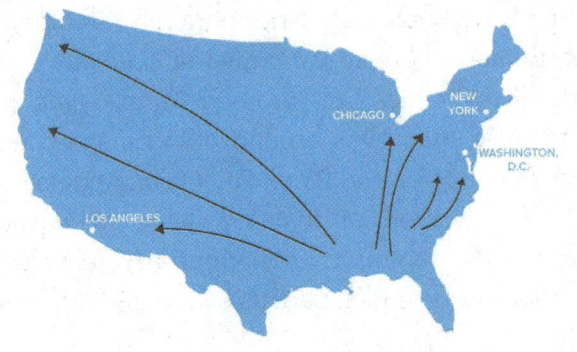

By the 1920s, recording labels saw a market for "race records," or music created by and for African Americans. After establishing her career as a touring musician, Ma Rainey recorded over 100 songs with Paramount in the span of 1923 to 1928 (Timmel). However, in 1928 Paramount stopped recording with Rainey after determining that race records like hers were no longer profitable. One could argue that Paramount exploited Ma Rainey for corporate gain. Still, making a phonograph record with Paramount did help Rainey's audience and success grow. Over the course of her career, she performed alongside various bands and other renowned Harlem Renaissance musicians, such as Louis Armstrong and Bessie Smith.

10 In an era when the possibilities for women of color were limited, the "Mother of Blues," Ma Rainey, surpassed expectations by taking advantage of the modes of performance that were available to her to build a long-lasting career. Rainey used the public platforms of vaudeville and recorded music to tell the stories of Southern African Americans during the post-Reconstruction Era. Her lyrics also revealed her own stories and sentiments that are unique to the experiences of black women at that time. Her deeply emotional vocal style appealed to many people. Ma Rainey's blues music demanded recognition through simple portrayals of authenticity. She brought the silenced narratives of African Americans into the scope of mainstream American culture.

Works Cited

Biography.com Editors. "Ma Rainey Biography." *The Biography.com Website*, A&E Television Networks, 27 Apr. 2017, https://www.biography.com/people/ma-rainey-9542413. Accessed 20 Sept. 2018.

Davis, Angela Y. *Blues Legacies and Black Feminism: Gertrude "Ma" Rainey, Bessie Smith, and Billie Holiday. Google Books*. 2nd ed., Vintage Books, 1999.

Orr, N. Lee. "Gertrude 'Ma' Rainey (1886-1939)." 9 May 2003. *New Georgia Encyclopedia*, Georgia State University, 9 Aug. 2018, https://www.georgiaencyclopedia.org/articles/arts-culture/gertrude-ma-rainey-1886–1939. Accessed 20 Sep. 2018.

Rainey, Ma. "Bo-Weavil Blues." *Harry's Blues Lyrics & Tabs Online*, Recorded December 1923, http://blueslyrics.tripod.com/lyrics/ma_rainey/bo_weavil_blues.htm. Accessed 25 Sep. 2018.

Timmel, Lisa. "The Music of Ma Rainey." *Huntington Theater Company*, https://www.huntingtontheatre.org/articles/Ma-Raineys-Black-Bottom/music-ma-rainey/. Accessed 20 Sep. 2018.

"The Great Migration, 1910 to 1970." The United States Census Bureau, September 13, 2012, https://www.census.gov/dataviz/visualizations/020/. Sep. 2018.

"Understanding the 12-Bar Blues." *PBS: The Blues*, 2003, www.pbs.org/theblues/classroom/essays12bar.html. Accessed 21 Sep. 2018.

"Vaudeville: About Vaudeville." *PBS: American Masters*, 8 Oct. 1999, www.pbs.org/wnet/americanmasters/vaudeville-about-vaudeville/721/. Accessed 20 Sept. 2018.

"What Is the Blues?" *PBS: The Blues*, 2003, www.pbs.org/theblues/classroom/essaysblues.html. Accessed 21 Sep. 2018.

WRITE

Writers often take notes about ideas before they sit down to write. Think about what you've learned so far about organizing informative research writing to help you begin prewriting.

- **Purpose:** Which Harlem Renaissance writer or artist do you find most influential? What do you want to learn about your chosen subject?
- **Audience:** Who is your audience, and what information do you want your audience to learn?
- **Questions:** How can you use a research question to focus your research?
- **Sources:** What kinds of sources will help you answer that question?
- **Structure:** How can you share the information you find with readers?

Response Instructions

Use the questions in the bulleted list to write a one-paragraph research summary. Your summary should describe what you plan to research and discuss in this research paper. Include possible research questions of your own based on the prompt.

Don't worry about including all of the details now; focus only on the most essential and important elements. You will refer to this short summary as you continue through the steps of the writing process.

Extended Writing Project and Grammar

Skill: Planning Research

••• CHECKLIST FOR PLANNING RESEARCH

In order to conduct a short or more sustained research project to answer a question or solve a problem, do the following:

- select a topic or problem to research
- think about what you want to find out and what kind of research can contribute to the project
- start to formulate your major research question by asking open-ended questions that begin "How . . .?" and "Why . . . ?" and then choose a question that you are interested in exploring
- narrow or broaden your inquiry when appropriate, sorting information or items into clear categories
- synthesize multiple sources on the subject to look at information from different points of view, while demonstrating understanding of the subject under investigation

In order to conduct a short or more sustained research project to answer a question or solve a problem, consider the following questions:

- Does my major research question allow me to explore a new issue, an important problem worth solving, or a fresh perspective on a topic?
- Can I research my question within my given time frame and with the resources available to me?
- Have I synthesized multiple sources on the question or problem, looking for different points of view?
- Have I demonstrated understanding of the subject under investigation in my research project?

YOUR TURN

Read the research questions below. Then, complete the chart by sorting the questions into the correct category. Write the corresponding letter for each question in the appropriate column.

	Research Questions
A	What is Louis Armstrong remembered for?
B	Why did Louis Armstrong specialize in playing the trumpet?
C	How does Nella Larsen's literary work relate to her personal life?
D	What are the events in Nella Larsen's novel *Passing*?
E	How did Louis Armstrong's artistry influence jazz?
F	What was Langston Hughes's poetry about?
G	What beliefs are reflected in Langston Hughes's poetry?
H	Why do people still read Nella Larsen's work today?
I	Who were Langston Hughes's literary inspirations?

Topic	Too Narrow	Appropriate	Too Broad
Louis Armstrong			
Nella Larsen			
Langston Hughes			

Extended Writing Project and Grammar

YOUR TURN

Develop a research question for formal research. Then, write a short plan of how you will go about doing research for your essay. Include a note about how you might need to modify your plan during the research process.

Process	Plan
Research Question	
Step 1	
Step 2	
Step 3	

Skill: Evaluating Sources

••• CHECKLIST FOR EVALUATING SOURCES

Once you gather your sources, identify the following:

- where information seems inaccurate, biased, or outdated
- where information strongly relates to your task, purpose, and audience
- where information helps you make an informed decision or solve a problem

In order to conduct advanced searches to gather relevant, credible, and accurate print and digital sources, use the following questions as a guide:

- Is the material published by a well-established source or an expert author?
- Is the source material written by a recognized expert on the topic or a well-respected author or organization?
- Is the material up to date or based on the most current information?
- Is the source based on factual information that can be verified by another source?
- Is the source material objective and unbiased?
- Does the source contain omissions of important information that supports other viewpoints?
- Does the source contain faulty reasoning?
- Are there discrepancies between the information presented in different sources?

In order to refine your search process, consider the following questions:

- Are there specific terms or phrases that I can use to adjust my search?
- Can I use *and, or,* or *not* to expand or limit my search?
- Can I use quotation marks to search for exact phrases?

Extended Writing Project and Grammar

YOUR TURN

Read the sentences below. Then, complete the chart by sorting the sentences into two categories: those that are credible and reliable and those that are not. Write the corresponding letter for each sentence in the appropriate column.

	Sentences
A	The article states only the author's personal opinions and omits, or leaves out, other positions on the topic.
B	The article includes clear arguments and counterarguments that are supported by factual information.
C	The website is a personal blog or social media website.
D	The author holds a PhD in a discipline related to your topic of research.
E	The text is objective and includes many viewpoints that are properly cited.
F	The text makes unsupported assumptions to persuade readers.

Credible and Reliable	Not Credible or Reliable

Extended Writing Project and Grammar

YOUR TURN

Complete the chart below by filling in the title and author of a source for your informative research essay and answering the questions about this source.

Source Questions	Answers
Source Title and Author:	
Reliability: Has the source material been published in a well-established book or periodical or on a well-established website? Is the source material up to date or based on the most current information?	
Accuracy: Is the source based on factual information that can be verified by another source?	
Credibility: Is the source material written by a recognized expert on the topic? Is the source material published by a well-respected author or organization?	
Bias: Is the source material objective and unbiased?	
Omission: Does the source contain omissions of important information that supports other viewpoints?	
Faulty Reasoning: Does the source contain faulty reasoning?	
Decision: Should I use this source in my research report? Is it effective in answering the research question?	

Extended Writing Project and Grammar

Skill:
Research and Notetaking

••• CHECKLIST FOR RESEARCH AND NOTETAKING

In order to conduct short as well as more sustained research projects to answer a question (including a self-generated question) or solve a problem, note the following:

- Answer a question for a research project, or think of your own question that you would like to have answered.
- Look up your topic in an encyclopedia to find general information.
- Find specific, up-to-date information in books and periodicals or on the Internet. If appropriate, conduct interviews with experts to get information.
- Narrow or broaden your inquiry when appropriate.
  > If you find dozens of books on a topic, your research topic may be too broad.
  > If it is difficult to write a research question, narrow your topic so it is more specific.
- Synthesize your information by organizing your notes from various sources to see what the sources have in common and how they differ.

To conduct short as well as more sustained research projects to answer a question (including a self-generated question) or solve a problem, consider the following questions:

- Where could I look to find information?
- How does new information I have found affect my research question?
- How can I demonstrate my understanding of the subject I am investigating?

Extended Writing Project and Grammar

YOUR TURN

Read each point from a student's note cards below. Then, complete the chart by sorting the points into two categories: those that are relevant and those that are not relevant to the writing topic of recorded music during Ma Rainey's time. Write the corresponding letter for each point in the appropriate column.

	Points
A	Source 1: During the Great Migration, music labels sought to make a profit from the highly popular "race music," which was music recorded by African Americans (Timmel).
B	Source 2: According to *History of Minstrelsy,* the purpose of African American minstrel shows differed from those of white performers in that "black minstrel performers felt the added responsibility to counter stereotypes of black identity."
C	Source 3: In 1904, Ma Rainey met and married her husband, William "Pa" Rainey, while performing on tour (Orr).
D	Source 4: The music Rainey recorded with Paramount is of poor quality due to Paramount's "below average recording techniques" (USC Libraries).

Relevant	Not Relevant

Extended Writing Project and Grammar

YOUR TURN

Complete the chart by synthesizing information from sources relevant to your essay subject's work and personal life. Remember to cite and number each source.

Work	Personal Life

Research Writing Process: Draft

| PLAN | DRAFT | REVISE | EDIT AND PUBLISH |

You have already made progress toward writing your informative research essay. Now it is time to draft your informative research essay.

WRITE

Use your plan and other responses in your Binder to draft your essay. You may also have new ideas as you begin drafting. Feel free to explore those new ideas as you have them. You can also ask yourself these questions to ensure that your writing is **focused**, **organized**, and **developed**:

Draft Checklist:

☐ **Focused:** Have I made my topic clear to readers? Have I included only relevant information and details and nothing extraneous that might confuse my readers?

☐ **Organized:** Does the organizational structure in my essay make sense? Will readers be engaged by the organization and interested in the way I present information and evidence?

☐ **Developed:** Does my writing include relevant evidence? Will my readers be able to follow my ideas? Will they understand the purpose of my research?

Before you submit your draft, read it over carefully. You want to be sure that you've responded to all aspects of the prompt.

Extended Writing Project and Grammar

Here is Daniela's research essay draft. As you read, notice how Daniela develops her draft to be focused, organized, and developed. As she continues to revise and edit her research essay, she will find and improve weak spots in her writing, as well as correct any language or punctuation mistakes.

STUDENT MODEL: FIRST DRAFT

Post-Reconstruction Blues:

How Gertrude "Ma" Rainey Sang Black Rural Southerners into Popular American Culture

Legendary blues vocalist and Harlem Renaissance artist Gertrude "Ma" Rainey, known as the "Mother of Blues," introduced blues music to a mainstream audience, transforming the genre and expanding opportunities for African American artists. Through depictions of black Southern life and the complex experiences of African American women, Rainey's music increased the visibility of a people silenced in popular culture. While less well-known today, Rainey left a legacy that continues to influence and broaden our knowledge of the Post Reconstruction era.

Ella Pridget gave birth to Ma Rainey, originally Gertrude Malissa Nix Pridgett, on April 26, 1886, in Columbus, Georgia. Rainey posessed a musical talent from a young age and performed in public for the first time at age 14 at the Springer Opera House in Columbus. Soon after, she found her calling singing on tour in vaudeville and African American minstral shows. For more than thirty years, performed in troupes, such as F.S. Wolcott's Rabbit Foot Minstrels and Tolliver's Circus and Musical Extravaganza.

~~Ma Rainey used vaudeville and minstrel shows as a platform to showcase her talent. She also used them to share her life experiences. Vaudeville originated from minstrel shows. It became popular at the turn of the century. Vaudeville shows featured unrelated acts such as singing, dancing, comedy, acrobatics, and magic. While no video recordings of Ma Rainey exist, the memory of her vibrint performances have been passed down through written reviews. According to critic Mary L. Bogumil in *Understanding August Wilson*, Rainey wore "flamboyant" jewelry and costmes and performed in front of a~~

~~backdrop that featured a large gramophone designe, "which gave the appearance of Ma emerging right from the speaker, issuing from and manifesting the music itself" (Timmel). Such extravagant details show the sensational nature of vaudeville shows. Rainey's bold and brilliant stage persona was magnetic she forced the audience, who were often men, to listen to what she had to say.~~

Vaudeville: Ma Rainey's Early Career

Ma Rainey used vaudeville and minstrel shows as a platform to showcase her talent and share her life experiences. Originating from minstrel shows, vaudeville became popular at the turn of the century and featured unrelated acts such as singing, dancing, comedy, acrobatics, and magic. While no video recordings of Ma Rainey exist, the memory of her vibrant performances has been passed down through written reviews. According to critic Mary L. Bogumil in *Understanding August Wilson*, Rainey wore "flamboyant" jewelry and costumes and performed in front of a backdrop that featured a large gramophone design, "which gave the appearance of Ma emerging right from the speaker, issuing from and manifesting the music itself" (qtd. in Timmel). Such extravagant details exemplify the sensational nature of vaudeville shows. Rainey's bold and brilliant stage persona was magnetic. She forced the audience, who were often men, to listen to what she had to say.

~~The variety show format of vaudeville allowed performers to communicate larger themes to the audience. For example, PBS's *American Masters* says of immigrant performers, "Their acts were a form of assimilation, in which they could become active parts of popular culture through representations of their heritage" ("Vaudeville: About Vaudeville"). However, as an African American woman, she belonged to a class of citizens who were underrepresented, misunderstood, and discriminated against. Ma Rainey was not an immigrant. Like the immigrants, she used the modes of performance available to her to cross racial and class boundaries and bring the experiences of a Southern African American women into the main stream ("Vaudeville: About Vaudeville").~~

Skill: Print and Graphic Features

Daniela decides that while her body paragraphs flow together, she could make her points clearer by using headings. So she inserts a heading between her second and third paragraphs. As she continues to reread her essay, she will add a heading wherever she discusses a new aspect of Ma Rainey's work and life.

Skill: Paraphrasing

Daniela realizes she has taken the phrase "to cross racial and class boundaries" word-for-word from her source. To avoid plagiarism, she can either paraphrase the information or quote it. Since she already has one quotation from this source in the paragraph, she decides to paraphrase.

Extended Writing Project and Grammar

NOTES

**Skill:
Critiquing Research**

Daniela notices that instead of synthesizing information from several sources, she has used only one source in the paragraph. To round out her explanation of vaudeville and Ma Rainey's role in it, she integrates another idea from a different source into the paragraph.

The variety show format of vaudeville allowed performers to communicate larger themes to the audience. For example, PBS's *American Masters* says of immigrant performers, "Their acts were a form of assimilation, in which they could become active parts of popular culture through representations of their heritage" ("Vaudeville: About Vaudeville"). In other words, immigrant performers used the highly adaptable and entertaining structure of vaudeville to disseminate information about where they came from. Ma Rainey was not an immigrant. However, as an African American woman, she belonged to a class of citizens who were underrepresented, misunderstood, and discriminated against. Like the immigrants, she used the modes of performance available to her to subvert boundaries and bring the experiences of a Southern African American women into the mainstream ("Vaudeville: About Vaudeville"). That Ma Rainey was also the first woman to include blues music in her act only further illustrates her ability to use this mode of performance to break barriers and convey an important message (Orr).

The blues played a central part in Rainey's performances. Originating in the South at the turn of the century, blues came from such African musical traditions as field hollers, work songs, spirituals, and country string ballads ("What Is the Blues?"). Most blues songs follow a 12 bar structure with an AAB verse pattern where "the first and second lines are repeated, and the third line is a response to them—often with a twist" ("Understanding the 12-Bar Blues"). Blues music tends to explore melancholy topics, such as sadness, desire, and longing. Many of Rainey's songs had a melancholy tone, her music served to empower women by approaching topics most women could not discuss freely. For example, Ma Rainey's candid discussion of love was unique to blues artists of her time. She was lonely but also embraced her independence ("I don't want no man to put sugar in my tea."). Rainey's rejection of a male partner was radical because women in this time period were expected to build their lives around being married and building a family. In *Blues Legacies and Black Feminism*, Angela Davis points out that "black women of that era were acknowledging and addressing issues central to contemporary feminist discourse" (Davis 28). Black female blues artists like Ma

Rainey were ahead of their time in terms of asserting their agency. Rainey's performance of this song introduced the idea of liberated black women into the mainstream.

~~Rainey's vocals had a deep and unbellished tone expressing raw emotion that resonated with a wide range of audiences. The gravelly timbre of her . . . raspy, deep voice (Orr) as well as her "moaning style" entranced listeners. Her flashy visual representation attracted the attention of the audience. Her measured and gripping delivery kept them waiting for more. Ma Rainey one of the first professional female blues artists to make a phonograph record. During the Great Migration, blues music spread from the South into other regions of the nation. By the 1920s, recording labels saw a market for "race records," or music created by and for African Americans. After establishing her career as a touring musician, Ma Rainey recorded over 100 songs with Paramount in the span of 1923 to 1928. One could argue that Paramount exploited Ma Rainey for corporate gane. However, in 1928 Paramount stopped recording with Rainey after determining that race records like hers were no longer profitable. Still, making a phonograph record with Paramount did help Rainey's audience and success grow. Over the course of her career, she performed alongside various bands and other renowned Harlem Renaissance muzicians, such as Louis Armstrong and Bessie Smith.~~

Rainey's vocals had a deep and unembellished tone expressing raw emotion that resonated with a wide range of audiences. "The gravelly timbre of her . . . raspy, deep voice" (Orr) as well as her "moaning style" (Timmel) entranced listeners. Her flashy visual representation attracted the attention of the audience. Her measured and gripping delivery kept them waiting for more. Ma Rainey was one of the first professional female blues artists to make a phonograph record. During the Great Migration, blues music spread from the South into other regions of the nation. [Include graphic] By the 1920s, recording labels saw a market for "race records," or music created by and for African Americans. After establishing her career as a touring musician, Ma Rainey

Skill: Sources and Citations

Daniela forgot to add quotation marks around the description from N. Lee Orr, so she adds them. In the same sentence, she forgot to add a parenthetical citation for the quotation "moaning style." She includes the author's name in the citation, but since the source is electronic, she doesn't add a page number.

recorded over 100 songs with Paramount in the span of 1923 to 1928 (Timmel). However, in 1928 Paramount stopped recording with Rainey after determining that race records like hers were no longer profitable. One could argue that Paramount exploited Ma Rainey for corporate gain. Still, making a phonograph record with Paramount did help Rainey's audience and success grow. Over the course of her career, she performed alongside various bands and other renowned Harlem Renaissance musicians, such as Louis Armstrong and Bessie Smith.

In an era when women of color had limited possibilities, "The Mother of Blues," Ma Rainey, was a musician who took advantage of the modes of performance that were available to her to build a long lasting career. Rainey used the public platforms of vaudeville and recorded music. Her lyrics talked about her experiences and feelings. Ma Rainey's unique style appealed to many people, helping bring the blues and her life experiences to a mainstream audience.

Works Cited

Biography.com Editors. "Ma Rainey Biography." *The Biography.com Website,* A&E Television Networks, Published 2 Apr. 2014, Updated 27 Apr. 2017, https://www.biography.com/people/ma-rainey-9542413. Accessed 20 Sep. 2018.

Davis, Angela Y. Blues Legacies and Black Feminism: Gertrude "Ma" Rainey, Bessie Smith, and Billie Holiday. *Google Books*. 2nd ed., Vintage Books, 1999.

Orr, N. Lee. "Gertrude 'Ma' Rainey (1886-1939)." *New Georgia Encyclopedia,* Georgia State University, 9 May 2003, https://www.georgiaencyclopedia.org/articles/arts-culture/gertrude-ma-rainey-1886–1939. Accessed 20 Sep. 2018.

Timmel, Lisa. "The Music of Ma Rainey." *Huntington Theater Company*, Accessed 20 Sep. 2018.

"Understanding the 12-Bar Blues." *PBS: The Blues,* 2003, www.pbs.org/theblues/classroom/essays12bar.html. Accessed 21 Sep. 2018.

"Vaudeville: About Vaudeville." *PBS: American Masters,* 8 Oct. 1999, www.pbs.org/wnet/americanmasters/vaudeville-about-vaudeville/721/. Accessed 20 Sep. 2018.

"What Is the Blues?" *PBS: The Blues,* 2003, www.pbs.org/theblues/classroom/essaysblues.html. Accessed 21 Sep. 2018.

Extended Writing Project and Grammar

Skill: Critiquing Research

••• CHECKLIST FOR CRITIQUING RESEARCH

In order to conduct short or sustained research projects to answer a question or solve a problem, drawing on several sources, do the following:

- narrow or broaden the question or inquiry as necessary when researching your topic
- use advanced search terms effectively when looking for information online, such as using unique terms that are specific to your topic (i.e., "daily life in Jamestown, Virginia" rather than just "Jamestown, Virginia")
- assess the strengths and limitations of each source in terms of the task, purpose, and audience
- synthesize and integrate multiple sources on a subject

To evaluate and use relevant information while conducting short or sustained research projects, consider the following questions:

- Did I narrow or broaden my research inquiry as needed?
- Are there specific terms or phrases in my research question that I can use to adjust my search?
- Can I use *and, or,* or *not* to expand or limit my search?
- Can I use quotation marks to search for exact phrases?
- Have I successfully synthesized and integrated multiple sources on my topic?

YOUR TURN

Read the previous draft of Daniela's research plan. Then, answer the multiple-choice questions.

> Major Research Question: Did Ma Rainey influence other musicians?
>
> List of Sources:
> 1. Facebook Post: Bessie Smith v. Ma Rainey
> 2. The Legacy of Blues Musicians: Mamie Smith, Ma Rainey, and Beyond (television documentary)
> 3. Britannica.com: Ma Rainey's Blues Style
> 4. Classic Blues Magazine: Classic Blues Traditions, Then and Now

1. Which revision of her major research question will best refocus her research plan?
   - A. What are the topics of Ma Rainey's lyrics?
   - B. How did Ma Rainey's blues style influence other musicians?
   - C. Why was Bessie Smith a successful blues singer?
   - D. The research question is already focused.

2. Which source should Daniela consider replacing?
   - A. 1
   - B. 2
   - C. 3
   - D. 4

WRITE

Write your major research question, and list your sources. Then, use the questions in the checklist to critique your research plan. In your critique, evaluate the appropriateness of your sources and determine whether your research plan needs a revision.

Extended Writing Project and Grammar

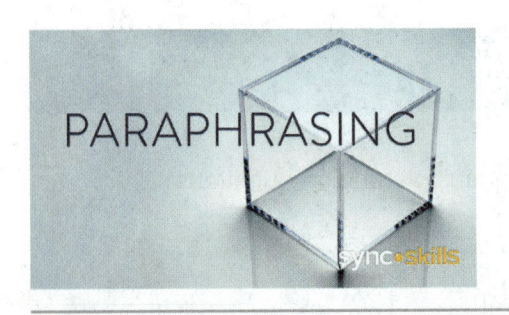

Skill: Paraphrasing

••• CHECKLIST FOR PARAPHRASING

In order to integrate information into your research essay, first make sure you understand what the author is saying after reading the text carefully. Then, note the following:

- any words or expressions that are unfamiliar
- words and phrases that are important to include in a paraphrase to maintain the meaning of the text
- potential instances of plagiarism; avoid plagiarism by acknowledging all sources for both paraphrased and quoted material, and avoid overly relying on any one source
- whether or not your integration of information maintains a logical flow of ideas

To integrate information into your research essay, consider the following questions:

- Do I understand the meaning of the text?
- Have I determined the meanings of any words in the text that are unfamiliar to me?
- Does my paraphrase of the text maintain the text's original meaning? Have I missed any key points or details?
- Have I avoided plagiarism by acknowledging all my sources for both paraphrased and quoted material and avoided overly relying on any one source?
- Did I integrate information selectively to maintain a logical flow of ideas?

YOUR TURN

Choose the best answer to each question.

1. The following is a quotation that Daniela is considering including in her essay. Which of the following sentences provides the best paraphrase of the source text?

   > "Today, the blues no longer commands the attention it once did; to many young listeners, traditional blues—if not contemporary blues—may sound antiquated and uninteresting."

   - A. Once a very popular genre, blues music is not as widely enjoyed by today's young listeners.
   - B. Many young listeners are unfamiliar with the blues today.
   - C. The history of traditional blues spans several generations.
   - D. Today, the blues no longer commands the attention it once did.

2. The following is a paragraph from a previous draft of Daniela's essay. How could paraphrasing best help Daniela improve this paragraph?

   > Rainey's vocals had a deep and unembellished tone expressing raw emotion that resonated with a wide range of audiences. "The gravelly timbre of her . . . raspy, deep voice" (Orr) as well as her "moaning style" (Timmel) entranced listeners. "Her material consisted of a variety of songs drawn from Southern traditions" (Timmel) and her flashy visual representation attracted the attention of the audience. Her measured and gripping delivery kept them waiting for more. Ma Rainey was one of the first professional female blues artists to make a phonograph record. During the Great Migration, blues music spread from the South into other regions of the nation. By the 1920s, recording labels saw a market for "race records," (Timmel) or music created by and for African Americans. After establishing her career as a touring musician, Ma Rainey "laid down over 100 tracks between 1923 and 1928" (Timmel).

   - A. Paraphrasing would help improve this paragraph by showing that Daniela thoroughly read each of her sources.
   - B. Paraphrasing would improve her paragraph by making it shorter and quicker to read.
   - C. Paraphrasing would increase Daniela's chances of plagiarizing information.
   - D. Paraphrasing would help improve her paragraph by avoiding so many back-to-back quotations and maintaining a logical flow of ideas.

WRITE

Use the questions in the checklist to paraphrase information from a source and integrate it into a paragraph of your informative research essay.

Extended Writing Project and Grammar

Skill: Sources and Citations

••• CHECKLIST FOR SOURCES AND CITATIONS

In order to gather relevant information from multiple authoritative print and digital sources and to cite the sources correctly, do the following:

- gather information from a variety of print and digital sources, using search terms to effectively narrow your search
- assess the strengths and limitations of each source in regard to your task, your purpose for writing, and your audience
  - > find information on authors to see if they are experts on a topic
  - > look at the publication date to see if the information is current
  - > avoid relying on any one source, and synthesize information from a variety of books, publications, and online resources
  - > quote or paraphrase the information you find, and cite it to avoid plagiarism
  - > integrate information selectively to maintain a logical flow of ideas in your essay, using transitional words and phrases
- include all sources in a bibliography, following a standard format:
  - > Halall, Ahmed. *The Pyramids of Ancient Egypt*. New York: Central Publishing, 2016.
  - > for a citation, footnote, or endnote, include the author, title, and page number

To check that you have gathered information and cited sources correctly, consider the following questions:

- Have I assessed the strengths and limitations of each source?
- Have I looked for different points of view, instead of relying on one source?
- Did I cite the information I found using a standard format to avoid plagiarism?
- Did I include all my sources in my bibliography?

Extended Writing Project and Grammar

YOUR TURN

Choose the best answer to each question.

1. Below is a section from a previous draft of Daniela's research paper. What change should Daniela make to improve the clarity of her citation?

   > Author Sandra R. Lieb writes, "The Classic Blues barely outlived the twenties, becoming engulfed in and utterly changed by the Depression and shifts in audience taste, but from 1920 to roughly 1928 Ma Rainey and [other women singers] were the greatest artists, enjoying a period of influence, wealth, popularity, and imitation by lesser performers."

   - A. Add the page number in parentheses after the quotation.
   - B. Add the author's last name in parentheses after the quotation.
   - C. Add the author's last name and page number in parentheses after the quotation.
   - D. No change needs to be made.

2. Below is a section from a previous draft of Daniela's works cited page in the MLA format. Which revision best corrects her style errors?

   > *Mother of Blues: A Study of Ma Rainey.* by Sandra R. Lieb. University of Massachusetts Press, 1981.

   - A. Lieb, Sandra R. Mother of Blues: A Study of Ma Rainey. University of Massachusetts Press, 1981.
   - B. University of Massachusetts Press, 1981. Lieb, Sandra R. *Mother of Blues: A Study of Ma Rainey.*
   - C. Lieb, Sandra R. *Mother of Blues: A Study of Ma Rainey.* University of Massachusetts Press.
   - D. Lieb, Sandra R. *Mother of Blues: A Study of Ma Rainey.* University of Massachusetts Press, 1981.

WRITE

Use the questions in the checklist to revise your in-text citations and works cited list.

Check that your information, whether quoted or paraphrased, is properly cited to avoid plagiarism. Refer to the *MLA Handbook* as needed.

Extended Writing Project and Grammar

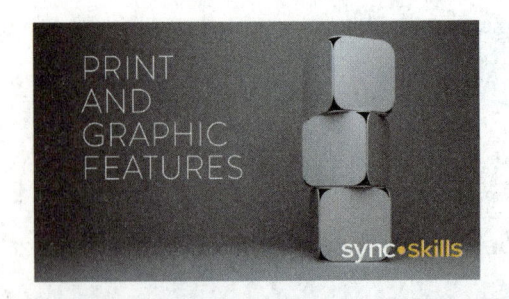

Skill:
Print and Graphic Features

••• CHECKLIST FOR PRINT AND GRAPHIC FEATURES

In order to check your draft for the inclusion of print and graphic features, first reread your draft and ask yourself the following questions:

- To what extent would including formatting, graphics, or multimedia be effective in achieving my purpose?
- Which formatting, graphics, or multimedia seem most important in conveying information to the reader?
- How is the addition of the formatting, graphics, or multimedia useful in aiding comprehension?

To include formatting, graphics, and multimedia, use the following questions as a guide:

- How can I use formatting to better organize information? Consider adding:

    > titles
    > headings
    > subheadings
    > bullets
    > boldface and italicized terms

- How can I use graphics to better convey information? Consider adding:

    > charts
    > graphs
    > tables
    > timelines
    > diagrams
    > maps
    > figures and statistics

- How can I use multimedia to add interest and variety? Consider adding a combination of:

    > photographs
    > art
    > audio
    > video

YOUR TURN

Choose the best answer to each question.

1. Read the following two paragraphs from another draft of Daniela's essay. Then, decide which of the possible headings below would best improve the flow of information between the two paragraphs.

> The variety show format of vaudeville allowed performers to communicate larger themes to the audience. For example, PBS's *American Masters* says of immigrant performers, "Their acts were a form of assimilation, in which they could become active parts of popular culture through representations of their heritage" ("Vaudeville: About Vaudeville"). In other words, immigrant performers used the highly adaptable and entertaining structure of vaudeville to disseminate information about where they came from. Ma Rainey was not an immigrant. However, as an African American woman, she belonged to a class of citizens who were underrepresented, misunderstood, and discriminated against. Like the immigrants, she used the modes of performance available to her "to cross racial and class boundaries" ("Vaudeville: About Vaudeville") and bring the experiences of a Southern African American women into the mainstream.
>
> The blues played a central part in Rainey's performances. Originating in the South at the turn of the century, blues emerged from such African musical traditions as field hollers, work songs, spirituals, and country string ballads ("What Is the Blues?"). Most blues songs follow a 12-bar structure with an AAB verse pattern where "the first and second lines are repeated, and the third line is a response to them—often with a twist" ("Understanding the 12-Bar Blues"). Blues music tends to explore melancholy topics, such as sadness, desire, and longing. While many of Rainey's songs had a melancholy tone, her music also served to empower women by approaching topics most women could not discuss freely.

- A. "Moving On From Vaudeville"
- B. "Ma Rainey and Her Influence on the Blues"
- C. "The Blues"
- D. Daniela does not need to include a heading between these two paragraphs.

WRITE

Use the questions in the checklist to review your informative research essay and locate where you can place headings to call out specific sections and topics. Then, note areas where you would like to add graphics or media, and describe what sort of features you might include and why.

Extended Writing Project and Grammar

Research Writing Process: Revise

| PLAN | DRAFT | **REVISE** | EDIT AND PUBLISH |

You have written a draft of your informative research essay. You have also received input from your peers about how to improve it. Now you are going to revise your draft.

⇐ REVISION GUIDE

Examine your draft to find areas for revision. Use the guide below to help you review:

Review	Revise	Example
Clarity		
Highlight a sentence that shows your purpose for writing.	Make sure the purpose is specific and clearly stated for your audience.	While less well-known today, Rainey left a legacy that continues to influence musicians and broaden our knowledge of life for African Americans in the Post-Reconstruction era.
Development		
Identify the textual evidence you quote in support of your thesis.	Rather than letting quotations speak for themselves, make sure you provide original commentary to build upon your evidence from sources.	For example, PBS's *American Masters* says of immigrant performers, "Their acts were a form of assimilation, in which they could become active parts of popular culture through representations of their heritage" ("Vaudeville: About Vaudeville"). In other words, immigrant performers used the highly adaptable and entertaining structure of vaudeville to disseminate information about where they came from.

Review	Revise	Example
\multicolumn{3}{c}{**Organization**}
Review your body paragraphs. Are they focused and logically organized? Identify and annotate any sentences within and across paragraphs that don't flow in a clear and logical way.	Rewrite the sentences so they appear in a clear and logical order.	One could argue that Paramount exploited Ma Rainey for corporate gane. However, in 1928 Paramount stopped recording with Rainey after determining that race records like hers were no longer profitable. ~~One could argue that Paramount exploited Ma Rainey for corporate gane.~~ Still, making a phonograph record with Paramount did help Rainey's audience and success grow.
\multicolumn{3}{c}{**Style: Word Choice**}
Identify any weak adjectives or verbs.	Replace weak adjectives and verbs with strong, descriptive adjectives and verbs.	Such extravagant details ~~show~~ exemplify the sensational nature of vaudeville shows.
\multicolumn{3}{c}{**Style: Sentence Fluency**}
Read aloud your writing and listen to the way the text sounds. Does it sound choppy? Or does it flow smoothly with rhythm, movement, and emphasis on important details and events?	Rewrite a key passage, making your sentences longer or shorter to achieve a better flow of writing.	Ma Rainey used vaudeville and minstrel shows as a platform to showcase her talent. ~~She also used them to~~ and share her life experiences. ~~Vaudeville originated~~ Originating from minstrel shows~~.~~, ~~It~~ vaudeville became popular at the turn of the century~~.~~ ~~Vaudeville shows~~ and featured unrelated acts such as singing, dancing, comedy, acrobatics, and magic.

✏️ WRITE

Use the revision guide, as well as your peer reviews, to help you evaluate your informative research essay to determine places that should be revised.

Extended Writing Project and Grammar

Skill:
Using a Style Guide

••• CHECKLIST FOR USING A STYLE GUIDE

In order to write your work so that it conforms to the guidelines in a style manual, do the following:

- Determine which style guide you should use before you write your draft.
  - > Follow the guidelines chosen by a teacher, for example.
  - > Familiarize yourself with that guide, and check your writing against the guide when you edit.
- Use the style guide for the overall formatting of your paper, citation style, bibliography format, and other style considerations for reporting research.

As you draft, use an additional style guide, such as *Artful Sentences: Syntax as Style* by Virginia Tufte, to help you vary your syntax, or the grammatical structure of sentences.

  - > Use a variety of simple, compound, complex, and compound-complex sentences to convey information.
  - > Be sure to punctuate your sentences correctly.
  - > Follow standard English language conventions to help you maintain a formal style for formal papers.

To edit your work so that it conforms to the guidelines in a style manual, consider the following questions:

- Have I followed the conventions for spelling, punctuation, capitalization, sentence structure, and formatting, according to the style guide?
- Have I varied my syntax to make my information clear for readers?
- Do I have an entry in my works cited or bibliography for each reference I used?
- Have I followed the correct style, including the guidelines for capitalization and punctuation, in each entry in my works cited or bibliography?

Extended Writing Project and Grammar

YOUR TURN

Read the types of information below. Then, complete the chart by sorting them into two categories: those that are found in a style guide and those that are not. Write the corresponding letter for each type of information in the appropriate column.

Types of Information	
A. proper punctuation for quotations	F. a list of possible research topics
B. synonyms for a word	G. how to format a bibliography
C. how to read a map	H. how to cite Internet sources
D. when to use a hyphen	I. the definition of a word
E. how to write an outline	J. when to use italics

In a Style Guide	Not in a Style Guide

WRITE

Use the checklist to help you choose a convention that you have found challenging to follow. Use a credible style guide to check and correct any errors related to that convention in your informative research essay.

Extended Writing Project and Grammar

Grammar: Contested Usage

For most formal writing, it is probably advisable to follow the traditional rules of grammar. In most cases, following the rules will improve both the clarity and effectiveness of your communication. However, there are a number of grammar "rules" that can be broken if you have a good reason to do so. The most important thing to keep in mind is that no rule of grammar should be broken unless it is done deliberately to improve the effectiveness of your writing.

The series comma is still widely used and preferred for a series of three or more items. However, in recent years, its necessity has come into question. Many authors of formal and informal writing find that they can use other strategies that eliminate the need for the series comma.

Strategy	Text
Sometimes you can omit a series comma if the wording clearly indicates a new phrase in the series.	Paul writes novels, paints pottery and designs gardens.
Sometimes you can omit a series comma if single words are clearly related to one reference or topic.	In an attempt to get to the bottom of the question once and for all, the *Guardian* has gathered writers from the fields of science, psychotherapy, literature, religion and philosophy to give their definition of the much-pondered word. What is Love?

The words *whom* and *who* are a great example of contested diction. *Who* is a subject pronoun, like *he, she,* or *they*. It is used as a subject in a main clause that asks a question or as the subject in a subordinate clause. *Whom* is an object pronoun, like *him, her,* or *them*. It is used in place of *who* as the direct object that receives the action of a verb or as the object of a preposition. If you are writing for an informational or research purpose, use *whom* when referring to a pronoun as an object. However, if you are writing informally, with contemporary dialogue, colloquialisms, or slang, it is appropriate to eliminate the use of *whom*.

Occasionally, writers choose to begin sentences with coordinating conjunctions. Writers use coordinating conjunctions as sentence openers when they want to indicate a relationship with the previous sentence but do not want to combine the two complete thoughts into one sentence. This is usually done to emphasize the second of two related ideas.

Strategy	Text
If you are writing two or three sentences that are closely related and have equal importance, you could use a coordinating conjunction such as *and* or *but* as a sentence opener.	So when Miss Lawington told me about the cakes I thought that I could bake them and earn enough at one time to increase the net value of the flock the equivalent of two head. And that by saving the eggs out one at a time, even the eggs wouldn't be costing anything. As I Lay Dying

YOUR TURN

1. When can a series comma be omitted?

   ○ A. A series comma must always be used, even if the objects are clearly related to one reference or topic.

   ○ B. A series comma can be omitted if single items are clearly related to one reference or topic.

2. Is the removal of the series comma in this sentence acceptable?

   > Would you like your eggs scrambled, fried or poached?

   ○ A. Yes, removing the series comma is acceptable.

   ○ B. No, removing the series comma is unacceptable.

3. Is this use of a coordinating conjunction as a sentence opener acceptable?

   > He spent his vacation in Naples, Florida. But he said it was a business trip, not a pleasure trip.

   ○ A. Yes, it is an acceptable use of a coordinating conjunction as a sentence opener.

   ○ B. No, it is an unacceptable use of a coordinating conjunction as a sentence opener.

4. Is this an acceptable use of *who*?

   > In 1864, Twain, who fortune still eluded, went to San Francisco where he worked on several newspapers.

   ○ A. Yes, it is an acceptable use of *who*.

   ○ B. No, it is an unacceptable use of *who*. It should be replaced with *whom*.

Extended Writing Project and Grammar

Grammar: Hyphens

Hyphens join words or parts of words. Do not use any type of dash where a hyphen is needed.

Rule	Text	Explanation
Use a hyphen after any prefix joined to a proper noun or a proper adjective, for example, *pre-Depression*. Use a hyphen after the prefixes *all-*, *ex-* (meaning "former"), and *self-* joined to any noun or adjective. Use a hyphen after the prefix *anti-* when it is joined to a word beginning with *i*. Also, use a hyphen after the prefix *vice-*, except in *vice president*.	Every Tory is a coward; for servile, slavish, **self-interested** fear is the foundation of Toryism; and a man under such influence, though he may be cruel, never can be brave. The Crisis	The prefix **self-** is joined to the word **interested** with a hyphen.
Hyphenate any compound word that is a spelled-out cardinal number (such as *twenty-one*) or ordinal number (such as *twenty-first*) up to *ninety-nine* or *ninety-ninth*. Hyphenate any spelled-out fraction.	**One-eighth** of the whole population were . . . slaves, not distributed generally over the Union, but localized in the southern part of it. Lincoln's Second Inaugural Address	**One-eighth** is a fraction.
Use a hyphen in a compound adjective that precedes a noun. Be sure to choose words carefully as the words should work together to provide a unified meaning.	It might be, too, that a witch, like old Mistress Hibbins, the **bitter-tempered** widow of the magistrate, was to die upon the gallows. The Scarlet Letter	The words **bitter-tempered** are hyphenated as a compound adjective that modifies the noun *widow*.

164 Reading & Writing Companion

YOUR TURN

1. How should this sentence be changed?

   > Sandra Wilson—the exmayor of our fair city—spoke warmly of the new, experienced mayor.

   - A. Change **exmayor** to **ex-mayor.**
   - B. Change the dashes to hyphens.
   - C. Change **new, experienced** to **new-experienced.**
   - D. No change needs to be made to this sentence.

2. How should this sentence be changed?

   > The short-tempered coach made the team do twenty five extra sit-ups before the end of practice—how unfair!

   - A. Remove the hyphen in **short-tempered.**
   - B. Change **twenty five** to **twenty-five.**
   - C. Change the dash to a hyphen.
   - D. No change needs to be made to this sentence.

3. How should this sentence be changed?

   > My grandfather—a two-tour veteran—loves telling stories about how newfound optimism spread through post–World War II America.

   - A. Change the dashes to hyphens.
   - B. Change **newfound** to **new-found.**
   - C. Change **post–World War II** to **post World War II.**
   - D. No change needs to be made to this sentence.

Extended Writing Project and Grammar

Research Writing Process: Edit and Publish

| PLAN | DRAFT | REVISE | **EDIT AND PUBLISH** |

You have revised your informative research essay based on your peer feedback and your own examination.

Now, it is time to edit your essay. When you revised, you focused on the content of your essay. You probably critiqued your research and made sure you paraphrased sources correctly and avoided plagiarism. When you edit, you focus on the mechanics of your writing, paying close attention to things like grammar and punctuation.

Use the checklist below to guide you as you edit:

☐ Have I followed all the rules for hyphens?

☐ Have I checked for contested usage and selected the usage that is most appropriate for my purpose?

☐ Do I have any sentence fragments or run-on sentences?

☐ Have I spelled everything correctly?

Notice some edits Daniela has made:

- Used the passive voice to remove less important information
- Corrected spelling errors
- Added a subject to correct a sentence fragment

~~Ella Pridget gave birth to Ma Rainey, originally~~ Ma Rainey was born Gertrude Malissa Nix Pridgett, on April 26, 1886, in Columbus, Georgia. Rainey ~~posessed~~ possessed a musical talent from a young age and performed in public for the first time at age 14 at the Springer Opera House in Columbus. Soon after, she found her calling singing on tour in vaudeville and African American ~~minstral~~ minstrel shows. For more than thirty years, Rainey performed in troupes, such as F.S. Wolcott's Rabbit Foot Minstrels and Tolliver's Circus and Musical Extravaganza.

WRITE

Use the questions in the checklist, as well as your peer reviews, to help you evaluate your informative research essay to determine areas that need editing. Then, edit your essay to correct those errors.

Once you have made all your corrections, you are ready to publish your work. You can distribute your writing to family and friends, hang it on a bulletin board, or post it on your blog. If you publish online, share the link with your family, friends, and classmates.

studysync

Life, Liberty, and the Pursuit of Happiness

UNIT 5

Life, Liberty, and the Pursuit of Happiness

How do our goals inform our actions?

Literary Focus: **THE POSTWAR AND CIVIL RIGHTS ERAS**

Texts

Paired Readings

174	Literary Focus: **THE POSTWAR AND CIVIL RIGHTS ERAS**
182	Hiroshima **INFORMATIONAL TEXT** *John Hersey*
186	A Good Man Is Hard to Find **FICTION** *Flannery O'Connor*
209	The Marshall Plan Speech **ARGUMENTATIVE TEXT** *George Marshall*
224	On the Road **FICTION** *Jack Kerouac*
228	Death of a Salesman **DRAMA** *Arthur Miller*
231	A Raisin in the Sun **DRAMA** *Lorraine Hansberry*
241	Literary Seminar: The Writings of Pauli Murray
248	Theme for English B **POETRY** *Langston Hughes*
251	On Listening to Your Teacher Take Attendance Talk Back Text **POETRY** *Aimee Nezhukumatathil*
254	Brown v. Board of Education **ARGUMENTATIVE TEXT** *U.S. Supreme Court*
265	Civil Rights Act of 1964 **INFORMATIONAL TEXT** *Lyndon B. Johnson with U.S. Congress*
269	I've Been to the Mountaintop **ARGUMENTATIVE TEXT** *Martin Luther King, Jr.*

Reading & Writing Companion

Please note that excerpts and passages in the StudySync® library and this workbook are intended as touchstones to generate interest in an author's work. The excerpts and passages do not substitute for the reading of entire texts, and StudySync® strongly recommends that students seek out and purchase the whole literary or informational work in order to experience it as the author intended. Links to online resellers are available in our digital library. In addition, complete works may be ordered through an authorized reseller by filling out and returning to StudySync® the order form enclosed in this workbook.

Extended Writing Project and Grammar

288   Argumentative Writing Process: Plan

Thesis Statement
Organizing Argumentative Writing
Reasons and Relevant Evidence

303   Argumentative Writing Process: Draft

Introductions
Transitions
Conclusions

315   Argumentative Writing Process: Revise

Style
Grammar: Sentence Fragments
Grammar: Run-On Sentences
Grammar: Parallel Structure

326   Argumentative Writing Process: Edit and Publish

Talk Back Text

Talk Back Texts are works from a later period that engage with the themes and tropes of the unit's literary focus. Demonstrating that literature is always in conversation, these texts provide dynamic new perspectives to complement the unit's more traditional chronology.

Unit 5: Life, Liberty, and the Pursuit of Happiness

How do our goals inform our actions?

LORRAINE HANSBERRY

Lorraine Hansberry (1930–1965) was born in the South Side of Chicago to a prominent African American family that called W. E. B. Du Bois, Langston Hughes, and Duke Ellington friends. Her father had founded one of Chicago's first banks for African Americans, yet the family faced opposition and violence when they bought a new home. Her family's experience with discrimination led to a case that ultimately went to the Supreme Court.

JOHN HERSEY

Born to American missionary parents in Tianjin, China, John Hersey (1914–1993) spoke Chinese before learning English. After moving to the United States at the age of ten, Hersey attended Yale University where he played football and was coached by Gerald Ford, the future president. As a journalist, Hersey pioneered what became known as New Journalism, a style of writing that uses the storytelling techniques of fiction to relate nonfiction events. This technique was later adopted by twentieth-century writers such as Truman Capote and Norman Mailer.

LANGSTON HUGHES

A leader of the Harlem Renaissance, Langston Hughes (1902–1967) was born in Missouri and raised by his grandmother until he was sixteen when he moved to Illinois with his mother and her husband and began to write. Hughes eventually moved to New York City, attended Columbia University, and worked various jobs, including one on a freight ship that sailed down the coast of Africa. In 1921 he saw his first published piece, "The Negro Speaks of Rivers," in the pages of *The Crisis*. Hughes would go on to write eleven plays and numerous works of prose and poetry.

LYNDON BAINES JOHNSON

The 36th president of the United States, Lyndon Baines Johnson (1908–1973) took the office after President Kennedy was assassinated. Born in Stonewall, Texas, Johnson worked as a schoolteacher before joining the House of Representatives in 1937. He is best known for championing the expansion of Civil Rights and a "War on Poverty." He helped pass the Voting Rights Act and also escalated U.S. involvement in the Vietnam War. He did not seek re-election, left office in 1969, and died of a heart attack four years later at his ranch in Texas.

JACK KEROUAC

Jack Kerouac attended Columbia University in New York at the same time as friend and poet Allen Ginsberg (*Howl*). Although Kerouac dropped out, he continued to live in Morningside Heights and became friends with author William S. Burroughs, collaborating with him on the novel *And the Hippos Were Boiled in Their Tanks*. Kerouac's best known work is *On the Road*, which *The New York Times* called "the clearest and most important utterance yet made by the generation Kerouac himself named years ago as 'beat.'"

MARTIN LUTHER KING, JR.

Martin Luther King, Jr. (1929–1968) entered college at the age of fifteen and received a bachelor of arts from Morehouse College. After earning a bachelor of divinity degree and earning his doctorate, he moved to Montgomery, Alabama, in 1954 to become pastor of the Dexter Avenue Baptist Church. Known for his oratorical skills, he led numerous nonviolent protests, including the 1955 bus boycott, the 1963 Birmingham protests, and the March on Washington, where he gave his "I Have a Dream" speech. King was assassinated in Memphis, Tennessee, on April 4, 1968.

GEORGE MARSHALL

General George C. Marshall's (1880–1959) eponymous plan to rebuild Europe in the aftermath of World War II promised funding, which exceeded $12 billion ($125+ billion in 2018), and earned him the 1953 Nobel Peace Prize. Marshall proposed the plan in a speech given at Harvard University in 1947. The plan aimed to thwart the Soviet Union's influence over Western Europe and to accelerate economic development and productivity back to pre-war levels; however, the extent to which the plan deserves credit for affecting growth is disputed among economists.

ARTHUR MILLER

Arthur Miller (1915–2005) was born into a wealthy Manhattan family that had a vacation home in Far Rockaway and a successful business, but his family lost everything when the Stock Market crashed in 1929. They moved to Brooklyn, and Miller delivered bread before school to help his family make ends meet. He eventually attended the University of Michigan, returned to New York City, and wrote his first play, which received poor reviews and closed after a few performances. Undeterred, Miller wrote his next play, *All My Sons*, which won him the Tony Award for Best Author.

AIMEE NEZHUKUMATATHIL

Born in Chicago, Illinois, Aimee Nezhukumatathil (b. 1974) attended The Ohio State University where she received a bachelor's degree in English and a master of fine arts in poetry and creative nonfiction. She received the Diane Middlebrook Poetry Fellowship at the Wisconsin Institute for Creative Writing at University of Wisconsin–Madison and served as the writer-in-residence at the University of Mississippi MFA program from 2016–2017. She is the poetry editor of *Orion* magazine, and her poems have appeared in *Ploughshares*, *Tin House*, and the Best American Poetry series.

FLANNERY O'CONNOR

Flannery O'Connor (1925–1964) was born in Savannah, Georgia. She graduated from the Georgia State College for Women in three years, and in 1946 she was accepted into the Iowa Writers' Workshop. Known for her short stories, she published *A Good Man Is Hard to Find* in 1955 and *Everything That Rises Must Converge* in 1965. O'Connor often wrote in the Southern Gothic style and stated, "Anything that comes out of the South is going to be called grotesque by the Northern reader, unless it is grotesque, in which case it is going to be called realistic."

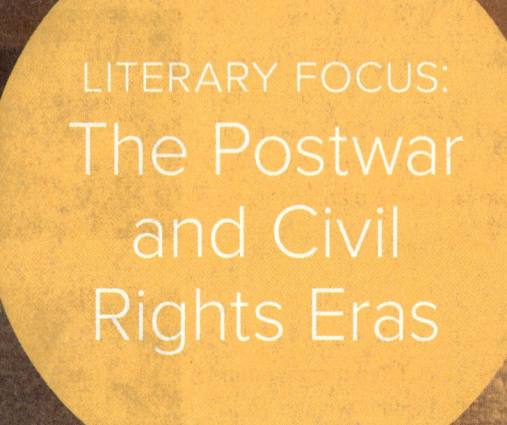

LITERARY FOCUS:
The Postwar and Civil Rights Eras

Introduction

This overview explains how Americans grappled with both empowerment and disillusionment in the wake of war, and how a national movement for civil rights grew from this angst. After defending their country on the front lines of World War II, African Americans continued to live in a racially divisive society. The text also describes how the political climate impacted literature and journalism, along with other artistic avenues, and how segregation and inequality shifted in the midst of change and progress.

Literary Focus: The Postwar and Civil Rights Eras

"Communities came together in acts of self-determination to seek equity."

A Global Catastrophe

1 In the 1930s, Italy's Fascists, Germany's Nazis, and Japan's military leadership all aggressively expanded their empires. Expansion by these countries, known as the Axis powers, contributed to the beginning of World War II in 1939. Early in the war, the German forces overwhelmed their enemies, quickly occupying much of Western Europe until only Britain remained unconquered. However, as Axis expansion took place in Europe and Asia, many Americans still believed in the idea of isolationism, especially so soon after World War I.

2 This attitude changed abruptly after the Japanese attack on Pearl Harbor, and the United States mobilized for war against the Axis powers. On the battlefront, U.S. forces turned the tide on the Western Front of Europe and the Pacific, and played a crucial role in the victory of the Allies. At home, United States workers quickly transformed the U.S. economy into the most productive and efficient war machine in the world.

3 *"We are now in this war. We are all in it—all the way. Every single man, woman, and child is a partner in the most tremendous undertaking of our American history."*

4 *—Franklin D. Roosevelt, wartime radio broadcast December 9, 1941*

5 The United States engaged in nearly four years of global warfare, ending with the defeat of the Axis Powers in 1945. The end of the war, which ultimately became the deadliest conflict of all time, left Europe and Japan in tatters. The United States however, experienced an economic boom, cementing its ascent as a global superpower.

The Good War?

6 World War II has become enshrined in the American public memory as "the good war"—a heroic crusade against an evil enemy. But the United States' fight against **Fascism** highlighted the tension between a commitment to democracy and the experience of people of color in America. The Double V Campaign emerged as African American soldiers, fighting in segregated

units, believed that if Americans could defeat Fascism abroad, then they could surely **eradicate** racism and Jim Crow rule at home.

Japanese Americans are moved from their homes into internment camps, supervised by American troops.

7   After Pearl Harbor, the United States forcefully relocated 120,000 people of Japanese ancestry—77,000 of whom were U.S. citizens—into internment camps in early 1942. The renewed migration of African Americans from the South to the big cities in the North and West, continuing the Great Migration, sometimes resulted in racial violence. In Detroit, twenty-five African Americans and nine whites were killed during riots in June 1943. During that same month, riots in Los Angeles occurred after hundreds of U.S. soldiers and sailors attacked a group of young Mexican American men.

Postwar Affluence

8   Wartime production helped restore prosperity to the United States after the long Depression, and postwar legislation continued to fuel the economy. Passed in 1944, the Servicemen's Readjustment Act, more commonly known as the G.I. Bill, expanded opportunities for many Americans. The G.I. Bill provided veterans money for college tuition and weekly unemployment benefits for those seeking a job. Furthermore, the federal government guaranteed loans for veterans who wished to purchase a home, business, or farm. This public policy enabled some veterans unprecedented access to upward mobility, and suddenly, the American Dream was increasingly attainable for a new middle class of white Americans.

Literary Focus: The Postwar and Civil Rights Eras

Franklin D. Roosevelt signing the G.I. Bill

9   While the G.I. Bill itself did not include racially **discriminatory** language, the execution of the bill was largely unequal. State and local communities chose how to distribute many of the bill's benefits, which resulted in severe inequities in many communities. For example, by the summer of 1947, over 3,000 home loans had been disbursed to veterans. Only two of those loans went to African American veterans. Similarly, veterans of color were denied admission to many "white-only" colleges and institutions, or were simply denied access to G.I. benefits by their local Veterans' Affairs boards. Ultimately, many African American veterans were denied the same economic opportunities that provided **affluence** to their white counterparts.

A Fight for Equity

10 The National Association for the Advancement of Colored People (NAACP) and the Urban League fought against discrimination during the war. Organizer A. Philip Randolph began organizing a march on Washington in 1941 to protest the lack of jobs for African Americans during the war. Randolph met with President Roosevelt, who signed Executive Order 8802, banning discrimination in the defense industry. As a result, Randolph called off the march. Although the military desegregated in 1948, this postwar optimism quickly faded as many veterans were denied benefits from the G.I. Bill, and lawmakers praised the Ku Klux Klan on the floor of Congress. These conditions galvanized the African American community to organize and continue fighting for racial equality.

11 In 1954, the U.S. Supreme Court ruled in its landmark *Brown v. Board of Education* decision that segregated education for whites and blacks was unconstitutional. Progress in desegregating schools was very slow and most schools remained segregated until African American communities took direct action. Inspired by the recent Supreme Court ruling, the NAACP began challenging the segregation of public facilities. On December 1, 1955, the

secretary of the Montgomery, Alabama, NAACP refused to give up her seat on a bus to a white passenger. Rosa Parks's action started a successful, year-long boycott of the city's segregated buses. Leaders such as Parks, a young minister named Martin Luther King Jr., and Ralph Abernathy organized the African American community and advocated for nonviolent direct action through their powerful actions, speeches, and writing.

12 Following the success of the Montgomery Bus Boycott, King and other civil rights leaders soon engaged in a strategic campaign of nonviolent resistance and civil disobedience to end segregation and secure voting rights. In 1957, nine black students attempted to integrate Central High School in Little Rock, Arkansas. When state authorities and a mob blocked the entrance, President Eisenhower called in federal troops to ensure that students could attend school according to the law. College students in Greensboro, North Carolina, engaged in another version of nonviolent resistance when they staged a "sit-in" at a segregated lunch counter. The four young men refused to move from their stool at the counter without being served. Leaders also used tactics such as peaceful marches. In 1963, A. Philip Randolph began to work towards another march, alongside his chief aid Bayard Rustin. This time, he did not call off his efforts, and there was a massive public demonstration, the "March on Washington for Freedom and Jobs." There, Martin Luther King Jr. delivered his famous "I Have a Dream" speech to a crowd of over 250,000 people.

13 African American communities continued to fight for equal treatment under the law, eventually leading to landmark legislation, such as the Civil Rights Act of 1964 and the Voting Rights Act of 1965. While the new legislation offered protections against discrimination in employment and nullified restrictive Jim Crow voting laws, African American communities continued their efforts to make sure that federal legislation was followed. Many of these efforts continue to the present day.

A. Philip Randolph (left) and Bayard Rustin (right) appearing before a Senate subcommittee in 1966

Literary Focus: The Postwar and Civil Rights Eras

Major Concepts

- **The United States and the World**—In 1941, aggression by the Axis Powers led the United States to enter World War II. During this period, American writers examined both wartime struggles and postwar anxieties.

- **Postwar Optimism and Pessimism**—The war united many Americans in the belief that they were saving the world against the evil forces of Fascism in Germany, Italy, and Japan. The G.I. Bill allowed millions of Americans to enter the middle class. Yet the carnage and horror of wartime atrocities, such as the firebombing of Dresden, the Nazi Death Camps, and the use of the atomic bomb on Hiroshima and Nagasaki, left many Americans searching for meaning. The denial of equal opportunities to minority groups, such as African Americans, Latinos, Japanese Americans, and Native Americans, led to further alienation.

- **Suburbia**—Despite the importance of cities in the development of the United States, a deep distrust of urban life has also been a part of the U.S. character. By 1900, U.S. cities were ringed with suburbs. The growth of suburbia continued to accelerate throughout the twentieth century. For millions of people in the United States, a home in the suburbs came to symbolize the American dream. Nevertheless, some writers have depicted suburbia as a cultural wasteland inhabited by conformists. John Cheever and John Updike are two writers who have explored the culture of suburbs in the United States.

- **Civil Rights Era**—African American veterans returned home to segregation and inequality after fighting for democracy and freedom abroad. Communities came together in acts of self-determination to seek equity. Writers and journalists during this period advocated for change in order to move the country to support an end to segregation.

Style & Form

New Journalism

- Journalists began to experiment with the form and function of reporting in order to more fully capture the nuance of current events. Writers such as John Hersey, Joan Didion, and Tom Wolfe began to incorporate devices from literature into their feature articles for newspapers and magazines.

- New journalists borrowed literary techniques such as telling a story in scenes, incorporating dialogue, developing the voice of the narrator, presenting the story through various points of view, and employing **characterization** techniques to bring the subject alive to the reader.

Literary Focus: The Postwar and Civil Rights Eras

16. **Postwar Realism**

    - Postwar legislation dramatically changed American society and American literature with it. Playwrights such as Lorraine Hansberry and Arthur Miller sought to capture the experience of the new middle class, and included new voices and themes to reflect the various experiences within an upwardly mobile society.

17. **Beat Fiction and Poetry**

    - Beat writers often found it difficult to connect with the optimism of the 1950s and rejected suburban complacency. Known as the Beat Generation, writers such as Allen Ginsberg and Jack Kerouac engaged in experimental forms of writing, attempting to capture the reality of each moment on the page, often with very little planning or revision.

18. **Aspirational Rhetoric**

    - As victors of World War II, Americans developed a new consciousness as protectors of freedom and democracy. This attitude found its way into the writings of politicians, journalists, and activists. Writing from this time appealed to a higher moral purpose and often charged the United States with a duty to spread freedom, democracy, and free trade at home and abroad.

    - Biblical rhetoric was often employed by leaders within the civil rights movement. For example, Martin Luther King Jr. frequently wove imagery and context from the Bible into his speeches.

19. The period after World War II and into the civil rights movement was full of changes for the United States and the world, and the social and political actions of this time remain relevant. Communities continue to grapple with the implications of landmark legislation and decisions, such as the Civil Rights Acts of 1964, and modern politicians evoke the rhetoric of the civil rights movement. How do you feel the postwar and civil rights eras continue to shape society today?

Literary Focus: The Postwar and Civil Rights Eras

Read "Literary Focus: The Postwar and Civil Rights Eras." After you read, complete the Think Questions below.

THINK QUESTIONS

1. Why did Americans change their minds about isolationism following the Japanese attack on Pearl Harbor? Explain, citing evidence from the text.

2. What is the disparity between WWII's nickname, "the good war," and the reality for marginalized citizens in American society? Explain, citing evidence from the text.

3. In which ways did the desegregation of the U.S. military in 1948 symbolize that it was just the beginning of the civil rights movement? Support your response with evidence from the text.

4. Use context clues to determine the meaning of **affluence** as it is used in the text. Write your best definition of *affluence* here, using evidence to explain your understanding.

5. What is the meaning of the word **discriminatory** as it is used in the text? Write your best definition of *discriminatory* here, along with a brief explanation of how you arrived at its meaning. Then, check a dictionary to confirm your understanding.

Hiroshima

INFORMATIONAL TEXT
John Hersey
1946

Introduction

John Hersey (1914–1993) collected eyewitness accounts of life in Hiroshima after the detonation of a nuclear bomb and intended to release them in serial form in *The New Yorker* until the editors made a last-minute decision to devote an entire issue to Hersey's reporting. The 1946 article was an immediate sensation, giving Americans their first real understanding of the impact of a nuclear weapon. In this excerpt, Hersey describes some of the aftermath of the bombing.

"The bomb had not only left the underground organs of plants intact; it had stimulated them."

Excerpt from *Chapter Four: Panic Grass and Feverfew*

1   The hospitals and aid stations around Hiroshima were so crowded in the first weeks after the bombing and staffs were so variable, depending on their health and on the unpredictable arrival of outside help, that patients had to be constantly shifted from place to place. Miss Sasaki, who had already been moved three times, twice by ship, was taken at the end of August to an engineering school, also at Hatsukaichi[1]. Because her leg did not improve but swelled more and more, the doctors at the school bound it with **crude** splints and took her by car, on September 9th, to the Red Cross Hospital in Hiroshima. This was the first chance she had had to look at the ruins of Hiroshima; the last time she had been carried through the city's streets, she had been hovering on the edge of unconsciousness. Even though the wreckage had been described to her, and though she was still in pain, the sight horrified and amazed her, and there was something she noticed about it that particularly gave her the creeps. Over everything—up through the wreckage of the city, in gutters, along the riverbanks, tangled among tiles and tin roofing, climbing on charred tree trunks—was a blanket of fresh, vivid, lush, optimistic green; the verdancy rose even from the foundations of ruined houses. Weeds already hid the ashes, and wild flowers were in bloom among the city's bones. The bomb had not only left the underground organs of plants intact; it had **stimulated** them. Everywhere were bluets and Spanish bayonets, goosefoot, morning glories and day lilies, the hairy-fruited bean, purslane and clotbur and sesame and panic grass and feverfew. Especially in a circle at the center, sickle senna grew in extraordinary **regeneration**, not only standing among the charred remnants of the same plant but pushing up in new places, among bricks and through cracks in the asphalt. It actually seemed as if a load of sickle-senna seed had been dropped along with the bomb. . . .

2   A year after the bomb was dropped, Miss Sasaki was a cripple; Mrs. Nakamura was **destitute**; Father Kleinsorge was back in the hospital; Dr. Sasaki was not capable of the work he once could do; Dr. Fujii had lost the thirty-room hospital it

---

1. **Hatsukaichi** a city near Hiroshima

took him many years to acquire, and had no prospects of rebuilding it; Mr. Tanimoto's church had been ruined and he no longer had his exceptional vitality. The lives of these six people, among the luckiest in Hiroshima, would never be the same. What they thought of their experiences and of the use of the atomic bomb was, of course, not unanimous. One feeling they did seem to share, however, was a **curious** kind of elated community spirit, something like that of the Londoners after their blitz—a pride in the way they and their fellow survivors had stood up to a dreadful ordeal. Just before the anniversary, Mr. Tanimoto wrote in a letter to an American some words which expressed this feeling: "What a heartbreaking scene this was the first night! About midnight I landed on the riverbank. So many injured people lied on the ground that I made my way by striding over them. Repeating 'Excuse me,' I forwarded and carried a tub of water with me and gave a cup of water to each of them. They raised their upper bodies slowly and accepted a cup of water with a bow and drunk quietly and, spilling any remnants gave back a cup with hearty expression of their thankfulness, and said, 'I couldn't help my sister, who was buried under the house, because I had to take care of my mother who got a deep wound on her eye and our house soon set fire and we hardly escaped. Look, I lost my home, my family, and at last myself bitterly injured. But now I have gotten my mind to dedicate what I have and to complete the war for our country's sake.' Thus they pledged to me, even women and children did the same. Being entirely tired I lied down on the ground among them, but couldn't sleep at all. Next morning I found many men and women dead, whom I gave water last night. But to my great surprise, I never heard any one cried in disorder, even though they suffered in great agony. They died in silence, with no grudge, setting their teeth to bear it. All for the country." . . .

3   It would be impossible to say what horrors were embedded in the minds of the children who lived through the day of the bombing in Hiroshima. On the surface their recollections, months after the disasters, were of an exhilarating adventure. Toshio Nakamura, who was ten at the time of the bombing, was soon able to talk freely, even gaily, about the experience, and a few weeks before the anniversary he wrote the following matter-of-fact essay for his teacher at No-bori-cho Primary School: "The day before the bomb, I went for a swim. In the morning, I was eating peanuts. I saw a light. I was knocked to little sister's sleeping place. When we were saved, I could only see as far as the tram. My mother and I started to pack our things. The neighbors were walking around burned and bleeding. Hataya-*san* told me to run away with her. I said I wanted to wait for my mother. We went to the park. A whirlwind came. At night a gas tank burned and I saw the reflection in the river. We stayed in the park one night. Next day I went to Taiko Bridge and met my girl friends Kikuki and Murakami. They were looking for their mothers. But Kikuki's mother was wounded and Murakami's mother, alas, was dead."

Excerpted from *Hiroshima* by John Hersey, published by Ishi Press.

WRITE

PERSONAL RESPONSE: The excerpt from *Hiroshima* addresses the experiences of survivors who experienced a horrific tragedy on a national scale. Consider a time you or someone you know witnessed a tragedy at a national or global level. How does perspective influence the way we experience tragedy? Include the most relevant evidence from the text and your own commentary to develop your response.

A Good Man Is Hard to Find

FICTION
Flannery O'Connor
1953

Introduction

Flannery O'Connor (1925–1964) was one of a kind. A lifelong resident of Milledgeville, Georgia, and a devout Catholic, she produced in her short career some of the best American writing of the postwar period. Her style of Southern Gothic writing was characterized by elements of religion, morality, violence, and redemption. In this, her most famous story, a disgruntled family on a grudging trip to Florida takes a detour with devastating consequences. Have they met the Devil himself? Or merely wandered into a predestined fate?

". . . Why you're one of my babies. You're one of my own children!"

> *Note: The text you are about to read contains offensive language. Remember to be mindful of the thoughts and feelings of your peers as you read and discuss this text. Please consult your teacher for additional guidance and support.*

1 THE GRANDMOTHER didn't want to go to Florida. She wanted to visit some of her connections in east Tennessee and she was seizing at every chance to change Bailey's mind. Bailey was the son she lived with, her only boy. He was sitting on the edge of his chair at the table, bent over the orange sports section of the Journal. "Now look here, Bailey," she said, "see here, read this," and she stood with one hand on her thin hip and the other rattling the newspaper at his bald head. "Here this fellow that calls himself The Misfit is aloose from the Federal Pen and headed toward Florida and you read here what it says he did to these people. Just you read it. I wouldn't take my children in any direction with a criminal like that aloose in it. I couldn't answer to my conscience if I did."

2 Bailey didn't look up from his reading so she wheeled around then and faced the children's mother, a young woman in slacks, whose face was as broad and innocent as a cabbage and was tied around with a green head-kerchief that had two points on the top like rabbit's ears. She was sitting on the sofa, feeding the baby his apricots out of a jar. "The children have been to Florida before," the old lady said. "You all ought to take them somewhere else for a change so they would see different parts of the world and be broad. They never have been to east Tennessee."

3 The children's mother didn't seem to hear her but the eight-year-old boy, John Wesley, a stocky child with glasses, said, "If you don't want to go to Florida, why dontcha stay at home?" He and the little girl, June Star, were reading the funny papers on the floor.

4 "She wouldn't stay at home to be queen for a day," June Star said without raising her yellow head.

5 "Yes and what would you do if this fellow, The Misfit, caught you?" the grandmother asked.

NOTES

Skill: Story Structure

The grandmother is determined to get what she wants. She points out that a criminal has escaped in Florida to manipulate her son. She even brings up her conscience. This creates tension and foreshadows the ending of the story.

A Good Man Is Hard to Find

6. "I'd smack his face," John Wesley said.

7. "She wouldn't stay at home for a million bucks," June Star said. "Afraid she'd miss something. She has to go everywhere we go."

8. "All right, Miss," the grandmother said. "Just remember that the next time you want me to curl your hair."

9. June Star said her hair was naturally curly.

10. The next morning the grandmother was the first one in the car, ready to go. She had her big black valise that looked like the head of a hippopotamus in one corner, and underneath it she was hiding a basket with Pitty Sing, the cat, in it. She didn't intend for the cat to be left alone in the house for three days because he would miss her too much and she was afraid he might brush against one of the gas burners and accidentally asphyxiate himself. Her son, Bailey, didn't like to arrive at a motel with a cat.

11. She sat in the middle of the back seat with John Wesley and June Star on either side of her. Bailey and the children's mother and the baby sat in front and they left Atlanta at eight forty-five with the mileage on the car at 55890. The grandmother wrote this down because she thought it would be interesting to say how many miles they had been when they got back. It took them twenty minutes to reach the outskirts of the city.

12. The old lady settled herself comfortably, removing her white cotton gloves and putting them up with her purse on the shelf in front of the back window. The children's mother still had on slacks and still had her head tied up in a green kerchief, but the grandmother had on a navy blue straw sailor hat with a bunch of white violets on the brim and a navy blue dress with a small white dot in the print. Her collars and cuffs were white organdy trimmed with lace and at her neckline she had pinned a purple spray of cloth violets containing a sachet. In case of an accident, anyone seeing her dead on the highway would know at once that she was a lady.

13. She said she thought it was going to be a good day for driving, neither too hot nor too cold, and she cautioned Bailey that the speed limit was fifty-five miles an hour and that the patrolmen hid themselves behind billboards and small clumps of trees and sped out after you before you had a chance to slow down. She pointed out interesting details of the scenery: Stone Mountain; the blue granite that in some places came up to both sides of the highway; the brilliant red clay banks slightly streaked with purple; and the various crops that made rows of green lace-work on the ground. The trees were full of silver-white sunlight and the meanest of them sparkled. The children were reading comic magazines and their mother had gone back to sleep.

14. "Let's go through Georgia fast so we won't have to look at it much," John Wesley said.

15 "If I were a little boy," said the grandmother, "I wouldn't talk about my native state that way. Tennessee has the mountains and Georgia has the hills."

16 "Tennessee is just a hillbilly dumping ground," John Wesley said, "and Georgia is a lousy state too."

17 "You said it," June Star said.

18 "In my time," said the grandmother, folding her thin veined fingers, "children were more respectful of their native states and their parents and everything else. People did right then. Oh look at the cute little pickaninny!"[1] she said and pointed to a Negro child standing in the door of a shack. "Wouldn't that make a picture, now?" she asked and they all turned and looked at the little Negro out of the back window. He waved.

19 "He didn't have any britches on," June Star said.

20 "He probably didn't have any," the grandmother explained. "Little n-----s in the country don't have things like we do. If I could paint, I'd paint that picture," she said.

21 The children exchanged comic books.

22 The grandmother offered to hold the baby and the children's mother passed him over the front seat to her. She set him on her knee and bounced him and told him about the things they were passing. She rolled her eyes and screwed up her mouth and stuck her leathery thin face into his smooth bland one. Occasionally he gave her a faraway smile. They passed a large cotton field with five or six graves fenced in the middle of it, like a small island. "Look at the graveyard!" the grandmother said, pointing it out. "That was the old family burying ground. That belonged to the plantation."

23 "Where's the plantation?" John Wesley asked.

24 "Gone With the Wind," said the grandmother. "Ha. Ha."

25 When the children finished all the comic books they had brought, they opened the lunch and ate it. The grandmother ate a peanut butter sandwich and an olive and would not let the children throw the box and the paper napkins out the window. When there was nothing else to do they played a game by choosing a cloud and making the other two guess what shape it suggested. John Wesley took one the shape of a cow and June Star guessed a cow and John Wesley said, no, an automobile, and June Star said he didn't play fair, and they began to slap each other over the grandmother.

---

1. **pickaninny** an old-fashioned term for an African American child, now considered a racist slur

A Good Man Is Hard to Find

26 The grandmother said she would tell them a story if they would keep quiet. When she told a story, she rolled her eyes and waved her head and was very dramatic. She said once when she was a maiden lady she had been courted by a Mr. Edgar Atkins Teagarden from Jasper, Georgia. She said he was a very good-looking man and a gentleman and that he brought her a watermelon every Saturday afternoon with his initials cut in it, E. A. T. Well, one Saturday, she said, Mr. Teagarden brought the watermelon and there was nobody at home and he left it on the front porch and returned in his buggy to Jasper, but she never got the watermelon, she said, because a n----- boy ate it when he saw the initials, E. A. T.! This story tickled John Wesley's funny bone and he giggled and giggled but June Star didn't think it was any good. She said she wouldn't marry a man that just brought her a watermelon on Saturday. The grandmother said she would have done well to marry Mr. Teagarden because he was a gentleman and had bought Coca-Cola stock when it first came out and that he had died only a few years ago, a very wealthy man.

27 They stopped at The Tower for barbecued sandwiches. The Tower was a part stucco and part wood filling station and dance hall set in a clearing outside of Timothy. A fat man named Red Sammy Butts ran it and there were signs stuck here and there on the building and for miles up and down the highway saying, TRY RED SAMMY'S FAMOUS BARBECUE. NONE LIKE FAMOUS RED SAMMY'S! RED SAM! THE FAT BOY WITH THE HAPPY LAUGH. A VETERAN! RED SAMMY'S YOUR MAN!

28 Red Sammy was lying on the bare ground outside The Tower with his head under a truck while a gray monkey about a foot high, chained to a small chinaberry tree, chattered nearby. The monkey sprang back into the tree and got on the highest limb as soon as he saw the children jump out of the car and run toward him.

29 Inside, The Tower was a long dark room with a counter at one end and tables at the other and dancing space in the middle. They all sat down at a board table next to the nickelodeon and Red Sam's wife, a tall burnt-brown woman with hair and eyes lighter than her skin, came and took their order. The children's mother put a dime in the machine and played "The Tennessee Waltz," and the grandmother said that tune always made her want to dance. She asked Bailey if he would like to dance but he only glared at her. He didn't have a naturally sunny disposition like she did and trips made him nervous. The grandmother's brown eyes were very bright. She swayed her head from side to side and pretended she was dancing in her chair. June Star said play something she could tap to so the children's mother put in another dime and played a fast number and June Star stepped out onto the dance floor and did her tap routine.

30 "Ain't she cute?" Red Sam's wife said, leaning over the counter. "Would you like to come be my little girl?"

Skill: Connotation and Denotation

The word *glared* has a negative connotation and is in contrast with the words *sunny* and *bright*. I think Bailey is annoyed by the grandmother, and she seems to be pretending everything is cheerful.

A Good Man Is Hard to Find

31 "No I certainly wouldn't," June Star said. "I wouldn't live in a broken-down place like this for a minion bucks!" and she ran back to the table.

32 "Ain't she cute?" the woman repeated, stretching her mouth politely.

33 "Arn't you ashamed?" hissed the grandmother.

34 Red Sam came in and told his wife to quit lounging on the counter and hurry up with these people's order. His khaki trousers reached just to his hip bones and his stomach hung over them like a sack of meal swaying under his shirt. He came over and sat down at a table nearby and let out a combination sigh and yodel. "You can't win," he said. "You can't win," and he wiped his sweating red face off with a gray handkerchief. "These days you don't know who to trust," he said. "Ain't that the truth?"

35 "People are certainly not nice like they used to be," said the grandmother.

36 "Two fellers come in here last week," Red Sammy said, "driving a Chrysler. It was a old beat-up car but it was a good one and these boys looked all right to me. Said they worked at the mill and you know I let them fellers charge the gas they bought? Now why did I do that?"

37 "Because you're a good man!" the grandmother said at once.

38 "Yes'm, I suppose so," Red Sam said as if he were struck with this answer.

39 His wife brought the orders, carrying the five plates all at once without a tray, two in each hand and one balanced on her arm. "It isn't a soul in this green world of God's that you can trust," she said. "And I don't count nobody out of that, not nobody," she repeated, looking at Red Sammy.

40 "Did you read about that criminal, ==The Misfit, that's escaped?==" asked the grandmother.

41 "I wouldn't be a bit surprised if he didn't ==attack this place right here==," said the woman. "If he hears about it being here, I wouldn't be none surprised to see him. If he hears it's two cent in the cash register, I wouldn't be a tall surprised if he . . ."

42 "That'll do," Red Sam said. "Go bring these people their Co'-Colas," and the woman went off to get the rest of the order.

43 "==A good man is hard to find==," Red Sammy said. "==Everything is getting terrible.== I remember the day you could go off and leave your screen door unlatched. Not no more."

44 He and the grandmother discussed better times. The old lady said that in her opinion Europe was entirely to blame for the way things were now. She said the way Europe acted you would think we were made of money and Red

Skill: Story Structure

The Misfit is mentioned again, and the wife says that he would "attack" them. Red Sam feels that there are few good men and that the world is terrible. This is a dark view of humanity, which is sad and scary.

Sam said it was no use talking about it, she was exactly right. The children ran outside into the white sunlight and looked at the monkey in the lacy chinaberry tree. He was busy catching fleas on himself and biting each one carefully between his teeth as if it were a **delicacy**.

45   They drove off again into the hot afternoon. The grandmother took cat naps and woke up every few minutes with her own snoring. Outside of Toombsboro she woke up and recalled an old plantation that she had visited in this neighborhood once when she was a young lady. She said the house had six white columns across the front and that there was an avenue of oaks leading up to it and two little wooden trellis arbors on either side in front where you sat down with your suitor after a stroll in the garden. She recalled exactly which road to turn off to get to it. She knew that Bailey would not be willing to lose any time looking at an old house, but the more she talked about it, the more she wanted to see it once again and find out if the little twin arbors were still standing. "There was a secret panel in this house," she said craftily, not telling the truth but wishing that she were, "and the story went that all the family silver was hidden in it when Sherman came through but it was never found . . ."

46   "Hey!" John Wesley said. "Let's go see it! We'll find it! We'll poke all the woodwork and find it! Who lives there? Where do you turn off at? Hey Pop, can't we turn off there?"

47   "We never have seen a house with a secret panel!" June Star shrieked. "Let's go to the house with the secret panel! Hey Pop, can't we go see the house with the secret panel!"

48   "It's not far from here, I know," the grandmother said. "It wouldn't take over twenty minutes."

49   Bailey was looking straight ahead. His jaw was as rigid as a horseshoe. "No," he said.

50   The children began to yell and scream that they wanted to see the house with the secret panel. John Wesley kicked the back of the front seat and June Star hung over her mother's shoulder and whined desperately into her ear that they never had any fun even on their vacation, that they could never do what THEY wanted to do. The baby began to scream and John Wesley kicked the back of the seat so hard that his father could feel the blows in his kidney.

51   "All right!" he shouted and drew the car to a stop at the side of the road. "Will you all shut up? Will you all just shut up for one second? If you don't shut up, we won't go anywhere."

52   "It would be very educational for them," the grandmother murmured.

53 "All right," Bailey said, "but get this: this is the only time we're going to stop for anything like this. This is the one and only time."

54 "The dirt road that you have to turn down is about a mile back," the grandmother directed. "I marked it when we passed."

55 "A dirt road," Bailey groaned.

56 After they had turned around and were headed toward the dirt road, the grandmother recalled other points about the house, the beautiful glass over the front doorway and the candle-lamp in the hall. John Wesley said that the secret panel was probably in the fireplace.

57 "You can't go inside this house," Bailey said. "You don't know who lives there."

58 "While you all talk to the people in front, I'll run around behind and get in a window," John Wesley suggested.

59 "We'll all stay in the car," his mother said. They turned onto the dirt road and the car raced roughly along in a swirl of pink dust. The grandmother recalled the times when there were no paved roads and thirty miles was a day's journey. The dirt road was hilly and there were sudden washes in it and sharp curves on dangerous embankments. All at once they would be on a hill, looking down over the blue tops of trees for miles around, then the next minute, they would be in a red depression with the dust-coated trees looking down on them.

60 "This place had better turn up in a minute," Bailey said, "or I'm going to turn around."

61 The road looked as if no one had traveled on it in months.

62 "It's not much farther," the grandmother said and just as she said it, a horrible thought came to her. The thought was so embarrassing that she turned red in the face and her eyes dilated and her feet jumped up, upsetting her valise in the corner. The instant the valise moved, the newspaper top she had over the basket under it rose with a snarl and Pitty Sing, the cat, sprang onto Bailey's shoulder.

63 The children were thrown to the floor and their mother, clutching the baby, was thrown out the door onto the ground; the old lady was thrown into the front seat. The car turned over once and landed right-side-up in a gulch off the side of the road. Bailey remained in the driver's seat with the cat—gray-striped with a broad white face and an orange nose—clinging to his neck like a caterpillar.

64 As soon as the children saw they could move their arms and legs, they scrambled out of the car, shouting, "We've had an ACCIDENT!" The

grandmother was curled up under the dashboard, hoping she was injured so that Bailey's wrath would not come down on her all at once. The horrible thought she had had before the accident was that the house she had remembered so vividly was not in Georgia but in Tennessee.

65 Bailey removed the cat from his neck with both hands and flung it out the window against the side of a pine tree. Then he got out of the car and started looking for the children's mother. She was sitting against the side of the red gutted ditch, holding the screaming baby, but she only had a cut down her face and a broken shoulder. "We've had an ACCIDENT!" the children screamed in a frenzy of delight.

66 "But nobody's killed," June Star said with disappointment as the grandmother limped out of the car, her hat still pinned to her head but the broken front brim standing up at a **jaunty** angle and the violet spray hanging off the side. They all sat down in the ditch, except the children, to recover from the shock. They were all shaking.

67 "Maybe a car will come along," said the children's mother hoarsely.

68 "I believe I have injured an organ," said the grandmother, pressing her side, but no one answered her. Bailey's teeth were clattering. He had on a yellow sport shirt with bright blue parrots designed in it and his face was as yellow as the shirt. The grandmother decided that she would not mention that the house was in Tennessee.

69 The road was about ten feet above and they could see only the tops of the trees on the other side of it. Behind the ditch they were sitting in there were more woods, tall and dark and deep. In a few minutes they saw a car some distance away on top of a hill, coming slowly as if the occupants were watching them. The grandmother stood up and waved both arms dramatically to attract their attention. The car continued to come on slowly, disappeared around a bend and appeared again, moving even slower, on top of the hill they had gone over. It was a big black battered hearse-like automobile. There were three men in it.

70 It came to a stop just over them and for some minutes, the driver looked down with a steady expressionless gaze to where they were sitting, and didn't speak. Then he turned his head and muttered something to the other two and they got out. One was a fat boy in black trousers and a red sweat shirt with a silver stallion embossed on the front of it. He moved around on the right side of them and stood staring, his mouth partly open in a kind of loose grin. The other had on khaki pants and a blue striped coat and a gray hat pulled down very low, hiding most of his face. He came around slowly on the left side. Neither spoke.

71. The driver got out of the car and stood by the side of it, looking down at them. He was an older man than the other two. His hair was just beginning to gray and he wore silver-rimmed spectacles that gave him a scholarly look. He had a long creased face and didn't have on any shirt or undershirt. He had on blue jeans that were too tight for him and was holding a black hat and a gun. The two boys also had guns.

72. "We've had an ACCIDENT!" the children screamed.

73. The grandmother had the peculiar feeling that the bespectacled man was someone she knew. His face was as familiar to her as if she had known him all her life but she could not recall who he was. He moved away from the car and began to come down the embankment, placing his feet carefully so that he wouldn't slip. He had on tan and white shoes and no socks, and his ankles were red and thin. "Good afternoon," he said. "I see you all had you a little spill."

74. "We turned over twice!" said the grandmother.

75. "Oncet," he corrected. "We seen it happen. Try their car and see will it run, Hiram," he said quietly to the boy with the gray hat.

76. "What you got that gun for?" John Wesley asked. "Whatcha gonna do with that gun?"

77. "Lady," the man said to the children's mother, "would you mind calling them children to sit down by you? Children make me nervous. I want all you all to sit down right together there where you're at."

78. "What are you telling US what to do for?" June Star asked.

79. Behind them the line of woods gaped like a dark open mouth. "Come here," said their mother.

80. "Look here now," Bailey began suddenly, "we're in a predicament! We're in . . ."

81. The grandmother shrieked. She scrambled to her feet and stood staring. "You're The Misfit!" she said. "I recognized you at once!"

82. "Yes'm," the man said, smiling slightly as if he were pleased in spite of himself to be known, "but it would have been better for all of you, lady, if you hadn't of reckernized me."

83. Bailey turned his head sharply and said something to his mother that shocked even the children. The old lady began to cry and The Misfit reddened.

84. "Lady," he said, "don't you get upset. Sometimes a man says things he don't mean. I don't reckon he meant to talk to you thataway."

A Good Man Is Hard to Find

85 "You wouldn't shoot a lady, would you?" the grandmother said and removed a clean handkerchief from her cuff and began to slap at her eyes with it.

86 The Misfit pointed the toe of his shoe into the ground and made a little hole and then covered it up again. "I would hate to have to," he said.

87 "Listen," the grandmother almost screamed, "I know you're a good man. You don't look a bit like you have common blood. I know you must come from nice people!"

88 "Yes mam," he said, "finest people in the world." When he smiled he showed a row of strong white teeth. "God never made a finer woman than my mother and my daddy's heart was pure gold," he said. The boy with the red sweat shirt had come around behind them and was standing with his gun at his hip. The Misfit squatted down on the ground. "Watch them children, Bobby Lee," he said. "You know they make me nervous." He looked at the six of them huddled together in front of him and he seemed to be embarrassed as if he couldn't think of anything to say. "Ain't a cloud in the sky," he remarked, looking up at it. "Don't see no sun but don't see no cloud neither."

89 "Yes, it's a beautiful day," said the grandmother. "Listen," she said, "you shouldn't call yourself The Misfit because I know you're a good man at heart. I can just look at you and tell."

90 "Hush!" Bailey yelled. "Hush! Everybody shut up and let me handle this!" He was squatting in the position of a runner about to sprint forward but he didn't move.

91 "I prechate that, lady," The Misfit said and drew a little circle in the ground with the butt of his gun.

92 "It'll take a half a hour to fix this here car," Hiram called, looking over the raised hood of it.

93 "Well, first you and Bobby Lee get him and that little boy to step over yonder with you," The Misfit said, pointing to Bailey and John Wesley. "The boys want to ast you some-thing," he said to Bailey. "Would you mind stepping back in them woods there with them?"

94 "Listen," Bailey began, "we're in a terrible predicament! Nobody realizes what this is," and his voice cracked. His eyes were as blue and intense as the parrots in his shirt and he remained perfectly still.

95 The grandmother reached up to adjust her hat brim as if she were going to the woods with him but it came off in her hand. She stood staring at it and after a second she let it fall on the ground. Hiram pulled Bailey up by the arm as if he were assisting an old man. John Wesley caught hold of his father's

hand and Bobby Lee followed. They went off toward the woods and just as they reached the dark edge, Bailey turned and supporting himself against a gray naked pine trunk, he shouted, "I'll be back in a minute, Mamma, wait on me!"

96 "Come back this instant!" his mother shrilled but they all disappeared into the woods.

97 "Bailey Boy!" the grandmother called in a tragic voice but she found she was looking at The Misfit squatting on the ground in front of her. "I just know you're a good man," she said desperately. "You're not a bit common!"

98 "Nome, I ain't a good man," The Misfit said after a second as if he had considered her statement carefully, "but I ain't the worst in the world neither. My daddy said I was a different breed of dog from my brothers and sisters. 'You know,' Daddy said, 'it's some that can live their whole life out without asking about it and it's others has to know why it is, and this boy is one of the latters. He's going to be into every-thing!'" He put on his black hat and looked up suddenly and then away deep into the woods as if he were embarrassed again. "I'm sorry I don't have on a shirt before you ladies," he said, hunching his shoulders slightly. "We buried our clothes that we had on when we escaped and we're just making do until we can get better. We borrowed these from some folks we met," he explained.

99 "That's perfectly all right," the grandmother said. "Maybe Bailey has an extra shirt in his suitcase."

100 "I'll look and see terrectly," The Misfit said.

101 "Where are they taking him?" the children's mother screamed.

102 "Daddy was a card himself," The Misfit said. "You couldn't put anything over on him. He never got in trouble with the Authorities though. Just had the knack of handling them."

103 "You could be honest too if you'd only try," said the grandmother. "Think how wonderful it would be to settle down and live a comfortable life and not have to think about some-body chasing you all the time."

104 The Misfit kept scratching in the ground with the butt of his gun as if he were thinking about it. "Yes'm, somebody is always after you," he murmured.

105 The grandmother noticed how thin his shoulder blades were just behind his hat because she was standing up looking down on him. "Do you ever pray?" she asked.

106 He shook his head. All she saw was the black hat wiggle between his shoulder blades. "Nome," he said.

A Good Man Is Hard to Find

107 There was a pistol shot from the woods, followed closely by another. Then silence. The old lady's head jerked around. She could hear the wind move through the tree tops like a long satisfied insuck of breath. "Bailey Boy!" she called.

108 "I was a gospel singer for a while," The Misfit said. "I been most everything. Been in the arm service, both land and sea, at home and abroad, been twict married, been an undertaker, been with the railroads, plowed Mother Earth, been in a tornado, seen a man burnt alive oncet," and he looked up at the children's mother and the little girl who were sitting close together, their faces white and their eyes glassy; "I even seen a woman flogged," he said.

109 "Pray, pray," the grandmother began, "pray, pray . . ."

110 "I never was a bad boy that I remember of," The Misfit said in an almost dreamy voice, "but somewheres along the line I done something wrong and got sent to the **penitentiary**. I was buried alive," and he looked up and held her attention to him by a steady stare.

111 "That's when you should have started to pray," she said. "What did you do to get sent to the penitentiary that first time?"

112 "Turn to the right, it was a wall," The Misfit said, looking up again at the cloudless sky. "Turn to the left, it was a wall. Look up it was a ceiling, look down it was a floor. I forget what I done, lady. I set there and set there, trying to remember what it was I done and I ain't recalled it to this day. Oncet in a while, I would think it was coming to me, but it never come."

113 "Maybe they put you in by mistake," the old lady said vaguely.

114 "Nome," he said. "It wasn't no mistake. They had the papers on me."

115 "You must have stolen something," she said.

116 The Misfit sneered slightly. "Nobody had nothing I wanted," he said. "It was a head-doctor at the penitentiary said what I had done was kill my daddy but I known that for a lie. My daddy died in nineteen ought nineteen of the epidemic flu and I never had a thing to do with it. He was buried in the Mount Hopewell Baptist churchyard and you can go there and see for yourself."

117 "If you would pray," the old lady said, "Jesus would help you."

118 "That's right," The Misfit said.

119 "Well then, why don't you pray?" she asked trembling with delight suddenly.

120 "I don't want no hep," he said. "I'm doing all right by myself."

121 Bobby Lee and Hiram came **ambling** back from the woods. Bobby Lee was dragging a yellow shirt with bright blue parrots in it.

122 "Thow me that shirt, Bobby Lee," The Misfit said. The shirt came flying at him and landed on his shoulder and he put it on. The grandmother couldn't name what the shirt reminded her of. "No, lady," The Misfit said while he was buttoning it up, "I found out the crime don't matter. You can do one thing or you can do another, kill a man or take a tire off his car, because sooner or later you're going to forget what it was you done and just be punished for it."

123 The children's mother had begun to make heaving noises as if she couldn't get her breath. "Lady," he asked, "would you and that little girl like to step off yonder with Bobby Lee and Hiram and join your husband?"

124 "Yes, thank you," the mother said faintly. Her left arm dangled helplessly and she was holding the baby, who had gone to sleep, in the other. "Hep that lady up, Hiram," The Misfit said as she struggled to climb out of the ditch, "and Bobby Lee, you hold onto that little girl's hand."

125 "I don't want to hold hands with him," June Star said. "He reminds me of a pig."

126 The fat boy blushed and laughed and caught her by the arm and pulled her off into the woods after Hiram and her mother.

127 Alone with The Misfit, the grandmother found that she had lost her voice. There was not a cloud in the sky nor any sun. There was nothing around her but woods. She wanted to tell him that he must pray. She opened and closed her mouth several times before anything came out. Finally she found herself saying, "Jesus. Jesus," meaning, Jesus will help you, but the way she was saying it, it sounded as if she might be cursing.

128 "Yes'm," The Misfit said as if he agreed. "Jesus thown everything off balance. It was the same case with Him as with me except He hadn't committed any crime and they could prove I had committed one because they had the papers on me. Of course," he said, "they never shown me my papers. That's why I sign myself now. I said long ago, you get you a signature and sign everything you do and keep a copy of it. Then you'll know what you done and you can hold up the crime to the punishment and see do they match and in the end you'll have something to prove you ain't been treated right. I call myself The Misfit," he said, "because I can't make what all I done wrong fit what all I gone through in punishment."

129 There was a piercing scream from the woods, followed closely by a pistol report. "Does it seem right to you, lady, that one is punished a heap and another ain't punished at all?"

130 "Jesus!" the old lady cried. "You've got good blood! I know you wouldn't shoot a lady! I know you come from nice people! Pray! Jesus, you ought not to shoot a lady. I'll give you all the money I've got!"

131 "Lady," The Misfit said, looking beyond her far into the woods, "there never was a body that give the undertaker a tip."

132 There were two more pistol reports and the grandmother raised her head like a parched old turkey hen crying for water and called, "Bailey Boy, Bailey Boy!" as if her heart would break.

133 "Jesus was the only One that ever raised the dead," The Misfit continued, "and He shouldn't have done it. He thown everything off balance. If He did what He said, then it's nothing for you to do but thow away everything and follow Him, and if He didn't, then it's nothing for you to do but enjoy the few minutes you got left the best way you can—by killing somebody or burning down his house or doing some other meanness to him. No pleasure but meanness," he said and his voice had become almost a snarl.

134 "Maybe He didn't raise the dead," the old lady mumbled, not knowing what she was saying and feeling so dizzy that she sank down in the ditch with her legs twisted under her.

135 "I wasn't there so I can't say He didn't," The Misfit said. "I wisht I had of been there," he said, hitting the ground with his fist. "It ain't right I wasn't there because if I had of been there I would of known. Listen lady," he said in a high voice, "if I had of been there I would of known and I wouldn't be like I am now." His voice seemed about to crack and the grandmother's head cleared for an instant. She saw the man's face twisted close to her own as if he were going to cry and she murmured, "Why you're one of my babies. You're one of my own children!" She reached out and touched him on the shoulder. The Misfit sprang back as if a snake had bitten him and shot her three times through the chest. Then he put his gun down on the ground and took off his glasses and began to clean them.

136 Hiram and Bobby Lee returned from the woods and stood over the ditch, looking down at the grandmother who half sat and half lay in a puddle of blood with her legs crossed under her like a child's and her face smiling up at the cloudless sky.

137 Without his glasses, The Misfit's eyes were red-rimmed and pale and defenseless-looking. "Take her off and thow her where you thown the others," he said, picking up the cat that was rubbing itself against his leg.

138 "She was a talker, wasn't she?" Bobby Lee said, sliding down the ditch with a yodel.

139 "She would of been a good woman," The Misfit said, "if it had been somebody there to shoot her every minute of her life."

140 "Some fun!" Bobby Lee said.

141 "Shut up, Bobby Lee," The Misfit said. "It's no real pleasure in life."

"A Good Man Is Hard to Find" from *A Good Man Is Hard to Find and Other Stories* by Flannery O'Connor. Copyright 1953 by Flannery O'Connor; Copyright © Renewed 1981 by Regina O'Connor. Reprinted by Permission of Houghton Mifflin Harcourt Publishing Company. All rights reserved.

First Read

Read "A Good Man Is Hard to Find." After you read, complete the Think Questions below.

THINK QUESTIONS

1. How would you describe the grandmother's general outlook on the world? How does she think and act differently from her son, Bailey, and her grandchildren, John Wesley and June Star?

2. Why does the grandmother recognize the driver of the car? Explain the events in the story leading up to this moment that foreshadow the man's arrival.

3. What is The Misfit's philosophy? How does he see things differently from the grandmother?

4. Based on its context, what do you think the word **jaunty** means? Write your best definition of *jaunty* here, explaining how you determined its meaning.

5. What do you think the word **ambling** means? Look at the context in which the word is used in the story and write your own definition of *ambling* here.

Skill:
Story Structure

Use the Checklist to analyze Story Structure in "A Good Man Is Hard to Find." Refer to the sample student annotations about Story Structure in the text.

••• CHECKLIST FOR STORY STRUCTURE

In order to identify the choices an author makes when structuring specific parts of a text, note the following:

- ✓ the choices an author makes to organize specific parts of a text such as where to begin and end a story, or whether the ending should be tragic, comic, or inconclusive

- ✓ the author's use of any literary devices, such as:

    - foreshadowing: a way of hinting at what will come later
    - flashback: a part of a story that shows something that happened in the past
    - pacing: how quickly or slowly the events of a story unfold

- ✓ how the overall structure of the text contributes to its meaning as well as to its aesthetic impact

    - the effect structure has on the reader, such as the creation of suspense through the use of pacing
    - the use of flashback to reveal hidden dimensions of a character that affect the theme

To analyze how an author's choices concerning how to structure specific parts of a text contribute to its overall structure and meaning as well as its aesthetic impact, consider the following questions:

- ✓ How does the author structure the text overall? How does the author structure specific parts of the text?

- ✓ Does the author incorporate literary elements such as flashback or foreshadowing?

- ✓ How do these elements affect the overall text structure and the aesthetic impact of the text?

A Good Man Is Hard to Find

Skill:
Story Structure

Reread paragraphs 66–72 of "A Good Man Is Hard to Find." Then, using the Checklist on the previous page, answer the multiple-choice questions below.

YOUR TURN

1. What impact does the author's narration of this scene have on the reader?

   - A. It creates comfort, anticipation, and excitement in the reader and sets up the reader for the story's surprise ending.
   - B. It creates discomfort, anticipation, and fear in the reader and sets up the reader for the story's eerie, tragic ending.
   - C. It creates discomfort, anticipation, and fear in the reader and sets up the reader for the story's happy ending.
   - D. It creates comfort, anticipation, and excitement in the reader and sets up the reader for the story's eerie, tragic ending.

2. In this scene, the reader encounters The Misfit. How does the revelation about who he is contribute to the suspense of this scene?

   - A. To create suspense, the driver of the car is portrayed with vivid, descriptive details, and the grandmother is described as having a feeling that he is someone she knows, which gives the reader subtle hints about who he is.
   - B. To create suspense, the driver of the car is portrayed as a man with glasses that make him look like a scholar, which gives the reader subtle hints about who he is.
   - C. To create suspense, the driver of the car is described as getting out of the car and standing by it as the grandmother is screaming that they have had an accident, which gives the reader subtle hints about who he is.
   - D. To create suspense, the driver of the car is described as having a gun and no shirt. The grandmother is described as noting that the driver's face is very familiar to her, which gives the reader subtle hints about who he is.

204 Reading & Writing Companion

3. The grandmother has a feeling that she recognizes the driver. How does this realization lead to the story's climax?

   ○ A. The grandmother realizes that she is mistaken and begins to try to persuade the driver not to kill her, and this leads up to the story's climax.

   ○ B. The grandmother's recognition of the driver makes the reader wonder if he is The Misfit. She then realizes that the man whom she is looking to for help is The Misfit, which is the conflict in the story that leads to the climax.

   ○ C. The grandmother's recognition of the driver makes the reader wonder if he is The Misfit. She then realizes that the man whom she is looking to for help is The Misfit, and this leads up to the story's climax.

   ○ D. The grandmother's recognition of the driver makes the reader wonder if the man is related to her. She then realizes that the man whom she is looking to for help is her estranged nephew, and this leads up to the story's climax.

A Good Man Is Hard to Find

Skill:
Connotation and Denotation

Use the Checklist to analyze Connotation and Denotation in "A Good Man Is Hard to Find." Refer to the sample student annotation about Connotation and Denotation in the text.

••• CHECKLIST FOR CONNOTATION AND DENOTATION

In order to identify the denotative meanings of words, use the following steps:

- ✓ first, note unfamiliar words and phrases, key words used to describe important characters, events, and ideas, or words that inspire an emotional reaction

- ✓ next, determine and note the denotative meanings of words by consulting a reference material such as a dictionary, glossary, or thesaurus

- ✓ finally, analyze nuances in the meanings of words with similar denotations

To better understand the meanings of words and phrases as they are used in a text, including connotative meanings, use the following questions as a guide:

- ✓ What is the genre or subject of the text? Based on context, what do you think the meaning of the word is intended to be?

- ✓ Is your inference the same as or different from the dictionary definition?

- ✓ Does the word create a positive, negative, or neutral emotion?

- ✓ What synonyms or alternative phrasings help you describe the connotative meaning of the word?

To determine the meanings of words and phrases as they are used in a text, including connotative meanings, use the following questions as a guide:

- ✓ What is the denotative meaning of the word? Is that denotative meaning correct in context?

- ✓ What possible positive, neutral, or negative connotations might the word have, depending on context?

- ✓ What textual details signal a particular connotation for the word?

Skill: Connotation and Denotation

Reread paragraphs 49–53 of "A Good Man Is Hard to Find." Then, using the Checklist on the previous page, answer the multiple-choice questions below.

YOUR TURN

1. How does the description of Bailey's jaw as "rigid as a horseshoe" in paragraph 49 affect the reader's understanding of this part of the story?

   - A. The description of Bailey's jaw suggests that he is a rigid person but that he is also willing to do things to make his children and mother happy.
   - B. The description of Bailey's jaw suggests that he is determined not to stray off course and implies a lack of flexibility.
   - C. The description of Bailey's jaw suggests that he is determined not to stray off course and implies that he has opinions that he is unwilling to change.
   - D. The description of Bailey's jaw suggests that he is determined to stray off course and implies that although he is flexible he does not want to be told what to do.

2. Which word does not have a negative connotation as used in this excerpt of the text?

   - A. desperately
   - B. scream
   - C. blows
   - D. educational

A Good Man Is Hard to Find

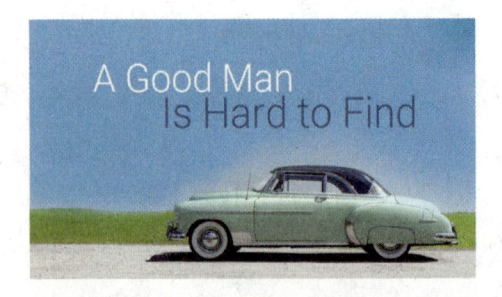

Close Read

Reread "A Good Man Is Hard to Find." As you reread, complete the Skills Focus questions below. Then use your answers and annotations from the questions to help you complete the Write activity.

SKILLS FOCUS

1. Identify the attitude the children have towards their grandmother. Find examples of words with negative connotations that reveal the kids' tone.

2. In what ways does the grandmother manipulate her family members? How do her manipulations contribute to the story's tragic ending?

3. How does the scene with Red Sam and his wife contribute to the overall structure of the story? Identify evidence from the text to support your answer.

4. How does the ending of the story contribute to its overall meaning? Identify evidence from the text to support your answer.

5. How does the grandmother's perspective change over the course of the story? Find evidence to support your answer.

WRITE

LITERARY ANALYSIS: Analyze the way the short story "A Good Man Is Hard to Find" uses story structure to express and contribute to the text's overall meaning. Be sure to include the most relevant evidence from the text to support your response.

The Marshall Plan Speech

ARGUMENTATIVE TEXT
George Marshall
1947

Introduction

In 1947, Europe was reeling from the devastation of World War II. Governments lacked funds to rebuild roads, bridges, and factories. People were sick and starving. At the same time, tensions were mounting between the Soviet Union and the United States. Although the superpowers had fought together against Nazi Germany during the war, the United States feared Russian expansion and the spread of Communism. The same year, Secretary of State George Marshall, a retired five-star general appointed to his position by President Truman, delivered a brief commencement address at Harvard University that would have an enormous impact on Europe's recovery. In the four years following Marshall's speech, the United States sent billions of dollars in assistance to European nations, helping countries rebuild infrastructure and restore financial institutions.

The Marshall Plan Speech

"Any government which maneuvers to block the recovery of other countries cannot expect help from us."

Stalingrad, USSR. Stalingrad during a German air raid in the Battle of Stalingrad on the Eastern Front of World War II. The battle marked a turning point in the war, and paved the way for the Red Army's advance on Berlin in 1945.

Warsaw in ruins at the end of World War II

Rebuilding Dresden
Women form a human chain to carry bricks used in the reconstruction of Dresden, March 1946, after Allied bombing had destroyed the city in February 1945. The steeple of the wrecked Roman Catholic cathedral can be seen in the background.

The Marshall Plan Speech

Skill: Informational Text Structure

The speaker, George Marshall, begins by introducing a problem, so this is likely a problem-solution structure. He uses words that suggest that the problem is very serious and that people will struggle to understand the problem's complexity.

Skill: Word Patterns and Relationships

The words *producing* and *produce* have the same base word, but *producing* is functioning as a verb and *produce* as a noun. I can infer that farm produce is produced by farmers and is what they sell.

1 I need not tell you gentlemen that the world situation is very serious. That must be apparent to all intelligent people. I think one difficulty is that the problem is one of such enormous complexity that the very mass of facts presented to the public by press and radio make it **exceedingly** difficult for the man in the street to reach a clear appraisement of the situation. Furthermore, the people of this country are distant from the troubled areas of the earth and it is hard for them to comprehend the plight and consequent reactions of the long-suffering peoples, and the effect of those reactions on their governments in connection with our efforts to promote peace in the world.

2 In considering the requirements for the rehabilitation of Europe the physical loss of life, the visible destruction of cities, factories, mines and railroads was correctly estimated, but it has become obvious during recent months that this visible destruction was probably less serious than the dislocation of the entire fabric of European economy. For the past ten years conditions have been highly abnormal. The feverish preparation for war and the more feverish maintenance of the war effort engulfed all aspects of national economies. Machinery has fallen into disrepair or is entirely obsolete. Under the **arbitrary** and destructive Nazi rule, virtually every possible enterprise was geared into the German war machine. Long-standing commercial ties, private institutions, banks, insurance companies and shipping companies disappeared, through loss of capital, absorption through nationalization or by simple destruction. In many countries, confidence in the local currency has been severely shaken. The breakdown of the business structure of Europe during the war was complete. Recovery has been seriously retarded by the fact that two years after the close of hostilities a peace settlement with Germany and Austria has not been agreed upon. But even given a more prompt solution of these difficult problems, the rehabilitation of the economic structure of Europe quite evidently will require a much longer time and greater effort than had been foreseen.

3 There is a phase of this matter which is both interesting and serious. The farmer has always produced the foodstuffs to exchange with the city dweller for the other necessities of life. This division of labor is the basis of modern civilization. At the present time it is threatened with breakdown. The town and city industries are not producing **adequate** goods to exchange with the food-producing farmer. Raw materials and fuel are in short supply. Machinery is lacking or worn out. The farmer or the peasant cannot find the goods for sale which he desires to purchase. So the sale of his farm produce for money which he cannot use seems to him an unprofitable transaction. He, therefore, has withdrawn many fields from crop cultivation and is using them for grazing. He feeds more grain to stock and finds for himself and his family an ample supply of food, however short he may be on clothing and the other ordinary gadgets of civilization. Meanwhile people in the cities are short of food and

The Marshall Plan Speech

fuel. So the governments are forced to use their foreign money and credits to procure these necessities abroad. This process exhausts funds which are urgently needed for reconstruction. Thus a very serious situation is rapidly developing which bodes no good for the world. The modern system of the division of labor upon which the exchange of products is based is in danger of breaking down.

4 The truth of the matter is that Europe's requirements for the next three or four years of foreign food and other essential products—principally from America—are so much greater than her present ability to pay that she must have substantial additional help, or face economic, social and political **deterioration** of a very grave character.

5 The remedy lies in breaking the vicious circle and restoring the confidence of the European people in the economic future of their own countries and of Europe as a whole. The manufacturer and the farmer throughout wide areas must be able and willing to exchange their products for currencies the continuing value of which is not open to question.

6 Aside from the demoralizing effect on the world at large and the possibilities of disturbances arising as a result of the desperation of the people concerned, the consequences to the economy of the United States should be apparent to all. It is logical that the United States should do whatever it is able to do to assist in the return of normal economic health in the world, without which there can be no political stability and no assured peace. Our policy is directed not against any country or doctrine but against hunger, poverty, desperation and chaos. Its purpose should be the revival of a working economy in the world so as to permit the emergence of political and social conditions in which free institutions can exist. Such assistance, I am convinced, must not be on a piece-meal basis as various crises develop. Any assistance that this Government may **render** in the future should provide a cure rather than a mere palliative. Any government that is willing to assist in the task of recovery will find full cooperation, I am sure, on the part of the United States Government. Any government which maneuvers to block the recovery of other countries cannot expect help from us. Furthermore, governments, political parties or groups which seek to perpetuate human misery in order to profit therefrom politically or otherwise will encounter the opposition of the United States.

7 It is already evident that, before the United States Government can proceed much further in its efforts to **alleviate** the situation and help start the European world on its way to recovery, there must be some agreement among the countries of Europe as to the requirements of the situation and the part those countries themselves will take in order to give proper effect to whatever action might be undertaken by this Government. It would be neither fitting nor efficacious for this Government to undertake to draw up **unilaterally** a

---

Skill: Author's Purpose and Point of View

Words like *demoralizing, consequences, apparent,* and *logical* strengthen Marshall's claim that inaction will prevent any chance of peace. These words support his argument, establish credibility, and appeal to his audience.

program designed to place Europe on its feet economically. This is the business of the Europeans. The initiative, I think, must come from Europe. The role of this country should consist of friendly aid in the drafting of a European program and of later support of such a program so far as it may be practical for U.S. to do so. The program should be a joint one, agreed to by a number, if not all European nations.

8   An essential part of any successful action on the part of the United States is an understanding on the part of the people of America of the character of the problem and the remedies to be applied. Political passion and prejudice should have no part. With foresight, and a willingness on the part of our people to face up to the vast responsibility which history has clearly placed upon our country, the difficulties I have outlined can and will be overcome.

The Marshall Plan Speech

First Read

Read "The Marshall Plan Speech." After you read, complete the Think Questions below.

THINK QUESTIONS

1. Speakers often try to persuade an audience to like them. They do this in order to get a point across. How does Marshall attempt to win over his audience in the opening paragraphs of his speech?

2. What are some of the reasons Marshall mentions in paragraph 2 for the economic instability in Europe?

3. What role does Marshall think the United States should play in the recovery of Europe?

4. Based on context clues in paragraph 7, what do you think the word **alleviate** means? Write your best definition of *alleviate* here, explaining how you arrived at its meaning.

5. The Latin word *lateralis* means "belonging to the side." With this in mind and using context from the text, try to infer the meaning of the word **unilaterally** as it is used in paragraph 7. Write your best definition of the word here.

The Marshall Plan Speech

Skill: Author's Purpose and Point of View

Use the Checklist to analyze Author's Purpose and Point of View in "The Marshall Plan Speech." Refer to the sample student annotation about Author's Purpose and Point of View in the text.

••• CHECKLIST FOR AUTHOR'S PURPOSE AND POINT OF VIEW

In order to identify author's purpose and point of view, note the following:

- ✓ whether the writer is attempting to establish trust by citing his or her experience or education
- ✓ whether the evidence the author provides is convincing and the argument or position is logical
- ✓ what words and phrases the author uses to appeal to the emotions
- ✓ the author's use of rhetoric, or the art of speaking and writing persuasively, such as the use of repetition to drive home a point, as well as allusion and alliteration
- ✓ the author's use of rhetoric to contribute to the power, persuasiveness, or beauty of the text

To determine the author's purpose and point of view, consider the following questions:

- ✓ How does the author try to convince me that he or she has something valid and important for me to read?
- ✓ What words or phrases express emotion or invite an emotional response? How or why are they effective or ineffective?
- ✓ What words and phrases contribute to the power, persuasiveness, or beauty of the text? Is the author's use of rhetoric successful? Why or why not?

Skill: Author's Purpose and Point of View

Reread paragraphs 6 and 7 of "The Marshall Plan Speech." Then, using the Checklist on the previous page, answer the multiple-choice questions below.

YOUR TURN

1. This question has two parts. First, answer Part A. Then, answer Part B.

   Part A: Based on Marshall's remarks in paragraph 6, the reader can conclude that Marshall's point of view is that it is imperative—

   - A. to proceed one step at a time.
   - B. that all countries receive help from the United States.
   - C. to encourage freedom throughout the world.
   - D. that America negotiate peace in Europe.

   Part B: Which line from the passage best supports your answer in Part A?

   - A. "Any government that is willing to assist in the task of recovery will find full cooperation, I am sure, on the part of the United States Government."
   - B. "Any government which maneuvers to block the recovery of other countries cannot expect help from us."
   - C. "Our policy is directed not against any country or doctrine but against hunger, poverty, desperation and chaos."
   - D. "Its purpose should be the revival of a working economy in the world so as to permit the emergence of political and social conditions in which free institutions can exist."

2. What is Marshall's purpose in paragraph 7?

   - A. He wants countries in Europe to reach an agreement before receiving help.
   - B. He is stating that the United States Government is ready to begin help immediately.
   - C. He wants to clarify the role of the countries involved in an agreement.
   - D. He is emphasizing the urgency in coming to an agreement.

The Marshall Plan Speech

Skill:
Informational Text Structure

Use the Checklist to analyze Informational Text Structure in "The Marshall Plan Speech." Refer to the sample student annotation about Informational Text Structure in the text.

••• CHECKLIST FOR INFORMATIONAL TEXT STRUCTURE

In order to determine the structure an author uses in his or her writing, note the following:

- ✓ where the author introduces and clarifies his or her argument

- ✓ sentences and paragraphs that reveal the text structure the author uses to frame the argument

- ✓ whether the text structure is effective in presenting all sides of the argument, and makes his or her points clear, convincing, and engaging

To analyze and evaluate the effectiveness of the structure an author uses in his or her writing, including whether the structure makes points clear, convincing, and engaging, consider the following questions:

- ✓ Did I have to read a particular sentence or paragraph over again? Where?

- ✓ Did I find myself distracted or uninterested while reading the text? When?

- ✓ Did the structure the author used make his or her points clear, convincing, and engaging? Why or why not?

- ✓ Was the author's exposition or argument effective? Why or why not?

- ✓ In what ways did the structure of the text enhance my understanding of the argument and its development?

Skill: Informational Text Structure

Reread paragraphs 7 and 8 of "The Marshall Plan Speech." Then, using the Checklist on the previous page, answer the multiple-choice questions below.

YOUR TURN

1. This question has two parts. First, answer Part A. Then, answer Part B.

   Part A: What is the purpose of paragraph 7 in relation to the overall structure of the text?

   - A. to ensure Americans that the U.S. government is prepared to do whatever it takes to aid in Europe's recovery
   - B. to ensure the American people that the U.S. involvement will be to provide programs to support Europe's economic recovery
   - C. to assure Americans that U.S. involvement will be limited as well as make it clear that he believes that Europe's economic recovery is their responsibility
   - D. to persuade the American people to give money to aid in Europe's recovery.

   Part B: Which line from the passage best supports your answer in Part A?

   - A. "The role of this country should consist of friendly aid in the drafting of a European program and of later support of such a program so far as it may be practical for us to do so."
   - B. "The program should be a joint one, agreed to by a number, if not all European nations."
   - C. "The initiative, I think, must come from Europe."
   - D. "It would be neither fitting nor efficacious for this Government to undertake to draw up unilaterally a program designed to place Europe on its feet economically. This is the business of the Europeans."

The Marshall Plan Speech

2. How does the final paragraph of the speech serve to make the speech more convincing?

   ○ A. It appeals to the character of the American people and explains the solutions that will be applied.
   ○ B. It appeals to the morality of the American people and suggests that Americans need to keep passion and prejudice out of this.
   ○ C. It appeals to the common sense of the American people and explains that they should understand the solutions being proposed.
   ○ D. It appeals to a sense of duty that Americans have to be a part of his proposed solution and makes it clear that the struggles they are facing will be overcome.

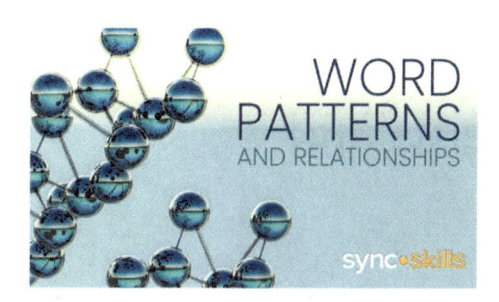

Skill: Word Patterns and Relationships

Use the Checklist to analyze Word Patterns and Relationships in "The Marshall Plan Speech." Refer to the sample student annotation about Word Patterns and Relationships in the text.

••• CHECKLIST FOR WORD PATTERNS AND RELATIONSHIPS

In order to identify patterns of word changes to indicate different meanings or parts of speech, do the following:

- ✓ determine the word's part of speech
- ✓ use context clues to make a preliminary determination of the meaning of the word
- ✓ identify other words in the text or that you are familiar with that share a base word with the word in question and may have a similar meaning
- ✓ use knowledge of common root words, prefixes, and suffixes to determine a word's part of speech or meaning
- ✓ consult a dictionary to verify your preliminary determination of the meanings and parts of speech
- ✓ be sure to read all the definitions, and then decide which definition, form, and part of speech makes sense within the context of the text

To identify and correctly use patterns of word changes that indicate different meanings or parts of speech, consider the following questions:

- ✓ What is the intended meaning of the word?
- ✓ Do I know that this word form is the correct part of speech? Do I understand the word patterns for this particular word?
- ✓ When I consult a dictionary, can I confirm that the meaning I have determined for this word is correct? Do I know how to use it correctly?

The Marshall Plan Speech

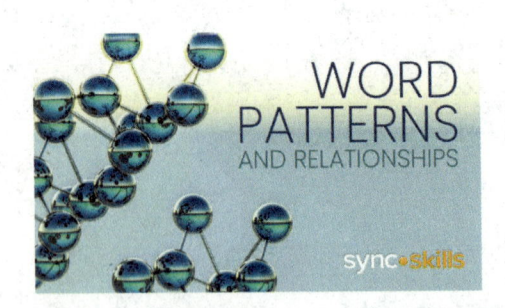

Skill: Word Patterns and Relationships

Reread paragraphs 6 and 7 of "The Marshall Plan Speech." Then, using the Checklist on the previous page, answer the multiple-choice questions below.

YOUR TURN

1. What is the relationship between the words *economy* and *economic*?

    - A. They have the same root word, and they are both used as nouns in the sentence. Both have to do with finances.
    - B. They have the same root word, but *economy* is a noun and *economic* is an adjective. Both have to do with finances.
    - C. They have the same root word, and *economy* is a noun and *economic* is an adverb. Both have to do with finances.
    - D. They do not share the same root word as the word endings for each are different.

2. Using your answer from question 1, what can you infer about the word part and meaning of the word *economically* in paragraph 7?

    - A. It is an adjective used to describe the way in which the United States will support European countries with money.
    - B. It is a verb used to show the action that the European countries will take to support European countries.
    - C. It is an adverb used to describe the way in which the United States will support European countries with money.
    - D. It is an adverb used to describe the way in which business will operate in Europe.

Close Read

Reread "The Marshall Plan Speech." As you reread, complete the Skills Focus questions below. Then use your answers and annotations from the questions to help you complete the Write activity.

SKILLS FOCUS

1. Identify a passage in which Marshall addresses his audience directly. Analyze how he connects his message to his audience.

2. Identify two words that share the same base word in paragraph 2. Identify the part of speech of each word and explain the relationship between their meanings.

3. Find a passage in which Marshall reinforces his message by pointing out that the recovery in Europe will take longer than people expected. Analyze his purpose for including this statement.

4. Identify a portion of the speech in which Marshall describes the problem he wants to solve. How does his use of structure in describing this problem help make his plea for support more convincing?

5. In this speech, Marshall describes his plan for helping Europe rebuild. How do you think Marshall would measure the success of his plan? Support your response with evidence from the text.

WRITE

RHETORICAL ANALYSIS: The Marshall Plan Speech was a rallying cry to America, a call to help Europe rebuild after the devastation of World War II. Write a rhetorical analysis in which you determine how Marshall structures his argument to Americans. Then, evaluate the effectiveness of this structure, as well as the rhetoric and reasoning Marshall uses to persuade his audience of his point of view. Use textual evidence and original commentary to support your response.

On the Road

FICTION
Jack Kerouac
1957

Introduction

Jack Kerouac (1922–1969) was a poet and novelist often celebrated as the voice of a generation. Along with his friends Allen Ginsberg and William S. Burroughs, Kerouac was a key figure in what is remembered as the "Beat Generation"—a literary movement that endeavored to give literature a freedom to stray from academics and rigid structure. This excerpt is from Kerouac's most widely read work, *On the Road*, a semi-autobiographical novel based on his own travels. As readers will come to witness in this excerpt, the beginning of a journey can often be the most challenging part.

"All I could see were smoky trees and dismal wilderness rising to the skies."

1   In the month of July 1947, having saved about fifty dollars from old veteran benefits, I was ready to go to the West Coast. My friend Remi Boncœur had written me a letter from San Francisco, saying I should come and ship out with him on an around-the-world liner. He swore he could get me into the engine room. I wrote back and said I'd be satisfied with any old freighter so long as I could take a few long Pacific trips and come back with enough money to support myself in my aunt's house while I finished my book. He said he had a shack in Mill City and I would have all the time in the world to write there while we went through the **rigmarole** of getting the ship. He was living with a girl called Lee Ann; he said she was a marvelous cook and everything would jump. Remi was an old prep-school friend, a Frenchman brought up in Paris and a really mad guy—I didn't know how mad at this time. So he expected me to arrive in ten days. My aunt was all in accord with my trip to the West; she said it would do me good, I'd been working so hard all winter and staying in too much; she even didn't complain when I told her I'd have to hitchhike some. All she wanted was for me to come back in one piece. So, leaving my big half-manuscript sitting on top of my desk, and folding back my comfortable home sheets for the last time one morning, I left with my canvas bag in which a few fundamental things were packed and took off for the Pacific Ocean with the fifty dollars in my pocket.

2   I'd been poring over maps of the United States in Paterson for months, even reading books about the pioneers and **savoring** names like Platte and Cimarron and so on, and on the roadmap was one long red line called Route 6 that led from the tip of Cape Cod clear to Ely, Nevada, and there dipped down to Los Angeles. I'll just stay on 6 all the way to Ely, I said to myself and confidently started. To get to 6 I had to go up to Bear Mountain. Filled with dreams of what I'd do in Chicago, in Denver, and then finally in San Fran, I took the Seventh Avenue subway to the end of the line at 242nd Street, and there took a trolley into Yonkers; in downtown Yonkers I transferred to an outgoing trolley and went to the city limits on the east bank of the Hudson River. If you drop a rose in the Hudson River at its mysterious source in the Adirondacks, think of all the places it journeys by as it goes out to sea forever—think of that wonderful Hudson Valley. I started hitching up the thing. Five scattered rides took me to the desired Bear Mountain Bridge, where Route 6 arched in from New England. It began to

rain in **torrents** when I was let off there. It was mountainous. Route 6 came over the river, wound around a traffic circle, and disappeared into the wilderness. Not only was there no traffic but the rain came down in buckets and I had no shelter. I had to run under some pines to take cover; this did no good; I began crying and swearing and socking myself on the head for being such a damn fool. I was forty miles north of New York; all the way up I'd been worried about the fact that on this, my big opening day, I was only moving north instead of the so-longed-for west. Now I was stuck on my northernmost hangup. I ran a quarter-mile to an abandoned cute English-style filling station and stood under the dripping eaves. High up over my head the great hairy Bear Mountain sent down thunderclaps that put the fear of God in me. All I could see were smoky trees and dismal wilderness rising to the skies. "What the hell am I doing up here?" I cursed, I cried for Chicago. "Even now they're all having a big time, they're doing this, I'm not there, when will I get there!"—and so on. Finally a car stopped at the empty filling station; the man and the two women in it wanted to study a map. I stepped right up and gestured in the rain; they consulted; I looked like a maniac, of course, with my hair all wet, my shoes sopping. My shoes, damn fool that I am, were Mexican huaraches, plantlike **sieves** not fit for the rainy night of America and the raw road night. But the people let me in and rode me north to Newburgh, which I accepted as a better alternative than being trapped in the Bear Mountain wilderness all night. "Besides," said the man, "there's no traffic passes through 6. If you want to go to Chicago you'd do better going across the Holland Tunnel in New York and head for Pittsburgh," and I knew he was right. It was my dream that screwed up, the stupid hearthside idea that it would be wonderful to follow one great red line across America instead of trying various roads and routes.

3 In Newburgh it had stopped raining. I walked down to the river, and I had to ride back to New York in a bus with a **delegation** of schoolteachers coming back from a weekend in the mountains—chatter-chatter blah-blah, and me swearing for all the time and the money I'd wasted, and telling myself, I wanted to go west and here I've been all day and into the night going up and down, north and south, like something that can't get started. And I swore I'd be in Chicago tomorrow, and made sure of that, taking a bus to Chicago, spending most of my money, and didn't give a damn, just as long as I'd be in Chicago tomorrow.

Excerpted from *On the Road* by Jack Kerouac, published by Penguin.

✏️ WRITE

PERSONAL NARRATIVE: *On the Road* relates the tale of a protagonist who sets a goal for his trip to the West Coast but is often diverted from his original plans and needs to adjust; sometimes he considers diversions a burden, other times he views them as a plus. Consider the ideas discussed in the texts of this unit, as well as your own experiences. Then write a personal narrative that describes a time you set a goal and had to adjust your plans to succeed. Be sure to include thoughtful details to convey a vivid picture of your experiences.

Death of a Salesman

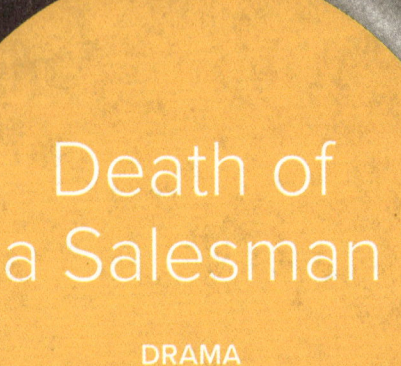

DRAMA
Arthur Miller
1949

Introduction

First performed in 1949, Arthur Miller's Pulitzer Prize–winning *Death of a Salesman* is a somber and penetrating exploration of the dark underbelly of the American Dream. Caught between his own overly romanticized past and the dimming promise of a brighter tomorrow, aging traveling salesman Willy Loman is slowly losing his grip on reality. In this scene, tensions are running high in the Loman household when estranged son Biff returns home a less successful man than Willy thinks he ought to be.

"No, no, some people—some people accomplish something."

from ACT ONE

1. WILLY: Figure it out. Work a lifetime to pay off a house. You finally own it, and there's nobody to live in it.

2. LINDA: Well, dear, life is a casting off. It's always that way.

3. WILLY: No, no, some people—some people accomplish something. Did Biff say anything after I went this morning?

4. LINDA: You shouldn't have criticised him, Willy, especially after he just got off the train. You mustn't lose your temper with him.

5. WILLY: When the hell did I lose my temper? I simply asked him if he was making any money. Is that a criticism?

6. LINDA: But, dear, how could he make any money?

7. WILLY (worried and angered): There's such an **undercurrent** in him. He became a moody man. Did he apologize when I left this morning?

8. LINDA: He was **crestfallen**, Willy. You know how he admires you. I think if he finds himself, then you'll both be happier and not fight any more.

9. WILLY: How can he find himself on a farm? Is that a life? A farmhand? In the beginning, when he was young, I thought, well, a young man, it's good for him to **tramp** around, take a lot of different jobs. But it's more than ten years now and he has yet to make thirty-five dollars a week!

10. LINDA: He's finding himself, Willy.

11. WILLY: Not finding yourself at the age of thirty-four is a disgrace!

12. LINDA: Shh!

13. WILLY: The trouble is he's lazy, goddammit!

Death of a Salesman

14 LINDA: Willy, please!

15 WILLY: Biff is a lazy bum!

16 LINDA: They're sleeping. Get something to eat. Go on down.

17 WILLY: Why did he come home? I would like to know what brought him home.

18 LINDA: I don't know. I think he's still lost, Willy. I think he's very lost.

19 WILLY: Biff Loman is lost. In the greatest country in the world a young man with such—personal attractiveness, gets lost. And such a hard worker. There's one thing about Biff—he's not lazy.

20 LINDA: Never.

21 WILLY (with pity and **resolve**): I'll see him in the morning; I'll have a nice talk with him. I'll get him a job selling. He could be big in no time. My God! Remember how they used to follow him around in high school? When he smiled at one of them their faces lit up. When he walked down the street . . . (He loses himself in **reminiscences**.)

22 LINDA (trying to bring him out of it): Willy, dear, I got a new kind of American-type cheese today. It's whipped.

23 WILLY: Why do you get American when I like Swiss?

24 LINDA: I just thought you'd like a change . . .

25 WILLY: I don't want a change! I want Swiss cheese. Why am I always being contradicted?

26 LINDA (with a covering laugh): I thought it would be a surprise.

Excerpted from *Death of a Salesman* by Arthur Miller, published by the Penguin Group.

✏ WRITE

PERSONAL RESPONSE: This excerpt focuses on Willy's rigid idea of success and the way it conflicts with his son Biff's actions. Consider the ideas you have read in this text, as well as individuals you admire. In your opinion, what makes a person successful? How do our definitions of success inform our goals? Provide evidence from the text to support your response.

A Raisin in the Sun

DRAMA
Lorraine Hansberry
1959

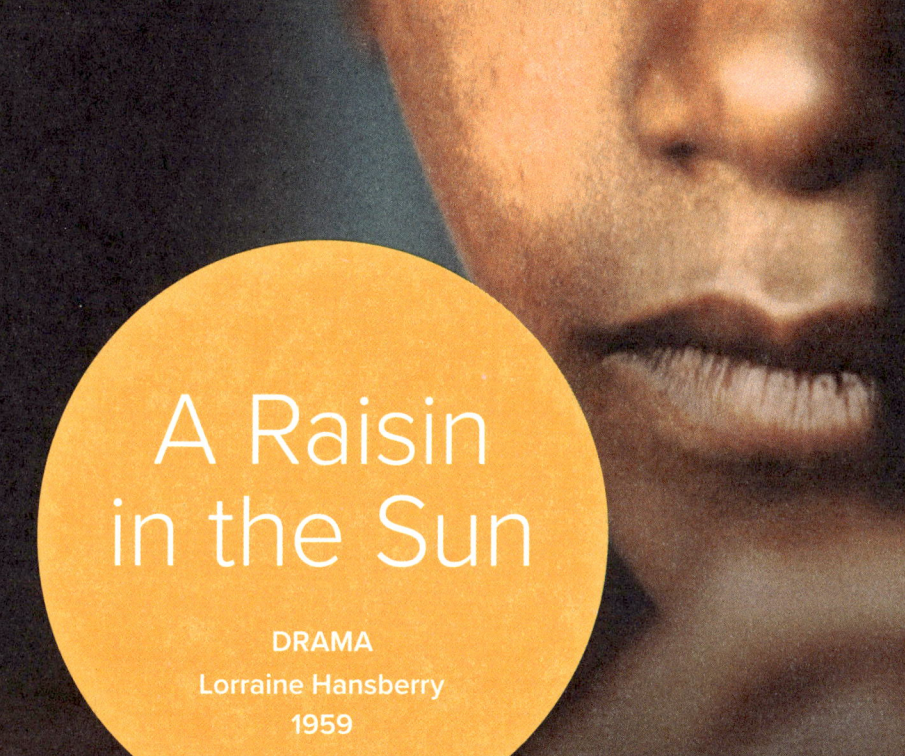

Introduction

studysync®

Set in the years after World War II, *A Raisin in the Sun* is an award-winning play by Lorraine Hansberry (1930–1965) about the Youngers, a fictional black family in Chicago struggling to keep things together during difficult financial times. In this excerpt from the third act of the play, son Walter has made a bad business decision and has lost the insurance money the family received from their father's death. He now comes up with a scheme to get some of the money back—but at what price?

A Raisin in the Sun

"There is always something left to love. And if you ain't learned that you ain't learned nothing."

Note: The text you are about to read contains offensive language. Remember to be mindful of the thoughts and feelings of your peers as you read and discuss this text. Please consult your teacher for additional guidance and support.

from Act III

1   RUTH: What did you call that man for, Walter Lee?

2   WALTER: Called him to tell him to come on over to the show. Gonna put on a show for the man. Just what he wants to see. You see, Mama, the man came here today and he told us that them people out there where you want us to move—well they so upset they willing to pay us not to move! *[He laughs.]* And—and oh, Mama you would have been proud of the way me and Ruth and Bennie acted. We told him to get out . . . . Lord have mercy! We told the man to get out! Oh, we was some proud folks this afternoon, yeah. *[He lights a cigarette.]* We were still full of that old-time stuff . . . .

3   RUTH (Walter's wife) *[coming toward him slowly]*: You talking 'bout taking them people's money to keep us from moving in that house?

4   WALTER: I ain't just talking 'bout it baby—I'm telling you that's what's going to happen!

5   BENEATHA (Walter's sister): Oh, God! Where is the bottom! Where is the real honest-to-God bottom so he can't go any farther!

6   WALTER: See—that's the old stuff. You and that boy was here today. You all want everybody to carry a flag and a spear and sing some marching songs, huh? You wanna spend your life looking into things and trying to find the right and wrong part, huh? Yeah. You know what's going to happen to that boy someday—he'll find himself sitting in a dungeon, locked in forever—and the takers will have the key! Forget it, baby! There ain't no causes—there ain't nothing but taking in this world, and he who takes most is smartest—and it don't make a damn bit of difference *how*.

Skill: Dramatic Elements and Structure

Walter explains what happened earlier in the day, establishing context. Walter's behavior, relayed through stage directions, is flippant. Ruth's action and dialogue build tension, advancing the plot into the rising action.

7 MAMA: You making something inside me cry, son. Some awful pain inside me.

8 WALTER: Don't cry, Mama. Understand. That white man is going to walk in that door able to write checks for more money than we ever had. It's important to him and I'm going to help him . . . I'm going to put on the show, Mama.

9 MAMA: Son—I come from five generations of people who was slaves and **sharecroppers**—but ain't nobody in my family never let nobody pay 'em no money that was a way of telling us we weren't fit to walk the earth. We ain't never been that poor. [*Raising her eyes and looking at him*] We ain't never been that—dead inside.

10 BENEATHA: Well—we are dead now. All the talk about dreams and sunlight that goes on in this house. It's all dead now.

11 WALTER: What's the matter with you all! I didn't make this world! It was give to me this way! Hell, yes, I want me some yachts someday! Yes, I want to hang some real pearls 'round my wife's neck. Ain't she supposed to wear no pearls? Somebody tell me—tell me, who decides which women is suppose to wear pearls in this world. I tell you I am a *man*—and I think my wife should wear some pearls in this world!

12 [*This last line hangs a good while and WALTER begins to move about the room. The word "Man" has penetrated his consciousness; he mumbles it to himself repeatedly between strange agitated pauses as he moves about.*]

13 MAMA: Baby, how you going to feel on the inside?

14 WALTER: Fine! . . . Going to feel fine . . . a man . . .

15 MAMA: You won't have nothing left then, Walter Lee.

16 WALTER [*coming to her*]: I'm going to feel fine, Mama. I'm going to look that son-of-a-bitch in the eyes and say—[*He falters.*]—and say, "All right, Mr. Lindner—[*He falters even more.*]—that's *your* neighborhood out there! You got the right to keep it like you want! You got the right to have it like you want! Just write the check and—the house is yours." And—and I am going to say—[*His voice almost breaks.*] "And you—you people just put the money in my hand and you won't have to live next to this bunch of stinking n------!"

17 . . . And maybe I'll just get down on my black knees . . . [*He does so,* RUTH *and* BENNIE *and* MAMA *watch him in frozen horror.*] "Captain, Mistuh, Bossman—[**groveling** *and grinning and wringing his hands in profoundly anguished imitation of the slow-witted movie stereotype*] Oh, yassuh boss! Yasssssuh! Great white—[*Voice breaking, he forces himself to go on.*]—Father, just gi' ussen de money, fo' God's sake, and we's—we's ain't gwine come out deh and dirty up yo' white folks neighborhood . . ." [*He breaks down completely.*] And I'll feel fine! Fine! FINE! [*He gets up and goes into the bedroom.*]

Skill: Dramatic Elements and Structure

Walter's words seem defiant, but the pauses and repetition in his speech, combined with the stage directions, undermine what he is saying. Walter's conscience is breaking through his rant, marking the beginning of the climax.

A Raisin in the Sun

NOTES

Skill: Theme

The characters' dialogue in response to Walter's decision creates conflict. Mama reminds Beneatha about the value of unconditional love. This reveals one of the play's themes about the importance of family.

18 BENEATHA: That is not a man. That is nothing but a toothless rat.

19 MAMA: Yes—death done come in this here house. [*She is nodding, slowly, reflectively.*] Done come walking in my house on the lips of my children. You what supposed to be my beginning again. You—what supposed to be my harvest. [*to* BENEATHA] You—you mourning your brother?

20 BENEATHA: He's no brother of mine.

21 MAMA: What you say?

22 BENEATHA: I said that that individual in that room is no brother of mine.

23 MAMA: That's what I thought you said. You feeling like you better than he is today?

24 [BENEATHA *does not answer.*]

25 MAMA: Yes? What you tell him a minute ago? That he wasn't a man? Yes? You give him up for me? You done wrote his **epitaph** too—like the rest of the world? Well who give you the privilege?

26 BENEATHA: Be on my side for once! You saw what he just did, Mama! You saw him—down on his knees. Wasn't it you who taught me—to **despise** any man who would do that? Do what he's going to do?

27 MAMA: Yes—I taught you that. Me and your daddy. But I thought I taught you something else too . . . I thought I taught you to love him.

28 BENEATHA: Love him? There is nothing left to love.

29 MAMA: There is always something left to love. And if you ain't learned that you ain't learned nothing. [*looking at her*] Have you cried for that boy today? I don't mean for yourself and for the family 'cause we lost the money. I mean for him; what he been through and what it done to him. Child, when do you think is the time to love somebody the most; when they done good and made things easy for everybody? Well then, you ain't through learning—because that ain't the time at all. It's when he's at his lowest and can't believe in hisself 'cause the world done whipped him so! When you starts measuring somebody, measure him right, child, measure him right. Make sure you done taken into account what hills and valleys he come through before he got to wherever he is.

Excerpted from *A Raisin in the Sun* by Lorraine Hansberry, published by Vintage Books.

First Read

Read *A Raisin in the Sun*. After you read, complete the Think Questions below.

THINK QUESTIONS

1. Based on the text, what can you infer about Mr. Lindner's motivations for paying Walter and his family not to move?

2. How does Walter define manhood? Cite specific quotes or passages from the text to support your answer.

3. Why is Mama upset at Beneatha? Refer to specific moments in the text in your answer.

4. Use context to determine the meaning of the word **groveling** as it is used in *A Raisin in the Sun*. Write your definition of *groveling* here and explain how you arrived at it.

5. Use context to determine the meaning of the word **epitaph** as it is used in *A Raisin in the Sun*. Double check your answer using a dictionary. In your own words, write a definition of *epitaph* here.

Skill: Dramatic Elements and Structure

Use the Checklist to analyze Dramatic Elements and Structure in *A Raisin in the Sun*. Refer to the sample student annotations about Dramatic Elements and Structure in the text.

CHECKLIST FOR DRAMATIC ELEMENTS AND STRUCTURE

In order to determine the author's choices regarding the development of a drama, note the following:

- ✓ the names of all the characters, how they are introduced, and their relationships with one another
- ✓ character development, including personality traits, motivations, decisions they make, and actions they take
- ✓ the setting(s) of the story and how it influences the characters and the events of the plot
- ✓ how characters' choices and dialogue affect the plot
- ✓ the stage directions and how they are used to reveal character and plot development

To analyze the impact of the author's choices regarding how to develop and relate elements of a story or drama, consider the following questions:

- ✓ How does the order of events in the play affect the development of the drama?
- ✓ How are characters introduced, and what does it reveal about them?
- ✓ In what ways do the characters change over the course of the drama?
- ✓ How do the choices the characters make help advance the plot?
- ✓ How does the setting affect the characters and plot?
- ✓ How do the characters' actions help develop the theme or message of the play?

Skill: Dramatic Elements and Structure

Reread paragraph 17 of *A Raisin in the Sun*. Then, using the Checklist on the previous page, answer the multiple-choice questions below.

YOUR TURN

1. Which of the following sentences best describes the relationship between the dialogue and the stage directions in this passage?

    ○ A. The dialogue and the stage directions complement each other to reinforce that Walter feels confident about his accepting the money from Mr. Lindner.

    ○ B. The aggressive mockery in the dialogue and the anguished horror of the stage directions reflect the extreme pain of Walter's conflict.

    ○ C. The dialogue and the stage directions work together to show that Ruth, Bennie, and Mama agree with Walter.

    ○ D. The painful dialogue and emotional stage directions show that the family is falling apart.

2. The relationship between the dialogue and the stage directions in this passage advances the plot by—

    ○ A. bringing the plot in this scene to its climax, or the point at which the conflict reaches its highest tension.

    ○ B. providing a resolution to the conflict.

    ○ C. giving background information, or exposition, about Walter's emotional state.

    ○ D. wrapping up loose ends in the falling action.

A Raisin in the Sun

Skill: Theme

Use the Checklist to analyze Theme in *A Raisin in the Sun*. Refer to the sample student annotation about Theme in the text.

••• CHECKLIST FOR THEME

In order to identify two or more themes, or central ideas, of a text, note the following:

✓ the subject and how it relates to the themes in the text

✓ if one or more themes is stated directly in the text

✓ details in the text that help reveal each theme:

- the title and chapter headings
- details about the setting
- the narrator's or speaker's tone
- characters' thoughts, actions, and dialogue
- the central conflict, climax, and resolution of the conflict
- shifts in characters, setting, or plot events

✓ when the themes interact with each other

To determine two or more themes, or central ideas, of a text and to analyze their development over the course of the text, including how they interact and build on one another to produce a complex account, consider the following questions:

✓ What are the themes in the text? When do they emerge?

✓ How does each theme develop over the course of the text?

✓ How do the themes interact and build on one another?

Skill: Theme

Reread paragraphs 9–15 of *A Raisin in the Sun*. Then, using the Checklist on the previous page, answer the multiple-choice questions below.

YOUR TURN

1. Which inference best demonstrates the relationship between characters and the theme about manhood as seen in paragraph 11?

   - A. Walter does not think sharecroppers are considered men.
   - B. Walter wants to win over his wife's affection by buying her pearls.
   - C. Walter acknowledges that all men want to own a yacht.
   - D. Walter prioritizes the expectation of proving his manhood by providing for his wife.

2. Beneatha's comments in paragraph 10 reveal that—

   - A. the characters live in a racially segregated neighborhood.
   - B. someone died in the house.
   - C. their home used to have a hopeful atmosphere.
   - D. there is no natural lighting in the house.

3. Which paragraph best communicates the message that being poor doesn't necessitate a loss of dignity and self-respect?

   - A. 9
   - B. 12
   - C. 13
   - D. 14

A Raisin in the Sun

Close Read

Reread *A Raisin in the Sun*. As you reread, complete the Skills Focus questions below. Then use your answers and annotations from the questions to help you complete the Write activity.

SKILLS FOCUS

1. Highlight an exchange of dialogue between Beneatha and Walter that shows how Beneatha feels about the family's dreams and Walter's reaction. Analyze the relationship between plot and theme in these lines.

2. Identify a passage that includes dialogue and stage directions that show what Walter thinks it means to be a man. Analyze how these dramatic elements help advance the plot of the play.

3. Locate a passage that contains clues about the setting of *A Raisin in the Sun*. How does the setting affect the characters and influence the plot?

4. Identify dialogue between Beneatha and Mama near the end of the scene in which they discuss respect, dignity, and love. Analyze the relationship between characters, and explain how their exchange reveals a theme of the play.

5. Why is owning a home so important to Mama? What makes a home so important to a family? Identify textual evidence to support your answer.

WRITE

LITERARY ANALYSIS: In both *Death of a Salesman* and *A Raisin in the Sun*, dialogue plays an important role in the development of the texts' themes. Analyze how dialogue reflects each text's message about the importance of family and the relevance of the American Dream. Support your response with the most relevant evidence from the text and your own analysis.

LITERARY SEMINAR:
The Writings of Pauli Murray

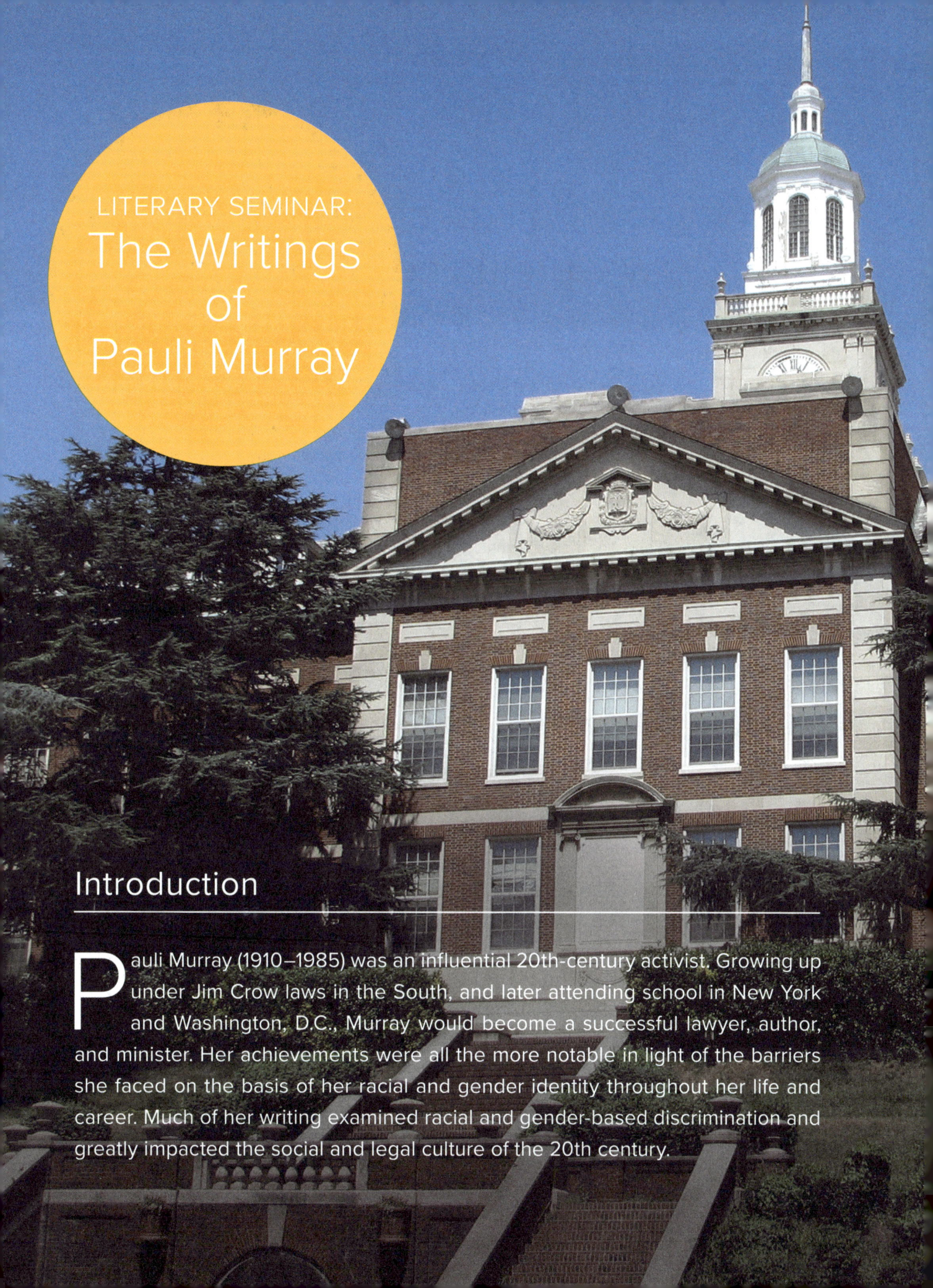

Introduction

Pauli Murray (1910–1985) was an influential 20th-century activist. Growing up under Jim Crow laws in the South, and later attending school in New York and Washington, D.C., Murray would become a successful lawyer, author, and minister. Her achievements were all the more notable in light of the barriers she faced on the basis of her racial and gender identity throughout her life and career. Much of her writing examined racial and gender-based discrimination and greatly impacted the social and legal culture of the 20th century.

Literary Seminar: The Writings of Pauli Murray

"Now, how do I go about killing 'Jane Crow'—prejudice against sex."

1   One of the most influential members of the civil rights movement is a person whose name might not be familiar: the activist, lawyer, and writer Pauli Murray. She wrote the book Thurgood Marshall referred to as the bible of the civil rights movement and her work on sex **discrimination** inspired Ruth Bader Ginsburg to cite her in the first legal brief Ginsburg argued before the Supreme Court. She was friends with Eleanor Roosevelt and Langston Hughes, served on a Presidential Commission appointed by John F. Kennedy, and she helped launch the National Organization for Women with Betty Friedan, as well as the Congress for Racial Equality. Murray's impact can be traced through a dynamic body of writing increasingly available to readers today.

Pauli Murray, c. 1940s

Early Advocacy

2   Pauli Murray's desire to fight against racial and sex discrimination began early, as she encountered barrier after barrier that restricted her personal, educational, and career opportunities. As a young woman, she hoped to escape the segregation of Jim Crow laws in the South and attend Columbia in New York City, but discovered that the school did not admit women and

attended Hunter College instead. Graduating at the height of the Great Depression, she struggled to find work, and decided to return home and apply for a graduate program in sociology at the University of North Carolina–Chapel Hill.

3   However, Murray was denied her admission to the graduate school because of her race. She leveraged writing as a tool to challenge the decision, waging a letter-writing campaign in 1938 protesting UNC's decision. Coincidentally, two days prior to UNC's rejection of Murray, the Supreme Court had ruled that colleges must either admit or supply equivalent education to non-white students. Murray published letters she sent and received to the school's officials and to prominent public figures, such as President Roosevelt, bringing national attention to the issue. Eventually, UNC avoided having to admit Murray or other African American students when it made **provisions** for what it deemed an equivalent program in Durham, North Carolina, and so satisfied the court's ruling. While she was frustrated by the outcome, Murray's efforts earned the attention of Eleanor Roosevelt, with whom she eventually became friends. Murray advised on matters of civil and human rights until Roosevelt's passing.

4   Although her writing brought attention to her ideas and intellect, one particular aspect of her identity often kept her from the activist spotlight. Murray often expressed her gender identity as male, though she frequently saw her experiences through the female lens. On a bus trip in 1940 to visit her aunt in Virginia, Murray and a female companion were arrested for refusing to move to the back of the bus. At the time, Murray was passing as male and gave her name as Oliver Fleming to the arresting officer. Murray and her companion were jailed for three days, and during their time in jail, used the principles of *satyagraha* (passive political resistance) to write three letters: one to their jailers, one to their fellow prisoners, and another detailing the facts of the case as Murray saw them. Although lawyers from the NAACP remarked her notes were "as good as a lawyer's brief," the NAACP ultimately elected to not support an appeal. Murray suspected that the NAACP's hesitance to become involved was due to fears they would need to discuss her gender performance as a man. The writing she generated throughout the experience, however, demonstrates the developing nonviolent resistance strategies she **espoused**.

The Challenges of Jane Crow

5   Through Murray's passion for social justice and eloquent speaking, she gained respect from important figures of the day and learned the nuances of the legal issues behind segregation. She worked for the Workers Defense League, a non-profit labor organization that campaigned to commute the death sentence of Odell Waller, who had been convicted of first-degree murder in a one-day trial by an all-white jury. She toured the South, speaking

publicly and meeting with lawyers, including Dr. Leon Ransom, the dean of Howard University School of Law. Dr. Ransom was so impressed with her arguments that he promised her a fellowship to study law at Howard.

6   It was at Howard that Murray gained the personal experience that helped build her influential legal arguments against sex discrimination. While Murray was no longer in the racial minority at Howard University Law, she was the only female student, and was blocked from opportunities despite her high achievement, a phenomenon she began to refer to as "Jane Crow." Upon graduating top of her class, she was denied from post-graduate studies at Harvard Law School due to her sex, and engaged in another campaign like the one against UNC to challenge this discrimination. Even with a letter of support from President Franklin Roosevelt, however, she lost her appeal.

7   While in law school, Murray wrote a paper for Dr. Ransom, arguing that segregation violated the Thirteenth and Fourteenth Amendments of the United States Constitution because "separate" was inherently not "equal." Murray's argument shifted the focus away from the equality of various segregated institutions, a legal strategy that the NAACP had been working to combat segregationist policies for years. As she submitted this paper to Dr. Ransom, Murray included a short note that revealed her beliefs about the relationship between race and sex and predicted a major legacy of her work, asking, "Now, how do I go about killing 'Jane Crow'—prejudice against sex."

Writing Change

8   After being denied from Harvard and completing a Master's of Law at University of California—Berkeley, Murray wrote one of her most consequential texts. The Women's Division of the Methodist Church asked Murray to research the laws of segregation, with the expectation being a simple pamphlet. Murray went above and beyond, writing the *States' Laws on Race and Color*, a several hundred page examination of all state laws that involved race. Murray went against the grain of historical precedent that relied almost exclusively on legal arguments, and used psychological and sociological evidence to argue that race was an **arbitrary** classification, and therefore racial segregation was unconstitutional.

9   Thurgood Marshall, who would later become the first African American justice on the Supreme Court, called the book the bible of civil rights, lawyers keeping stacks of it around the NAACP offices as his team argued *Brown v. Board of Education*. A member of Marshall's legal team and a former professor of Murray's at Howard, Spottswood Robinson remembered Murray's paper for Dr. Ransom on the Thirteenth and Fourteenth Amendments and shared it with his colleagues. The lawyers on the case were inspired by Murray's

arguments, and the Supreme Court overturned *Plessy v. Ferguson*, the case from which "separate but equal" had come.

10 Murray continued to use legal arguments to fight race and sex discrimination. Some in the civil rights movement believed that including sex as a protected class would prevent the Civil Rights Act of 1964 from passing, but Murray wrote a widely circulated memo arguing that without the inclusion of sex as a protected class, black women would not be protected under the bill. Murray's memo helped convince **skeptics** in the White House and Congress that the provision regarding sex was not just an add-on, and in fact, was necessary to achieving the bill's goals. The bill passed, banning segregation in public places and employment discrimination, including sex discrimination.

(Back, left to right) Professor Albert M. Sacks, Pauli Murray, Dr. Mary Bunting; (seated) Alma Lutz, Betty Friedan. Harvard Law School Forum speaking event

11 Murray's writing would further influence policy. While finishing her doctorate in law at Yale University, Murray co-wrote "Jane Crow and the Law: Sex Discrimination and Title VII," which helped create a legal basis for ending sex discrimination. Murray would go on to serve as co-counsel on a highly influential case, *White v. Crook*, with Dorothy Kenyon in 1965 that would successfully eliminate the use of sex and race discrimination in jury selection. Eventually, this work would get recognition, with Ruth Bader Ginsburg naming Pauli Murray and Dorothy Kenyon as co-authors on the *Reed v. Reed* brief to the Supreme Court in 1971, acknowledging their contributions to the fight against sex discrimination.

Considering Murray's Legacy

12. The question must be asked: Why isn't Pauli Murray a more well-known figure? Recently, Murray's contributions to, and her personal involvement in, the civil rights movement have been more widely recognized. For example, the 2018 movie dramatizing Ruth Bader Ginsburg's first gender-discrimination argument in court, *On the Basis of Sex*, depicted Murray, played by Sharon Washington, advising on Ginsburg's strategy in court. One possible reason that much of Murray's work was behind-the-scenes is that contemporary attitudes about her identity as a queer[1] African American woman kept her from the spotlight.

13. Fortunately for today's readers, Murray generated a great deal of writing, including over 300 letters with Eleanor Roosevelt, two autobiographies, and a book of poetry. The publication of these works has led to renewed interest in her work. Murray's writings provide insight into a multifaceted leader, who had a hand in many social and legal advances during the twentieth century.

---

1. Murray's memoirs and history suggest that today she most likely would have identified as "queer" or "transgender." Here, the term "queer" is used in the modern sense as an all-encompassing term for individuals who do not identify as heterosexual or are gender non-conforming.

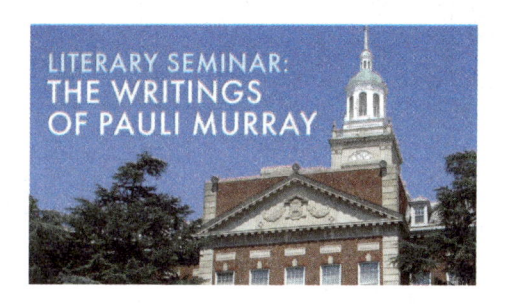

Literary Seminar: The Writings of Pauli Murray

Read "Literary Seminar: The Writings of Pauli Murray." After you read, complete the Think Questions below.

THINK QUESTIONS

1. Who is Dr. Leon Ransom, and how did he help Pauli Murray along her journey to achieve social and legal advancements? Support your answer with evidence from the text.

2. What is *satyagraha*, and how was it successful in Pauli Murray's case? Cite evidence from the text to support your answer.

3. What is Pauli Murray's most consequential achievement, and how did it come about? Explain using relevant evidence from the text.

4. What is the meaning of the word **arbitrary** as it is used in the text? Write your best definition here, along with a brief explanation of how you arrived at its meaning.

5. Read the following dictionary entry:

   provision
   pro•vi•sion /pruh-vizh-uhn/

   noun

   1. the ability to produce something useful
   2. a quantity that is furnished or supplied

   verb

   1. to present with sustenance, namely meals, liquids, or supplies, particularly for a trip
   2. to put something out of the way, especially a quantity that is specifically designated to cover an organization's finances of a known debt or liability

   Which definition most closely matches **provision** as it is used in the text? Write that definition of *provision* here and indicate which clues found in the text helped you determine its meaning.

Theme for English B

POETRY
Langston Hughes
1949

Introduction

The writing of Langston Hughes (1902–1967) captured African American experiences and explored ideas that have resonated with generations of readers. Born and raised in the Midwest, Hughes relocated to New York in 1921 to attend Columbia University. Once there, he was introduced to Harlem, the place that would define his career as a writer. As he mingled with African American artists, including writers, musicians, and painters, he drew inspiration from his surroundings. Hughes eventually established himself as one of the leaders of the cultural movement known as the Harlem Renaissance.

Theme for English B

> "Sometimes perhaps you don't want to be a part of me. / Nor do I often want to be a part of you."

1. The instructor said,
2. Go home and write
3. a page tonight.
4. And let that page come out of you—
5. Then, it will be true.

6. I wonder if it's that **simple**?
7. I am twenty-two, **colored**[1], born in Winston-Salem.
8. I went to school there, then Durham, then here
9. to this college on the hill above Harlem.
10. I am the only colored student in my class.
11. The steps from the hill lead down into Harlem,
12. through a park, then I cross St. Nicholas,
13. Eighth Avenue, Seventh, and I come to the Y,
14. the Harlem Branch Y, where I take the elevator
15. up to my room, sit down, and write this page:

16. It's not easy to know what is true for you or me
17. at twenty-two, my age. But I guess I'm what
18. I feel and see and hear, Harlem, I hear you:
19. hear you, hear me—we two—you, me, talk on this page.
20. (I hear New York, too.) Me—who?
21. Well, I like to eat, sleep, drink, and be in love.
22. I like to work, read, learn, and understand life.
23. I like a pipe for a Christmas present,
24. or records—Bessie[2], bop, or Bach.
25. I guess being colored doesn't make me not like
26. the same things other folks like who are other races.
27. So will my page be colored that I write?

---

1. **colored** a term that was common at the time, used to describe someone who was racially non-white, usually black
2. **Bessie** Bessie Smith, a well-known jazz and blues singer from the 1920s and 1930s

28 Being me, it will not be white.
29 But it will be
30 a part of you, instructor.
31 You are white—
32 yet a part of me, as I am a part of you.
33 That's American.
34 Sometimes perhaps you don't want to be a part of me.
35 Nor do I often want to be a part of you.
36 But we are, that's true!
37 As I learn from you,
38 I guess you learn from me—
39 although you're older—and white—
40 and somewhat more free.

41 This is my page for English B.

"Theme for English B" from THE COLLECTED POEMS OF LANGSTON HUGHES by Langston Hughes, edited by Arnold Rampersad with David Roessel, Associate Editor, copyright © 1994 by the Estate of Langston Hughes. Used by permission of Alfred A. Knopf, an imprint of the Knopf Doubleday Publishing Group, a division of Random House LLC. All rights reserved.

By permission of Harold Ober Associates Incorporated.
Copyright © 1994 by The Estate of Langston Hughes.

WRITE

PERSONAL RESPONSE: Throughout his poem "Theme for English B," Langston Hughes addresses the complicated dynamics of the speaker's experience as the only student of color in his college class. Write a personal response in which you reflect on your own experience with a contemporary social issue. Include descriptive details and figurative language to create a rich and meaningful response.

On Listening to Your Teacher Take Attendance

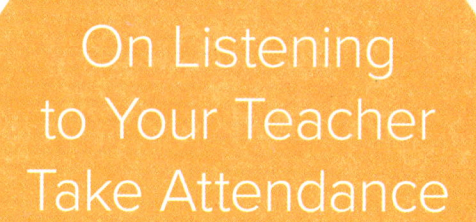

POETRY
Aimee Nezhukumatathil
2018

Introduction

Aimee Nezhukumatathil (b. 1974) was born in Chicago to a Filipina mother and an Indian father. She is the author of three collections of poetry and currently serves as a professor in the MFA program at the University of Mississippi. In this poem, Nezhukumatathil uses vivid imagery and detail to evoke the speaker's feelings as her last name is mispronounced by yet another teacher.

". . . And when / everyone turns around to check out / your face, no need to flush red and warm."

1. Breathe deep even if it means you wrinkle
2. your nose from the fake-lemon **antiseptic**
3. of the mopped floors and wiped-down
4. doorknobs. The freshly soaped necks
5. and armpits. Your teacher means well,
6. even if he **butchers** your name like
7. he has a bloody sausage casing stuck
8. between his teeth, handprints
9. on his white, sloppy apron. And when
10. everyone turns around to check out
11. your face, no need to flush red and warm.
12. Just picture all the eyes as if your classroom
13. is one big scallop with its dozens of icy blues
14. and you will remember that winter your family

15. took you to the China Sea and you sank
16. your face in it to gaze at baby clams and sea stars

17. the size of your **outstretched** hand. And when
18. all those necks start to **crane**, try not to forget

19. someone once **lathered** their bodies, once patted them
20. dry with a fluffy towel after a bath, set out their clothes

21. for the first day of school. Think of their pencil cases
22. from third grade, full of sharp pencils, a pink pearl eraser.

23. Think of their handheld pencil sharpener and its tiny blade.

Aimee Nezhukumatathil, "On Listening to Your Teacher Take Attendance" from *Oceanic*. Copyright © 2018 by Aimee Nezhukumatathil. Used with the permission of The Permissions Company, Inc. on behalf of Copper Canyon Press, www.coppercanyonpress.org.

✏️ WRITE

POETRY: Sometimes writing in the second person makes describing painful situations easier because it takes the focus off the speaker. The second person can also be used to give comfort, advice, or instruction to others. Using "On Listening to Your Teacher Take Attendance" as a guide, write a poem in the second person about a real or imagined embarrassing or uncomfortable situation in which the narrator describes personal memories, thoughts, or actions that help alleviate the discomfort. Be sure to maintain the second-person voice and use descriptive language throughout your poem.

Brown v. Board of Education

ARGUMENTATIVE TEXT
U.S. Supreme Court
1954

Introduction

A class-action suit filed by 13 Topeka, Kansas, parents on behalf of their children, *Brown v. Board of Education* was a landmark 1954 U.S. Supreme Court case that declared unanimously, with no dissenting opinions, that establishing separate public schools for African American students was unconstitutional. The ruling overturned the previous *Plessy v. Ferguson* decision from 1896, which sanctioned segregation in public institutions.

"A sense of inferiority affects the motivation of a child to learn."

from the unanimous decision of the Court, delivered by Chief Justice Earl Warren:

1. In approaching this problem, we cannot turn the clock back to 1868, when the [Fourteenth] Amendment was adopted, or even to 1896, when *Plessy v. Ferguson* was written. We must consider public education in the light of its full development and its present place in American life throughout the Nation. Only in this way can it be determined if segregation in public schools deprives these plaintiffs of the equal protection of the laws.

2. Today, education is perhaps the most important function of state and local governments. Compulsory school attendance laws and the great expenditures for education both demonstrate our recognition of the importance of education to our democratic society. It is required in the performance of our most basic public responsibilities, even service in the armed forces. It is the very **foundation** of good citizenship. Today it is a principal instrument in awakening the child to cultural values, in preparing him for later professional training, and in helping him to adjust normally to his environment. In these days, it is doubtful that any child may reasonably be expected to succeed in life if he is denied the opportunity of an education. Such an opportunity, where the state has undertaken to provide it, is a right which must be made available to all on equal terms.

3. We come then to the question presented: Does segregation of children in public schools solely on the basis of race, even though the physical facilities and other **"tangible"** factors may be equal, deprive the children of the minority group of equal educational opportunities? We believe that it does.

Elizabeth Eckford ignores the hostile screams and stares of fellow students on her first day of school at Little Rock's Central High School.

Skill: Technical Language

The author mentions segregation in schools. *Segregation* shares a root with *segregate*, so it likely has to do with separating. The author does not mention who was separated or by what criteria.

Skill: Word Meaning

What does *facilities* mean here? I know the term is used as a noun in this sentence. The facilities are described as physical and have to do with public schools. Maybe the word refers to the school building.

Brown v. Board of Education

Skill: Reasons and Evidence

The claim is strengthened by citing previous court cases. Both cases point out that there are negative effects of segregation, which are hard to measure. This supports the claim that segregation is inherently unequal.

4 In *Sweatt v. Painter,* in finding that a segregated law school for Negroes could not provide them equal educational opportunities, this Court relied in large part on "those qualities which are incapable of objective measurement but which make for greatness in a law school." In *McLaurin v. Oklahoma State Regents,* the Court, in requiring that a Negro admitted to a white graduate school be treated like all other students, again resorted to intangible considerations: ". . . his ability to study, to engage in discussions and exchange views with other students, and, in general, to learn his profession." Such considerations apply with added force to children in grade and high schools. To separate them from others of similar age and qualifications solely because of their race generates a feeling of inferiority as to their status in the community that may affect their hearts and minds in a way unlikely ever to be undone. The effect of this separation on their educational opportunities was well stated by a finding in the Kansas case by a court which nevertheless felt compelled to rule against the Negro plaintiffs: Segregation of white and colored children in public schools has a **detrimental** effect upon the colored children. The impact is greater when it has the **sanction** of the law, for the policy of separating the races is usually interpreted as denoting the inferiority of the negro group. A sense of inferiority affects the motivation of a child to learn. Segregation with the sanction of law, therefore, has a tendency to [retard] the educational and mental development of negro children and to deprive them of some of the benefits they would receive in a racial[ly] integrated school system. Whatever may have been the extent of psychological knowledge at the time of *Plessy v. Ferguson,* this finding is amply supported by modern authority. Any language in *Plessy v. Ferguson* contrary to this finding is rejected.

5 We conclude that, in the field of public education, the doctrine of "separate but equal" has no place. Separate educational facilities are **inherently** unequal. Therefore, we hold that the plaintiffs and others similarly situated for whom the actions have been brought are, by reason of the segregation complained of, deprived of the equal protection of the laws guaranteed by the Fourteenth Amendment.

First Read

Read *Brown v. Board of Education*. After you read, complete the Think Questions below.

THINK QUESTIONS

1. Why might the Supreme Court have thought that this ruling, overturning *Plessy v. Ferguson,* was important for the country? Refer to one or more details from the text to support your explanation.

2. According to Chief Justice Warren, what effect did a court ruling such as *Plessy v. Ferguson* have on educational opportunities for students? Support your answer with textual evidence.

3. Use details and evidence provided in the text to explain what Chief Justice Warren means by the phrase "modern authority" at the end of the next-to-last paragraph.

4. What is the meaning of the word **tangible** as it is used in the text? Write your best definition here, along with a brief explanation of how you arrived at its meaning.

5. What is the meaning of the word **detrimental** as it is used in the text? Write your best definition here, along with a brief explanation of how you arrived at its meaning.

Brown v. Board of Education

Skill:
Reasons and Evidence

Use the Checklist to analyze Reasons and Evidence in *Brown v. Board of Education*. Refer to the sample student annotations about Reasons and Evidence in the text.

••• CHECKLIST FOR REASONS AND EVIDENCE

In order to delineate and evaluate the reasoning and evidence in seminal U.S. texts, note the following:

- ✓ the writer's position and how he or she uses legal reasoning to interpret the law
  - legal reasoning includes the thinking processes and strategies used by lawyers and judges when arguing and deciding legal cases and is based on constitutional principles, or laws written down in the U.S. Constitution
- ✓ whether the premise is based on legal reasoning and constitutional principles
- ✓ the precision of the author's argument or how exactly he or she identifies conflicts, claims, objections, and supporting evidence
- ✓ how compelling the writer's argument is, including the elements that give the argument force and power and those that lessen its strength and viability

To evaluate the reasoning and evidence in seminal U.S. texts, including the application of constitutional principles and use of legal reasoning, consider the following questions:

- ✓ What position does the writer take?
- ✓ How does the writer use constitutional principles and legal reasoning to support his or her position?
- ✓ What evidence does the author use to support his or her claim?

Skill: Reasons and Evidence

Reread paragraphs 4 and 5 of *Brown v. Board of Education*. Then, using the Checklist on the previous page, answer the multiple-choice questions below.

YOUR TURN

1. What is the main claim made in the closing of this decision?

   - A. That the doctrine of "separate but equal" is unconstitutional as stipulated by the Fourteenth Amendment.
   - B. That the doctrine of "separate but equal" is constitutional as stipulated by the Fourteenth Amendment.
   - C. That the doctrine of "separate but equal" has no place in public education and is inherently racist.
   - D. That the doctrine of "separate but equal" has deprived the plaintiffs of a high-quality education.

2. Which line from the passage best represents the reasoning that Chief Justice Warren uses to support the claim of this unanimous decision?

   - A. "Segregation of white and colored children in public schools has a detrimental effect upon the colored children."
   - B. "The impact is greater when it has the sanction of the law, for the policy of separating the races is usually interpreted as denoting the inferiority of the negro group."
   - C. "A sense of inferiority affects the motivation of a child to learn."
   - D. "Whatever may have been the extent of psychological knowledge at the time of *Plessy v. Ferguson,* this finding is amply supported by modern authority."

Brown v. Board of Education

Skill: Technical Language

Use the Checklist to analyze Technical Language in *Brown v. Board of Education*. Refer to the sample student annotations about Technical Language in the text.

••• CHECKLIST FOR TECHNICAL LANGUAGE

In order to determine the meanings of words and phrases as they are used in a text, including technical meanings, note the following:

- ✓ the subject of the text
- ✓ any unfamiliar words that you think might be technical terms
- ✓ words that have multiple meanings that change when used with a specific subject
- ✓ the possible contextual meaning of a word, or the definition from a dictionary

To determine the meanings of words and phrases as they are used in a text, including technical meanings, consider the following questions:

- ✓ What is the subject of the informational text?
- ✓ How does the use of technical language help establish the author as an authority on a subject?
- ✓ Are there any technical words that have an impact on the meaning and tone of the text?
- ✓ Does the author use the same term several times, refining its meaning and adding layers to it over the course of the text?

Skill: Technical Language

Reread this passage from paragraph 4 of *Brown v. Board of Education*. Then, using the Checklist on the previous page, answer the multiple-choice questions below.

YOUR TURN

from *Brown v. Board of Education* by U.S. Supreme Court

. . . The impact is greater when it has the sanction of the law, for the policy of separating the races is usually interpreted as denoting the inferiority of the negro group. A sense of inferiority affects the motivation of a child to learn. Segregation with the sanction of law, therefore, has a tendency to [retard] the educational and mental development of negro children and to deprive them of some of the benefits they would receive in a racial[ly] integrated school system. Whatever may have been the extent of psychological knowledge at the time of *Plessy v. Ferguson,* this finding is amply supported by modern authority. Any language in *Plessy v. Ferguson* contrary to this finding is rejected.

1. How does the author further refine the meaning of the word *segregation* as it is used in this passage?

    - ○ A. The author refines the meaning of the word *segregation* by mentioning it several times, illustrating the importance of the word in the text.
    - ○ B. The phrase "segregation with the sanction of law" confirms that as it is used here, the word does not describe mere discrimination but institutionalized racism.
    - ○ C. The author refines the meaning of the word *segregation* by defining it for the audience.
    - ○ D. The phrase "separating the races" serves to clarify by what means people are being segregated.

2. Using context clues, determine the meaning of *integrated* as it is used in this passage.

    - ○ A. with various parts or aspects linked or coordinated
    - ○ B. desegregated
    - ○ C. indicating the mean value or total sum of a measurement
    - ○ D. two things combined so that they become a whole

Brown v. Board of Education

Skill:
Word Meaning

Use the Checklist to analyze Word Meaning in *Brown v. Board of Education*. Refer to the sample student annotations about Word Meaning in the text.

••• CHECKLIST FOR WORD MEANING

In order to find the pronunciation of a word or to determine or clarify its precise meaning, do the following:

- ✓ determine the word's part of speech
- ✓ use context clues to make an inferred meaning of the word or phrase
- ✓ consult a dictionary to verify your preliminary determination of the meaning of a word or phrase
- ✓ be sure to read all of the definitions, and then decide which definition makes sense within the context of the text

In order to determine or to clarify a word's part of speech, do the following:

- ✓ determine what the word is describing
- ✓ identify how the word is being used in the phrase or sentence

In order to determine the etymology of a word, its origin, or its standard usage, do the following:

- ✓ use reference materials, such as a dictionary, to determine the word's origin and history
- ✓ consider how the historical context of the word clarifies its usage

To determine or to clarify the etymology or standard usage of a word, consider the following questions:

- ✓ How formal or informal is this word?
- ✓ What is the word describing? What inferred meanings can I make?
- ✓ In what context is the word being used?
- ✓ Is this slang? An example of vernacular? In what other contexts might this word be used?
- ✓ What is the etymology of this word?

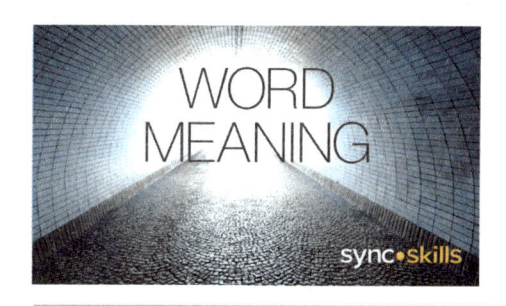

Skill: Word Meaning

Reread paragraph 4 of *Brown v. Board of Education*. Then, using the Checklist on the previous page as well as the dictionary entry below, answer the multiple-choice questions.

YOUR TURN

intangible /in'tan jə b(ə)l/ *adjective*

1. difficult or impossible to define or understand; vague and abstract
2. unable to be touched or grasped; not having physical presence
3. unearthly, supernatural

1. This question has two parts. First, answer Part A. Then, answer Part B.

   Part A: Which definition best fits the way the word *intangible* is used in paragraph 4?
   - A. Definition 1
   - B. Definition 2
   - C. Definition 3
   - D. None of the above

   Part B: Which of the following phrases provides context that best explains the meaning of *intangible* as identified in Part A?
   - A. "could not provide them equal educational opportunities"
   - B. "incapable of objective measurement"
   - C. "a Negro admitted to a white graduate school"
   - D. "be treated like all other students"

Close Read

Reread *Brown v. Board of Education*. As you reread, complete the Skills Focus questions below. Then use your answers and annotations from the questions to help you complete the Write activity.

SKILLS FOCUS

1. Infer the meaning of the word *plaintiffs* as it is used in the text. Explain why the use of this technical language is appropriate for this text.

2. Write a definition for the word *instrument* as it is used in paragraph 2. Highlight the clues in the text that helped you arrive at this definition. Then confirm your definition in a dictionary or online resource.

3. Identify an instance in the text where the author references another court case. How does the author use this piece of evidence to support his claim?

4. Identify one reason the author gives to support the idea that "separate" can never be "equal." Explain how the author's reasoning makes his argument more convincing.

5. Identify the goal(s) that the *Brown v. Board of Education* decision hoped to accomplish. Include information from the text to support your answer.

WRITE

LITERARY ANALYSIS: After reading *Brown v. Board of Education*, "On Listening to Your Teacher Take Attendance," and "Theme for English B," write a brief essay in which you analyze the language of the court's decision. Make an argument about how it affects students' real-life experiences in school, using Nezhukumatathil's, Hughes's, and your own point of view to inform your argument. What was the intention conveyed by the ruling's language, and what does school look like in our country today? Demonstrate your understanding of the language of the ruling and support your argument using the most relevant evidence from the texts.

Civil Rights Act of 1964

INFORMATIONAL TEXT
Lyndon B. Johnson
with U.S. Congress
1964

Introduction

Easily the most memorable achievement of United States President Lyndon B. Johnson (1908–1973) was his role in the Civil Rights Act of 1964. Johnson famously signed the act into law, which banned discrimination based on race, national origin, religion, and gender in public places. The signing of this act also paved the way for Congress to pass the Voting Rights Act in 1965. Although the Civil Rights Act of 1964 was initially introduced during the presidency of Johnson's predecessor, John F. Kennedy, Johnson continued the fight against segregation in America in the wake of Kennedy's assassination. The following text includes the sections of the legislation that address the banning of discrimination in public places

Civil Rights Act of 1964

"All persons shall be entitled to be free, at any establishment or place, from discrimination..."

1   **SEC. 201.** (a) All persons shall be entitled to the full and equal enjoyment of the goods, services, facilities, and privileges, advantages, and accommodations of any place of public accommodation, as defined in this section, without **discrimination** or segregation on the ground of race, color, religion, or national origin.

Clergy members stand in front as a crowd protesting for civil rights moves toward the Boston Common in Boston, April 23, 1965.

2   (b) Each of the following establishments which serves the public is a place of public accommodation within the meaning of this title if its operations affect commerce, or if discrimination or segregation by it is supported by State action:

3   (1) any inn, hotel, motel, or other establishment which provides lodging to **transient** guests, other than an establishment located within a building which contains not more than five rooms for rent or hire and which is actually occupied by the proprietor of such establishment as his residence;

4   (2) any restaurant, cafeteria, lunchroom, lunch counter, soda fountain, or other facility principally engaged in selling food for consumption on the premises, including, but not limited to, any such facility located on the premises of any retail establishment; or any gasoline station;

5   (3) any motion picture house[1], theater, concert hall, sports arena, stadium or other place of exhibition or entertainment; and

6   (4) any establishment (A)(i) which is physically located within the premises of any establishment otherwise covered by this subsection, or (ii) within the premises of which is physically located any such covered establishment, and (B) which holds itself out as serving patrons of such covered establishment.

---

1. **motion picture house** a single-screen movie theater

7   (c) The operations of an establishment affect commerce within the meaning of this title if (1) it is one of the establishments described in paragraph (1) of subsection (b); (2) in the case of an establishment described in paragraph (2) of subsection (b), it serves or offers to serve interstate travelers or a **substantial** portion of the food which it serves, or gasoline or other products which it sells, has moved in commerce; (3) in the case of an establishment described in paragraph (3) of subsection (b), it customarily presents films, performances, athletic teams, exhibitions, or other sources of entertainment which move in commerce; and (4) in the case of an establishment described in paragraph (4) of subsection (b), it is physically located within the premises of, or there is physically located within its premises, an establishment the operations of which affect commerce within the meaning of this subsection. For purposes of this section, "commerce" means travel, trade, traffic, commerce, transportation, or communication among the several States, or between the District of Columbia and any State, or between any foreign country or any territory or possession and any State or the District of Columbia, or between points in the same State but through any other State or the District of Columbia or a foreign country.

8   (d) Discrimination or segregation by an establishment is supported by State action within the meaning of this title if such discrimination or segregation (1) is carried on under color of any law[2], statute, ordinance, or regulation; or (2) is carried on under color of any custom or usage required or enforced by officials of the State or political subdivision thereof; or (3) is required by action of the State or political subdivision thereof.

9   (e) The provisions of this title shall not apply to a private club or other establishment not in fact open to the public, except to the extent that the facilities of such establishment are made available to the customers or patrons of an establishment within the **scope** of subsection (b).

10 **SEC. 202.** All persons shall be entitled to be free, at any establishment or place, from discrimination or segregation of any kind on the ground of race, color, religion, or national origin, if such discrimination or segregation is or purports to be required by any law, statute, ordinance, regulation, rule, or order of a State or any agency or political subdivision thereof.

11 **SEC. 203.** No person shall (a) withhold, deny, or attempt to withhold or deny, or deprive or attempt to deprive, any person of any right or privilege secured by section 201 or 202, or (b) intimidate, threaten, or coerce, or attempt to intimidate, threaten, or coerce any person with the purpose of interfering with

---

2. **under color of any law** with the appearance of legal power where it doesn't exist

Civil Rights Act of 1964

any right or privilege secured by section 201 or 202, or (c) punish or attempt to punish any person for exercising or attempting to exercise any right or privilege secured by section 201 or 202.

✏️ WRITE

RESEARCH: The scope and specificity of the places named in this excerpt of the Civil Rights Act of 1964 serve not only to define the broad reach of the new law but also to recognize the particular battlegrounds where the fight for civil rights occurred. Research an event that took place in one of the locations mentioned in this portion of the Civil Rights Act of 1964. Then, write about how your research impacts your understanding of the text and the civil rights movement as a whole.

I've Been to the Mountaintop

ARGUMENTATIVE TEXT
Martin Luther King Jr.
1968

Introduction

studysync

Dr. Martin Luther King Jr. (1929–1968) delivered "I've Been to the Mountaintop" at Mason Temple in Memphis, Tennessee, on April 3, 1968. King had been to Memphis a number of times in the spring of 1968 to show his support for African American sanitation workers who were striking to protest unfair working conditions. On March 29, the situation in Memphis exploded when looters broke away from a protest march led by King and vandalized businesses on Beale Street. Chaos ensued, resulting in injuries, arrests, and the death of one man. Devastated by the violence, King returned to Memphis several days later to refocus the campaign on nonviolence and the plight of the sanitation workers. "I've Been to the Mountaintop" was King's last speech. He was assassinated on the evening of

I've Been to the Mountaintop

"We have an opportunity to make America a better nation."

NOTES

1 Thank you very kindly, my friends. As I listened to Ralph Abernathy[1] in his eloquent and generous introduction and then thought about myself, I wondered who he was talking about. It's always good to have your closest friend and associate to say something good about you. And Ralph Abernathy is the best friend that I have in the world.

2 I'm delighted to see each of you here tonight in spite of a storm warning. You reveal that you are determined to go on anyhow. Something is happening in Memphis; something is happening in our world.

3 And you know, if I were standing at the beginning of time, with the possibility of taking a kind of general and panoramic view of the whole of human history up to now, and the Almighty said to me, "Martin Luther King, which age would you like to live in?" I would take my mental flight by Egypt and I would watch God's children in their magnificent **trek** from the dark dungeons of Egypt through or rather across the Red Sea, through the wilderness on toward the promised land[2]. And in spite of its magnificence, I wouldn't stop there. I would move on by Greece and take my mind to Mount Olympus[3]. And I would see Plato, Aristotle, Socrates, Euripides and Aristophanes[4] assembled around the Parthenon, and I would watch them around the Parthenon[5], as they discussed the great and eternal issues of reality.

4 But I wouldn't stop there. I would go on, even to the great hey-day of the Roman Empire. And I would see **developments** around there, through various emperors and leaders. But I wouldn't stop there. I would even come up to the

---

1. **Ralph Abernathy** Civil rights leader Ralph Abernathy (1926–1990) was a mentor to Dr. King, and his successor as president of the Southern Christian Leadership Conference.
2. **"through the wilderness on toward the promised land"** a reference to the Book of Numbers in the Old Testament, in which the Israelites are made to wander in the wilderness for forty years before reaching their destination
3. **Mount Olympus** the highest mountain in Greece and the mythical residence of the Greek gods
4. **Plato, Aristotle, Socrates, Euripides and Aristophanes** great ancient Greek philosophers and playwrights, and the founders of Western thought
5. **Parthenon** 5th century B.C.E. temple on the Acropolis dedicated to the goddess Athena and dominating central Athens

day of the Renaissance, and get a quick picture of all that the Renaissance did for the cultural and esthetic life of man. But I wouldn't stop there. I would even go by the way that the man for whom I am named had his habitat. And I would watch Martin Luther as he tacked his ninety-five theses[6] on the door at the church of Wittenberg.

5   But I wouldn't stop there. I would come on up even to 1863, and watch a **vacillating** President by the name of Abraham Lincoln finally come to the conclusion that he had to sign the Emancipation Proclamation. But I wouldn't stop there. I would even come up to the early thirties, and see a man grappling with the problems of the bankruptcy of his nation. And come with an eloquent cry that we have nothing to fear but fear itself.

6   But I wouldn't stop there. Strangely enough, I would turn to the Almighty, and say, "If you allow me to live just a few years in the second half of the Twentieth Century, I will be happy." Now that's a strange statement to make, because the world is all messed up. The nation is sick. Trouble is in the land. Confusion all around. That's a strange statement. But I know, somehow, that only when it is dark enough can you see the stars. And I see God working in this period of the Twentieth Century in a way that men, in some strange way, are responding—something is happening in our world. The masses of people are rising up. And wherever they are assembled today, whether they are in Johannesburg, South Africa; Nairobi, Kenya; Accra, Ghana; New York City; Atlanta, Georgia; Jackson, Mississippi; or Memphis, Tennessee—the cry is always the same—"We want to be free."

7   Another reason that I'm happy to live in this period is that we have been forced to a point where we are going to have to grapple with the problems that men have been trying to grapple with through history, but the demands didn't force them to do it. Survival demands that we grapple with them. Men, for years now, have been talking about war and peace. But now, no longer can they just talk about it. It is no longer a choice between violence and nonviolence in this world, it's nonviolence or nonexistence.

8   That is where we are today. And also in the human rights revolution, if something isn't done, and done in a hurry, to bring the colored peoples of the world out of their long years of poverty, their long years of hurt and neglect, the whole world is doomed. Now, I'm just happy that God has allowed me to live in this period to see what is unfolding. And I'm happy that He's allowed me to be in Memphis.

---

6. **ninety-five theses** proposals by theologian Martin Luther (1483–1546) that began the Protestant split from the Catholic Church

Skill: Language, Style, and Audience

Grapple is used three times, and this repetition intensifies the call to action, as survival now depends on it. This engages the audience, and the serious tone suggests that choosing not to act peacefully could lead to nonexistence.

I've Been to the Mountaintop

NOTES

⚙ Skill: Central or Main Idea

King's main idea is introduced here. He is strongly stating that all people are God's children and should be treated equally. All human beings deserve to be treated decently, and he is determined to make this happen.

9   I can remember, I can remember when Negroes were just going around as Ralph has said so often, scratching where they didn't itch, and laughing when they were not tickled. But that day is all over. We mean business now, and we are determined to gain our rightful place in God's world.

10 And that's all this whole thing is about. We aren't engaged in any negative protest and in any negative arguments with anybody. We are saying that we are determined to be men. We are determined to be people. We are saying that we are God's children. And if we're God's children, we don't have to live like we are forced to live.

11 Now, what does all of this mean in this great period of history? It means that we've got to stay together. We've got to stay together and maintain unity. You know, whenever Pharaoh wanted to prolong the period of slavery in Egypt, he had a favorite, favorite formula for doing it. What was that? He kept the slaves fighting among themselves. But whenever the slaves get together, something happens in Pharaoh's court, and he cannot hold the slaves in slavery. When the slaves get together, that's the beginning of getting out of slavery. Now let us maintain unity.

12 Secondly, let us keep the issues where they are. The issue is injustice. The issue is the refusal of Memphis to be fair and honest in its dealings with its public servants, who happen to be sanitation workers. Now we've got to keep attention on that. That's always the problem with a little violence. You know what happened the other day, and the press dealt only with the window breaking. I read the articles. They very seldom got around to mentioning the fact that one thousand, three hundred sanitation workers are on strike, and that Memphis is not being fair to them, and that Mayor Loeb is in dire need of a doctor. They didn't get around to that.

13 Now we're going to march again, and we've got to march again, in order to put the issue where it is supposed to be. And force everybody to see that there are thirteen hundred of God's children here suffering, sometimes going hungry, going through dark and dreary nights wondering how this thing is going to come out. That's the issue. And we've got to say to the nation, "We know how it's coming out." For when people get caught up with that which is right and they are willing to sacrifice for it, there is no stopping point short of victory.

14 We aren't going to let any mace stop us. We are masters in our nonviolent movement in disarming police forces; they don't know what to do. I've seen them so often. I remember in Birmingham, Alabama, when we were in that majestic struggle there we would move out of the 16th Street Baptist Church

day after day, by the hundreds we would move out. And Bull Connor[7] would tell them to send the dogs forth, and they did come; but we just went before the dogs singing, "Ain't gonna let nobody turn me 'round." Bull Connor next would say, "Turn the fire hoses on." And as I said to you the other night, Bull Connor didn't know history. He knew a kind of physics that somehow didn't relate to the transphysics that we knew about. And that was the fact that there was a certain kind of fire that no water could put out. And we went before the fire hoses; we had known water. If we were Baptist or some other denominations, we had been immersed. If we were Methodist, and some others, we had been sprinkled, but we knew water.

15 That couldn't stop us. And we just went on before the dogs and we would look at them; and we'd go on before the water hoses and we would look at it, and we'd just go on singing "Over my head I see freedom in the air." And then we would be thrown in the paddy wagons, and sometimes we were stacked in there like sardines in a can. And they would throw us in, and old Bull would say, "Take them off," and they did; and we would just go in the paddy wagon singing, "We Shall Overcome." And every now and then we'd get in jail, and we'd see the jailers looking through the windows being moved by our prayers, and being moved by our words and our songs. And there was a power there which Bull Connor couldn't adjust to; and so we ended up transforming Bull into a steer, and we won our struggle in Birmingham.

16 Now we've got to go on in Memphis just like that. I call upon you to be with us when we go out Monday. Now about injunctions: We have an injunction and we're going into court tomorrow morning to fight this illegal, unconstitutional injunction. All we say to America is, "Be true to what you said on paper." If I lived in China or even Russia, or any totalitarian country, maybe I could understand some of these illegal injunctions. Maybe I could understand the denial of certain basic First Amendment privileges, because they hadn't committed themselves to that over there. But somewhere I read of the freedom of assembly. Somewhere I read of the freedom of speech. Somewhere I read of the freedom of press. Somewhere I read that the greatness of America is the right to protest for right. And so just as I say, we aren't going to let any dog or water hose turn us around, we aren't going to let any injunction turn us around. We are going on.

17 We need all of you. And you know what's beautiful to me, is to see all of these ministers of the Gospel. It's a marvelous picture. Who is it that is supposed to articulate the longings and aspirations of the people more than the preacher? Somehow the preacher must have a kind of fire shut up in his bones. And

---

7. **Bull Connor** Theophilus Eugene 'Bull' Connor (1897–1973) was Commissioner of Public Safety of Birmingham, Alabama, when he ordered the use of attack dogs and fire hoses against civil rights demonstrators in May of 1963.

Skill: Rhetoric

King establishes credibility—uses *ethos*—by describing his persistence and victory in Birmingham, even in the face of extreme adversity. He uses *ethos* to persuade the audience to continue their nonviolent protests in Memphis.

whenever injustice is around he must tell it. Somehow the preacher must be an Amos, and say, "When God speaks who can but prophesy?" Again with Amos[8], "Let justice roll down like waters and righteousness like a mighty stream." Somehow the preacher must say with Jesus, "The Spirit of the Lord is upon me, because He hath anointed me to deal with the problems of the poor."

18   And I want to commend the preachers, under the leadership of these noble men: James Lawson, one who has been in this struggle for many years; he's been to jail for struggling; he's been kicked out of Vanderbilt University for this struggle, but he's still going on, fighting for the rights of his people. Reverend Ralph Jackson, Billy Kiles. I could just go right on down the list, but time will not permit. But I want to thank all of them. And I want you to thank them, because so often, preachers aren't concerned about anything but themselves. And I'm always happy to see a relevant ministry.

19   It's all right to talk about "long white robes over yonder,"[9] in all of its symbolism. But ultimately people want some suits and dresses and shoes to wear down here! It's all right to talk about "streets flowing with milk and honey,"[10] but God has commanded us to be concerned about the slums down here, and his children who can't eat three square meals a day. It's all right to talk about the New Jerusalem[11], but one day, God's preacher must talk about the new New York, the new Atlanta, the new Philadelphia, the new Los Angeles, the new Memphis, Tennessee. This is what we have to do.

20   Now the other thing we'll have to do is this. Always anchor our external direct action with the power of economic withdrawal. Now, we are poor people. Individually, we are poor when you compare us with white society in America. We are poor. Never stop and forget, that collectively, that means all of us together, collectively, we are richer than all the nations in the world, with the exception of nine. Did you ever think about that? After you leave the United States, Soviet Russia, Great Britain, West Germany, France, and I could name the others, the American Negro collectively is richer than most nations of the world. We have an annual income of more than thirty billion dollars a year, which is more than all of the exports of the United States, and more than the national budget of Canada. Did you know that? That's power right there, if we know how to pool it.

8. **Amos** one of the twelve prophets of the Old Testament
9. **"long white robes over yonder"** a reference to the belief in an afterlife in heaven as reward for earthly suffering
10. **"streets flowing with milk and honey"** In the Old Testament, God promised Abraham the land of Canaan (Israel) would "flow with milk and honey."
11. **New Jerusalem** In the Old Testament, Ezekiel says that there will one day be a New Jerusalem as capital of God's kingdom on Earth.

21. We don't have to argue with anybody. We don't have to curse and go around acting bad with our words. We don't need any bricks and bottles, we don't need any Molotov cocktails. We just need to go around to these stores, and to these massive industries in our country, and say, "God sent us by here to say to you that you're not treating his children right. And we've come here to ask you to make the first item on your agenda—fair treatment where God's children are concerned. Now if you are not prepared to do that, we do have an agenda that we must follow. And our agenda calls for withdrawing economic support from you."

22. And so far, as a result of this, we are asking you tonight, to go out and tell your neighbors not to buy Coca-Cola in Memphis. Go by and tell them not to buy Sealtest Milk. Tell them not to buy—what is the other bread?—Wonder Bread. And what is the other bread company, Jesse? Tell them not to buy Hart's Bread. As Jesse Jackson has said, "Up to now, only the garbage men have been feeling pain, now we must kind of redistribute the pain." We are choosing these companies because they haven't been fair in their hiring policies; and we are choosing them because they can begin the **process** of saying they are going to support the needs and the rights of these men who are on strike. And then they can move downtown and tell Mayor Loeb to do what is right.

23. But not only that, we've got to strengthen black institutions. I call upon you to take your money out of the banks downtown and deposit your money in Tri-State Bank. We want a "bank-in" movement in Memphis. Go by the Savings and Loan Association. I'm not asking you something that we don't do ourselves at SCLC. Judge Hooks and others will tell you that we have an account here in the savings and loan association from the Southern Christian Leadership Conference. We are telling you to follow what we are doing. Put your money there. You have six or seven black insurance companies here in the city of Memphis. Take out your insurance there. We want to have an "insurance-in."

24. Now these are some practical things that we can do. We begin the process of building a greater economic **base**. And at the same time, we are putting pressure where it really hurts. I ask you to follow through here.

25. Now, let me say as I move to my conclusion, that we've got to give ourselves to this struggle until the end. Nothing would be more tragic than to stop at this point, in Memphis. We've got to see it through. And when we have our march, you need to be there. If it means leaving work, if it means leaving school—be there. Be concerned about your brother. You may not be on strike. But either we go up together, or we go down together.

26 Let us develop a kind of dangerous unselfishness. One day a man came to Jesus; and he wanted to raise some questions about some vital matters of life. At points, he wanted to trick Jesus, and show him that he knew a little more than Jesus knew, and through this throw him off base. Now that question could have easily ended up in a philosophical and theological debate. But Jesus immediately pulled that question from mid-air, and placed it on a dangerous curve between Jerusalem and Jericho. And he talked about a certain man, who fell among thieves. You remember that a Levite and a priest passed by on the other side. They didn't stop to help him. And finally a man of another race came by. He got down from his beast, decided not to be compassionate by proxy. But he got down with him, administered first aid, and helped the man in need. Jesus ended up saying, "This was the good man, this was the great man, because he had the capacity to project the 'I' into the 'thou,' and to be concerned about his brother" Now you know, we use our imagination a great deal to try to determine why the priest and the Levite didn't stop. At times we say they were busy going to a church meeting—an ecclesiastical gathering—and they had to get on down to Jerusalem so they wouldn't be late for their meeting. At other times we would speculate that there was a religious law that "One who was engaged in religious ceremonials was not to touch a human body twenty-four hours before the ceremony." And every now and then we begin to wonder whether maybe they were not going down to Jerusalem, or down to Jericho, rather to organize a "Jericho Road Improvement Association." That's a possibility. Maybe they felt that it was better to deal with the problem from the causal root, rather than to get bogged down with an individual effect.

27 But I'm going to tell you what my imagination tells me. It's possible that those men were afraid. You see, the Jericho road is a dangerous road. I remember when Mrs. King and I were first in Jerusalem. We rented a car and drove from Jerusalem down to Jericho. And as soon as we got on that road, I said to my wife, "I can see why Jesus used this as the setting for his parable." It's a winding, meandering road. It's really conducive for ambushing. You start out in Jerusalem, which is about 1200 miles, or rather 1200 feet above sea level. And by the time you get down to Jericho, fifteen or twenty minutes later, you're about 2200 feet below sea level. That's a dangerous road. In the days of Jesus it came to be known as the "Bloody Pass." And you know, it's possible that the priest and the Levite looked over that man on the ground and wondered if the robbers were still around. Or it's possible that they felt that the man on the ground was merely faking. And he was acting like he had been robbed and hurt, in order to seize them over there, lure them there for quick and easy seizure. And so the first question that the Priest asked, the first question that the Levite asked was, "If I stop to help this man, what will happen to me?" But then the Good Samaritan came by. And he reversed the question: "If I do not stop to help this man, what will happen to him?"

28. That's the question before you tonight. Not, "If I stop to help the sanitation workers, what will happen to my job." Not, "If I stop to help the sanitation workers what will happen to all of the hours that I usually spend in my office every day and every week as a pastor?" The question is not, "If I stop to help this man in need, what will happen to me?" The question is, "If I do not stop to help the sanitation workers, what will happen to them?" That's the question.

29. ==Let us rise up tonight with a greater readiness. Let us stand with a greater determination. And let us move on in these powerful days, these days of challenge to make America what it ought to be. We have an opportunity to make America a better nation.== And I want to thank God, once more, for allowing me to be here with you.

30. You know, several years ago, I was in New York City autographing the first book that I had written. And while sitting there autographing books, a demented black woman came up. The only question I heard from her was, "Are you Martin Luther King?"

31. And I was looking down writing, and I said, "Yes." And the next minute I felt something beating on my chest. Before I knew it I had been stabbed by this demented woman. I was rushed to Harlem Hospital. It was a dark Saturday afternoon. And that blade had gone through, and the X-rays revealed that the tip of the blade was on the edge of my aorta, the main artery. And once that's punctured, you drown in your own blood—that's the end of you.

32. It came out in the *New York Times* the next morning, that if I had merely sneezed, I would have died. Well, about four days later, they allowed me, after the operation, after my chest had been opened, and the blade had been taken out, to move around in the wheel chair in the hospital. They allowed me to read some of the mail that came in, and from all over the states and the world, kind letters came in. I read a few, but one of them I will never forget. I had received one from the President and the Vice-President. I've forgotten what those telegrams said. I'd received a visit and a letter from the Governor of New York, but I've forgotten what that letter said. But there was another letter that came from a little girl, a young girl, who was a student at the White Plains High School. And I looked at that letter, and I'll never forget it. It said simply, "Dear Dr. King, I am a ninth-grade student at the White Plains High School." She said, "While it should not matter, I would like to mention that I'm a white girl. I read in the paper of your misfortune, and of your suffering. And I read that if you had sneezed, you would have died. And I'm simply writing you to say that I'm so happy that you didn't sneeze."

NOTES

Skill: Central or Main Idea

Achieving King's goal of universal equality will require determination and unity, two ideas that are emphasized through much of the speech. Here, he asks his audience to rise and stand together to demand equality.

I've Been to the Mountaintop

Skill: Rhetoric

King uses the same repeating phrase to emphasize and memorialize the successes of the civil rights movement. The repetition of these accomplishments serves to persuade the audience that victory is possible and to keep fighting.

33 And I want to say tonight—I want to say tonight that I, too, am happy that I didn't sneeze. Because if I had sneezed, I wouldn't have been around here in 1960, when students all over the South started sitting-in at lunch counters. And I knew that as they were sitting in, they were really standing up for the best in the American dream. And taking the whole nation back to those great wells of democracy which were dug deep by the Founding Fathers in the Declaration of Independence and the Constitution. If I had sneezed, I wouldn't have been around here in 1961, when we decided to take a ride for freedom, and ended segregation in interstate travel. If I had sneezed, I wouldn't have been around here in 1962, when Negroes in Albany, Georgia decided to straighten their backs up. And whenever men and women straighten their backs up, they are going somewhere, because a man can't ride your back unless it is bent. If I had sneezed, if I had sneezed, I wouldn't have been here in 1963, when the black people of Birmingham, Alabama aroused the conscience of this nation, and brought into being the Civil Rights Bill. If I had sneezed, I wouldn't have had a chance later that year, in August, to try to tell America about a dream that I had had. If I had sneezed, I wouldn't have been down in Selma, Alabama, to see the great movement there. If I had sneezed, I wouldn't have been in Memphis to see a community rally around those brothers and sisters who are suffering. I'm so happy that I didn't sneeze.

34 And they were telling me, now, it doesn't matter, now. It really doesn't matter what happens now. I left Atlanta this morning, and as we got started on the plane, there were six of us, the pilot said over the public address system, "We are sorry for the delay, but we have Dr. Martin Luther King on the plane. And to be sure that all of the bags were checked, and to be sure that nothing would be wrong on the plane, we had to check out everything carefully. And we've had the plane protected and guarded all night."

35 And then I got into Memphis. And some began to say the threats, or talk about the threats that were out. What would happen to me from some of our sick white brothers?

36 Well, I don't know what will happen now. We've got some difficult days ahead. But it really doesn't matter with me now, because I've been to the mountaintop. And I don't mind. Like anybody, I would like to live a long life. Longevity has its place. But I'm not concerned about that now. I just want to do God's will. And He's allowed me to go up to the mountain. And I've looked over. And I've seen the Promised Land. I may not get there with you. But I want you to know tonight that we, as a people, will get to the promised land. And I'm happy tonight. I'm not worried about anything. I'm not fearing any man. Mine eyes have seen the glory of the coming of the Lord.

@ 1968 Dr. Martin Luther King, Jr. © renewed 1996 Coretta Scott King.

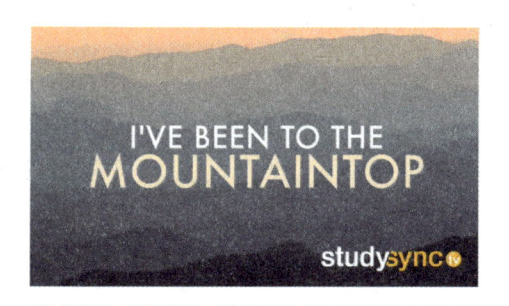

First Read

Read "I've Been to the Mountaintop." After you read, complete the Think Questions below.

THINK QUESTIONS

1. What is "this whole thing about," according to the speaker? Cite evidence from paragraph 10 to support your answer.

2. What specific actions does the speaker propose the audience take in order to exercise their "power of economic withdrawal"? Support your answer with evidence from the text.

3. Citing evidence from the text to support your answer, explain why the speaker tells the parable of the Good Samaritan in "I've Been to the Mountaintop."

4. What is the meaning of the word **vacillating** as it is used in the text? Write your best definition here, along with a brief explanation of how you arrived at its meaning.

5. Read the following dictionary entry:

   base
   base /bās/ *noun*

   1. the bottom part of something that provides structural support
   2. any one of the four stations in a softball or baseball infield
   3. something from which people draw support

   Use context to determine which of these definitions most closely matches the use of **base** in the text. Write the correct definition of *base* here and explain how you figured out its meaning.

Skill:
Central or Main Idea

Use the Checklist to analyze Central or Main Idea in "I've Been to the Mountaintop." Refer to the sample student annotations about Central or Main Idea in the text.

••• CHECKLIST FOR CENTRAL OR MAIN IDEA

In order to identify two or more central ideas of a text, note the following:

- ✓ the main idea in each paragraph or group of paragraphs
- ✓ key details in each paragraph or section of text, distinguishing what they have in common
- ✓ whether the details contain information that could indicate more than one main idea in a text
    - A science text, for example, may provide information about a specific environment and also a message on ecological awareness.
    - A biography may contain equally important ideas about a person's achievements, influence, and the time period in which the person lives or lived.
- ✓ when each central idea emerges
- ✓ ways that the central ideas interact and build on one another

To determine two or more central ideas of a text and analyze their development over the course of the text, including how they interact and build on one another to provide a complex analysis, consider the following questions:

- ✓ What main idea(s) do the details in each paragraph explain or describe?
- ✓ What central or main ideas do all the paragraphs support?
- ✓ How do the central ideas interact and build on one another? How is that affected when they emerge?
- ✓ How might you provide an objective summary of the text? What details would you include?

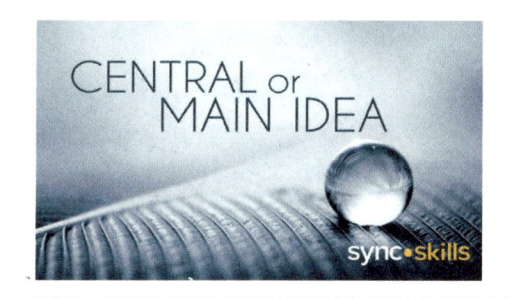

Skill: Central or Main Idea

Reread paragraphs 34–36 of "I've Been to the Mountaintop." Then, using the Checklist on the previous page, answer the multiple-choice questions below.

⟳ YOUR TURN

1. How does sharing the threats he has received help King add to one of the central ideas of the text?

    - A. It helps the reader understand that Dr. King is in grave danger and could be harmed.
    - B. It strengthens his argument that the path to equality won't be easy, but it is worth it.
    - C. It builds on the themes of unity and opportunity, even in times of instability.
    - D. It helps strengthen his argument that equal rights should be granted to all Americans.

2. What is the central idea of King's closing paragraph?

    - A. That regardless of what happens next, Dr. King has seen what could be and has faith in God that one day African Americans will achieve equality.
    - B. That the Promised Land is a place all African Americans will get to no matter what, as King has already been there.
    - C. That African Americans should come together to make the world a better place.
    - D. That nothing matters to Dr. King now, as he has been to the mountaintop and feels that he is now free.

I've Been to the Mountaintop

Skill: Rhetoric

Use the Checklist to analyze Rhetoric in "I've Been to the Mountaintop." Refer to the sample student annotations about Rhetoric in the text.

••• CHECKLIST FOR RHETORIC

In order to identify a speaker's reasoning, point of view, and use of evidence and rhetoric, note the following:

- ✓ the stance, or position, the speaker takes on a topic
- ✓ the use of rhetorical appeals, including appeals to *logos* (logic), *ethos* (trust), and *pathos* (emotions)
- ✓ the use of rhetorical devices, such as:
  - sensory language that appeals to the senses and creates a vivid picture in the minds of readers and listeners
  - repetition of the same word or phrase to emphasize an idea or claim. Look for:
    - > anaphora, or repetition at the start of a sentence or clause
    - > anadiplosis, or repetition of the last word in a sentence or clause
- ✓ the speaker's choice of words, the points he or she chooses to emphasize, and the tone, or general attitude

To evaluate a speaker's point of view, reasoning, and use of evidence and rhetoric, consider the following questions:

- ✓ What is the speaker's point of view? Is their stance based on sound, logical reasoning? Why or why not?
- ✓ Does the speaker use facts and evidence to make a point? Are they exaggerated? How do you know?
- ✓ Does the speaker use rhetorical devices? If so, are they effective? Why or why not?
- ✓ What points does the speaker choose to emphasize? How does the speaker's choice of words affect his or her tone?

Skill: Rhetoric

Reread paragraphs 3–6 of "I've Been to the Mountaintop." Then, using the Checklist on the previous page, answer the multiple-choice questions below.

YOUR TURN

1. The speaker repeats the phrase "I wouldn't stop there" seven times in paragraphs 3–6. This rhetorical device is called—

    - A. the rhetorical appeal known as *pathos*.
    - B. anaphora.
    - C. rhetorical shift.
    - D. antithesis.

2. Which statement best describes the effect of the rhetorical device in question 1 on how the passage is read and understood?

    - A. It powerfully calls attention to the progress of human history while creating a personal connection between the speaker and his audience that is intended to convince listeners that remarkable progress is yet to come right there in Memphis.
    - B. It reveals that the speaker will soon move on and that the people must commit to carrying on his nonviolent approach to achieving equality for all.
    - C. It alerts listeners to the fact that the speaker knows a lot about history and they should be honored that he has come back to Memphis to help fight for workers' rights and civil rights nationwide.
    - D. It tells listeners that they should be wary of participating in marches or protests as they are likely to be part of only one small moment in history.

3. The speaker says, "But I know, somehow, that only when it is dark enough can you see the stars." Why does the speaker use the rhetorical device evident in this sentence?

    - A. He uses it to change the audience's focus from the historic times he mentioned to the importance of the march that is to take place the next day.
    - B. He uses it as a way to logically defend the troubled times in the United States and around the world.
    - C. He uses it to help convince the audience to fight for civil rights by describing a figurative contrast between keeping hope in the troubled times they live in.
    - D. He uses it to provide proof that nonviolent protests are not always effective and therefore not necessary.

I've Been to the Mountaintop

Skill: Language, Style, and Audience

Use the Checklist to analyze Language, Style, and Audience in "I've Been to the Mountaintop." Refer to the sample student annotations about Language, Style, and Audience in the text.

CHECKLIST FOR LANGUAGE, STYLE, AND AUDIENCE

In order to determine an author's style and possible intended audience, do the following:

- ✓ identify instances where the author uses key terms throughout the course of a text
- ✓ examine surrounding words and phrases to determine the context, connotation, style, and tone of the term
- ✓ analyze how the author's treatment of the key term affects the reader's understanding of the text
- ✓ note the audience—both intended and unintended—and possible reactions to the author's word choice, style, and treatment of key terms

To analyze how an author's treatment of language and key terms affect the reader's understanding of the text, consider the following questions:

- ✓ How do the author's word choices enhance or change what is being described?
- ✓ How do the author's word choices affect the reader's understanding of key terms and ideas in the text?
- ✓ How do choices about language affect the author's style and audience?
- ✓ How often does the author use this term or terms?

Skill: Language, Style, and Audience

Reread paragraphs 32 and 33 of "I've Been to the Mountaintop." Then, using the Checklist on the previous page, answer the multiple-choice questions below.

YOUR TURN

1. How does the repetition of the phrase "if I had sneezed" enhance the meaning of these paragraphs?

   - A. It emphasizes that King is excited about the next chapter of the civil rights movement.
   - B. It enhances the reader's understanding of how King felt happy to be alive.
   - C. It emphasizes that King is proud and feels lucky to have been part of many great moments in the civil rights struggle.
   - D. It enhances the reader's understanding of the impact of the events of the civil rights movement that occurred over the years.

2. What is the effect of this summary of successes on the audience?

   - A. It reminds the audience of the gradual progress that has been made, which inspires action, hope, and the need to keep fighting.
   - B. It teaches the audience about the major events of the civil rights movement.
   - C. It helps the reader understand how close King was to dying and how happy he is to be alive.
   - D. It builds tension by foreshadowing King's assassination.

I've Been to the Mountaintop

Close Read

Reread "I've Been to the Mountaintop." As you reread, complete the Skills Focus questions below. Then use your answers and annotations from the questions to help you complete the Write activity.

SKILLS FOCUS

1. What is one of King's central or main ideas in this text? Support your answer with textual evidence.

2. Identify a passage in "I've Been to the Mountaintop" that reveals the audience of the speech. Analyze how King communicates his purpose to this audience.

3. Highlight a rhetorical device that King uses in his speech. Then, analyze the effect the rhetorical devices have on the way the text is read and understood.

4. Identify an example in the text where King urges his audience to partake in nonviolent forms of resistance. Explain why you believe nonviolence is important for King in the fight for equality.

WRITE

RHETORICAL ANALYSIS: What makes rhetoric effective? Identify King's main idea and purpose in this speech. Then discuss what aspect of King's rhetoric is most crucial to convincing his audience of his main idea. Cite examples of rhetoric from the text and explain how they are used to support King's central idea.

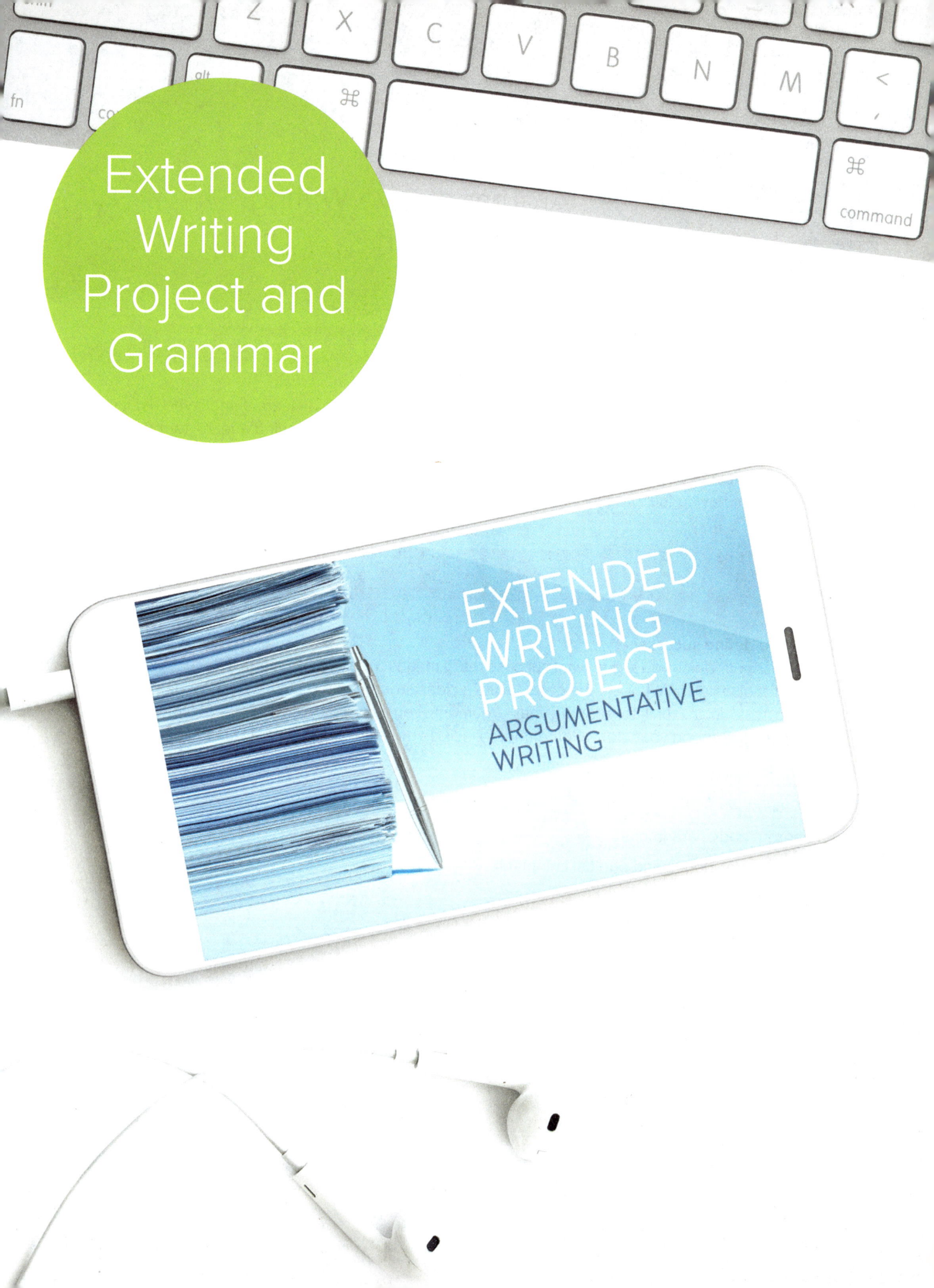

Extended Writing Project and Grammar

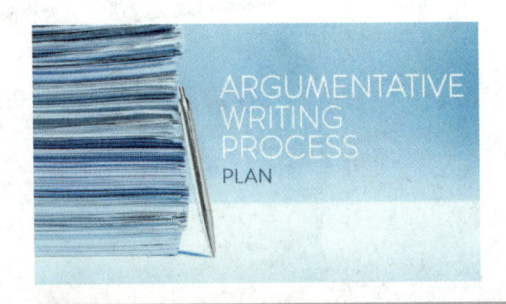

Argumentative Writing Process: Plan

| PLAN | DRAFT | REVISE | EDIT AND PUBLISH |

John Green once said that he defines success by asking himself, "What did I learn?" and "Who did it help?" Many authors in this unit argue what success in pursuit of their goals, or winning, means to them—at the workplace, in the classroom, or even in life itself. For some, winning means achieving a hard-earned victory or achieving a certain economic status. For others, winning carries an altruistic meaning, working towards equity for others or having the integrity to forsake political power.

WRITING PROMPT

How do we define success?
Write an essay in which you argue what success really means. What does it mean to "win"? What are the benefits of winning? What are the costs? Write a clear, arguable thesis, and use evidence from at least two texts in the unit to support your argument. You may also draw on relevant personal experiences to support your ideas. Remember to include the following in your argumentative essay:

- an introduction
- a thesis statement
- coherent body paragraphs
- supporting evidence and original commentary
- a counterargument
- a conclusion

Writing to Sources

As you gather ideas and information from the texts in the unit, be sure to:

- include a claim,
- address counterarguments,
- use evidence from multiple sources, and
- avoid overly relying on one source.

Introduction to Argumentative Writing

Argumentative writing aims to persuade an audience to agree with a writer's point of view on a topic or issue. In an argumentative essay, a writer states a claim and then provides facts, details, examples, and quotations to support it. Strong argumentative writing effectively uses genre characteristics and craft such as relevant evidence, and a clear organizational structure to persuade readers to accept and agree with the writer's claim. The characteristics of argumentative writing include:

- an introduction
- a thesis statement
- evidence
- transitions
- a conclusion

In addition to these characteristics, argumentative writers also carefully craft their work through their use of a clear and persuasive organizational structure as well as counterarguments and a strong, confident tone. These choices help make the text more persuasive. Effective arguments combine these genre characteristics and craft to engage and convince the reader.

As you continue with this Extended Writing Project, you'll receive more instruction and practice in crafting each of the characteristics of argumentative writing to create your own argumentative essay.

Extended Writing Project and Grammar

Before you get started on your own argumentative essay, read this essay that one student, Alex, wrote in response to the writing prompt. As you read the Model, highlight and annotate the features of argumentative writing that Alex included in his essay.

STUDENT MODEL

Champions of Change

1   When you envision "winning," you might see a runner crossing a finish line with his or her arms extended into the air. Perhaps you visualize the first-place winner of a science fair holding a gold medal with a confident smile. Wins such as these are personal achievements. Individual wins are certainly worthy of praise, but they do not embody what success really means. A true winner takes courageous action and, through his or her fortitude, inspires a series of incremental achievements toward a future goal. This courageous action can take many forms. The decision in the Supreme Court case *Brown v. Board of Education* and George Marshall's speech at Harvard University demonstrate how speakers and writers use words to publicly express ideals. These texts show that winning can mean the courageous act of publicly declaring a need for change in society.

2   In 1951, Oliver Brown's daughter, Linda, was denied entry into Topeka, Kansas's all-white elementary schools on the basis of the "separate but equal" doctrine. The doctrine was set in place in 1896 after the verdict in *Plessy v. Ferguson* legalized racial segregation of public facilities ("Documents Related to Brown v. Board of Education"). In practice, the separate facilities were not actually equal. Schools for African American students received significantly less funding than white schools did ("*Brown v. Board at Fifty*"). After decades of mandated segregation, Oliver Brown, along with others seeking justice, filed a class action suit against the city's board of education. They claimed that segregated schools violated the Fourteenth Amendment, or the right to equal protection under the law ("Documents Related to Brown v. Board of Education"). The children and families who risked their lives to go to school and the lawyers who stuck with the case combined their efforts in defense of African Americans' access to education and, more broadly, their civil rights.

3   The case made it to the Supreme Court of the United States, and in 1952, the justices unanimously ruled that segregation in schools was unconstitutional. Chief Justice Warren opens the decision by stating, "We cannot turn the clock back" and "We must consider public education in the light of its full development and its present place in American life throughout the Nation." Warren's references to time serve multiple purposes. First, he states the simple truth that the past cannot not be changed. Then, by saying, "in the light of its full development," he implies that public education has transformed over time. Life in mid-twentieth century America differed from how it was in "1868, when the [Fourteenth] Amendment was adopted." Yet, by 1952, many people had grown accustomed to segregational practices. The Supreme Court justices challenge this way of thinking by acknowledging that change in this country is inevitable. Thus, it was necessary to honor this inevitability by re-evaluating public education and the laws that regulate it in the present.

4   The decision of the court goes on to demonstrate that the doctrine of "separate but equal" is unequal because it "generates a feeling of inferiority" in African American students. The laws mandated by *Plessy v. Ferguson* had great influence over American life. By declaring "separate but equal" as "inherently unequal," the court risked inciting outrage, but made the determination that they felt was right. Many of those who benefited from segregation did not want it to change. Nonetheless, the justices fulfilled their role of interpreting the law through the Constitution. With this landmark case, the Supreme Court reminded citizens that their way of life can and will evolve. The language in the Supreme Court's verdict further encouraged people to question the legality of segregation in general. The court's bold decision was a win because it motivated more people to continue to fight for civil rights and greater equality on a larger scale. As the ACLU stated upon the 50th anniversary of the decision, Brown v. Board of Education changed America "as a nation, and for the better, and as a result African Americans made tremendous gains in access to education, income, and civic participation, out of which grew a generation of black middle-class leaders in all spheres of our nation's life."

5   George Marshall also uses the power of words to inspire change. Unlike the United States Supreme Court justices who rely on the

clarity of their reasoning to make a point, Marshall uses an emotional appeal to generate meaning, make a point, and persuade his audience in his speech about rebuilding Europe after World War II. Marshall, who was appointed to the position of Secretary of State by President Truman, delivered a commencement address at Harvard University after the Paris Peace Treaties were signed in 1947. In the speech's first sentences, Marshall says, ". . . the world situation is very serious." Here, the author is laying out the purpose for delivering his speech: although the United States and its allies have sacrificed much to win the war, peace cannot be ensured while Europe is on the brink of chaos. Marshall makes a stirring case for the United States to aid their former enemies, and he starts by showing just how high the stakes are for Europe and the world.

6   Marshall then sets out to describe the problem in economic terms and appeal to the patriotic values of his audience. He explains how the Nazi state incorporated the entire German economy into the war effort, disrupting the normal flow of goods between farmers and city dwellers. Marshall argues that unless the United States intervenes, "there can be no political stability and no assured peace." Although Americans may be weary from war, the fight must continue. Marshall charges his audience to continue the war, stating that the United States has a "vast responsibility which history has clearly placed upon our country." With financial assistance from the United States, Europe can re-emerge from devastation. The use of an emotional appeal throughout the speech reminds the audience that the United States is uniquely positioned to champion the rise of free and democratic nations.

7   Marshall had a long history with the European theater before he gave this speech. A five-star general during World War II, Marshall was the creator of the strategy that achieved military victory ("History of the Marshall Plan"). However, he was was convinced that there could be no triumph with Europe in ruins. In its weakened state, it was prey to Russia and communist ideas ("History of the Marshall Plan"). Consequently, the only way the United States could truly win was to assist Europe in recovering politically through economic revitalization. Winning the war for capitalism and free trade meant further sacrifice.

8   Some might say that the mere act of expressing ideas in public hardly constitutes winning, particularly if those words do not incite immediate change. To illustrate, George Marshall's audience was recent Harvard graduates and their families. One might argue that there is no win gained from this speech and that, ultimately, his audience had limited control over the US's aid to foreign countries. This however, misses the purpose of the speech. Marshall may have shared his thinking to an audience at Harvard, but he used this speech to publicly launch his plan for recovery with the full backing of the US State Department. Furthermore, it is important to consider that lasting change rarely happens overnight. Instead, it takes the combined effort of focused leaders like George Marshall to rally others around their vision for progress. Winning comes not just from the final outcome but from the allies and partners gained along the way.

9   When writers make a declaration that challenges the status quo, they put their reputations on the line. They make themselves a target for ridicule and risk alienation. The Supreme Court knew the implications of their verdict. They knew that their decision went against many people's core beliefs. Nevertheless, they made a choice in support of those fighting for civil rights and kick-started a series of changes to American life. Likewise, George Marshall was well aware of the fact that his speech about rebuilding Europe— especially Germany— might be met with resistance, but he continued to move forward with his plans, garnering national attention and international assistance. When writers go against the grain, they can influence more people to share their opinions. Through their declarations, they exhibit the fortitude required to enact change. Courageous writers like Chief Justice Earl Warren and George Marshall embody what it means to win because they effectively challenged entrenched mindsets, inspired their audiences, and built momentum for further growth and change.

Works Cited

"Brown v. Board at Fifty: 'With an Even Hand': A Century of Racial Segregation, 1849–1950." The Library of Congress. www.loc.gov/exhibits/brown/brown-segregation.html#obj20. Accessed 9 November 2019.

"Documents Related to Brown v. Board of Education: Background." U.S. National Archives and Records Administration, 15 August 2016. www.archives.gov/education/lessons/brown-v-board. Accessed 9 November 2019.

"History of the Marshall Plan." The George C. Marshall Foundation. https://www.marshallfoundation.org/marshall/the-marshall-plan/history-marshall-plan/. Accessed 9 November 2019.

WRITE

Writers often take notes about essay ideas before they sit down to write. Think about what you've learned so far about organizing argumentative writing to help you begin prewriting.

- **Purpose:** What does it mean to win? How do the texts support your argument?

- **Audience:** Who is your audience? How do you want them to view the texts differently?

- **Introduction:** How will you introduce the topic and thesis of your essay? Do your topic and thesis present a unique perspective on the texts?

- **Thesis Statement:** What is your claim about the topic or issue? How can you word your claim so it is clear to readers?

- **Evidence:** What evidence will you use to support your claim? What facts, details, examples, and quotations will persuade your audience to agree with your claim?

- **Transitions:** How will you smoothly transition from one idea to another within and across paragraphs?

- **Conclusion:** How will you wrap up your argument? How can you rephrase the main ideas in your argument without being redundant?

Response Instructions

Use the questions in the bulleted list to write a one-paragraph summary. Your summary should describe what you will argue in your argumentative essay like the one above.

Don't worry about including all of the details now; focus only on the most essential and important elements. You will refer to this short summary as you continue through the steps of the writing process.

Extended Writing Project and Grammar

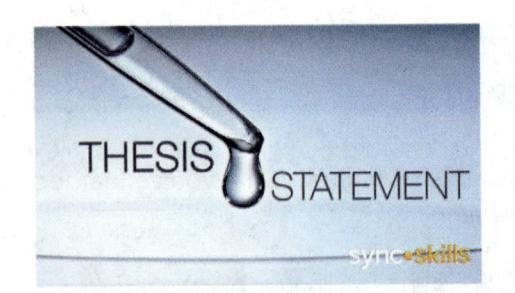

Skill: Thesis Statement

••• CHECKLIST FOR THESIS STATEMENT

Before you begin writing your thesis statement, ask yourself the following questions:

- What is the prompt asking me to write about?
- What claim do I want to make about the topic of this essay?
- Is my claim precise and informative? Is it specific to my topic? How does it inform the reader about my topic?
- Does my thesis statement introduce the body of my essay?
- Where should I place my thesis statement?

Here are some methods for introducing and developing a topic as well as a precise and informative claim:

- think about the central claim of your essay
  - > identify a clear claim you want to introduce, thinking about:
    - o how closely your claim is related to your topic and how specific it is to your supporting details
    - o how your claim includes necessary information to guide the reader through your argument

- your thesis statement should:
  - > let the reader anticipate the content of your essay
  - > help you begin your essay in an organized manner
  - > present your opinion clearly
  - > respond completely to the writing prompt

- consider the best placement for your thesis statement
  - > if your response is short, you may want to get right to the point and present your thesis statement in the first sentence
  - > if your response is longer (as in a formal essay), you can build up to your thesis statement and place it at the end of your introductory paragraph

Extended Writing Project and Grammar

YOUR TURN

Read the thesis statements below. Then, complete the chart by sorting the statements into two categories: effective thesis statements and ineffective thesis statements. Write the corresponding letter for each statement in the appropriate column.

	Thesis Statements
A	In his speech at Harvard University, George Marshall uses emotional appeals to generate sympathy and convince America to help its former enemies.
B	George Marshall's speech was a response to the Paris Peace Treaties in 1947.
C	References to similar cases such as *Sweatt v. Painter* are what ultimately convince the reader of the Supreme Court's claim about segregation in *Brown v. Board of Education*.
D	In the verdict of *Brown v. Board of Education*, the Supreme Court determined that segregation is detrimental to African American students.

Effective Thesis Statements	Ineffective Thesis Statements

WRITE

Follow the steps in the checklist to draft a thesis statement for your argumentative essay.

Extended Writing Project and Grammar

Skill: Organizing Argumentative Writing

••• CHECKLIST FOR ORGANIZING ARGUMENTATIVE WRITING

As you consider how to organize your writing for your argumentative essay, use the following questions as a guide:

- What evidence can I find that would support my claim?
- What information can I look for to establish the significance of my claim?
- What approach can I use to distinguish my claim from any alternate or opposing claims?
- Did I choose an organizing structure that establishes clear relationships between claims and evidence?

Follow these steps to organize your argumentative essay in a way that logically sequences claim(s), counterclaims, reasons, and evidence:

- identify your precise, or specific, claim or claims and the evidence that supports them
- establish the significance of your claim
    > find what others may have written about the topic, and learn why they feel it is important
- distinguish the claim or claims from alternate or opposing claims
- find evidence that distinguishes counterclaims from your own claim
- choose an organizing structure that logically sequences and establishes clear relationships between claims and the evidence presented to support the claims

YOUR TURN

Read the thesis statements below. Then, choose the organizational structure that would be most appropriate for the purpose, topic, and context of the corresponding essay, as well as the audience, and write it in the chart.

Organizational Structure Options			
cause and effect	list advantages and disadvantages	problem and solution	compare and contrast

Thesis Statement	Organizational Structure
Eliminating the use of electronics before going to bed is the most effective method for resolving frequent nightmares.	
The benefits of remodeling the college's library outweigh the cost of construction.	
If people did not obey traffic laws, there would be chaos on the roads.	
Homeschooled students and students who attend school on a campus have more in common than most people may think.	

Extended Writing Project and Grammar

YOUR TURN

Complete the outline by writing an introductory statement, thesis statement, three main ideas for body paragraphs, and concluding ideas for your argumentative essay. Make sure your ideas are appropriate for the purpose, topic, and context of your essay, as well as your audience.

Outline	Summary
Introductory Statement	
Thesis	
Main Idea 1	
Main Idea 2	
Main Idea 3 (present and refute counterargument)	
Conclusion	

Extended Writing Project and Grammar

Skill: Reasons and Relevant Evidence

••• CHECKLIST FOR REASONS AND RELEVANT EVIDENCE

As you determine the reasons and relevant evidence you will need to support your claim, use the following questions as a guide:

- What is my claim (or claims)? What are the strengths and limitations of my claim(s)?
- What relevant evidence do I have? Where could I add more support for my claim(s)?
- What do I know about the audience's:
  - > knowledge about my topic?
  - > concerns and values?
  - > possible biases toward the subject matter?

Use the following steps to help you develop claims fairly and thoroughly:

- establish a claim and counterclaim, which is another claim that attempts to disprove the opposing opinion. Then, evaluate:
  - > how precise, specific, and clear the claim and counterclaim are
  - > the strengths and limitations of both
  - > any biases you have toward both
  - > any gaps in support for your claim, so that your support can be more thorough

- consider your audience and their perspective on your topic. Determine:
  - > their probable prior knowledge about the topic
  - > their concerns and values
  - > any biases they may have toward the subject matter
  - > how you will need to approach your claim to accommodate your audience

- find the most relevant evidence that supports the claim

Extended Writing Project and Grammar

YOUR TURN

Read each quotation from *Brown v. Board of Education* below. Then, complete the chart by sorting the quotations into two categories: those that are relevant and those that are not relevant to the writing topic of "Why segregated public schools are detrimental to a student's ability to learn." Write the corresponding letter for each quotation in the appropriate column.

	Quotations
A	"education is perhaps the most important function of state and local governments"
B	"the policy of separating the races is usually interpreted as denoting the inferiority of the negro group"
C	"a feeling of inferiority . . . may affect their hearts and minds in a way unlikely ever to be undone"
D	"Any language in *Plessy v. Ferguson* contrary to this finding is rejected."

Relevant to Topic	Not Relevant to Topic

YOUR TURN

Complete the chart below by identifying evidence from each text you've chosen. Identifying evidence will help you support your thesis. Then, explain why this evidence is relevant to your thesis.

Text	Relevant Evidence	Explanation

Extended Writing Project and Grammar

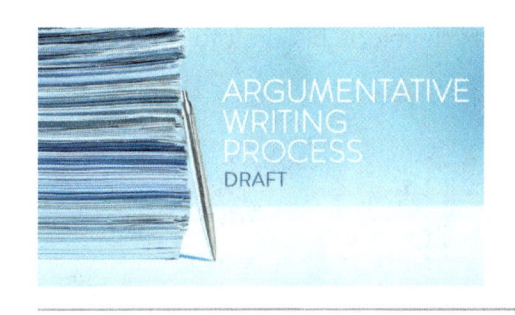

Argumentative Writing Process: Draft

| PLAN | **DRAFT** | REVISE | EDIT AND PUBLISH |

You have already made progress toward writing your argumentative essay. Now it is time to draft your argumentative essay.

✎ WRITE

Use your plan and other responses in your Binder to draft your argumentative essay. You may also have new ideas as you begin drafting. Feel free to explore those new ideas as you have them. You can also ask yourself these questions to ensure that your writing is focused, organized, and developed:

Draft Checklist:

☐ **Focused:** Have I introduced my claim clearly in a thesis statement? Have I included only relevant evidence to support my claim and nothing extraneous that might confuse my readers?

☐ **Organized:** Have I organized my analysis in a way that makes sense? Have I established clear relationships among claims, counterclaims, reasons, and evidence?

☐ **Developed:** Have I clearly stated reasons that support my claim? Have I identified counterclaims in a way my audience can follow? Is my evidence sufficient?

Extended Writing Project and Grammar

Here is Alex's argumentative essay draft. As you read, notice how Alex develops his draft to be focused, organized, and developed.

STUDENT MODEL: FIRST DRAFT

Student Model: First Draft

1 ~~There are lots of ways to win, such as winning a race or a science fair. Wins such as these are isolated achievements. Individual wins are certainly worthy of prase. A true winner takes courageous action and, through his or her fortitude, inspires a series of incremental achievements toward a future goal. This courageous act can take many forms as seen in the decision in the Supreme Court case Brown v. Board of Education and George Marshall's speech at Harvard University demonstrate how speakers and writers use words to publicly express ideals. These texts show that winning can mean the act of declaring a need for change in society.~~

When you envision "winning," you might see a runner crossing a finish line with his or her arms extended into the air. Perhaps you visualize the first-place winner of a science fair holding a gold medal with a confident smile. Wins such as these are personal achievements. Individual wins are certainly worthy of praise, but they do not embody what success really means. A true winner takes courageous action and, through his or her fortitude, inspires a series of incremental achievements toward a future goal. This courageous action can take many forms. The decision in the Supreme Court case *Brown v. Board of Education* and George Marshall's speech at Harvard University demonstrate how speakers and writers use words to publicly express ideals. These texts show that winning can mean the courageous act of publicly declaring a need for change in society.

2 In 1951, Oliver Brown's daughter, Linda, was denied entry into Topeka, Kansas's all-white elementary schools on the basis of the "separate but equal" doctrine. The doctrine was set in place in 1896 after the verdict in *Plessy v. Ferguson* legalized racial segregation of public facilities ("Documents Related to *Brown v. Board of Education*"). In practice, the separate facilities were not actually equal. Schools for African American students received significantly less funding than white schools did ("*Brown v. Board at Fifty*"). After decades of

---

Skill: Introductions

After discussing his introduction with a partner, Alex understands that he needs to add a more interesting "hook." He decides to provide some examples of winning that his reader will be able to envision. Alex also adds clarifying language about individual wins and adjusts his thesis to be more specific, including the words *courageous* and *publicly*.

mandated segregation, Oliver Brown, along with others seeking justice, filed a class action suit against the city's board of education. They claimed that segregated schools violated the Fourteenth Amendment, or the right to equal protection under the law ("Documents Related to *Brown v. Board of Education*"). The children and families who risked their lives to go to school and the lawyers who stuck with the case combined their efforts in defense of African Americans' access to education and, more broadly, their civil rights.

In 1952, the justices unanimously ruled that segregation in schools was unconstitutional. Chief Justice Warren opens the decision by stating, "We cannot turn the clock back" and "We must consider public education in the light of its full development and its present place in American life throughout the Nation." Warren's references to time serve multiple purposes. First, he states the simple truth that the past cannot not be changed. Then, by saying, "in the light of its full development," he implies that public education has transformed over time. Life in mid-twentieth century America differed from how it was in "1868, when the [Fourteenth] Amendment was adopted." Yet, by 1952, many people had grown accustomed to segregational practices. The Supreme Court justices challenge this way of thinking by acknowledging that change in this country is inevitable. Thus, it was necessary to honor this inevitability by re-evaluating public education and the laws that regulate it in the present.

The decision of the court goes on to demonstrate that the doctrine of "separate but equal" is unequal because it "generates a feeling of inferiority" in African American students. The laws mandated by *Plessy v. Ferguson* had great influence over American life. By declaring "separate but equal" as "inherently unequal," the court risked inciting outrage but made the determination that they felt was right. Many of those who benefited from segregation did not want it to change. Nonetheless, the justices fulfilled their role of interpreting the law through the Constitution. With this landmark case, the Supreme Court reminded citizens that their way of life can and will evolve. The language in the Supreme Court's verdict further encouraged people to question the legality of segregation in general. The court's bold decision was a win because it motivated more people to continue to fight for civil rights and greater equality on a larger scale. As the ACLU stated upon the 50th anniversary of the decision, *Brown v Board of Education* changed America "as a

Extended Writing Project and Grammar

NOTES

nation, and for the better, and as a result African Americans made tremendous gains in access to education, income, and civic participation, out of which grew a generation of black middle-class leaders in all spheres of our nation's life."

George Marshall also uses the power of words to inspire change. Unlike the United States Supreme Court justisses who rely on the clarity of their reasoning to make a point, Marshall uses an emotional appeal to generate meaning, make a point, and persuades his audience in his speech about rebuilding Europe after World War II. Marshall, appointed to the position of Secretary of State by President Truman, delivered a commencement address at Harvard University. In the speech's first sentences, Marshall says, "the world situation is very serious." Here, the author is laying out the purpose for delivering his speech. He argues that the United States and its allies have sacrificed much to win the war, peace cannot be ensured while Europe is on the brink of chaos. Marshall makes a stirring case for the United States to aid their former enemies. He starts by showing just how high the stakes are for Europe and the world.

Skill: Transitions

Alex revisits the checklist and realizes that the relationships between his ideas are not always clear. Alex reviews a list of transition words and adds phrases and words such as *however* and *consequently* to improve the flow and clarify the meaning of his paragraph.

Marshall then sets out to describe the problem in economic terms and appeal to the patriotic values of his audience. He explains how the Nazi state incorporated the entire German economy into the war effort, disrupting the normal flow of goods between farmers and city dwellers. Marshall argues that unless the United States intervenes, "there can be no political stability and no assured peace." Although Americans may be tired from war, the fight must continue. Marshall charges his audience to continue the war, stating that the United States has a "vast responsibility which history has clearly placed upon our country." With financial assistance from the United States, Europe can come out from devastation.

~~Marshall had a long history with the European theater before he gave this speech. Marshall was a five-star general during World War II. He created the strategy that achieved military victory ("History of the Marshall Plan"). Marshall was convinced that there could be no triumph with Europe in ruins. In its weakened state, it was prey to Russia and communist ideas ("History of the Marshall Plan). The only way the United States could truly win was to assist Europe in recovering politically through economic revitalization. Winning the war for capitalism and free trade meant further sacrifice.~~

306 Reading & Writing Companion

Marshall had a long history with the European theater before he gave this speech. A five-star general during World War II, Marshall was the creator of the strategy that achieved military victory ("History of the Marshall Plan"). However, he was was convinced that there could be no triumph with Europe in ruins. In its weakened state, it was prey to Russia and communist ideas ("History of the Marshall Plan). Consequently, the only way the United States could truly win was to assist Europe in recovering politically through economic revitalization. Winning the war for capitalism and free trade meant further sacrifice.

Some might say that the mere act of sharing one's ideals publicly doesn't really count as winning, particularly if those words don't work right away. For example, George Marshall presented his speech to a group of recent Harvard graduates and their families. One might argue that there is no win gained from this speech and that those people had no control of the U.S.'s aid to foreign countries. Marshall may have shared his thinking to an audience at Harvard, but he was the secretary of state. He just used this opportunity to tell the public about his ideas. He just used this opportunity to tell the public about his ideas. Also, lasting change rarely happens overnight. Instead, it takes the combined effort of focused leaders these to rally others around their vision for progress. Winning comes not just from the final outcome but from the allies and partners gained along the way.

~~When writers make a declaration that challenges the status quo, they put their reputations on the line. They make themselves a target for ridicule, being alienated, and discrimination. The Supreme Court knew the implications of their verdict. They knew that their decision went against many people's core beliefs. Nevertheless, they made a choice in support of those fighting for civil rights and kick started a series of changes to American life. When writers go against the grain they can influence more people to share their opinions through their declarations, these texts exemplify the fortitude required to enact change.~~

When writers make a declaration that challenges the status quo, they put their reputations on the line. They make themselves a target for ridicule and risk alienation. The Supreme Court knew the

---

Skill: Conclusions

Alex realizes he didn't include any summarizing thoughts for "The Marshall Plan Speech." He also notices that his final sentence could better capture his thesis, and he believes he can further improve his essay by leaving readers with a memorable final idea. He adds a reference to "The Marshall Plan Speech" to the conclusion and writes an additional closing sentence to more meaningfully capture his thesis.

implications of their verdict. They knew that their decision went against many people's core beliefs. Nevertheless, they made a choice in support of those fighting for civil rights and kick-started a series of changes to American life. Likewise, George Marshall was well aware of the fact that his speech about rebuilding Europe—especially Germany— might be met with resistance, but he continued to move forward with his plans, garnering national attention and international assistance. When writers go against the grain, they can influence more people to share their opinions. Through their declarations, they exhibit the fortitude required to enact change. Courageous writers like Chief Justice Earl Warren and George Marshall embody what it means to win because they effectively challenged entrenched mindsets, inspired their audiences, and built momentum for further growth and change.

Extended Writing Project and Grammar

Skill: Introductions

••• CHECKLIST FOR INTRODUCTIONS

Before you write your introduction, ask yourself the following questions:

- What is my claim? In addition:
  - > Do I state my claim in a clear and powerful thesis statement?
  - > How can I make my claim more precise and informative?
  - > Have I included why my claim is significant to discuss?
- How can I introduce my topic? Have I organized complex ideas, concepts, and information so that each new element builds on the previous element and creates a unified whole?
- How will I "hook" my reader's interest? I might:
  - > start with an attention-grabbing statement
  - > begin with an intriguing question
  - > use descriptive words to set a scene

Below are two strategies to help you introduce your precise claim and topic clearly in an introduction:

- Peer Discussion
  - > Talk about your topic with a partner, explaining what you already know and your ideas about your topic.
  - > Write notes about the ideas you have discussed and any new questions you may have.
  - > Review your notes, and think about what your claim or controlling idea will be.
  - > Write a possible "hook."

- Freewriting
  - > Freewrite for 10 minutes about your topic. Don't worry about grammar, punctuation, or having fully formed ideas. The point of freewriting is to discover ideas.
  - > Review your notes, and think about what your claim or controlling idea will be.
  - > Write a possible "hook."

Extended Writing Project and Grammar

YOUR TURN

Choose the best answer to each question.

1. Which of the following elements belongs in an introductory paragraph?

    ○ A. a counterargument with supporting evidence
    ○ B. a list of reasons to support a claim
    ○ C. relevant evidence to justify a claim
    ○ D. a thesis statement containing a claim

2. The following introduction is from a previous draft of Alex's essay. Alex needs to add a hook to grab his audience's attention and introduce his topic. Which sentence could he add to achieve this goal?

> A true winner takes courageous action and, through his or her fortitude, inspires a series of incremental achievements toward a future goal. This courageous act can take many forms. The decision in the Supreme Court case *Brown v. Board of Education* and George Marshall's speech at Harvard University demonstrate how speakers and writers use words to publicly express their ideals. These texts show that winning can mean the act of declaring a need for change in society.

    ○ A. The texts in this unit portrayed a range of individual experiences.
    ○ B. Have you ever wondered what makes someone a winner? Is it individual victory? Or personal growth? Or is it something more complex?
    ○ C. "The Marshall Plan Speech" was written to spark change in society.
    ○ D. The texts I will discuss cover a variety of arguments and points of view.

WRITE

Use the checklist to revise the introduction of your argumentative essay.

Extended Writing Project and Grammar

Skill: Transitions

••• CHECKLIST FOR TRANSITIONS

Before you revise your current draft to include transitions, think about:

- the key ideas you discuss in your body paragraphs
- the relationships among your claim(s), reasons, and evidence
- the relationship between your claim(s) and counterclaims
- the logical progression of your argument

Next, reread your current draft and note places in your essay where:

- the relationships among your claim(s), counterclaims, and reasons and evidence are unclear
- you could add linking words, vary sentence structure, or use other transitional devices to make your argument more cohesive. Look for:

  > sudden jumps in your ideas

  > breaks between paragraphs where the ideas in the next paragraph do not logically follow from the points in the previous paragraph

  > repetitive sentence structures

Revise your draft to use words, phrases, and clauses as well as varied syntax to link the major sections of your essay, create cohesion, and clarify the relationships between claim(s) and reasons, between reasons and evidence, and between claim(s) and counterclaims, using the following questions as a guide:

- Are there unifying relationships among the claims, reasons, and evidence I present in my argument?
- How do my claim(s) and counterclaim(s) relate?
- Have I made these relationships clear?
- How can I link major sections of my essay using words, phrases, clauses, and varied syntax?

Extended Writing Project and Grammar

YOUR TURN

Choose the best answer to each question.

1. Below is a passage from the next draft of Alex's essay. The connection between the ideas in the underlined sentence is unclear. What transition should Alex use to replace *and* after "The court's bold decision was a win" to make his writing more coherent?

> Nonetheless, the justices fulfilled their role of interpreting the law through the constitution. With this landmark case, the Supreme Court reminded citizens that their way of life can and will evolve. The language in the Supreme Court's verdict encouraged people to question the legality of segregation in general. <u>The court's bold decision was a win and the decision motivated more people to continue to fight for civil rights and greater equality on a larger scale.</u>

- A. another key point
- B. in the final analysis
- C. because
- D. prior to

2. Below is a passage from a previous draft of Alex's essay. Alex did not use an appropriate transition to show the relationship between the ideas in sentences 1 and 2. In sentence 2, which of the following transitions is the best replacement for *Conversely*?

> (1) Some might say that the mere act of expressing ideas in public hardly constitutes winning, particularly if those words do not incite immediate change. (2) Conversely, George Marshall delivered his speech at a small lunch to thirteen Harvard graduates. (3) One might argue that there is no win gained from this speech and that, ultimately, his audience had no control over the U.S.'s aid to foreign countries.

- A. Eventually
- B. To illustrate
- C. Consequently
- D. On balance

WRITE

Use the questions in the checklist to revise your use of transitions in a section of your argumentative essay.

Extended Writing Project and Grammar

Skill: Conclusions

••• CHECKLIST FOR CONCLUSIONS

Before you write your conclusion, ask yourself the following questions:

- How can I rephrase the thesis or main idea?
- How can I write my conclusion so that it supports and follows from the information I presented?
- How can I communicate the importance of my topic? What information do I need?

Below are two strategies to help you provide a concluding statement or section that follows from and supports the information or explanation you presented:

- Peer Discussion
  - > After you have written your introduction and body paragraphs, talk with a partner about what you want readers to remember, writing notes about your discussion.
  - > Think about how you can articulate, or express, the significance of your topic in the conclusion.
  - > Rephrase your main idea to show the depth of your knowledge and support for the information you presented.
  - > Write your conclusion.

- Freewriting
  - > Freewrite for 10 minutes about what you might include in your conclusion. Don't worry about grammar, punctuation, or having fully formed ideas. The point of freewriting is to discover ideas.
  - > Think about how you can articulate, or express, the significance of your topic in the conclusion.
  - > Rephrase your main idea to show the depth of your knowledge and support for the information you presented.
  - > Write your conclusion.

Extended Writing Project and Grammar

YOUR TURN

Choose the best answer to each question.

1. Which of the following elements belongs in a concluding paragraph?

   - A. a statement that rephrases the thesis
   - B. reasons and relevant evidence to support a claim
   - C. transitions to link major sections of a text
   - D. a "hook" and the first appearance of the thesis statement containing a claim

2. Below is Alex's conclusion from another draft. What is one piece of information that Alex needs to include as he continues to revise?

> When writers make a declaration that challenges the status quo, they put their reputations on the line. They make themselves a target for ridicule and risk alienation. The Supreme Court knew the implications of their verdict, but they did it anyways. Likewise, George Marshall was well aware of the fact that his speech about rebuilding Europe—especially Germany—might be met with resistance, but he continued to move forward with his plans, garnering national attention and international assistance.

   - A. Alex neglects to support his ideas with relevant evidence.
   - B. Alex neglects to discuss both of the texts that he has selected.
   - C. Alex needs to discuss other texts besides the two mentioned in his essay.
   - D. Alex needs to explain how these courageous actions connect to the idea of winning.

WRITE

Use the checklist to revise the conclusion of your argumentative essay.

Extended Writing Project and Grammar

Argumentative Writing Process: Revise

| PLAN | DRAFT | **REVISE** | EDIT AND PUBLISH |

You have written a draft of your argumentative essay. You have also received input from your peers about how to improve it. Now you are going to revise your draft.

⬅ REVISION GUIDE

Examine your draft to find areas for revision. Keep in mind your purpose and audience as you revise for clarity, development, organization, and style. Use the guide below to help you review:

Review	Revise	Example
	Clarity	
Identify all pronouns, and determine if it is clear to whom you are referring.	Use the authors' or individuals' names to identify whom you are talking about.	Instead, it takes the combined effort of focused leaders like ~~these~~ George Marshall and the members of the Supreme Court to rally others around their vision for progress.

Extended Writing Project and Grammar

Review	Revise	Example
\multicolumn{3}{c}{**Development**}
Identify the textual evidence that supports your claims as well as places where you have included commentary. Annotate places where you feel there is not enough textual evidence to support your ideas or where you have failed to provide commentary.	Focus on a single idea or claim, and add your personal reflections in the form of commentary or add support in the form of textual evidence.	Marshall charges his audience to continue the war, stating that the United States has a "vast responsibility which history has clearly placed upon our country." With financial assistance from the United States, Europe can re-emerge from devastation. The use of an emotional appeal throughout the speech reminds the audience that the United States is uniquely positioned to champion the rise of free and democratic nations.
\multicolumn{3}{c}{**Organization**}
Review your body paragraphs. Are they coherent? Identify and annotate any sentences within and across paragraphs that don't flow in a clear and logical way.	Rewrite the sentences so they are clear and flow logically.	The children and families who risked their lives to go to school and the lawyers who stuck with the case combined their efforts in defense of African Americans' access to education and, more broadly, their civil rights. ~~In 1952, the justices unanimously ruled that segregation in schools was unconstitutional.~~ The case made it to the Supreme Court of the United States, and in 1952 the justices unanimously ruled that segregation in schools was unconstitutional. Chief Justice Warren opens the decision by stating, "we cannot turn the clocks back" and "We must consider public education in the light of its full development and its present place in America."

Review	Revise	Example
Style: Word Choice		
Identify any weak adjectives, nouns, or verbs.	Replace weak adjectives, nouns, or verbs with strong, descriptive, and precise language.	Although Americans may be ~~tired~~ weary from war, the fight must continue. Marshall charges his audience to continue the war, stating that the United States has a "vast responsibility which history has clearly placed upon our country." With financial assistance from the United States, Europe can ~~come out~~ re-emerge from devastation.
Style: Sentence Fluency		
Read aloud your writing and listen to the way the text sounds. Does it sound choppy? Or does it flow smoothly with rhythm, movement, and emphasis on important details and events?	Rewrite a key passage, making your sentences longer or shorter to achieve a better flow of writing and the effect you want your reader to feel.	Here, the author is laying out the purpose for delivering his speech. ~~He argues that:~~ Although the United States and its allies have sacrificed much to win the war, peace cannot be ensured while Europe is on the brink of chaos. Marshall makes a stirring case for the United States to aid their former enemies. ~~He,~~ and he starts by showing just how high the stakes are for Europe and the world.

✏️ WRITE

Use the revision guide, as well as your peer reviews, to help you evaluate your argumentative essay to determine areas that should be revised.

Extended Writing Project and Grammar

Skill: Style

CHECKLIST FOR STYLE

First, reread the draft of your argumentative essay and identify the following:

- slang, colloquialisms, contractions, abbreviations, or a conversational tone
- places where you could use academic language in order to help persuade your readers
- the use of the first person (*I*) or the second person (*you*)
- statements that express judgment or emotion, rather than objective statements that rely on facts and evidence
- places where you could vary sentence structure and length by using compound, complex, and compound-complex sentences

    > for guidance on effective ways of varying syntax, use a style guide

- incorrect uses of the conventions of standard English for grammar, spelling, capitalization, and punctuation

Establish and maintain a formal style in your essay, using the following questions as a guide:

- Have I avoided slang in favor of academic language?
- Did I consistently use a third-person perspective, using third-person pronouns (*he*, *she*, *they*)?
- Have I maintained an objective tone without expressing my own judgments and emotions?
- Have I used varied sentence lengths and different sentence structures? Did I consider using style guides to learn about effective ways of varying syntax?

    > Where should I make some sentences longer by using conjunctions to connect independent clauses, dependent clauses, and phrases?

    > Where should I make some sentences shorter by separating independent clauses?

- Have I correctly used the conventions of standard English?

YOUR TURN

Choose the best answer to each question.

1. Which type of stylistic error did Alex make in this line from a previous draft?

> I think Marshall was a very strong person and he gives me hope.

- A. Alex's use of capitalization is incorrect.
- B. The sentence is too complex.
- C. Alex uses the pronouns *I* and *me* and makes a statement based on his feelings.
- D. Alex uses slang.

2. Below are two sentences from a previous draft of Alex's essay. How should these sentences be rewritten to address possible stylistic errors?

> The use of a series of emotional appeals throughout the speech challenges the complacency of allies who think the war is finished. And it also encourages listeners to really think hard about the decision at hand.

- A. The use of a series of emotional appeals throughout the speech challenges the complacency of allies who think the war is finished and I think it encourages listeners to think critically about the decision at hand.
- B. The use of a series of emotional appeals throughout the speech challenges the complacency of allies who think the war is finished encourages listeners to think critically about the decision at hand.
- C. The use of a series of emotional appeals throughout the speech challenges the complacency of allies who think the war is finished and encourages listeners to think critically about the decision at hand.
- D. These sentences should not be changed.

WRITE

Use the checklist to revise a paragraph of your argumentative essay to improve the style.

Extended Writing Project and Grammar

Grammar: Sentence Fragments

A sentence fragment is a group of words that lacks a subject, a predicate, or both. A fragment does not express a complete thought.

Every sentence must have a subject and a predicate to express a complete thought. The subject part of a sentence names whom or what the sentence is about. The predicate part tells what the subject does or has. It can also describe what the subject is or is like.

Term	Definition	Example
complete sentence	contains a subject and a predicate to express a complete thought	He objected to the T-shirt logo, calling it disgusting and vulgar. Catch the Moon
sentence fragment	a group of words that lacks a subject, a predicate, or both	Not too far. Call It Sleep

Extended Writing Project and Grammar

YOUR TURN

1. What change is needed to form a complete sentence?

   > Barked continually from midnight until 4:00 A.M.

   - A. Add the subject: *My neighbor's dog.*
   - B. Remove the words **from midnight.**
   - C. Change **continually** to *constantly.*
   - D. No change needs to be made.

2. What change is needed to form a complete sentence?

   > My older sister Becky, who had twins at the beginning of January.

   - A. Add *healthy* before **twins.**
   - B. Add the conjunction *but* after **twins.**
   - C. Add the predicate: *decided to work from home.*
   - D. No change needs to be made.

3. What change is needed to form a complete sentence?

   > No one but Marella was in the car when the accident occurred.

   - A. Add a detail about whose car it was.
   - B. Add a colon after **Marella.**
   - C. Remove the phrase **in the car.**
   - D. No change needs to be made.

4. What change is needed to form a complete sentence?

   > Walked along Sixth Street, looked up, and saw a hot-air balloon.

   - A. Before **walked,** add the subject: *My friends and I.*
   - B. Replace the period with a question mark.
   - C. Add *Wandered and* in front of **walked.**
   - D. No change needs to be made.

Reading & Writing Companion

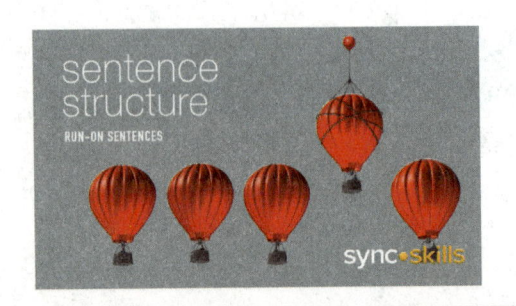

Grammar: Run-On Sentences

A run-on sentence is two or more sentences incorrectly written as one sentence. Correct a run-on sentence by doing one of the following:

- Change the independent clauses into two separate sentences with a period after each
- Separate the independent clauses with a semicolon (;)
- Separate the independent clauses with a comma and a coordinating conjunction (*and, or, but*)
- Separate the independent clauses with a subordinating conjunction (*because, although,* etc.)
- Separate the independent clauses with a semicolon or period and then add a conjunctive adverb followed by a comma (*however, finally, therefore,* etc.)

Run-On Sentence	Strategy	Text
Scot has arrived, and brings news that he expected to find all peace and Quietness here as he left them at home, you will have more particulars than I am able to send you, from much better hands.	Add a period to separate the independent clauses into two separate sentences.	Scot has arrived, and brings news that he expected to find all peace and Quietness here as he left them at home. You will have more particulars than I am able to send you, from much better hands. Letters to John Adams
They walked through the diningroom where the firebrick in the hearth was as yellow as the day it was laid, his mother could not bear to see it blackened.	Remove the comma and add a subordinating conjunction.	They walked through the diningroom where the firebrick in the hearth was as yellow as the day it was laid because his mother could not bear to see it blackened. The Road

YOUR TURN

1. How should this sentence be changed?

   > It is smaller than the crane it has a longer neck.

   - A. Add a comma after **crane**.
   - B. Add a comma and *but* after **crane**.
   - C. Put a period after **crane**.
   - D. No change needs to be made to this sentence.

2. How should this sentence be changed?

   > My aunt Debra owns three dogs she wants to get another one.

   - A. Add a comma after **dogs**.
   - B. Add *big* before **dogs**.
   - C. Add a comma and the word *but* after **dogs**.
   - D. No change needs to be made to this sentence.

3. How should this sentence be changed?

   > My jeans were hanging on the clothesline, and a wren tried to build a nest in them.

   - A. Replace **and** with *therefore*.
   - B. Delete the word **and**.
   - C. Change the comma to a semicolon.
   - D. No change needs to be made to this sentence.

4. How should this sentence be changed?

   > Sharon brought cheesecake to the class reunion Marla brought brownies.

   - A. Add a comma after **reunion**.
   - B. Add a comma and the word *and* after **reunion**.
   - C. Add a semicolon and the word *and* after **reunion**.
   - D. No change needs to be made to this sentence.

Extended Writing Project and Grammar

Grammar: Parallel Structure

Parallel structure, or parallelism, is a deliberate repetition of words, phrases, or other grammatical structures to achieve an effect. Parallel structure creates a pattern to show that two or more ideas have equal weight in a sentence. Words, phrases, or clauses joined by a conjunction should be parallel within a sentence. Using parallel structure also helps writers clarify their ideas and avoid extra unnecessary language. Read below to learn more about situations in which writers often use parallel structure.

Strategy	Not Parallel	Parallel
Use parallel structure when listing elements.	Some common gases are colorless, odorless, and **they won't hurt you**.	Some common gases are colorless, odorless, and **harmless**.
Use parallel structure when using correlative conjunctions. Correlative conjunctions are used in pairs and include the following: — either/or — neither/nor — not only/but also — both/and	The waterfall not only looked beautiful but also **was making a soothing sound**.	The waterfall not only looked beautiful but also **sounded soothing**.
Use parallel structure when comparing elements.	Running is just as effective exercise as **when you ride a bike**.	Running is just as effective exercise as **riding a bike**.
Use parallel structure when using the gerund, or -ing, form of words.	James enjoys outdoor activities such as hiking, camping, and **to play tennis**.	James enjoys outdoor activities such as hiking, camping, and **playing tennis**.
Use parallel structure with infinitive phrases, or verbs preceded by the word *to*. Note that it is necessary to write *to* only before the first infinitive, not before each one.	Thom liked to read the paper, cut out articles, and **taping** them to the wall.	Thom liked to read the paper, cut out articles, and **tape** them to the wall.

YOUR TURN

1. How should this sentence be changed?

   > Traveling over the winter holidays can be difficult because the airports are crowded, the lines are long, and bad weather.

   - A. Replace **the airports are crowded** with **crowded airports.**
   - B. Replace **bad weather** with **the weather is bad.**
   - C. Replace **the lines are long** with **long lines.**
   - D. No change needs to be made to this sentence.

2. How should this sentence be changed?

   > The campers had to dive off the dock, swim across the lake, and paddle back in a canoe.

   - A. Insert **to** before **swim.**
   - B. Insert **to** before **paddle.**
   - C. Replace **to dive** with **diving.**
   - D. No change needs to be made to this sentence.

3. How should this sentence be changed?

   > William looked behind the door, in the closet, and checked under the bed, but he could not find his other sneaker.

   - A. Delete **checked.**
   - B. Replace **looked** with **is looking.**
   - C. Insert **still** after **he.**
   - D. No change needs to be made to this sentence.

4. How should this sentence be changed?

   > Mom's morning routine is to make coffee, read the paper, and getting dressed for work.

   - A. Replace **to make** with **making.**
   - B. Replace **read** with **reading.**
   - C. Replace **getting** with **get.**
   - D. No change needs to be made to this sentence.

Extended Writing Project and Grammar

Argumentative Writing Process: Edit and Publish

| PLAN | DRAFT | REVISE | **EDIT AND PUBLISH** |

You have revised your argumentative essay based on your peer feedback and your own examination.

Now, it is time to edit your argumentative essay. When you revised, you focused on the content of your argumentative essay. You probably looked at your essay's clarity and development. When you edit, you focus on the mechanics of your essay, paying close attention to things like grammar and punctuation.

Use the checklist below to guide you as you edit:

- ☐ Does each sentence express a complete thought?
- ☐ Have I properly structured sentences with more than one independent clause?
- ☐ Have I used parallel structure properly?
- ☐ Have I spelled everything correctly?

Notice some edits Alex has made:

- Corrected a spelling mistake
- Changed a verb form to create parallelism
- Added a verb to correct a sentence fragment

Extended Writing Project and Grammar

George Marshall also uses the power of words to inspire change. Unlike the United States Supreme Court ~~justisses~~ justices who rely on the clarity of their reasoning to make a point, Marshall uses an emotional appeal to generate meaning, make a point, and ~~persuades~~ persuade his audience in his speech about rebuilding Europe after World War II. Marshall, who was appointed to the position of Secretary of State by President Truman, delivered a commencement address at Harvard University after the Paris Peace Treaties were signed in 1947. In the speech's first sentences, Marshall says, "the world situation is very serious." Here, the author is laying out the purpose for delivering his speech.

WRITE

Use the questions in the checklist, as well as your peer reviews, to help you evaluate your argumentative essay to determine places that need editing. Then, edit your essay to correct those errors.

Once you have made all your corrections, you are ready to publish your work. You can distribute your writing to family and friends, hang it on a bulletin board, or post it on your blog. If you publish online, share the link with your family, friends, and classmates.

studysync

We Hold These Truths

UNIT 6

We Hold These Truths

How do stories capture change?

Literary Focus: **POSTMODERNISM**

Texts

🔗 Paired Readings

334	Literary Focus: **POSTMODERNISM**
342	**Song of Solomon** FICTION Toni Morrison
348	**The Warmth of Other Suns: The Epic Story of America's Great Migration** INFORMATIONAL TEXT Isabel Wilkerson
352	**Fences** DRAMA August Wilson
364	**American Horse** Talk Back Text FICTION Louise Erdrich
382	**So Much Happiness** POETRY Naomi Shihab Nye
385	**Literary Seminar: Democratizing Literature**
391	**Little Miss Sunshine** DRAMA Michael Arndt
397	**Hyperbole and a Half** INFORMATIONAL TEXT Allie Brosh
403	**Hunger: A Memoir of (My) Body** INFORMATIONAL TEXT Roxane Gay
410	**Boyhood** DRAMA Richard Linklater
419	**The Immortal Horizon** INFORMATIONAL TEXT Leslie Jamison
428	**The Four Foods** FICTION Dalia Rosenfeld
434	**Gaman** POETRY Christine Kitano
437	**Demeter's Prayer to Hades** POETRY Rita Dove

Reading & Writing Companion

Please note that excerpts and passages in the StudySync® library and this workbook are intended as touchstones to generate interest in an author's work. The excerpts and passages do not substitute for the reading of entire texts, and StudySync® strongly recommends that students seek out and purchase the whole literary or informational work in order to experience it as the author intended. Links to online resellers are available in our digital library. In addition, complete works may be ordered through an authorized reseller by filling out and returning to StudySync® the order form enclosed in this workbook.

Extended Oral Project and Grammar

444 | **Oral Presentation Process: Plan**

Organizing an Oral Presentation
Evaluating Sources
Considering Audience and Purpose
Persuasive Techniques

468 | **Oral Presentation Process: Draft**

Transitions
Reasons and Evidence
Sources and Citations
Communicating Ideas
Engaging in Discourse

490 | **Oral Presentation Process: Revise**

Grammar: Commonly Misspelled Words
Grammar: Sentence Variety—Openings
Grammar: Sentence Variety—Sentence Length

499 | **Oral Presentation Process: Edit and Present**

Talk Back Text

Talk Back Texts are works from a later period that engage with the themes and tropes of the unit's literary focus. Demonstrating that literature is always in conversation, these texts provide dynamic new perspectives to complement the unit's more traditional chronology.

504 | Text Fulfillment through StudySync

Unit 6: We Hold These Truths
How do stories capture change?

MICHAEL ARNDT

American screenwriter Michael Arndt (b. 1970) is best known for his Academy Award–winning screenplay *Little Miss Sunshine*, but he was also nominated for Best Adapted Screenplay for *Toy Story 3*, which made him the first screenwriter to be nominated for these awards for his first two scripts. He graduated from New York University and worked as a personal assistant to actor Matthew Broderick (*Ferris Bueller's Day Off, Glory, The Producers*) until Arndt focused on writing full time. Arndt wrote the original script for *Little Miss Sunshine* in just three days.

RITA DOVE

The youngest person and first African American appointed Poet Laureate Consultant by the Library of Congress, Rita Dove (b. 1952) was born in Akron, Ohio. She was a top student and was invited to the White House as a Presidential Scholar. Dove graduated from Miami University in Ohio and received a Fulbright Scholarship, which allowed her to study in Germany. She returned to the United States to earn her master of fine arts from the University of Iowa. Her book *Thomas and Beulah* won the Pulitzer Prize for Poetry in 1987.

LOUISE ERDRICH

Louise Erdrich (b. 1954) was born in Little Falls, Minnesota, and attended Dartmouth College, where she was one of the first women admitted to the school. In 1979 she earned a master of arts from Johns Hopkins University. She won numerous awards, including the Pushcart Prize in Poetry, the National Book Award for Fiction (*The Round House*), and the Anisfield-Wolf Book Award (*The Plague of Doves,* which was also a finalist for the Pulitzer Prize for Fiction). She currently lives in Minnesota and owns a small, independent bookstore.

ROXANE GAY

Best-selling author of *Bad Feminist* and *Hunger*, Roxane Gay (b. 1974) was born in Nebraska. A Yale graduate, she later attended the University of Nebraska (MA) and Michigan Technological Institute, where she earned her PhD. She wrote a dissertation titled "Subverting the Subject Position: Toward a New Discourse About Students as Writers and Engineering Students as Technical Communicators." Her work has appeared in *Tin House* and *McSweeney's*, and Gay now serves as a contributing opinion writer for the *New York Times* and is essays editor for *The Rumpus*.

LESLIE JAMISON

Author of *The Recovering: Intoxication and Its Aftermath*, *The Empathy Exams*, and *The Gin Closet*, California native, and director of Columbia University's graduate nonfiction writing program Leslie Jamison attended Harvard University as an undergraduate. She earned her MFA from the Iowa Writers' Workshop and her PhD from Yale University. Jamison's writing has appeared in the *New York Times*, *Harper's*, and *The Believer*. She lives in Brooklyn, New York.

CHRISTINE KITANO

Christine Kitano (b. 1985) was raised in Los Angeles, California, to a first-generation immigrant mother from Korea and a second-generation Japanese American father. She received her master of fine arts in creative writing from Syracuse University and her PhD in creative writing from Texas Tech University. She teaches at Ithaca College, where she serves as an assistant professor of creative writing, poetry, and Asian American literature. She is the author of the collections of poetry *Sky Country* and *Birds of Paradise*. Kitano lives in Ithaca, New York.

RICHARD LINKLATER

Born in Texas, Richard Linklater (b. 1960) is an American filmmaker and storyteller. Although a college dropout, Linklater wrote, directed, and produced *Dazed and Confused* (1993), a film that captured the angst of teenagers on their last day of high school. In 2002 he began filming *Boyhood*, a magnum opus that took more than a decade to make. The film, released in 2014, tracks the coming of age of one boy and his absent father, with a cast that ages throughout the film. *Boyhood* won the Golden Globe for Best Motion Picture, Drama, and Linklater won Best Director.

TONI MORRISON

"A writer's life and work are not a gift to mankind," says author Toni Morrison (b. 1931), "they are a necessity." Over the course of her nearly five-decade-long career, Morrison's writing has been both a beautiful gift to American culture and necessary to its moral conscience. Born in Ohio, Morrison grew up in a family that celebrated the stories, songs, and folktales of African American culture. In her acclaimed novels, Morrison draws inspiration from this rich tradition to create lyrical tales of black life in America.

NAOMI SHIHAB NYE

Both songwriter and poet, Naomi Shihab Nye (b. 1952) uses her work to explore the power of place and identity. Her book *Habibi* charts an autobiographical course, following an Arab American teenager's move to Jerusalem. Nye's collection *Never in a Hurry: Essays on People and Places* follows Nye on her travels across the world as she meets people and learns about what connects each of us to a greater shared humanity. The Pushcart Prize-winning author lives in San Antonio, Texas.

DALIA ROSENFELD

Graduate of the Iowa Writers' Workshop, freelance journalist, and creative writing instructor at Bar Ilan University in Israel, Dalia Rosenfeld has seen her work published in the *Atlantic*, *Los Angeles Review*, *Mississippi Review*, *The Forward*, and the *Michigan Quarterly Review*. She received her bachelor of arts in Jewish studies from Oberlin College. Rosenfeld has won the Tobias Wolff Award for Fiction and the Mississippi Review Prize. She is the author of the short story collection *The Worlds We Think We Know* and lives in Tel Aviv with her three children.

ISABEL WILKERSON

Pulitzer Prize–winning author Isabel Wilkerson (b. 1961) interviewed more than twelve hundred people over the course of fifteen years for *The Warmth of Other Suns*, a book that examines the lives of three people searching for a better life after fleeing oppression and violence in the South. She was the first black woman to win the Pulitzer Prize for Journalism for her work in 1994 as the Chicago Bureau Chief of the *New York Times*. Toni Morrison called the *The Warmth of Other Suns*, a *New York Times* Best Seller, "profound, necessary, and a delight to read."

AUGUST WILSON

August Wilson (1945–2005) was born in Pittsburgh, Pennsylvania, the fourth of seven children. At age sixteen he dropped out of school to work but visited the library when he could. Through reading books, especially the works of Langston Hughes, Wilson discovered his passion and decided to become a writer, much to his mother's dismay. Wilson eventually helped establish a theater company, moved to Minnesota, worked as a chef to finance his art, and won two Pulitzer Prizes for his plays *Fences* and *The Piano Lesson*.

ALLIE BROSH

Allie Brosh (b. 1985) created the webcomic and blog that evolved into the book *Hyperbole and a Half: Unfortunate Situations, Flawed Coping Mechanisms, Mayhem, and Other Things That Happened*, a *New York Times* Best Seller. Brosh's writing covers topics that include depression, anxiety, and the chasm that can separate people suffering from mental illness from feeling accepted or understood. When Brosh isn't writing, she enjoys spending time with her pets at her home in Oregon.

LITERARY FOCUS:
Postmodernism

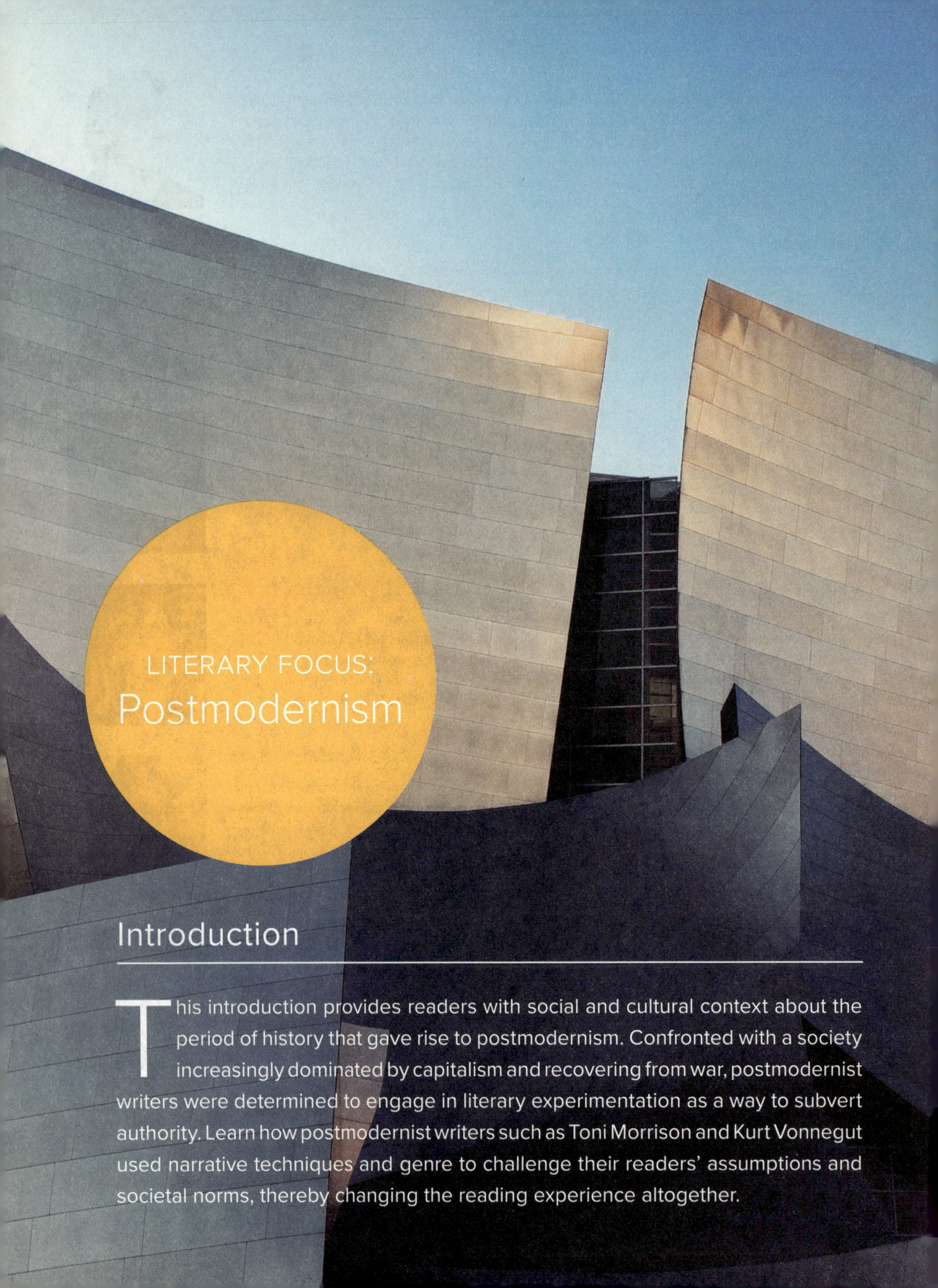

Introduction

This introduction provides readers with social and cultural context about the period of history that gave rise to postmodernism. Confronted with a society increasingly dominated by capitalism and recovering from war, postmodernist writers were determined to engage in literary experimentation as a way to subvert authority. Learn how postmodernist writers such as Toni Morrison and Kurt Vonnegut used narrative techniques and genre to challenge their readers' assumptions and societal norms, thereby changing the reading experience altogether.

Literary Focus: Postmodernism

"... a single text can embody a multiplicity of meanings."

1 Have you ever read a text and struggled to figure out which character was the protagonist? Have you had difficulty recounting the plot of a film because it was not presented in chronological order? Perhaps in your inability to categorize such a text or film you simply described it as "experimental." It's possible that these representations of dismantled narrative techniques were examples of postmodernism, a trend that rejects universalities and embraces instability. Postmodernist writing can be difficult to identify because it is the nature of postmodernism to evade categorization. Much of today's popular media that seem to defy genre characteristics operate within the realm of postmodernism. Even these texts, however, have patterns and common characteristics. Learning the history of how postmodernist trends emerged and how they function in contemporary society will better prepare you to see the influence of postmodernism in your daily life.

Capitalism

2 Postmodernism is not a clear-cut movement with a definitive start and end date. As with other literary trends, many scholars choose to trace the development of postmodernism in relation to major events in history and their effect on the economy and patterns of cultural expression. For example, comparative literature professor and scholar Fredric Jameson outlines the evolution of realism, Modernism, and postmodernism according to economist Ernest Mandel's three stages of capitalism:

- The first stage is free market capitalism, a system in which goods and services are privately owned by individuals or businesses rather than controlled by an authority. In the eighteenth and late nineteenth centuries, Western Europe, England, and the United States witnessed fast-paced technological advancements, such as the growth of the steel industry and steam-driven motors, that made it possible to transport goods and people more efficiently. This period is associated with the development of literary realism and naturalism.

Literary Focus: Postmodernism

- The next stage of capitalism is monopoly capitalism, a system from the late nineteenth century until the mid-1900s in which corporations became larger and more powerful and international markets were developed. This phase of capitalism is connected to literary modernism.

- The third stage, **late capitalism**, started after World War II and is still happening now. Late capitalism is a post-industrial economic system characterized by globalization, mass media, and consumption. In this modern era of capitalism, the media, consumerism, mass communication, and computer technology are ingrained in everyday life.

3   Many critics agree that the development of postmodernist thought is concurrent with the emergence of late capitalism. Postmodernists respond to late capitalism with an anti-authoritarian attitude. They reject generalizing theories, universalities, all-encompassing narratives, and ideals constructed by authoritative entities. Early postmodern writers, such as Kurt Vonnegut, reacted to post-war, post-atomic America in their expressions of antiwar and anti-establishment feelings. Contemporary postmodern works such as the television series *Black Mirror* often express a distrust in society's reliance on digital networks and surveillance.

Beyond Modernism

4   The postmodern lens has been applied to such disciplines as philosophy, literature, art, and architecture. The "post" in postmodern does not identify a time period, but rather a departure from Modernist principles. Modernist texts feature subversive techniques in an effort to demonstrate the inadequacy of outdated literary conventions and to make sense of the chaos in modern life. Modernist writers portray disorder to express their interest in overcoming their disillusionment through the use of new literary forms. Postmodernists engage in similar forms of literary experimentation. For example, **fragmentation**, or the breaking down of narrative conventions, is a common technique in both modern and postmodern literature. A text might employ fragmentation through non-linear storytelling to disrupt the audiences' reliance on chronology to make sense of events. Or, an author might incorporate an unreliable narrator or multiple narrators to discourage dependency on the experiences of a single character for understanding. However, Modernists and postmodernists use similar techniques for different purposes. On the one hand, a Modernist might use fragmentation to express a sense of meaninglessness and a desire to ultimately restore order and meaning through new forms. On the other hand, postmodernists might use fragmentation to underscore the incoherent nature of life and the world. They encourage readers to not only challenge conventions but also to deconstruct literature and to question how meaning is produced.

Hol en Bol by M.C. Escher, 1955. Displayed at the Escher Museum in The Hague, Netherlands

5   Another key difference between the attitudes of Modernism and postmodernism is how they conceptualize the roles of the author and the reader. Modernist texts call attention to the author and the control he or she exerts over the text. More emphasis is placed on the inherent subjectivity of a text and how it reflects the interiority of the author or characters. This is exemplified by Modernism's use of interior monologue and stream-of-consciousness narration. Postmodernism is more concerned with how external forces shape what is perceived about a text. Postmodernists often abandon the practice of examining how the author crafted the text to produce a certain meaning and, instead, welcome a new objective purpose in which the meaning of language transforms depending on the perspective of the reader. They generally do not subscribe to the belief that there can be a singular truth or unified means of engagement. As a result, a single text can embody a **multiplicity** of meanings.

Major Concepts

Traditions of Non-Tradition

6   Postmodern writers frequently reject overarching interpretations of events that provide a foundation for people's beliefs and give meaning to their experiences. For example, a postmodernist might respond with skepticism to the claim that anything can be accomplished through hard work and determination. The postmodernist might seek to point out that such generalizations fail to account for experiences that do not fit within the singular narrative presented.

Literary Focus: Postmodernism

7   In their efforts to dismantle authority, postmodern narrators often have a self-reflexive voice that draws attention to the text's status as a written work. Self-reflexivity is a characteristic of **metafiction**, or fiction in which the author self-consciously references the fact that the work presented is a literary construction. Examples of postmodern metafiction include the novel and film *Atonement* which is a story about an author writing a story. The cult classic *The Princess Bride* is a story about a reader reading a story. Lemony Snicket's *A Series of Unfortunate Events* and Roald Dahl's *James and the Giant Peach* both have a narrator that purposefully reveals himself as the author. A metafictional work might also feature a story within a story such as in *The Fault in Our Stars*.

Heterogenous Storytelling

8   Postmodernist literature places an emphasis on multiplicity of voices and experiences. As such, postmodernism rejects homogenous storytelling and embraces difference by demanding more visibility for people of color, women, and LGBTQ communities.

9   Some postmodern authors have engaged with the question of multiplicity of experience with the genre of historiographic metafiction. A term coined by literary theorist Linda Hutcheon, historiographic metafiction is a type of postmodern literature which combines the techniques of metafiction and historical fiction. According to Hutcheon, such works "are both intensely self-reflexive and yet paradoxically lay claim to historical events." Works of historiographic metafiction, such as Toni Morrison's Pulitzer Prize-winning novel *Beloved,* blend elements of fiction and history to reconsider the past. Historiographic metafiction is just one example of how postmodern thinking can be used to re-evaluate history and prioritize voices that may have been marginalized in other narratives for a more nuanced view of society.

Adaptation and Amalgamation

10   **Pastiche** is the practice of combining elements of previous works to create something new. This is a common element in postmodern texts, which tend to imitate the style of, make reference to, or adapt texts from the past. Pastiche can be used to honor the ideas from a previous text or to reinvent them with a unique representation. Stephen Sondheim's musical *Into the Woods* uses pastiche to weave the characters and plots of fairy tales such as "Little Red Riding Hood," "Cinderella," "Rapunzel," and "Jack and the Beanstalk" into one story.

Literary Focus: Postmodernism

American actor Gene Wilder (1933–2016) stars as the grandson of the original Frankenstein, with Peter Boyle (1935–2006) as the new monster in the Mel Brooks film 'Young Frankenstein', 1974.

11 Postmodern works also make use of **parody**, or work that mimics a style of a work, artist or genre in an exaggerated manner for comedic effect. *Young Frankenstein* (1974), directed by Mel Brooks and starring Gene Wilder, adapts Mary Shelley's novel *Frankenstein* in a parody of the horror film genre. The film, shot entirely in black and white, borrows from the style of classic 1930's horror films. Postmodern works can also employ a playful or critical tone through a mixture of highbrow and lowbrow genres that question the value of such distinctions. Highbrow genres are generally considered to be intellectual, sophisticated, and serious. Lowbrow genres are regarded as easily accessible and sometimes unrefined. *Young Frankenstein* plays with this hierarchy by repositioning a "classic" text in a new popular culture context. Postmodernists also blend highbrow and lowbrow genres when they play with low- and high-register vocabularies and grammatical structures; through mixing characteristics and structures of screenwriting, literature, poems, music, ads, news, comics, lists, text messages, etc.; through the use of slang; and by incorporating pop-culture and Americana.

12 Postmodernists encourage audiences to doubt the notion that any text can exist in isolation. They embrace intertextuality, or the references, allusions, and relationships to other texts, to demonstrate how our conceptions of who we are and the world we live in is subject to an endless array of influences.

Literary Focus: Postmodernism

13. Postmodern texts also encourage their audience to take themselves less seriously by denying the existence of set rules or principles and blurring the boundaries between genres.

A piece of graffiti street art, claimed to be by Banksy, shows three stencil figures listening into a conversation in an existing telephone box.

14. **Style and Form**

    - Postmodern writing sometimes uses clear, everyday language, though the structure of the text might be very involved. Postmodern writing can include non-traditional or interwoven narratives.
    - Popular postmodernist techniques include an unreliable narrator, ironic narrator, or multiple narrators.
    - Postmodernist literature is often easily recognizable through a departure from genre structures, with the incorporation and intermixing of multiple genres.

15. Postmodernism is a far-reaching term that can be applied to a wide range of disciplines. In theory, any text can be read from a postmodern perspective regardless of whether or not the creator intended it to be ambiguous. Postmodern thinkers interrogate objective proclamations of truth, embracing the echo of interpretation. Where do you draw the line between what is meaningful and what is meaningless? What is purposeful and what is coincidence?

Literary Focus: Postmodernism

Read "Literary Focus: Postmodernism." After you read, complete the Think Questions below.

THINK QUESTIONS

1. What is the relationship between late capitalism and postmodernism? Cite evidence from the text to support your answer.

2. Postmodernists reject overarching concepts about how the world works. How does the use of fragmentation in narratives reflect this purpose? Cite evidence from the text to support your answer.

3. How do modernists and postmodernists interpret the roles of the author and the reader differently? Cite evidence from the text to support your answer.

4. The word **multiplicity** likely stems from the Latin *multiplico*, meaning "to increase." With this information in mind and using context clues, write your best definition of the word *multiplicity* as it is used in this text. Cite any words or phrases that were particularly helpful in coming to your conclusion.

5. Use context clues to determine the meaning of the word **pastiche**. Write your best definition here, along with the words and phrases that were most helpful in determining the word's meaning. Then, check a dictionary to confirm your understanding.

Song of Solomon

FICTION
Toni Morrison
1977

Introduction

Song of Solomon is the third novel by Nobel Prize-winning author Toni Morrison (1931–2019). It traces the life of Milkman Dead—son of Macon Dead II, a rich and ruthless landlord—as he grows up to become a greedy man, interested in accumulating wealth at the expense of his family members. In this excerpt from the novel's beginning, a North Carolina Mutual Life Insurance agent named Robert Smith is perched on the roof of Mercy Hospital wearing blue silk wings, getting ready to jump. Below him, among a crowd of protesters who are upset that the hospital only admits white patients, is Ruth Foster Dead. When the crowd begins to sing, Ruth, who is pregnant with Milkman, goes into labor.

Song of Solomon

"'I knew it. Soon's I get two dimes back to back, here you come. More regular than a reaper.'"

1. "Ma'am?"

2. "Send one around back to the emergency office. Tell him to tell the guard to get over here quick. That boy there can go. That one." She pointed to a cat-eyed boy about five or six years old.

3. The stout woman slid her eyes down the nurse's finger and looked at the child she was pointing to.

4. "Guitar[1], ma'am."

5. "What?"

6. "Guitar."

7. The nurse gazed at the stout woman as though she had spoken Welsh. Then she closed her mouth, looked again at the cat-eyed boy, and lacing her fingers, spoke her next words very slowly to him.

8. "Listen. Go around to the back of the hospital to the guard's office. It will say 'Emergency Admissions' on the door. A-D-M-I-S-I-O-N-S. But the guard will be there. Tell him to get over here—on the double. Move now. Move!" She unlaced her fingers and made scooping notions with her hands, the palms pushing against the wintry air.

9. A man in a brown suit came toward her, puffing little white clouds of breath. "Fire truck's on its way. Get back inside. You'll freeze to death."

10. The nurse nodded.

11. "You left out a *s*, ma'am," the boy said. The North was new to him and he had just begun to learn he could speak up to white people. But she'd already gone, rubbing her arms against the cold.

---

1. **Guitar** Guitar Bains, a childhood friend of Milkman

Song of Solomon

12 "Granny, she left out a *s*."

13 "And a 'please.'"

14 "You reckon he'll jump?"

15 "A nutwagon do anything."

16 "Who is he?"

17 "Collects insurance. A nutwagon."

18 "Who is that lady singing?"

19 "That, baby, is the very last thing in pea-time." But she smiled when she looked at the singing woman, so the cat-eyed boy listened to the musical performance with at least as much interest as he devoted to the man flapping his wings on top of the hospital.

20 The crowd was beginning to be a little nervous now that the law was being called in. They each know Mr. Smith. He came to their houses twice a month to collect one dollar and sixty-eight cents and write down on a little yellow card both the date and their eighty-four cents a week payment. They were always half a month or so behind, and talked endlessly to him about paying ahead—after they had a preliminary discussion about what he was doing back so soon anyway.

21 "You back in here already? Look like I just got rid of you."

22 "I'm tired of seeing your face. Really tired."

23 "I knew it. Soon's I get two dimes back to back, here you come. More regular than a reaper. Do Hoover know about you?"

24 They kidded him, abused him, told their children to tell him they were out or sick or gone to Pittsburgh. But they held on to those little yellow cards as though they meant something—laid them gently in the shoe box along with the rent receipts, marriage licenses, and expired factory identification badges. Mr. Smith smiled through it all, managing to keep his eyes focused almost the whole time on his customers' feet. He wore a business suit for his work, but his house was no better than theirs. He never had a woman that any of them knew about and said nothing in church but an occasional "Amen." He never beat anybody up and he wasn't seen after dark, so they thought he was probably a nice man. But he was heavily associated with illness and death, neither of which was distinguishable from the brown picture of the North Carolina Mutual Life Building on the back of their yellow cards. Jumping from

Song of Solomon

the roof of Mercy was the most interesting thing he had done. None of them had suspected he had it in him. Just goes to show, they murmured to each other, you never really do know about people.

25 The singing woman quieted down and, humming the tune, walked through the crowd toward the rose-petal lady, who was still cradling her stomach.

26 "You should make yourself warm," she whispered to her, touching her lightly on the elbow. "A little bird'll be here with the morning."

27 "Oh?" said the rose-petal lady. "Tomorrow morning?"

28 "That's the only morning coming."

29 "It can't be," the rose-petal lady said. "It's too soon."

30 "No it ain't. Right on time."

31 The women were looking deep into each other's eyes when a loud roar went up from the crowd—a kind of wavy *oo* sound. Mr. Smith had lost his balance for a second, and was trying gallantly to hold on to a triangle of wood that jutted from the cupola. Immediately the singing woman began again:

> *O Sugarman done fly*
> *O Sugarman done gone . . .*

32 Downtown the firemen pulled on their greatcoats, but when they arrived at Mercy, Mr. Smith had seen the rose petals, heard the music, and leaped on into the air.

. . .

33 The next day a colored[2] baby was born inside Mercy for the first time. Mr. Smith's blue silk wings must have left their mark, because when the little boy discovered, at four, the same thing Mr. Smith had learned earlier—that only birds and airplanes could fly—he lost all interest in himself. To have to live without that single gift saddened him and left his imagination so **bereft** that he appeared **dull** even to the women who did not hate his mother. The ones who did, who accepted her invitations to tea and **envied** the doctor's big dark house of twelve rooms and the green sedan, called him "peculiar." The others, who knew that the house was more prison than palace, and that the Dodge sedan was for Sunday drives only, felt sorry for Ruth Foster and her dry daughters, and called her son "deep." Even mysterious.

2. **colored** a term that was common at the time, used to describe someone who was racially non-white, usually black

Song of Solomon

34 "Did he come with a caul?"

35 "You should have dried it and made him some tea from it to drink. If you don't he'll see ghosts."

36 "You believe that?"

37 "I don't, but that's what the old people say."

38 "Well, he's a deep one anyways. Look at his eyes."

39 And they pried pieces of baked-too-fast sunshine cake from the roofs of their mouths and looked once more into the boy's eyes. He met their gaze as best he could until, after a pleading glance toward his mother, he was allowed to leave the room.

40 It took some planning to walk out of the parlor, his back washed with the hum of their voices, open the heavy double doors leading to the dining room, slip up the stairs past all those bedrooms, and not arouse the attention of Lena and Corinthians sitting like big baby dolls before a table heaped with scraps of red velvet. His sisters made roses in the afternoon. Bright, lifeless roses that lay in peck baskets for months until the specialty buyer at Gerhardt's sent Freddie the janitor over to tell the girls that they could use another gross. If he did manage to slip by his sisters and avoid their **casual malice**, he knelt in his room at the window sill and wondered again and again why he had to stay level on the ground. The quiet that suffused the doctor's house then, broken only by the murmur of the women eating sunshine cake, was only that: quiet. It was not peaceful, for it was preceded by and would soon be terminated by the presence of Macon Dead.

41 Solid, rumbling, likely to erupt without prior notice, Macon kept each member of his family awkward with fear. His hatred of his wife glittered and sparkled in every word he spoke to her. The disappointment he felt in his daughters sifted down on them. Like ash, dulling their buttery complexions and choking the lilt out of what should have been girlish voices. Under the frozen heat of his glance they tripped over doorsills and dropped the salt cellar into the yolks of their poached eggs. The way he mangled their grace, wit, and self-esteem was the single excitement of their days. Without the tension and drama he ignited, they might not have known what to do with themselves. In his absence his daughters bent their necks over blood-red squares of velvet and waited eagerly for any hint of him, and his wife, Ruth, began her days stunned into stillness by her husband's contempt and ended them wholly animated by it.

Excerpted from *Song of Solomon* by Toni Morrison, published by Vintage Publishers.

WRITE

LITERARY ANALYSIS: In this excerpt from *Song of Solomon*, Toni Morrison juxtaposes the death of Robert Smith with the birth of Milkman Dead. Why does Morrison make this choice, and how does it deviate from the reader's expectations? In a brief response, analyze the author's decisions in structuring the narrative in this way. Be sure to cite evidence from the text and explain how the author's choices elicited a response in the reader.

The Warmth of Other Suns:
The Epic Story of America's Great Migration

INFORMATIONAL TEXT
Isabel Wilkerson
2013

Introduction

Between 1915 and 1970, over six million African Americans migrated from the rural southern United States to the Northeast, Midwest, and West to escape racial oppression and pursue economic and social opportunities. One of the largest migrations ever to take place on national soil, the Great Migration changed the food, music, culture, and social fabric of American cities. In *The Warmth of Other Suns*, Pulitzer Prize-winning journalist Isabel Wilkerson (b. 1961) tells the history, intertwining the personal stories of three young African Americans who left family and home to participate in this epic migration.

"He wasn't going to lose his life over them. He had come close enough as it was."

1.

Chickasaw County, Mississippi, Late October 1937

Ida Mae Brandon Gladney

1   The night clouds were closing in on the salt licks east of the oxbow lakes along the folds in the earth beyond the Yalobusha River. The cotton was at last cleared from the field. Ida Mae tried now to get the children ready and to gather the clothes and quilts and somehow keep her mind off the churning within her. She had sold off the turkeys and **doled** out in secret the old stools, the wash pots, the tin tub, the bed pallets. Her husband was settling with Mr. Edd over the worth of a year's labor, and she did not know what would come of it. None of them had been on a train before—not unless you counted the clattering local from Bacon Switch to Okolona, where, "by the time you sit down, you there," as Ida Mae put it. None of them had been out of Mississippi. Or Chickasaw County, for that matter.

2   There was no explaining to little James and Velma the stuffed bags and chaos and all that was at stake or why they had to put on their shoes and not cry and bring undue attention from anyone who might happen to see them leaving. Things had to look normal, like any other time they might ride into town, which was rare enough to begin with.

3   Velma was six. She sat with her ankles crossed and three braids in her hair and did what she was told. James was too little to understand. He was three. He was upset at the commotion. Hold still now, James. Lemme put your shoes on, Ida Mae told him. James wriggled and kicked. He did not like shoes. He ran free in the field. What were these things? He did not like them on his feet. So Ida Mae let him go barefoot.

4   Miss Theenie stood watching. One by one, her children had left her and gone up north. Sam and Cleve to Ohio. Josie to Syracuse. Irene to Milwaukee. Now the man Miss Theenie had tried to keep Ida Mae from marrying in the first place was taking her away, too. Miss Theenie had no choice but to accept it and let Ida Mae and the grandchildren go for good. Miss Theenie drew them close to her, as she always did whenever anyone was leaving. She had them

The Warmth of Other Suns: The Epic Story of America's Great Migration

bow their heads. She whispered a prayer that her daughter and her daughter's family be protected on the long journey ahead in the Jim Crow[1] car.

5 "May the Lord be the first in the car," she prayed, "and the last out."

6 When the time had come, Ida Mae and little James and Velma and all that they could carry were loaded into a brother-in-law's truck, and the three of them went to meet Ida Mae's husband at the train depot in Okolona for the night ride out of the bottomland.

2.

Wildwood, Florida, April 14, 1945

George Swanson Starling

7 A man named Roscoe Colton gave Lil George Starling a ride in his pickup truck to the train station in Wildwood through the fruit-bearing scrubland of central Florida. And Schoolboy, as the toothless orange pickers mockingly called him, boarded the Silver Meteor pointing north.

8 A railing divided the stairs onto the train, one side of the railing for white passengers, the other for colored, so the soles of their shoes would not touch the same stair. He boarded on the colored side of the railing, a final reminder from the place of his birth of the **absurdity** of the world he was leaving.

9 He was getting out alive. So he didn't let it bother him. "I got on the car where they told me to get on," he said years later.

10 He hadn't had time to bid farewell to everyone he wanted to. He stopped to say good-bye to Rachel Jackson, who owned a little café up on what they called the Avenue and the few others he could safely get to in the little time he had. He figured everybody in Egypt town, the colored section of Eustis, probably knew he was leaving before he had climbed onto the train, small as the town was and as much as people talked.

11 It was a clear afternoon in the middle of April. He folded his tall frame into the hard surface of the seat, his knees knocking against the seat back in front of him. He was packed into the Jim Crow car, where the railroad stored the luggage, when the train pulled away at last. He was on the run, and he wouldn't rest easy until he was out of range of Lake County, beyond the reach of the grove owners whose invisible laws he had broken.

12 The train rumbled past the forest of citrus trees that he had climbed since he was a boy and that he had tried to wrestle some **dignity** out of and, for a time,

---

1. **Jim Crow** refers to the areas and times of the American South in which there were mandated segregation laws

had. They could have their trees. He wasn't going to lose his life over them. He had come close enough as it was.

13. He had lived up to his family's accidental **surname**. Starling. Distant cousin to the mockingbird. He had spoken up about what he had seen in the world he was born into, like the **starling** that sang Mozart's own music back to him or the starling out of Shakespeare that tormented the king by speaking the name of Mortimer. Only, George was paying the price for tormenting the ruling class that owned the citrus groves. There was no place in the Jim Crow South for a colored starling like him.

14. He didn't know what he would do once he got to New York or what his life would be. He didn't know how long it would take before he could send for Inez. His wife was mad right now, but she'd get over it once he got her there. At least that's what he told himself. He turned his face to the North and sat with his back to Florida.

15. Leaving as he did, he figured he would never set foot in Eustis again for as long as he lived. And as he settled in for the twenty-three-hour train ride up the coast of the Atlantic, he had no desire to have anything to do with the town he grew up in, the state of Florida, or the South as a whole, for that matter.

Excerpted from *The Warmth of Other Suns: The Epic Story of America's Great Migration* by Isabel Wilkerson, published by Vintage Books.

✏ WRITE

RESEARCH: In *The Warmth of Other Suns,* Wilkerson relates the tale of young African Americans who left family and home to participate in the Great Migration. Research the events that helped launch the Great Migration, and then write a response in which you explain how the two perspectives in the selected text reflect your research.

Fences

DRAMA
August Wilson
1985

Introduction

Fences is a Pulitzer Prize-winning play by August Wilson (1945–2005), one of his ten plays collectively referred to as "The Pittsburgh Cycle." Each play in the cycle focuses on the African American experience during a particular decade in 20th-century America; though it premiered in 1985, *Fences* is set in the latter half of the 1950s. In this scene, Cory, a high school senior, confronts his father, a garbage collector and former Negro League baseball player named Troy, about pursuing a future in college football. The ensuing argument escalates quickly, and despite Cory's mother Rose's interruption, Troy lands several verbal blows.

"I'm the boss around here. I do the only saying that counts."

> Note: The text you are about to read contains offensive language. Remember to be mindful of the thoughts and feelings of your peers as you read and discuss this text. Please consult your teacher for additional guidance and support.

1. Troy: Where's Cory? That boy brought his butt home yet?

2. Rose: He's in the house doing chores. *(calling)* Cory! Get your butt out here, boy!
   (Troy goes over to a pile of wood, picks up a board, and starts sawing. Cory enters from the house.)

3. Troy: You just now coming in here from leaving this morning?

4. Cory: Yeah, I had to go to football practice.

5. Troy: Yeah, what?

6. Cory: Yessir.

7. Troy: I ain't but two seconds off you noway. The garbage sitting in there overflowing . . . you ain't done none of your chores . . . and you come in here talking about "Yeah."

8. Cory: I was just getting ready to do my chores now, Pop . . .

9. Troy: Your first chore is to help me with this fence on Saturday. Everything else come after that. Now get that saw and cut them boards.

10. *(Cory begins to get out the boards. There's a long pause.)*

11. Troy: Your mama told me you done got **recruited** by a college football team? Is that right?

12. Cory: Yeah, Coach Zellman say the recruiter gonna be coming by to talk to you. Get you to sign the permission papers.

13. Troy: I thought you supposed to be working down there at the A&P. Ain't you supposed to be working down there after school?

Skill: Dramatic Elements and Structure

Troy is agitated and starts sawing boards, which seems menacing and tense. Cory enters the scene from the house. His dismissive "yeah" response upsets Troy even more. Troy demands he say "yessir," suggesting he expects respect.

Fences

14 Cory: Mr. Stawicki say he gonna hold my job for me until after the football season. Say starting next week I can work weekends.

15 Troy: I thought we had an understanding about this football stuff? You supposed to keep up with your chores and hold that job down at the A&P. Ain't been around here all Saturday. Ain't none of your chores done . . . now you telling me you done quit your job.

16 Cory: I'm gonna be working weekends.

17 Troy: You damn right you are! And ain't no need for nobody coming around here to talk to me about signing for nothing.

18 Cory: Hey, Pop . . . you can't do that. He coming all the way from North Carolina.

19 Troy: I don't care where he coming from. The white man ain't gonna let you nowhere with that football noway. You go on and get your book-learning so you can work yourself up in that A&P or learn how to fix cars or build houses or something, get you a **trade**. That way you have something can't nobody take away from you. You go on and learn how to put your hands to some good use. Besides **hauling** people's garbage.

20 Cory: I get good grades, Pop. That's why the recruiter wants to talk with you. You got to keep up your grades to get recruited. This way I'll be going to college. I'll get a chance.

21 Troy: First you gonna get your butt down there to the A&P and get your job back.

22 Cory: Mr. Stawicki done already hired somebody else 'cause I told him I was playing football.

23 Troy: You a bigger fool than I thought . . . to let somebody take away your job so you can play some football. Where you gonna get your money to take out your girlfriend and whatnot? What kind of foolishness is that to let somebody take away your job?

24 Cory: I'm still gonna be working weekends.

25 Troy: Naw . . . naw. You getting your butt out of here and finding another job.

26 Cory: Come on, Pop! I got to practice. I can't work after school and play football too. The team needs me. That's what Coach Zellman say . . .

27 Troy: I don't care what nobody else say, I'm the boss . . . you understand? I'm the boss around here. I do the only saying that counts.

28 Cory: Come on, Pop!

29 Troy: I asked you . . . did you understand?

Skill: Summarizing

Without telling his father, Cory quits his job. Troy finds out after the fact, tells Cory to get his job back, finds out it isn't available, and insists Cory get another job.

Fences

30 Cory: Yessir.

31 Troy: You go on down there to that A&P and see if you can get your job back. If you can't do both . . . then you quit the football team. You've got to take the crookeds with the straights.

32 Cory: Yessir.
    (Pause)
    . . . Can I ask you a question?

33 Troy: What the hell you wanna ask me? Mr. Stawicki the one you got the questions for.

34 Cory: How come you ain't never liked me?

35 Troy: Liked you? Who the hell say I got to like you? What law is there say I got to like you? Wanna stand up in my face and ask a damn fool ass question like that. Talking about liking somebody. Come here, boy, when I talk to you . . . Straighten up dammit! I asked you a question . . . what law is there say I got to like you?

36 Cory: None.

37 Troy: Well, all right then! Don't you eat every day? (Pause) Answer me when I talk to you! Don't you eat every day?

38 Cory: Yeah.

39 Troy: N-----, as long as you in my house, you put that sir on the end of it when you talk to me!

40 Cory: Yes . . . sir.

41 Troy: You eat every day.

42 Cory: Yessir!

43 Troy: You got clothes on your back.

44 Cory: Yessir.

45 Troy: Why you think that is?

46 Cory: Cause of you.

47 Troy: Ah, hell I know it's cause of me . . . but why do you think that is?

48 Cory (hesitant): Cause you like me.

Skill: Dramatic Elements and Structure

Troy wants Cory to keep the job and quit the team. I think Troy's message about the "crookeds and straights" is about taking the good with the bad. Cory's pause implies he disagrees but is hesitant to further anger Troy.

Fences

49 **Troy:** Like you? I go out of here every morning . . . bust my butt putting up with them crackers everyday . . . 'cause I like you? You about the biggest fool I ever saw. *(Pause)* It's my job, it's my responsibility! You understand that? A man got to take care of his family. You live in my house, sleep on my bedclothes, fill your belly up on my food . . . cause you my son. You my flesh and blood. Not cause I like you! Cause it's my duty to take care of you. I owe a responsibility to you! Let's get this straight here, before it go along any further . . . I ain't got to like you. Mr. Rand don't give me my money come payday 'cause he likes me. He gives me 'cause he owes me. I done given you everything I had to give you. I gave you your life! Me and your mama worked that out between us. And liking your black ass wasn't part of the bargain. Don't you try and go through life worrying about if somebody like you or not. You best be making sure they doing right by you. You understand what I'm saying, boy?

50 **Cory:** Yessir.

51 **Troy:** Then get the hell out of my face, and get on down to that A&P.

52 *(Rose has been standing behind the screen door for much of the scene. She enters as Cory exits.)*

53 **Rose:** Why don't you let the boy go ahead and play football, Troy? Ain't no harm in that. He's just trying to be like you with the sports.

54 **Troy:** I don't want him to be like me! I want him to move as far away from my life as he can get. You the only decent thing that's ever happened to me. I wish him that. But I don't wish him a thing else from my life. I decided seventeen years ago that boy wasn't getting involved in no sports. Not after what they did to me.

55 **Rose:** Everything that boy do . . . he do it for you. He wants you to say "Good job, son." That's all.

56 **Troy:** Rose, I ain't got time for that. He's alive. He's healthy. He's got to make his own way. I made mine. Ain't nobody gonna hold his hand when he get out there in the real world.

57 **Rose:** Times have changed from when you was young, Troy. People change. The world is changing around you and you can't even see it.

58 **Troy** *(slow, **methodical**)*: Woman . . . I do the best I can do. I come home every Friday. I carry a sack of potatoes and a bucket of lard. You all line up at the door with your hands out. I give you the lint from my pockets. I give you my sweat and blood. I ain't got no tears. I done spent them. I get up on Monday morning . . . find my lunch on the table. I go out. Make my way. Find my strength to carry me through to the next Friday. *(Pause)* That's all I've got Rose. That's all I've got to give. I can't give nothing else.

Excerpted from *Fences* by August Wilson, published by Samuel French, Inc.

Fences

First Read

Read *Fences*. After you read, complete the Think Questions below.

THINK QUESTIONS

1. Cory answers "Yessir" to most of his father's statements. What can you infer about Cory's character based on his responses? Use evidence from the text to support your answer.

2. Troy says Rose is the "only decent thing that's ever happened" to him. Why does he say this? How would you describe Troy and Rose's relationship? Use evidence from the text to support your answer.

3. There are not many stage directions included in the text. How do you imagine Troy's tone of voice during this scene? Use evidence from the text to support your answer.

4. Read the following dictionary entry:

   trade
   trade /trād/ *noun*
   1. the action of buying and selling goods and services
   2. a skilled job
   3. an exchange between two people

   Decide which definition best matches **trade** as it is used in *Fences*. Write that definition of *trade* here, and indicate which clues found in the text helped you determine the meaning.

5. What is the meaning of the word **hauling** as it is used in paragraph 19 of *Fences*? Write your best definition here, along with a brief explanation of how you arrived at its meaning.

Fences

Skill: Dramatic Elements and Structure

Use the Checklist to analyze Dramatic Elements and Structure in *Fences*. Refer to the sample student annotations about Dramatic Elements and Structure in the text.

••• CHECKLIST FOR DRAMATIC ELEMENTS AND STRUCTURE

In order to determine the author's choices regarding the development of a drama, note the following:

- ✓ the names of all the characters, how they are introduced, and their relationships with one another
- ✓ character development, including personality traits, motivations, decisions they make, and actions they take
- ✓ the setting(s) of the story and how it influences the characters and the events of the plot
- ✓ how character choices and dialogue affect the plot
- ✓ the stage directions and how they are used to reveal character and plot development

To analyze the impact of the author's choices regarding how to develop and relate elements of a story or drama, consider the following questions:

- ✓ How does the order of events in the play affect the development of the drama?
- ✓ How are characters introduced, and what does it reveal about them?
- ✓ In what ways do the characters change over the course of the drama?
- ✓ How do the choices the characters make help advance the plot?
- ✓ How does the setting affect the characters and plot?
- ✓ How do the characters' actions help develop the theme or message of the play?

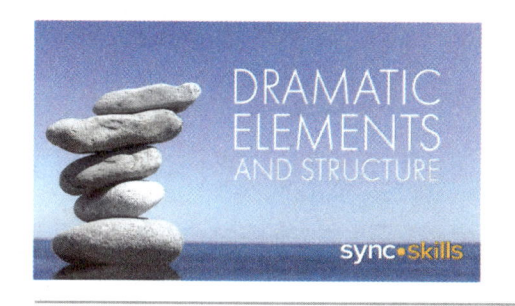

Skill: Dramatic Elements and Structure

Reread paragraphs 45–51 of *Fences*. Then, using the Checklist on the previous page, answer the multiple-choice questions below.

YOUR TURN

1. Based on the stage direction and dialogue between Troy and Cory in paragraphs 45 through 48, the reader can conclude that—

   - A. Troy and Cory feel at ease around each other.
   - B. Cory feels intimidated by his father's exertion of authority.
   - C. Both Troy and Cory have explosive personalities.
   - D. Cory is trying to apologize to Troy, but Troy is unwilling to listen to him.

2. The dialogue in paragraph 49 reveals that Troy—

   - A. supports his family out of love, even if he doesn't always show it.
   - B. likes and is proud of his job.
   - C. believes he has a duty to take care of Cory but that doesn't mean he has to like him.
   - D. wants to protect Cory from hardships in life.

3. The dramatic elements in this passage advance the plot in the overall scene by—

   - A. adding tension to the rising action.
   - B. providing a resolution to the conflict.
   - C. giving background information about Troy's past and how it influences his parenting style.
   - D. portraying the highest moment of tension, or climax, of the scene.

Fences

Skill: Summarizing

Use the Checklist to analyze Summarizing in *Fences*. Refer to the sample student annotation about Summarizing in the text.

CHECKLIST FOR SUMMARIZING

In order to determine how to write an objective summary of a text, consider the following:

- ✓ find details that answer the basic questions *who*, *what*, *where*, *when*, *why*, and *how*
- ✓ identify key details that support theme, plot, and other major story elements
- ✓ exclude from summaries minor details that don't contribute to the theme or plot
- ✓ exclude from summaries personal thoughts, judgments, or opinions to ensure that the summaries are objective

To provide an objective summary of a text, consider the following questions:

- ✓ What are the answers to basic *who*, *what*, *where*, *when*, *why*, and *how* questions?
- ✓ Have I included key details that support major story elements?
- ✓ Have I avoided including minor details that don't contribute to the theme or plot?
- ✓ Is my summary objective, or have I added my own thoughts, judgments, and personal opinions?

Skill: Summarizing

Reread paragraphs 52–56 of *Fences*. Then, using the Checklist on the previous page, answer the multiple-choice questions below.

YOUR TURN

1. This question has two parts. First, answer Part A. Then, answer Part B.

   Part A: Summarize how Troy feels about Cory playing college football.
   - A. Troy decided many years ago that Cory would not play sports in college because of the bad experience Troy had, which had a negative impact on his life.
   - B. Rose tries to convince Troy to allow Cory to play football by telling him that Cory wants to be like him.
   - C. Troy feels that playing football is too dangerous. Playing football in college could hurt Cory as it did Troy, and he does not want this for his son.
   - D. Troy does not want Cory to be at all like him because his life is miserable and because Cory needs to find his own way.

   Part B: What textual evidence best supports the correct answer to Part A?
   - A. "I don't want him to be like me! I want him to move as far away from my life as he can get."
   - B. "Why don't you let the boy go ahead and play football, Troy? Ain't no harm in that."
   - C. "I decided seventeen years ago that boy wasn't getting involved in no sports. Not after what they did to me."
   - D. "Everything that boy do . . . he do it for you. He wants you to say 'Good job, son.' That's all."

2. Which statement provides the most objective summary of the information from this passage?

   ○ A. Cory storms off. Rose rushes in to tell Troy that all Cory wants is for Troy to show that he is proud of him by saying "Good job, son." Troy agrees that he should do this.

   ○ B. Rose overhears Troy and Cory's conversation. She jumps to Cory's defense. She tells Troy that their son just wants to hear some encouragement from his father, that's all. Troy says he doesn't want his son to get involved in sports. Rose says Cory only wants to play sports because he wants to be like Troy.

   ○ C. Rose enters as Cory exits. Troy tells Rose that she is the best thing that's ever happened to him but he disagrees with her about Cory's future.

   ○ D. Rose tells Troy privately that Cory wants to be like Troy. Troy doesn't want Cory to be like him or to have the same bad experience with sports. Rose says Cory wants encouragement from Troy. Troy rebuffs her, explaining that Cory needs to learn the hard truths of the real world.

Fences

Close Read

Reread *Fences*. As you reread, complete the Skills Focus questions below. Then use your answers and annotations from the questions to help you complete the Write activity.

SKILLS FOCUS

1. Locate lines at the beginning of the scene in which Troy demands that Cory address him formally and then asks Cory about being recruited. Explain how dramatic elements in this passage, such as dialogue and stage directions, work together to advance the plot.

2. Identify a section in the middle of the excerpt in which Troy insults Cory by calling him a fool. Analyze how the economic context of the setting influences Troy's characterization.

3. Identify evidence from the latter part of the excerpt in which Troy discusses duty and responsibility. Based on this evidence, analyze how the economic context influences an important theme in the play.

4. Highlight the stage directions for Rose near the end of the scene, as well as the dialogue between Rose and Troy immediately following those stage directions. Objectively summarize the conflict occurring between Rose and Troy.

5. Highlight a section of the text in which Troy explains what it means to him to be a father. According to Troy, what is the relationship between a man and his home? What responsibilities does he have in the face of a changing world?

WRITE

LITERARY ANALYSIS: Think about the setting and the action in this excerpt from *Fences*, as well as the context provided by your reading of the excerpt from *The Warmth of Other Suns*. How does the literal action—Troy constructing a fence in the backyard and enlisting Cory to join him—coincide with what is happening in the dialogue? Analyze how the author uses dramatic elements and structure to develop the connection between literal action and the deeper relationship between the characters.

American Horse

FICTION
Louise Erdrich
1991

Introduction

A National Book Award winner, bookstore owner, and member of the Turtle Mountain Band of Chippewa Indians, Louise Erdrich (b. 1954) explores themes of poverty, family, and Native American intercultural dynamics in "American Horse." In this nuanced and empathic work, Erdrich tells the story of Buddy American Horse, a boy torn between the conflicting beliefs of a social worker and the family he loves dearly.

"Look at his family life—the old man crazy as a bedbug, the mother intoxicated somewhere."

Note: Content Advisory: Please be advised that this text contains mature themes, violence, and mildly explicit language.

1. The woman sleeping on the cot in the woodshed was Albertine American Horse. The name was left over from her mother's short marriage. The boy was the son of a man she had loved and let go. Buddy was on the cot too, sitting on the edge because he'd been awake three hours watching out for his mother and besides, she took up the whole cot. Her feet hung over the edge, limp and brown as two trout. Her long arms reached out and slapped at things she saw in her dreams.

2. Buddy had been knocked awake out of hiding in a washing machine while herds of policemen with dogs searched through the large building with many tiny rooms. When the arm came down, Buddy screamed because it had a blue cuff and sharp silver buttons. "Tss," his mother mumbled, half awake, "wasn't nothing." But Buddy sat up after her breathing went deep again, and he watched.

3. There was something coming and he knew it.

4. It was coming from very far off but he had a picture of it in his mind. It was a large thing made of metal with many barbed hooks, points, and drag chains[1] on it, something like a giant potato peeler that rolled out of the sky, scraping clouds down with it and jabbing or crushing everything that lay in its path on the ground.

5. Buddy watched his mother. If he woke her up, she would know what to do about the thing, but he thought he'd wait until he saw it for sure before he shook her. She was pretty, sleeping, and he liked knowing he could look at her as long and close up as he wanted. He took a strand of her hair and held it in his hands as if it was the rein to a delicate beast. She was strong enough and could pull him along like the horse their name was.

---

1. **drag chains** chains put on a horse to attach it to a harrow rake, used to smooth ground after planting

> **Skill: Story Structure**
>
> The story opens with Buddy having a nightmare about being hunted by the police. His mother tells him not to worry. He knows something bad is coming. This scene creates immediate tension and seems to foreshadow something bad.

American Horse

NOTES

6 Buddy had his mother's and his grandmother's name because his father had been a big mistake.

7 "They're all mistakes, even your father. But *you* are the best thing that ever happened to me."

8 That was what she said when he asked.

9 Even Kadie, the boyfriend crippled from being in a car wreck, was not as good a thing that happened to his mother as Buddy was. "He was a medium-sized mistake," she said. "He's hurt and I shouldn't even say that, but it's the truth." At the moment, Buddy knew that being the best thing in his mother's life, he was also the reason they were hiding from the cops.

10 He wanted to touch the satin roses sewed on her pink T-shirt, but he knew he shouldn't do that even in her sleep. If she woke up and found him touching the roses, she would say, "Quit that, Buddy." Sometimes she told him to stop hugging her like a gorilla. She never said that in the mean voice she used when he oppressed her, but when she said that he loosened up anyway.

Skill: Point of View

Buddy seems to have complicated emotions toward his mother. Due to this unexpected point of view, it is hard to tell how much Buddy can be trusted in his opinions of her. This story seems to be looking at the complexity of point of view.

11 There were times he felt like hugging her so hard and in such a special way that she would say to him, "Let's get married." There were also times he closed his eyes and wished that she would die, only a few times, but still it haunted him that his wish might come true. He and Uncle Lawrence would be left alone. Buddy wasn't worried, though, about his mother getting married to somebody else. She had said to her friend, Madonna, "All men suck," when she thought Buddy wasn't listening. He made an uncertain sound, and when they heard him they took him in their arms.

12 "Except for you, Buddy," his mother said. "All except for you and maybe Uncle Lawrence, although he's pushing it."

13 "The cops suck the worst, though," Buddy whispered to his mother's sleeping face, "because they're after us." He felt tired again, slumped down, and put his legs beneath the blanket. He closed his eyes and got the feeling that the cot was lifting up beneath him, that it was arching its canvas back and then traveling, traveling very fast and in the wrong direction for when he looked up he saw three of them were advancing to meet the great metal thing with hooks and barbs and all sorts of sharp equipment to catch their bodies and draw their blood. He heard its insides as it rushed toward them, purring softly like a powerful motor and then they were right in its shadow. He pulled the reins as hard as he could and the beast reared, lifting him. His mother clapped her hand across his mouth.

14 "Okay," she said. "Lay low. They're outside and they're gonna hunt."

15 She touched his shoulder and Buddy leaned over with her to look through the cracks in the boards.

16 They were out there all right, Albertine saw them. Two officers and that social worker woman. Vicki Koob. There had been no whistle, no dream, no voice to warn her that they were coming. There was only the crunching sound of cinders in the yard, the engine purring, the dust sifting off their car in a fine light brownish cloud and settling around them.

17 The three people came to a halt in their husk of metal—the car emblazoned with the North Dakota State Highway Patrol emblem which is the glowing profile of the Sioux policeman, Red Tomahawk, the one who killed Sitting Bull. Albertine gave Buddy the blanket and told him that he might have to wrap it around him and hide underneath the cot. "We're gonna wait and see what they do." She took him in her lap and hunched her arms around him. "Don't you worry," she whispered against his ear. "Lawrence knows how to fool them."

18 Buddy didn't want to look at the car and the people. He felt his mother's heart beating beneath his ear so fast it seemed to push the satin roses in and out. He put his face to them carefully and breathed the deep, soft powdery woman smell of her. That smell was also in her little face cream bottles, in her brushes, and around the washbowl after she used it. The satin felt so unbearably smooth against his cheek that he had to press closer. She didn't push him away, like he expected, but hugged him still tighter until he felt as close as he had ever been to back inside her again where she said he came from. Within the smells of her things, her soft skin, and the satin of her roses, he closed his eyes then, and took his breaths softly and quickly with her heart.

19 They were out there, but they didn't dare get out of the car yet because of Lawrence's big, ragged dogs. Three of these dogs had loped up the dirt driveway with the car. They were **rangy**, alert, and bounced up and down on their cushioned paws like wolves. They didn't waste their energy barking, but positioned themselves quietly, one at either car door and the third in front of the bellied-out screen door to Uncle Lawrence's house. It was six in the morning but the wind was up already, blowing dust, ruffling their short moth-eaten coats. The big brown one on Vicki Koob's side had unusual black and white markings, stripes almost, like a hyena and he grinned at her, tongue out and teeth showing.

20 "Shoo!" Miss Koob opened her door with a quick jerk.

21 The brown dog sidestepped the door and jumped before her, tiptoeing. Its dirty white muzzle curled and its eyes crossed suddenly as if it were zeroing its cross-hair sights in on the exact place it would bite her. She ducked back and slammed the door.

American Horse

22 "It's mean," she told Officer Brackett. He was printing out some type of form. The other officer, Harmony, a slow man, had not yet reacted to the car's halt. He had been sitting quietly in the back seat, but now he rolled down his window and with no change in expression unsnapped his holster and drew his pistol out and pointed it at the dog on his side. The dog smacked down on its belly, wiggled under the car and was out and around the back of the house before Harmony drew his gun back. The other dogs vanished with him. From wherever they had disappeared to they began to yap and howl, and the door to the low shoebox-style house fell open.

23 "Heya, what's going on?"

24 Uncle Lawrence put his head out the door and opened wide the one eye he had in working order. The eye bulged impossibly wider in outrage when he saw the police car. But the eyes of the two officers and Miss Vicki Koob were wide open too because they had never seen Uncle Lawrence in his sleeping get-up or, indeed, witnessed anything like it. For his ribs, which were cracked from a bad fall and still mending, Uncle Lawrence wore a thick white corset laced up the front with a striped sneakers' lace. His glass eye and his set of dentures were still out for the night so his face puckered here and there, around its absences and scars, like a damaged but fierce little cake. Although he had a few gray streaks now, Uncle Lawrence's hair was still thick, and because he wore a special contraption of elastic straps around his head every night, two oiled waves always crested on either side of his middle part. All of this would have been sufficient to astonish, even without the most striking part of his outfit—the smoking jacket. It was made of black satin and hung open around his corset, dragging a tasseled belt. Gold thread dragons struggled up the lapels and blasted their furry red breath around his neck. As Lawrence walked down the steps, he put his arms up in surrender and the gold tassels in the inner seams of his sleeves dropped into view.

25 "My heavens, what a sight." Vicki Koob was impressed.

26 "A character," apologized Officer Harmony.

27 As a tribal police officer who could be counted on to help out the State Patrol, Harmony thought he always had to explain about Indians or get twice as tough to show he did not favor them. He was slow-moving and shy but two jumps ahead of other people all the same, and now, as he watched Uncle Lawrence's splendid approach, he gazed speculatively at the torn and bulging pocket of the smoking jacket. Harmony had been inside Uncle Lawrence's house before and knew that above his draped orange-crate shelf of war medals a blue-black German luger was hung carefully in a net of flat-headed nails and fishing line. Thinking of this deadly exhibition, he got out of the car and shambled toward Lawrence with a dreamy little smile of welcome

Skill: Point of View

Harmony uses understatement when he describes Uncle Lawrence, a fellow Native American, as "a character." Harmony feels the need to explain Lawrence to Vicki.

on his face. But when he searched Lawrence, he found that the bulging pocket held only the lonesome-looking dentures from Lawrence's empty jaw. They were still dripping denture polish.

28 "I had been cleaning them when you arrived," Uncle Lawrence explained with acid dignity.

29 He took the toothbrush from his other pocket and aimed it like a rifle.

30 "Quit that, you old idiot." Harmony tossed the toothbrush away. "For once you ain't done nothing. We came for your nephew."

31 Lawrence looked at Harmony with a faint air of puzzlement.

32 "Ma Frere, listen," threatened Harmony **amiably**, "those two white people in the car came to get him for the welfare. They got papers on your nephew that give them the right to take him."

33 "Papers?" Uncle Lawrence puffed out his deeply pitted cheeks. "Let me see them papers."

34 The two of them walked over to Vicki's side of the car and she pulled a copy of the court order from her purse. Lawrence put his teeth back in and adjusted them with busy workings of his jaw.

35 "Just a minute," he reached into his breast pocket as he bent close to Miss Vicki Koob. "I can't read these without I have in my eye." He took the eye from his breast pocket delicately, and as he popped it into his face the social worker's mouth fell open in a **consternated** O.

36 "What is this," she cried in a little voice.

37 Uncle Lawrence looked at her mildly. The white glass of the eye was cold as lard. The black iris was strangely charged and menacing.

38 "He's nuts," Brackett huffed along the side of Vicki's neck. "Never mind him."

39 Vicki's hair had sweated down her nape in tiny corkscrews and some of the hairs were so long and dangly now that they disappeared into the zippered back of her dress. Brackett noticed this as he spoke into her ear. His face grew red and the backs of his hands prickled. He slid under the steering wheel and got out of the car. He walked around the hood to stand with Leo Harmony.

40 "We could take you in too," said Brackett roughly. Lawrence eyed the officers in what was taken as defiance. "If you don't cooperate, we'll get out the handcuffs," they warned.

41 One of Lawrence's arms was stiff and would not move until he'd rubbed it with witch hazel in the morning. His other arm worked fine though, and he stuck it out in front of Brackett.

42 "Get them handcuffs," he urged them. "Put me in a welfare home." Brackett snapped one side of the handcuffs on Lawrence's good arm and the other to the handle of the police car.

43 "That's to hold you," he said. "We're wasting our time. Harmony, you search that little shed over by the tall grass and Miss Koob and myself will search the house."

44 "My rights is violated!" Lawrence shrieked suddenly. They ignored him. He tugged at the handcuff and thought of the good heavy file he kept in his tool box and the German luger oiled and ready but never loaded, because of Buddy, over his shelf. He should have used it on these bad ones, even Harmony in his big-time white man job. He wouldn't last long in that job anyway before somebody gave him what for.

45 "It's a damn scheme," said Uncle Lawrence, rattling his chains against the car. He looked over at the shed and thought maybe Albertine and Buddy had sneaked away before the car pulled into the yard. But he sagged, seeing Albertine move like a shadow within the boards. "Oh, it's all a damn scheme," he muttered again.

46 "I want to find that boy and salvage him," Vicki Koob explained to Officer Brackett as they walked into the house. "Look at his family life—the old man crazy as a bedbug, the mother intoxicated somewhere."

47 Brackett nodded, energetic, eager. He was a short hopeful redhead who failed consistently to win the hearts of women. Vicki Koob intrigued him. Now, as he watched, she pulled a tiny pen out of an ornamental clip on her blouse. It was attached to a retractable line that would suck the pen back, like a child eating one strand of spaghetti. Something about the pen on its line excited Brackett to the point of discomfort. His hand shook as he opened the screen door and stepped in, beckoning Miss Koob to follow.

48 They could see the house was empty at first glance. It was only one rectangular room with whitewashed walls and a little gas stove in the middle. They had already come through the cooking lean-to with the other stove and washstand and rusty old refrigerator. That refrigerator had nothing in it but some wrinkled

potatoes and a package of turkey necks. Vicki Koob noted that in her perfect-bound notebook. The beds along the walls of the big room were covered with quilts that Albertine's mother, Sophie, had made from bits of old wool coats and pants that the Sisters sold in bundles at the mission. There was no one hiding beneath the beds. No one was under the little aluminum dinette table covered with a green oilcloth, or the soft brown wood chairs tucked up to it. One wall of the big room was filled with neatly stacked crates of things—old tools and springs and small half-dismantled appliances. Five or six television sets were stacked against the walls. Their control panels spewed colored wires and at least one was cracked all the way across. Only the topmost set, with coathanger antenna angled sensitively to catch the bounding signals around Little Shell, looked like it could possibly work.

49   Not one thing escaped Vicki Koob's trained and cataloguing gaze. She made note of the cupboard that held only commodity flour and coffee. The unsanitary tin oil drum beneath the kitchen window, full of empty surplus pork cans and beer bottles, caught her eye as did Uncle Lawrence's physical and mental deteriorations. She quickly described these "benchmarks of alcoholic dependency within the extended family of Woodrow (Buddy) American Horse" as she walked around the room with the little notebook open, pushed against her belly to steady it. Although Vicki had been there before, Albertine's presence had always made it difficult for her to take notes.

50   "Twice the maximum allowable space between door and threshold," she wrote now. "Probably no insulation. Two three-inch cracks in walls inadequately sealed with whitewashed mud." She made a mental note but could see no point in describing Lawrence's stuffed reclining chair that only reclined, the shadeless lamp with its plastic orchid in the bubble glass base, or the three-dimensional picture of Jesus that Lawrence had once demonstrated to her. When plugged in, lights rolled behind the water the Lord stood on so that he seemed to be strolling although he never actually went forward, of course, but only pushed the glowing waves behind him forever like a poor tame rat in a treadmill.

51   Brackett cleared his throat with a nervous rasp and touched Vicki's shoulder.

52   "What are you writing?"

53   She moved away and continued to scribble as if thoroughly absorbed in her work. "Officer Brackett displays an undue amount of interest in my person," she wrote. "Perhaps?"

54   He snatched playfully at the book, but she hugged it to her chest and moved off smiling. More curls had fallen, wetted to the base of her neck. Looking out the window, she sighed long and loud. "All night on brush rollers for this. What

a joke." Brackett shoved his hands in his pockets. His mouth opened slightly, then shut with a small throttled cluck.

55 When Albertine saw Harmony ambling across the yard with his big brown thumbs in his belt, his placid smile, and his tiny black eyes moving back and forth, she put Buddy under the cot. Harmony stopped at the shed and stood quietly. He spread his arms to show her he hadn't drawn his big police gun.

56 "Ma Cousin," he said in the Michif dialect[2] that people used if they were relatives or sometimes if they needed gas or a couple of dollars, "why don't you come out here and stop this foolishness?"

57 "I ain't your cousin," Albertine said. Anger boiled up in her suddenly. "I ain't related to no pigs."

58 She bit her lip and watched him through the cracks, circling, a big tan punching dummy with his boots full of sand so he never stayed down once he fell. He was empty inside, all stale air. But he knew how to get to her so much better than a white cop could. And now he was circling because he wasn't sure she didn't have a weapon, maybe a knife or the German luger that was the only thing that her father, Albert American Horse, had left his wife and daughter besides his name. Harmony knew that Albertine was a tall strong woman who took two big men to subdue when she didn't want to go in the drunk tank. She had hard hips, broad shoulders, and stood tall like her Sioux father, the American Horse who was killed threshing in Belle Prairie.

59 "I feel bad to have to do this," Harmony said to Albertine. "But for godsakes, let's nobody get hurt. Come on out with the boy, why don't you? I know you got him in there."

60 Albertine did not give herself away this time. She let him wonder. Slowly and quietly she pulled her belt through its loops and wrapped it around and around her hand until only the big oval buckle with turquoise chunks shaped into a butterfly stuck out over her knuckles. Harmony was talking but she wasn't listening to what he said. She was listening to the pitch of his voice, the tone of it that would tighten or tremble at a certain moment when he decided to rush the shed. He kept talking slowly and reasonably, flexing the dialect from time to time, even mentioning her father.

61 "He was a damn good man. I don't care what they say, Albertine, I knew him."

---

2. **Michif dialect** also known as French Cree, spoken generally by older descendents of indigenous people and European fur trappers on the central plains of Canada and in the upper central continental United States

62 Albertine looked at the stone butterfly that spread its wings across her fist. The wings looked light and cool, not heavy. It almost looked like it was ready to fly. Harmony wanted to get to Albertine through her father but she would not think about American Horse. She concentrated on the sky blue stone.

63 Yet the shape of the stone, the color, betrayed her.

64 She saw her father suddenly, bending at the grille of their old gray car. She was small then. The memory came from so long ago it seemed like a dream— narrowly focused, snapshot-clear. He was bending by the grille in the sun. It was hot summer. Wings of sweat, dark blue, spread across the back of his work shirt. He always wore soft blue shirts, the color of shade cloudier than this stone. His stiff hair had grown out of its short haircut and flopped over his forehead. When he stood up and turned away from the car, Albertine saw that he had a butterfly.

65 "It's dead," he told her. "Broke its wings and died on the grille." She must have been five, maybe six, wearing one of the boy's tee-shirts Mama bleached in hilex-water.[3] American Horse took the butterfly, a black and yellow one, and rubbed it on Albertine's collarbone and chest and arms until the color and the powder of it were blended into her skin.

66 "For grace," he said.

67 And Albertine had felt a strange lightening in her arms, in her chest, when he did this and said, "For grace." The way he said it, grace meant everything the butterfly was. The sharp delicate wings. The way it floated over grass. The way its wings seemed to breathe fanning in the sun. The wisdom of the way it blended into the flowers or changed into a leaf. In herself she felt the same kind of possibilities and closed her eyes almost in shock or pain, she felt so light and powerful at that moment.

68 Then her father had caught her and thrown her high into the air. She could not remember landing in his arms or landing at all. She only remembered the sun filling her eyes and the world tipping crazily behind her, out of sight.

69 "He was a damn good man," Harmony said again.

70 Albertine heard his starched uniform gathering before his boots hit the ground. Once, twice, three times. It took him four solid jumps to get right where she wanted him. She kicked the plank door open when he reached for the handle and the corner caught him on the jaw. He faltered, and Albertine hit him flat on the chin with the butterfly. She hit him so hard the shock of it

---

3. **hilex-water** referring to Hilex, a brand of bleach

went up her arm like a string pulled taut. Her fist opened, numb, and she let the belt unloop before she closed her hand on the tip end of it and sent the stone butterfly swooping out in a wide circle around her as if it was on the end of a leash. Harmony reeled backward as she walked toward him swinging the belt. She expected him to fall but he just stumbled. And then he took the gun from his hip.

71   Albertine let the belt go limp. She and Harmony stood within feet of each other, breathing. Each heard the human sound of air going in and out of the other person's lungs. Each read the face of the other as if **deciphering** letters carved into softly eroding veins of stone. Albertine saw the pattern of tiny arteries that age, drink, and hard living had blown to the surface of the man's face. She saw the spoked wheels of his iris and the arteries like tangled threads that sewed him up. She saw the living net of springs and tissue that held him together, and trapped him. She saw the random, intimate plan of his person. She took a quick shallow breath and her face went strange and tight. She saw the black veins in the wings of the butterfly, roads burnt into a map, and then she was located somewhere in the net of veins and **sinew** that was the tragic complexity of the world so she did not see Officer Brackett and Vicki Koob rushing toward her, but felt them instead like flies caught in the same web, rocking it.

72   "Albertine!" Vicki Koob had stopped in the grass. Her voice was shrill and tight. "It's better this way, Albertine. We're going to help you." Albertine straightened, threw her shoulders back. Her father's hand was on her chest and shoulders lightening her wonderfully. Then on wings of her father's hands, on dead butterfly wings, Albertine lifted into the air and flew toward the others. The light powerful feeling swept her up the way she had floated higher, seeing the grass below. It was her father throwing her up into the air and out of danger. Her arms opened for bullets but no bullets came. Harmony did not shoot. Instead, he raised his fist and brought it down hard on her head.

73   Albertine did not fall immediately, but stood in his arms a moment. Perhaps she gazed still farther back behind the covering of his face. Perhaps she was completely stunned and did not think as she sagged and fell. Her face rolled forward and hair covered her features, so it was impossible for Harmony to see with just what particular expression she gazed into the head-splitting wheel of light, or blackness, that overcame her.

74   Harmony turned the vehicle onto the gravel road that led back to town. He had convinced the other two that Albertine was more trouble than she was worth, and so they left her behind, and Lawrence too. He stood swearing in his cinder driveway as the car rolled out of sight. Buddy sat between the social worker and Officer Brackett. Vicki tried to hold Buddy fast and keep her arm down at the same time, for the words she'd screamed at Albertine had

broken the seal of antiperspirant beneath her arms. She was sweating now as though she'd stored up an ocean inside of her. Sweat rolled down her back in a shallow river and pooled at her waist and between her breasts. A thin sheen of water came out on her forearms, her face. Vicki gave an irritated moan but Brackett seemed not to take notice, or take offense at least. Air-conditioned breezes were sweeping over the seat anyway, and very soon they would be comfortable. She smiled at Brackett over Buddy's head. The man grinned back. Buddy stirred. Vicki remembered the emergency chocolate bar she kept in her purse, fished it out, and offered it to Buddy. He did not react, so she closed his fingers over the package and peeled the paper off one end.

75 The car accelerated. Buddy felt the road and wheels pummeling each other and the rush of the heavy motor purring in high gear. Buddy knew that what he'd seen in his mind that morning, the thing coming out of the sky with barbs and chains, had hooked him. Somehow he was caught and held in the sour tin smell of the pale woman's armpit. Somehow he was pinned between their pounds of breathless flesh. He looked at the chocolate in his hand. He was squeezing the bar so hard that a thin brown trickle had melted down his arm. Automatically he put the bar in his mouth.

76 As he bit down he saw his mother very clearly, just as she had been when she carried him from the shed. She was stretched flat on the ground, on her stomach, and her arms were curled around her head as if in sleep. One leg was drawn up and it looked for all the world like she was running full tilt into the ground, as though she had been trying to pass into the earth, to bury herself, but at the last moment something had stopped her.

77 There was no blood on Albertine, but Buddy tasted blood now at the sight of her, for he bit down hard and cut his own lip. He ate the chocolate, every bit of it, tasting his mother's blood. And when he had the chocolate down inside him and all licked off his hands, he opened his mouth to say thank you to the woman, as his mother had taught him. But instead of thank you coming out he was astonished to hear a great rattling scream, and then another, rip out of him like pieces of his own body and whirl onto the sharp things all around him.

"American Horse" by Louise Erdrich. Copyright © 1983 Louise Erdrich, used by permission of The Wylie Agency LLC.

American Horse

First Read

Read "American Horse" After you read, complete the Think Questions below.

THINK QUESTIONS

1. What do we learn about Vicki Koob from the details she notices about Lawrence's home? Explain, supporting your answer with evidence from the text.

2. What does the memory of the butterfly in the grille add to the arc of the story? Cite evidence from the text to support your response.

3. At the end of the story, what attitude does Buddy have toward Vicki Koob? Provide evidence from the text to support your response.

4. The Latin word *consternare* means "to terrify." Keeping this in mind and using context from the story, what do you think the word **consternated** means? Write your best answer here.

5. What is the meaning of the word **sinew** as it is used in the text? Write your best definition here, along with a brief explanation of how you arrived at its meaning.

Skill: Story Structure

Use the Checklist to analyze Story Structure in "American Horse." Refer to the sample student annotation about Story Structure in the text.

••• CHECKLIST FOR STORY STRUCTURE

In order to identify the choices an author makes when structuring specific parts of a text, note the following:

- ✓ the author's use of any literary devices, such as:

    - foreshadowing: a way of hinting at what will come later
    - flashback: a part of a story that shows something that happened in the past
    - pacing: how quickly or slowly the events of a story unfold
    - tension: a way of evoking emotion such as fear, stress, or anxiety in both the reader and the characters

- ✓ how the overall structure of the text contributes to its meaning as well as its aesthetic impact

    - the effect structure has on the impact it makes on the reader, such as the creation of suspense through the use of pacing
    - the use of flashback to reveal hidden dimensions of a character that affect the theme

To analyze how an author's choices concerning how to structure specific parts of a text contribute to its overall structure and meaning as well as its aesthetic impact, consider the following questions:

- ✓ How does the author structure the text overall? How does the author structure specific parts of the text?

- ✓ Does the author incorporate literary elements such as flashback or foreshadowing?

- ✓ How do these elements affect the overall text structure and the aesthetic impact of the text?

American Horse

Skill: Story Structure

Reread paragraphs 63–70 of "American Horse." Then, using the Checklist on the previous page, answer the multiple-choice questions below.

YOUR TURN

1. The author uses a flashback to describes a memory that Albertine has about her father. What impact does this have on the reader and what does it reveal about Albertine's character?

   - A. The flashback reveals a memory of Albertine's father, which helps the reader better understand their relationship and shows how she is like her father.
   - B. The flashback reveals a memory of a dead butterfly, which helps the reader better understand how Albertine feels about death.
   - C. The flashback reveals an intimate experience between Albertine and her father, which reminds the reader of her humanity as well as her frailty and strength, despite her flaws and circumstances.
   - D. The flashback reveals a loving experience between Albertine and her father, which reminds the reader that she is like a butterfly who has been mistreated by society.

2. How does this flashback contribute to the overall meaning of the story?

   - A. The flashback captures the importance of dreams, memories, and the power of a mother.
   - B. The flashback captures the power of fathers, as well as the importance of the past.
   - C. The flashback captures the impact of memories on who we are, as well as the beauty of butterflies.
   - D. The flashback captures the importance of memories, human connections, and the power of familial love.

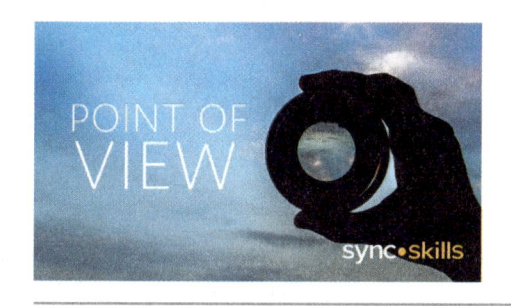

Skill:
Point of View

Use the Checklist to analyze Point of View in "American Horse." Refer to the sample student annotations about Point of View in the text.

••• CHECKLIST FOR POINT OF VIEW

In order to determine how a narrator's point of view through what is directly stated is different from what is really meant, note the following:

- ✓ literary techniques intended to provide humor or criticism. Examples include:
  - sarcasm, or the use of language that says one thing but means the opposite
  - irony, or a contrast between what one expects to happen and what happens
  - understatement, or an instance where a character deliberately makes a situation seem less important or serious than it is
  - satire, or the use of humor, irony, exaggeration, or ridicule to expose and criticize people's foolishness or vices

- ✓ possible critiques an author might be making about contemporary society

- ✓ an unreliable narrator or character whose point of view cannot be trusted

To analyze a case in which grasping a point of view requires distinguishing what is directly stated in a text from what is really meant, consider the following questions:

- ✓ How do the cultural lens and experiences of the narrator or speaker shape his or her point of view? How do the cultural lens and experiences of the narrator or speaker shape what the speaker says and how he says it?

- ✓ Is the narrator or speaker reliable? Why or why not?

- ✓ How does a character's or narrator's point of view contribute to a non-literal understanding of the text?

- ✓ How does the use of sarcasm, understatement, or satire add meaning to the story?

American Horse

Skill: Point of View

Reread paragraphs 55–61 of "American Horse." Then, using the Checklist on the previous page, answer the multiple-choice questions below.

YOUR TURN

1. This question has two parts. First, answer Part A. Then, answer Part B.

   Part A: What is Harmony's motivation for speaking to Albertine the way that he does in this passage?

   - A. He wants to connect with her about their shared heritage in order to convince her to surrender peacefully.
   - B. He has already exhausted all other approaches, and this is his only remaining option.
   - C. Albertine has indicated that she will negotiate with Harmony only if he speaks respectfully to her.
   - D. Harmony is fearful of Albertine and what she is capable of doing to him.

   Part B: Which line from the passage best supports your answer to Part A?

   - A. "But for godsakes, let's nobody get hurt. Come on out with the boy, why don't you? I know you got him in there."
   - B. "I ain't related to no pigs."
   - C. "He was a damn good man. I don't care what they say, Albertine, I knew him."
   - D. "'Ma Cousin,' he said in the Michif dialect that people used if they were relatives"

Close Read

Reread "American Horse." As you reread, complete the Skills Focus questions below. Then use your answers and annotations from the questions to help you complete the Write activity.

SKILLS FOCUS

1. Reread paragraph 1 of "American Horse." Explain how the author uses characterization and point of view to develop a theme in the text.

2. Identify a passage that describes Officer Brackett's thoughts about Vicki Koob. Analyze how Brackett's behaviors and underlying motivations contribute to a moral dilemma that influences the plot.

3. How does the structure the author uses to develop the setting contribute to the theme of the story?

4. Identify an instance in the text in which what a character says and what a character means are contradictory. How does this point of view add to your understanding of the story and its themes?

5. Each of the adults in this story believes he or she is pursuing a change that is on the right side of justice. Which adult do you believe is most motivated by justice and why? Support your answer with evidence from the text.

WRITE

LITERARY ANALYSIS: In "American Horse," author Louise Erdrich presents a Native American family experiencing a crisis. Towards the end of the story, Vicki Koob states: "It's better this way, Albertine. We're going to help you." Analyze Erdrich's use of story structure and point of view throughout the story to develop the perspectives of Vicki and Albertine. How are the perspectives of these characters integral to a theme about family identity? Use evidence from the text to support your analysis.

So Much Happiness

POETRY
Naomi Shihab Nye
1995

Introduction

Poet Naomi Shihab Nye (b. 1952) was born in St. Louis, Missouri, to a Palestinian refugee father and an American mother of German and Swiss descent. She is the recipient of numerous awards and honors, including a Lavan Award, several Pushcart Prizes, and a Guggenheim Fellowship. She also served as a Chancellor of the Academy of American Poets from 2010 to 2015. In her poem "So Much Happiness," Nye meditates on what it means to be happy, drawing on comparisons between sadness as an evocation of the past and happiness as a way to look to the future.

"Happiness lands on the roof of the next house, singing, and disappears when it wants to."

1. It is difficult to know what to do with so much happiness.
2. With sadness there is something to rub against,
3. a wound to tend with lotion and cloth.
4. When the world falls in around you, you have pieces to pick up,
5. something to hold in your hands, like ticket stubs or change.

6. But happiness floats.
7. It doesn't need you to hold it down.
8. It doesn't need anything.
9. Happiness lands on the roof of the next house, singing,
10. and disappears when it wants to.
11. You are happy either way.
12. Even the fact that you once lived in a peaceful tree house
13. and now live over a **quarry** of noise and dust
14. cannot make you unhappy.
15. Everything has a life of its own,
16. it too could wake up filled with possibilities
17. of coffee cake and **ripe** peaches,
18. and love even the floor which needs to be swept,
19. the soiled linens and scratched records...

20. Since there is no place large enough
21. To **contain** so much happiness,
22. you shrug, you **raise** your hands, and it flows out of you
23. into everything you touch. You are not responsible.
24. You take no **credit**, as the night sky takes no credit
25. for the moon, but continues to hold it, and share it,
26. and in that way, be known.

"So Much Happiness" from *Words Under the Words: Selected Poems* by Naomi Shihab Nye, copyright © 1995. Reprinted with the permission of Far Corner Books.

WRITE

DISCUSSION: Choose at least two examples of figurative language used in the poem and explain how they relate to the poem's meaning. Base your analysis on evidence from the text and original commentary.

LITERARY SEMINAR:
Democratizing Literature

Introduction

The Internet revolutionized publishing in the 21st century. What was once a lengthy and daunting process can now be done with the simple click of a button. Audiences and authors are closer than ever with the rise in popularity of "microblogging" sites such as Twitter and Instagram, which make self-publishing creative works quick, simple, and free. Authors have more creative control of their content than ever before, and audiences can even weigh in on the final product. What does the future of publishing look like, and what do these changes mean for print media?

Literary Seminar: Democratizing Literature

"... the distinction between creator and audience is breaking down..."

1   In the late twentieth century, authors who wanted their work in print often faced the **daunting** task of grabbing an agent's attention. If writers succeeded, their work faced further rounds of meticulous editing and workshopping for marketing strategies. All told, the production of a book could take about a year. On the Internet, however, an author can go from composing to publishing in a matter of seconds. New opportunities for digital publishing have lowered the traditional hurdles of the print publishing industry. Many have recognized a **democratizing** effect made possible by creative digital tools, which has resulted in more authors (2017 saw one million self-published books) as well as a greater diversity in authorship and content. Simultaneously, the distinction between creator and audience is breaking down, blurring the lines between writer and reader, creation and consumption.

On a modern printing press, putting a paperback book together can take several days, whereas on the Internet, a writer can share a book in an instant.

A Shift in Forms

2   One way to author content quickly on the Internet is via microblogging, that is, through short bursts of content released on services such as Twitter. Authors are meaningfully engaging with the platform to evolve new writing

forms with their own genre considerations and characteristics. Microblogging creates a reading experience akin to the evolution of thoughts and feelings over real time. Because readers must wait for the next bit of text, as opposed to print literature, the writer has the opportunity to create moments of almost film-like suspense. What's more, telling stories through microblogging requires the writer to be concise and allows the reader more interpretive room than they might have when there is more content to consider. David Mitchell, a best-selling British writer, was one of the first major novelists to release new content entirely on Twitter. His short story "The Right Sort" was released via twenty tweets per day, for seven days. The story was written in the voice of a character whose thoughts were short and scattered, so Twitter was the perfect medium. The platform allowed the reader to experience the character's thoughts one at a time as the character did.

Before she was a *New York Times* best-selling author, Rupi Kaur originally posted her poems to Instagram, pairing them with simple line drawings.

3   Poetry, in particular, has become immensely popular via microblogging sites like Instagram and Tumblr. For instance, Rupi Kaur, a best-selling poet, began posting short snippets of poetry with simple line drawings on Instagram. She would eventually elect to self-publish *Milk and Honey* in book form, as publishers wanted to pick and choose from her work, which she considered to be one long poem. By self-publishing, she was able to retain creative control, and the book made it to #1 on the *New York Times* Best Seller list, quickly selling over 3.5 million copies in print. Kaur's success reflects a larger trend: half of all books of poetry sold in 2017 are by so-called "Instapoets."

4   Podcasting, another mode of storytelling that has become available to content creators and audiences through the Internet, is composed of audio content. With over half a million podcasts released in 2018 alone, the format has proven to have a low barrier to entry. Many people who would never have been able to produce a traditional radio show have been able to launch a

podcast. The medium allows for elongated narratives and long-term fanbases. Similar to blogging, podcasts are released over time, allowing for the creator to control the schedule and speed at which the audience can engage with the content. One popular example, *Serial*, told the story of Adnan Syed, a young man who some believed was a wrongfully convicted murderer. The host of the podcast, Sarah Koenig, conducted hundreds of hours of interviews, re-investigating the case, and speaking with Adnan and others involved. Koenig pondered aloud for her more than 5 million listeners about the complexity of determining Adnan's guilt or innocence. These listeners tuned in for the suspenseful narrative and, week to week, engaged in conversations with each other on online message boards, fact-checking the podcast and sharing information. Listeners even tried to solve the case themselves, **reprocessing** the same evidence and primary sources that Koenig presented and creating new theories about what had happened, directly engaging the audience with the subject matter.

Blurring the Line Between Reader and Writer

5   Authors have **leveraged** innovations in form not just as a framework for composition, but also for crowdsourcing ideas, engaging audiences in ways that shift the traditional roles of content creator and content consumer. Neil Gaiman, a writer of speculative fiction and graphic novels, tweeted a first line of narration: "Sam was brushing her hair when the girl in the mirror put down the hairbrush, smiled, and said, 'We don't love you anymore.'" Afterwards, he solicited continuations of the story from Twitter users. The project culminated in *Hearts, Keys, and Puppetry*, an audiobook with the authors listed as "Neil Gaiman and the Twitterverse." For Gaiman's fans that participated in the composition, they were neither exclusively writers nor readers, but a mix of both.

Author Neil Gaiman on a panel at the Comic-Con International Convention in 2016. Gaiman has innovated in form to break down boundaries between writer and reader.

6   A **dynamic** relationship between reader and writer can also be seen in websites dedicated to long-form self-publishing, like Wattpad. These sites give budding writers access to an eager audience and have features, like annotations, that encourage specific interactions between audience and text. These platforms can even generate data to help determine what makes stories successful, helping authors produce more successful content and get published in the print industry. For example, Anna Todd, now a *New York Times'* best-seller, began by using a digital self-publishing site. She initially composed her 90-chapter One Direction fanfiction on her phone, transitioning content to the site and publishing one chapter at a time. After finishing a chapter, she would review readers' comments, using their reactions to construct the plot going forward. She felt an accountability towards her readers, and that relationship led her to produce writing informed by their feedback; in many ways, readers were part of the compositional process.

7   Such projects often beget questions about what makes someone an author. While some authors have chosen to release previously written content on these platforms to generate excitement and sales for their work, the examples above are part of a trend that makes the medium an important part of the creative process, wherein the relationship of creative ideation and consumption are more intertwined.

Twenty-First-Century Authorship

8   While in the past, the path to becoming a published author meant garnering the attention of a publisher, today, the evolution of digital self-publishing has allowed more and more people to create content and be read than ever before. For authors, this means a great deal of creative freedom, as well as a challenge to stand apart from the crowd. For readers, this provides opportunities to become involved in the development of content, whether as a consumer or as a part of the creative process.

9   Scholars suggest that future readers will continue to see experimentation with publication methods, more niche content, and more interaction between author and audience. Increasingly, narratives are told through combinations of printed and digital media, and stories are even being told in virtual reality, offering a fully immersive reader experience. As new technologies continue to emerge, modes of creating and consuming content will likewise change, but so long as authors offer rich and engrossing stories, they will continue to connect with their audiences.

Literary Seminar: Democratizing Literature

Read "Literary Seminar: Democratizing Literature." After you read, complete the Think Questions below.

THINK QUESTIONS

1. How has the Internet changed the world of publishing? Explain, citing specific evidence from the text to support your answer.

2. How does self-publishing benefit creators? Support your answer with evidence from the text.

3. How has the relationship between creators and consumers changed? Support your answer with evidence from the text.

4. What is the meaning of the word **reprocessing** as it is used in the text? Write your best definition here, along with a brief explanation of how you arrived at its meaning.

5. Use context clues to determine the meaning of the word **leveraged** as it is used in the text. Write your definition of *leveraged* here, along with those words from the text that helped you determine its meaning. Then check a dictionary to confirm your understanding.

Little Miss Sunshine

DRAMA
Michael Arndt
2006

Introduction

Little Miss Sunshine is a 2006 screenplay by Michael Arndt about a family from Albuquerque, New Mexico—the Hoovers—who set off to California in order for their youngest daughter, Olive, to compete in the "Little Miss Sunshine" beauty pageant. In the scene excerpted here, Olive and her grandfather play games in the back seat of their now-broken-down Volkswagen bus while the mother and father, Sheryl and Frank, strategize with a mechanic. Outside the car, Sheryl's brother Frank and her oldest son, Dwayne, look on.

"Dwayne watches bitterly—this is just one more fiasco he's been dragged into."

INT. VW BUS - PARKED - DAY

1   Sheryl is trying to back up the bus. She's grinding gears.

    RICHARD
2   Push the stick down hard!

    SHERYL
3   I'm pushing hard!

    RICHARD
4   Put the clutch in all the way!

    SHERYL
5   It's on the floor!

                                              JUMP CUT TO:

6   Richard tries. He keeps grinding gears as well. It's a horrible sound.

INT. SERVICE STATION GARAGE - DAY

7   Richard and Sheryl talk to a MECHANIC.

8   Behind them, Olive and Grandpa are playing that game where you try to slap the other person's wrists. When Grandpa gets hit, he reacts with cries of pain—much to Olive's delight.

9   In the background, across the lot, Dwayne and Frank sit on a cinderblock wall, waiting for the situation to **resolve** itself.

    MECHANIC
10 Well, you got a problem. Your clutch is shot.

    RICHARD
11 Can we get a new one?

      MECHANIC

12   Well, I tell you what: These old buses? We'd have to order it.

      RICHARD

13   How long'd that take?

      MECHANIC

14   Well, it's the weekend, so . . . Maybe Thursday?

15   Richard and Sheryl react.

EXT. SERVICE STATION - DAY

16   Frank and Dwayne sit silently. Dwayne watches bitterly--this is just one more **fiasco** he's been dragged into.

17   Frank looks on **wistfully** as Sheryl--thirty yards away--glances worriedly between Richard and the Mechanic. Frank notices Dwayne's stare. He speaks without looking at Dwayne.

      FRANK

18   I don't know if you know this, but growing up? Your Mom was the cool one. She turned me on to Proust. She could've done anything.

19   Dwayne looks at Frank—he can't quite believe this. He takes out his pad, half-smirking, and writes:

20   "What happened?"

21   Frank looks at the pad, then at Dwayne.

      FRANK (cont'd)

22   She had you, Dwayne.

23   He pats Dwayne on the leg, gets up, and walks back towards Richard and Sheryl. Dwayne is left alone, taking this in.

INT. SERVICE STATION GARAGE - DAY

24   Frank wanders in as Richard presses the Mechanic. Grandpa and Olive stop their game and join the conversation.

      RICHARD

25   Okay, look: we've come two hundred miles . . . Is there a dealership around here?

      MECHANIC

26   Well, you could call over to Clarksville, but they're probably closed. Y'know, it's the weekend.

Little Miss Sunshine

27   **RICHARD**
Yeah, we're all aware of that.

28 Silence. The Mechanic feels bad for them. Dwayne re-enters.

29   **MECHANIC**
Well, I tell you what: these old buses? You don't need a clutch to shift from third to fourth. You just ease up on the gas. You only really need the clutch for first and second.

30 Richard doesn't understand what he's getting at.

31   **MECHANIC (cont'd)**
What I'm sayin' is: as long as you keep parkin' on a hill, you get yourself goin' fifteen, twenty miles an hour, and you just start up in third. Then you shift between third and fourth.

32   **RICHARD**
And you can drive like that?

33   **MECHANIC**
Oh, yeah. The problem's just getting that speed up. As long as you keep parkin' it on a hill, you're fine. My brother and I once drove from here to Canada . . .

34   **RICHARD**
What if you're not on a hill?

35   **MECHANIC**
What?

36   **RICHARD**
I mean, it's sitting here right now. There's no hill. How do we . . . ?

37 The Mechanic considers this. He squints his eyes and runs his tongue back and forth across his teeth.

38   **MECHANIC**
Well, I tell you what: You get enough people—you just get behind there and push. Just push it up to ten, fifteen miles an hour, and you just go. Everybody jump inside, and you just go!

39 They all stare at him.

EXT. PARKING LOT - DAY

40 Richard's at the wheel of the bus. Everyone else, including the Mechanic, is behind the bus. The sliding door is open.

> RICHARD
41 Okay, ready?! Olive, Dad: I want you in the car first.

> OLIVE
42 I know. We know.

> RICHARD
43 Okay, is everyone ready?

> SHERYL
44 Yes! Let's go!

45 Richard starts up the bus. Frank turns to the others.

> FRANK
46 I just want everyone here to know I'm the **preeminent** Proust scholar in the United States.

> RICHARD
47 Okay, go! Push!

48 They all push. The van starts rolling, slow at first, then faster and faster. Finally, they're all running behind it.

> RICHARD (cont'd)
49 Olive, Dad, get in! Sheryl!

50 Olive, Grandpa, and Sheryl jump in the side door. The Mechanic fades. Frank and Dwayne keep pushing faster.

> RICHARD (cont'd)
51 Okay, I'm puttin' it into gear! Get ready!

52 He guns the engine and shifts from neutral to third. The bus is REVVING low but is powering itself nonetheless.

> SHERYL
53 Okay, get in! Get in!
> (to Richard)
54 Slow down! You're losing them!

> RICHARD
55 I can't! I can't slow down!

56 Dwayne runs up to the door. He sees Frank is fading.

57 He runs back to Frank, gets behind him, and pushes him up alongside the bus. Frank dives in. Dwayne dives after him.

INT. VW BUS - ON THE ROAD - DAY

58   Everyone cheers. Frank is panting. Dwayne shuts the door.

                    RICHARD
59   Is that it? Are we in?

                    FRANK
                (to Dwayne)
60   "No one gets left behind! No one gets left behind!" Outstanding, soldier! Outstanding!

61   Frank salutes him. Dwayne smiles, embarrassed.

Excerpted from *Little Miss Sunshine* by Michael Arndt, published by Newmarket Press.

WRITE

NARRATIVE: Write an account about a time, real or imagined, when something broke down. What was that experience like? How did those involved respond? Incorporate characteristics of literary texts such as characterization, point of view, setting, plot, and descriptive details in your narrative.

Hyperbole and a Half

INFORMATIONAL TEXT
Allie Brosh
2013

Introduction

First launched in 2009, *Hyperbole and a Half* is a quasi-autobiographical webcomic series. Creator Allie Brosh (b. 1985) humorously depicts personal everyday events from childhood to adulthood. In 2013, she published her first book, bringing her highly popular webcomic series to print. Brosh is perhaps best known for using purposefully simplistic imagery to accentuate the complex and anxiety-inducing absurdity of everyday life. In this excerpt, Brosh explores the agony of living in perpetual inaction.

"Surely I have more control over my life than this."

Motivation

One of the most terrifying things that has ever happened to me was watching myself decide over and over again—thirty-five days in a row—to not return a movie I had rented. Every day, I saw it sitting there on the arm of my couch. And every day, I thought, *I should really do something about that*... and then I just *didn't*.

After a week, I started to worry that it wasn't going to happen, but I thought, *Surely I have more control over my life than this. Surely I wouldn't allow myself to NEVER return the movie.*

But that's exactly what happened. After thirty-five days, I decided to just never go back to Blockbuster again.

Most people can motivate themselves to do things simply by knowing that those things need to be done. But not me. For me, motivation is this horrible, scary game where I try to make myself do something while I actively avoid doing it. If I win, I have to do something I don't want to do. If I lose, I'm one step closer to ruining my entire life. And I never know whether I'm going to win or lose until the last second.

Hyperbole and a Half

Hyperbole and a Half

Hyperbole and a Half

From HYPERBOLE AND A HALF: Unfortunate Situations, Flawed Coping Mechanisms, Mayhem, and other Things that Happened by Allie Brosh. Copyright © 2013 by Alexandra Brosh. Reprinted with the permission of Touchstone, a division of Simon & Schuster, Inc. All rights reserved.

WRITE

LITERARY ANALYSIS: In this excerpt from *Hyperbole and a Half,* Allie Brosh originally used a webcomic to explore the agony of living in perpetual inaction. In a brief essay, identify Brosh's message and analyze how it is impacted by the use of the webcomic format. How does technology complement literature? Make sure to reference the most relevant evidence from the text to support your response.

Hunger: A Memoir of (My) Body

INFORMATIONAL TEXT
Roxane Gay
2017

Introduction

Roxane Gay (b. 1974) is a Haitian American writer, professor, editor, and commentator. She is the author of the *New York Times* best-selling essay collection *Bad Feminist,* as well as the short story collections *Ayiti* and *Difficult Women*, and the novel *An Untamed State*. Her work centers on the female experience in society, sexuality, identity, and privilege. In her memoir *Hunger: A Memoir of (My) Body*, she discusses the lifelong consequences of being sexually assaulted when she was 12 years old. In this excerpt, Gay opens up about her struggle with self-image and feeling trapped in her own body.

Hunger: A Memoir of (My) Body

"My body is a cage of my own making. I am still trying to figure my way out of it."

7.

1. This is the reality of living in my body: I am trapped in a cage. The frustrating thing about cages is that you're trapped but you can see exactly what you want. You can reach out from the cage, but only so far.

2. It would be easy to pretend I am just fine with my body as it is. I wish I did not see my body as something for which I should apologize or provide explanation. I'm a feminist and I believe in doing away with the rigid beauty standards that force women to conform to unrealistic ideals. I believe we should have broader definitions of beauty that include diverse body types. I believe it is so important for women to feel comfortable in their bodies, without wanting to change every single thing about their bodies to find that comfort. I (want to) believe my worth as a human being does not **reside** in my size or appearance. I know, having grown up in a culture that is generally toxic to women and constantly trying to **discipline** women's bodies, that it is important to resist unreasonable standards for how my body or any body should look.

3. What I know and what I feel are two very different things.

4. Feeling comfortable in my body isn't entirely about beauty standards. It is not entirely about ideals. It's about how I feel in my skin and bones, from one day to the next.

5. I am not comfortable in my body. Nearly everything physical is difficult. When I move around, I feel every extra pound I am carrying. I have no stamina. When I walk for long periods of time, my thighs and calves ache. My feet ache. My lower back aches. More often than not, I am in some kind of physical pain. Every morning, I am so stiff I contemplate just spending the duration of the day in bed. I have a pinched nerve, and so if I stand for too long, my right leg goes numb and then I sort of lurch about until the feeling returns.

6. When it's hot, I sweat **profusely**, mostly from my head, and then I feel self-conscious and find myself constantly wiping the sweat from my face. Rivulets of sweat spring forth between my breasts and pool at the **base** of my spine.

Skill:
Connotation and Denotation

The choice of words like *ache, pain, stiff, pinched,* and *numb* all have slightly different denotations but all share a negative connotation. They describe the author's discomfort in her own body.

404 Reading & Writing Companion

My shirt gets damp and sweat stains begin seeping through the fabric. I feel like people are staring at me sweating and judging me for having an unruly body that perspires so wantonly, that dares to reveal the costs of its exertion.

7   There are things I want to do with my body but cannot. If I am with friends, I cannot keep up, so I am constantly thinking up excuses to explain why I am walking slower than they are, as if they don't already know. Sometimes, they pretend not to know, and sometimes, it seems like they are genuinely that oblivious to how different bodies move and take up space as they look back at me and suggest we do impossible things like go to an amusement park or walk a mile up a hill to a stadium or go hiking to an overlook with a great view.

8   My body is a cage. My body is a cage of my own making. I am still trying to **figure** my way out of it. I have been trying to figure a way out of it for more than twenty years.

Excerpted from *Hunger: A Memoir of (My) Body* by Roxane Gay, published by HarperCollins.

Hunger: A Memoir of (My) Body

First Read

Read *Hunger: A Memoir of (My) Body*. After you read, complete the Think Questions below.

THINK QUESTIONS

1. What does the author mean when she says, "I am trapped in a cage"? Cite evidence from the text to support your thinking.

2. What does the author think about how women and women's bodies are treated by society? What do you think contributes to her point of view? Refer to the text in your response.

3. According to the author, how does her body impact her daily life? Use evidence from the text to support your answer.

4. Use context clues to determine the meaning of the word **profusely**. Write your best definition here, along with the words or phrases from the text that helped you determine the meaning. Finally, check a dictionary to confirm your understanding.

5. The word **figure** comes from the Latin *figura*, which means "shape, figure, form." With that information in mind and using context clues, write the definition for *figure* as it is used in the text. How does your definition compare or contrast to the Latin definition? Explain, and cite any context clues that helped you arrive at your understanding.

Skill: Connotation and Denotation

Use the Checklist to analyze Connotation and Denotation in *Hunger: A Memoir of (My) Body*. Refer to the sample student annotations about Connotation and Denotation in the text.

••• CHECKLIST FOR CONNOTATION AND DENOTATION

In order to identify the denotative meanings of words, use the following steps:

- ✓ first, note unfamiliar words and phrases, key words, or words that inspire an emotional reaction
- ✓ next, determine and note the denotative meaning of words by consulting a reference material such as a dictionary, glossary, or thesaurus
- ✓ finally, analyze nuances in the meanings of words with similar denotations

To better understand the meanings of words and phrases as they are used in a text, including connotative meanings, use the following questions as a guide:

- ✓ What is the genre or subject of the text? Based on context, what do you think the meaning of the word is intended to be?
- ✓ Is your inference the same or different from the dictionary definition?
- ✓ Does the word create a positive, negative, or neutral emotion?
- ✓ What synonyms or alternative phrasing help you describe the connotative meaning of the word?

To determine the meanings of words and phrases as they are used in a text, including connotative meanings, use the following questions as a guide:

- ✓ What is the denotative meaning of the word? Is that denotative meaning correct in context?
- ✓ What possible positive, neutral, or negative connotations might the word have, depending on context?
- ✓ What textual details signal a particular connotation for the word?

Hunger: A Memoir of (My) Body

Skill: Connotation and Denotation

Reread paragraphs 6–8 of *Hunger: A Memoir of (My) Body*. Then, using the Checklist on the previous page, answer the multiple-choice questions below.

YOUR TURN

1. What is the connotation of the words *unruly, wantonly,* and *dares,* and what does this reveal to the reader about the struggles of the author?

   - A. These words have a positive connotation and reveal to the reader that the author feels that she is strong and daring.
   - B. These words have a neutral connotation and reveal to the reader that the author feels that she is physically unfit.
   - C. These words have a negative connotation and reveal to the reader that the author feels that she does not have control over her body.
   - D. These words have a negative connotation and reveal to the reader that the author feels that she is unattractive.

2. Why does the use of the word *cage* in this passage have a negative connotation?

   - A. The word has a negative connotation because it suggests that the author feels that she is trapped inside her own body, which is a cage.
   - B. The word has a negative connotation because it suggests that someone has robbed the author of her freedom.
   - C. The word has a negative connotation because it suggests that the author is trying to escape from her life.
   - D. The word has a positive connotation because it suggests that the author made a cage that helps her feel safe and protected.

Close Read

Reread *Hunger: A Memoir of (My) Body*. As you reread, complete the Skills Focus questions below. Then use your answers and annotations from the questions to help you complete the Write activity.

SKILLS FOCUS

1. Identify what metaphor the author uses to describe her body. Explain what the use of the metaphor reveals about the author's attitude toward her body.

2. Identify a word in paragraph 2 that has a positive connotation. Explain how you know the connotation of the word is positive.

3. To what extent do the author's friends described in this text understand her feelings and frustrations? Support your answer with evidence from the text.

4. The author makes it clear that success should not be measured by appearances. How do you imagine the author believes we should determine if a person is successful?

WRITE

LITERARY ANALYSIS: The author uses the metaphor of the cage to describe her experience. Why does she use this image? How does she use words with strong connotations to elaborate on this metaphor and convey her feelings? Analyze the author's use of words with strong connotative meanings to illustrate this metaphor throughout the text. Cite evidence from the text to support your analysis.

Boyhood

DRAMA
Richard Linklater
2014

Introduction

In 2014, more than a century into the history of motion pictures, director Richard Linklater (b. 1960) did something entirely new. He released a fictional narrative covering 12 years of a boy's life using the same actors. Instead of casting children of different ages who looked alike, Linklater shot the film for two weeks every year—over more than a decade—to imitate real time. The result was a film that incorporated news and pop culture as it happened but also tracked the subtler changes in its child, teen, and adult actors over time. *Boyhood* was nominated for six Oscars including Best Screenplay and Best Picture, and won the prize for Best Supporting Actress for Patricia Arquette. In an excerpt from the screenplay, we observe teenage Mason and his dad on one of their twice-a-month reunions, a narrow window of opportunity for the father to offer guidance and support, and for Mason to seek his help with the mysteries of life.

"Guy's got to be responsible. What do you think?"

INT. MOVING CAR - DAY

1 Dad and Mason are driving along the open road, listening to a song by Wilco.

DAD

2 Now . . . listen to this song, alright?

3 Sings along:

DAD (CONT'D)

4 "I try to stay busy." It's just straight up, the lyrics . . . it's a straight up old school country song.

SONG

5 "I do the dishes, I mow the lawn . . ."

DAD

6 Listen to the **production** of this. Production's like uh, like "Abbey Road" or something.

SONG

7 "I try to keep myself **occupied**."

8 Dad sings along.

DAD

9 "Even though I know you're not comin' home." You know, his old woman's gone . . . straight up. Nothin' fancy.

DAD AND SONG

10 "I try to keep the house nice and neat. Make my bed. I change the sheets."

EXT. RIVERBED - DAY

11 Mason and Dad walk along the rocks, mid-conversation. They sit down near the water and begin taking off socks and shoes.

Boyhood

Skill: Media

Mason "shrugs" and acts casual about his moving away, but in the video clip I notice he tries to avoid eye contact and his tone of voice is too offhanded. Because of the video, I see that Mason is trying to conceal his sadness.

12   MASON
Yeah, I think she's about to get her master's **degree.**

13   DAD
Well, then she's gonna start applying for teaching jobs?

14   MASON
I think she already has.

15   DAD
Really? Where?

                    MASON
(shrugs)

16   All over.

                    DAD
17   All over Texas?

18   MASON
Yeah.

19   DAD
Well, if you gotta move, you gotta move, you know? It's no big deal. We can handle that. I'll still come get you every other weekend. I mean, unless she moves 500 miles away or something, it'll just be a little more car time. No big deal.

20   MASON
I'm just kinda sick of moving.

21   DAD
Well, I bet you are. But you know, you never know. I mean, I might have to move, right? I'm working for this insurance company now. These places get bought and sold all the time. You know? We'll just roll with it.

22   They take off pants, walk up to the water in boxer shorts.

23   MASON
I thought you were a musician?

24   DAD
I am but . . . life is expensive, you know. Guy's got to be responsible. What do you think?

25   Mason pushes his Dad into the water, then dives in himself.

DAD (CONT'D)
Hey, hey, you bast — Oh you, punk kid! You got no respect!

Dad splashes his son and they both begin to swim.

. . .

DAD
(back to Mason)

I guarantee you, you didn't do anything wrong. These high school love things, they never work out. Here, come here.

(MORE)

I mean, everyone's just changing so much. The odds of two young people staying on the same wavelength are . . .

MASON
Yeah, but still--

DAD
Look, and I also guarantee you that every day of your life that you spend crying over some silly girl is a complete waste of time.

MASON
She wasn't a silly girl, though. I mean, she's a serious person. I really thought we were—

DAD
What?

MASON
I don't know.

DAD
Here's the truth. Women are never satisfied. Ok? They're always looking to potentially trade up and that's, I'm sorry to say, what I think has happened to you, my fine-feathered friend.

MASON
What does that even mean?

DAD
It means don't hand over the controls to your self-esteem to Sheila.

MASON

38   Sheena.

DAD

39   Alright. It means you are responsible for you, not your girlfriend, your mom, not me. You. And if you truly take care of you, you will be amazed at how much girls like Sheena start lining up at your front door.

MASON

40   Great.

DAD

41   Yeah, you know, you just gotta separate yourself from the pack in some way. **Excel** at something, you know, and then you have your pick of the litter when them front-running hussies start sniffing around.

MASON

42   So what you're saying is, I should take up lacrosse.

DAD

43   Exactly. Or you could, you know, start a band. Worked for me a long time ago. I think it's still working for Jimmy. Or you just keep taking pictures.

MASON

44   She hated the pictures I took of her.

DAD

45   Alright. I'm sick to death of her, okay? I only met her a few times and yes she was cute, alright. But, truth be told I always thought she was a little bit, you know, a little bit too square for you. Y'know, not quite the same vibe.

MASON

46   You really thought that?

© 2014 BOYHOOD INC./IFC PRODUCTIONS I, L.L.C.

First Read

Read *Boyhood*. After you read, complete the Think Questions below.

THINK QUESTIONS

1. How often do Mason and his dad see each other? What is their particular arrangement, and why does it exist? Do possible changes arise? Cite textual evidence from the selection to support your answer.

2. What does Mason's dad say that clues us in to his level of dedication to their relationship and its current schedule?

3. Do all the scenes included in the excerpt take place in one visit? If so, how do we know, and if not, how do we know that? How much time does the excerpt span?

4. Which context clues helped you determine the meaning of the word **production** as the dad uses it in the screenplay? Write your definition of *production*, and indicate the clues that helped you figure out the meaning of the word.

5. Which context clues helped you determine the meaning of the term **excel** as it is written in the dialogue? Write your definition of *excel*, and indicate the clues that helped you figure out the meaning of the word.

Boyhood

Skill: Media

Use the Checklist to analyze Media in *Boyhood*. Refer to the sample student annotation about Media in the text.

••• CHECKLIST FOR MEDIA

Before analyzing multiple interpretations of a story, drama, or poem, note the following:

✓ similarities and differences in types of media, such as the live production of a play as compared to the film version

✓ the similarities, differences, and nuances that can occur between the written version of a work and an audio version

✓ the different time periods and cultures in which the source material and interpretations were produced

To analyze multiple interpretations of a story, drama, or poem, evaluating how each version interprets the source text, consider the following questions:

✓ How does each version or medium interpret the source text? What are the main similarities and differences between the two (or more) versions?

✓ How does a media interpretation of a source text influence or change the audience's understanding of the text? Include how ways of accessing the text might affect the reading experience.

✓ If each version is from a different time period and/or culture, what does each version reveal about the time period and culture in which it was written? Does information about the time period and culture allow you to make any inferences about the authors' objectives or intentions?

Skill: Media

Reread paragraphs 21–27 of *Boyhood* and watch the StudySyncTV episode. Then, using the Checklist on the previous page, answer the multiple-choice questions below.

YOUR TURN

1. The interaction of visual and audio media in the video clip is most likely intended to—

    - A. show that Mason has no respect for his father.
    - B. show that Mason and his father are joking around.
    - C. persuade people to treasure time spent with their parents.
    - D. show that Mason's father is disrespectful.

2. How does the video help support the script's message about the significance of Mason's relationship with his father?

    - A. The video clip contains a montage of childhood photographs, visually representing the memories Mason describes in the clip.
    - B. The video clip uses sound effects to convey Mason's sorrow about his parents' divorce.
    - C. The video clip uses audio and visual media to show that Mason and his father can have serious conversations, as well as joke around with each other.
    - D. The video clip uses audio and visual media to show that Mason and his father often have deep, meaningful conversations about the future.

Boyhood

Close Read

Reread *Boyhood*. As you reread, complete the Skills Focus questions below. Then use your answers and annotations from the questions to help you complete the Write activity.

SKILLS FOCUS

1. Identify a stage direction from the middle of the scene when Mason is a child. Watch the first film clip, and see how this stage direction is executed in the film. Then, analyze how the characteristics of the text and media work to effectively convey a message about childhood.

2. Identify a portion of the screenplay in which the dialogue enhances your understanding of the characters' emotions. Explain the inferences you are able to make based on the dialogue.

3. Identify details from the script that reveal that Mason has matured and grown older. Analyze how viewing the film alongside the text helps readers understand how Mason has transformed from being a child to becoming a young man.

4. In this excerpt, to what extent is Mason's definition of home connected to a place? Who or what represents home for Mason, particularly in the face of change in his life? Identify evidence from the text to support your answer.

WRITE

PERSONAL RESPONSE: Mason struggles to balance his own individuality with what others expect of him. Choose a crucial time from your own life when you felt torn between what you wanted and what others expected of you. Then, write a journal entry describing that experience and how you responded.

The Immortal Horizon

INFORMATIONAL TEXT
Leslie Jamison
2011

Introduction

Leslie Jamison (b. 1983) is a writer known best for her 2014 essay collection, *The Empathy Exams*. In this long-form piece for *The Believer* magazine, Jamison explores the origins, motivations, and idiosyncrasies of the Barkley Marathons, an extremely brutal race that spans over 100 miles of rugged terrain in Tennessee. Through the specificity of the anecdotes that Jamison has assembled, she seeks to answer the question of what drives people to seek out seemingly impossible challenges and push their bodies to the limits—in the face of long odds and extreme discomfort.

"The event is considered extreme even by those who specialize in extremity."

1. On the western edge of Frozen Head State Park, just before dawn, a man in a rust brown trench coat blows a giant conch shell[1]. Runners stir in their tents. They fill their water pouches. They tape their blisters. They eat thousand-calorie breakfasts: Pop-Tarts and candy bars and geriatric energy drinks. Some of them pray. Others ready their fanny packs. The man in the trench coat sits in an ergonomic lawn chair beside a famous yellow gate, holding a cigarette. He calls the two-minute warning.

2. The runners gather in front of him, stretching. They are about to travel more than a hundred miles through the wilderness—if they are strong and lucky enough to make it that far, which they probably aren't. They wait anxiously. We, the watchers, wait anxiously. A pale wash of light is barely visible in the sky. Next to me, a skinny girl holds a skinny dog. She has come all the way from Iowa to watch her father disappear into this gray dawn.

3. All eyes are on the man in the trench coat. At precisely 7:12, he rises from his lawn chair and lights his cigarette. Once the tip glows red, the race known as Barkley Marathons has begun.

I.

4. The first race was a prison break. On June 10, 1977, James Earl Ray, the man who shot Martin Luther King Jr., escaped from Brushy Mountain State Penitentiary and fled across the briar-bearded hills of northern Tennessee. Fifty-four hours later he was found. He'd gone about eight miles. Some might hear this and wonder how he managed to squander his escape. One man heard this and thought: I need to see that terrain!

5. Over twenty years later, that man, the man in the trench coat—Gary Cantrell by birth, self-dubbed Lazarus Lake—has turned this terrain into the stage for a legendary ritual: the Barkley Marathons, held yearly (traditionally on Lazarus Friday or April Fool's Day) outside Wartburg, Tennessee. Lake (known as Laz) calls it "The Race That Eats Its Young." The runners' bibs say something

---

1. **conch shell** the shell of a large sea snail which can be made into a horn

different each year: SUFFERING WITHOUT A POINT; NOT ALL PAIN IS GAIN. Only eight men have ever finished. The event is considered extreme even by those who specialize in extremity.

II.

6   What makes it so bad? No trail, for one. A cumulative elevation gain that's nearly twice the height of Everest[2]. Native flora called saw briars[3] that can turn a man's leg to raw meat in meters. The tough hills have names like Rat Jaw, Little Hell, Big Hell—not to mention Stallion Mountain, Bird Mountain, Coffin Springs, Zip Line, and an uphill stretch, new this year, known simply as "the Bad Thing."

7   The race consists of five loops on a course that's been officially listed at twenty miles, but is probably more like twenty-six. The moral of this slanted truth is that standard metrics are **irrelevant**. The moral of a lot of Barkley's slanted truths is that standard metrics are irrelevant. The laws of physics and human tolerance have been replaced by Laz's personal whims. Even if the race was really "only" a hundred miles, these would still be "Barkley miles." Guys who could typically finish a hundred miles in twenty hours might not finish a single loop here. If you finish three, you've completed what's known as the Fun Run. If you happen not to finish—and, let's face it, you probably won't—Laz will play taps to commemorate your quitting. The whole camp, shifting and dirty and tired, will listen, except for those who are asleep or too weak to notice, who won't.

. . .

IV.

8   The day before the race, runners start arriving at camp like rainbow seals, sleekly gliding through the air in multi-colored bodysuits. They come in pickup trucks and rental cars, rusty vans and camper trailers. Their license plates say 100 RUNNR, ULT MAN, CRZY RUN. They bring camouflage tents and orange hunting vests and **skeptical** girlfriends and acclimated wives and tiny travel towels and tiny dogs. Laz himself brings a little dog (named "Little Dog") with a black spot like a pirate's patch over one eye. Little Dog almost loses her name this year, after encountering and trying to eat an even smaller dog, the skinny one from Iowa, who turns out to be two dogs rather than just one.

9   It's a male scene. There are a few female regulars, I learn, but they rarely manage more than a loop. Most of the women in sight, like me, are part of someone's support crew. I help sort Julian's supplies in the back of the car.

---

2. **Everest** Mount Everest, the tallest mountain on Earth (29,029 feet) on the border between Nepal and China in the Himalayan range
3. **saw briars** thorny vines of the genus Smilax known for their sawlike appearance and effect on anyone who might brush past them

The Immortal Horizon

10   He needs a compass. He needs pain pills and NO-DOZ pills and electrolyte pills and Ginger Chews for when he gets sleepy and a "kit" for popping blisters that basically includes a needle and Band-Aids. He needs tape for when his toenails start falling off. He needs batteries. We pay special attention to the batteries. Running out of batteries is the *must-avoid-at-all-costs worst possible thing that could happen.* But it has happened. It happened to Rich Limacher, whose night spent under a huge buckeye tree earned it the name "Limacher Hilton." Julian's coup de grâce[4] is a pair of duct-tape pants that we've fashioned in the manner of cowboy chaps. They will fend off saw briars, is the idea, and earn Julian the envy of the other runners.

11   Traditionally, the epicenter of camp is a chicken fire kindled on the afternoon before the race begins. This year's fire is blazing by four p.m. It's manned by someone name Doc Joe. Julian tells me Doc Joe's been wait-listed for several years and (Julian speculates) has offered himself as a helper in order to secure a spot for 2011. We arrive just as he's spearing the first thighs from the grill. He's got a two-foot can of beans in the fire pit, already bubbling, but the clear stars of this show are the birds, skin-blackened and smothered in red sauce. The chicken here (as legend has it) is served partway thawed, with only skins and "a bit more" cooked.

12   I ask Doc Joe how he plans to find the sweet spot between cooked and frozen. He looks at me like I'm stupid. That frozen chicken thing is just a myth, he says. This will not be the last time, I suspect, that I catch Barkley at the game of crafting its own legend.

13   At this particular potluck, small talk rarely stays banal for long. I fall into conversation with John Price, a bearded veteran who tells me he's sitting out the race this year, wait-listed, but has driven hundreds of miles just to be "a part of the action." Our conversation starts predictably. He asks where I'm from. I say Los Angeles. He says he loves Venice Beach. I say I love Venice Beach, too. Then he says: "Next fall I'm running from Venice Beach to Virginia Beach to celebrate my retirement."

14   I've learned not to pause at this kind of declaration. I've learned to proceed with practical questions. I ask, "Where will you sleep?"

15   "Mainly camping," he says. "A few motels."

16   "You'll carry the tent in a backpack?"

17   "God, no," he laughs. "I'll be pulling a small cart harnessed to my waist."

---

4. **coup de grâce** a final action or event which results in death or destruction (Origin: French)

18 I find myself at the picnic table, which has become a veritable bulimic's buffet, spread with store-bought cakes and sprinkle cookies and brownies. It's designed to feed men who will do little for the next few days besides burn an incredible number of calories.

19 The tall man next to me is tearing into a massive chicken thigh. His third, I've noticed. Its steam rises softly into the twilight.

20 "So that whole frozen thing?" I ask him. "It's really just a myth?"

21 "It *was* one year," he says. "It was honest-to-god frozen." He pauses. "Man! That year was a great race."

22 This guy introduces himself as Carl. Broad and good-looking, he's a bit less sinewy than many of his fellow runners. He tells me he runs a machine shop down in Atlanta. As best as I can gather, this means he uses his machines to build things that aren't machines—like bicycle parts or flyswatters. He works on commission. "The people who ask for crazy inventions," he says, sighing, "are never the ones who can afford them."

23 Carl tells me that he's got an ax to grind this time around. He's got a strong history at Barkley—one of the few runners who has finished a Fun Run under official time—but his performance last year was dismal. "I barely left camp," he says. Translated, this means he ran only thirty-five miles. But it was genuinely disappointing: he didn't even finish a second loop. He tells me he was dead-tired and heartbroken. He'd just gone through a nasty breakup.

24 But now he's back. He looks pumped. I ask him who he thinks the major contenders are to complete a hundred.

25 "Well," he says, "there's always Blake and A.T."

26 He means two of the "alumni" (former finishers) who are running this year: Blake Wood, class of 2001, and "A.T.", Andrew Thompson, class of 2009. Finishing the hundred twice would make history. Two years *in a row* is the stuff of fantasy.

27 Blake is a nuclear engineer at Los Alamos with a doctorate from Berkeley and an incredible Barkley record: six for six Fun Run completions, one finish, another near finish that was blocked only by a flooded creek. In person, he's just a friendly middle-aged dad with a salt-and-pepper mustache, eager to talk about his daughter's bid to qualify for the Olympic Marathon Trials, and about the new pair of checkered clown pants he'll wear this year to boost his spirits on the trail.

28. Andrew Thompson is a youngish guy from New Hampshire famous for a near finish in 2005, when he was strong heading into his fifth loop but literally lost his mind when he was out there—battered from fifty hours of sleep deprivation and physical strain. He completely forgot about the race. He spent an hour squishing mud in his shoes. He came back four more times until he finally finished the thing, in 2009.

29. There's "J.B.," Jonathan Basham, A.T.'s best support crew for years, at Barkley for his own race this time around. He's a strong runner, though I mainly hear him mentioned in the context of his relationship to A.T., who calls him "Jonboy."

30. Though Carl doesn't say it, I learn from others that he's a strong contender, too. He's one of the toughest runners in the pack, a D.N.F. (Did Not Finish) veteran hungry for a win. I picture him out there on the trails, a mud-splattered machinist, with mechanical claws picking granola bars from his pockets and bringing them to his mouth.

31. There are some strong newbies in the pack, including Charlie Engle, already an accomplished ultra-runner (he's "done" the Sahara) and inspirational speaker. Like many ultra-runners, he's a former addict. He's been sober for nearly twenty years, and many describe his recovery as the switch from one addiction to another—drugs for adrenaline, trading that extreme for this one.

32. If there's such a thing as the opposite of a newbie, it's probably John DeWalt. He's an old man in a black ski cap, seventy-three and wrinkled, with a gruff voice that sounds like it should belong to a smoker or a cartoon grizzly bear. He tells me that his nine-year-old grandson recently beat him in a 5K. Later, I will hear him described as an animal. He's been running the race for twenty years—never managing a finish or even a Fun Run.

33. I watch Laz from across the campfire. He's darkly regal in his trench coat, warming his hands over the flames. I want to meet him, but haven't yet summoned the courage to introduce myself. When I look at him I can't help thinking of *Heart of Darkness*. Like Kurtz, Laz is bald and charismatic, leader of a minor empire, trafficker in human pain. He's like a cross between the Colonel and your grandpa. There's certainly an Inner Station splendor to his orchestration of this whole hormone extravaganza, testosterone spread like fertilizer across miles of barren and brambled wilderness.

34. He speaks to "his runners" with comfort and fondness, as if they are a batch of wayward sons turned **feral** for each year at the flick of his lighter. Most have been running "for him" (their phrase) for years. All of them bring offerings. Everyone pays a $1.60 entry fee. Alumni bring Laz a pack of his favorite cigarettes (Camel Filters), veterans bring a new pair of socks, and newbies are responsible for a license plate. These license plates hang like laundry at the edge of camp, a wall of clattering metal flaps. Julian has brought one

from Liberia, where—in his non-superhero incarnation as a development economist—he is working on a microfinance project. I asked him how one manages to procure a spare license plate in Liberia. He tells me he asked a guy on the street and the guy said, "Ten dollars," and Julian gave him five and then it appeared. Laz immediately strings it in a place of honor, near the center, and I can tell Julian is pleased.

35   All through the potluck, runners pore over their instructions, five single-spaced pages that tell them "exactly where to go"—though every single runner, even those who've run the course for years, will probably get lost at least once, many of them for hours at a time. It's hard for me to understand this—*can't you just do what they say?*—until I look at the instructions themselves. They range from surprising ("the coal pond beavers have been very active this year, be careful not to fall on one of the sharpened stumps they have left") to self-evident ("all you have to do is keep choosing the steepest path up the mountain"). But the instructions tend to cite landmarks like "the ridge" or "the rock" that seem less than useful, considering. And then there's the issue of the night.

36   The official Barkley requirements read like a treasure hunt: there are ten books placed at various points along the course, and runners are responsible for ripping out pages that match their race number. Laz is playful in his book choices: *The Most Dangerous Game, Death by Misadventure, A Time to Die*—even *Heart of Darkness*, a choice that seems to vindicate my associative impulses.

37   The big talk this year is about Laz's latest addition to the course: a quarter-mile cement tunnel that runs directly under the grounds of the old penitentiary. There's a drop through a narrow concrete shaft to get in, a fifteen-foot climb to get out, and "plenty of" standing water once you're inside. There are also, rumor has it, rats the size of possums and—when it gets warmer—snakes the size of arms. Whose arms? I wonder. Most of the guys are pretty wiry.

38   The seventh course book has been hung between two poles next to the old penitentiary walls. "This is almost exactly the same place James Earl Ray went over," the instructions say. "Thanks a lot, James."

39   *Thanks a lot, James*—for getting all this business started.

• • •

IX.

40   Why this sense of stakes and heroism? Of course, I have been wondering the whole time: why do people *do* this, anyway? Whenever I pose the question directly, runners reply ironically: I'm a masochist; I need somewhere to put my

craziness; type A from birth; etc. I begin to understand that joking about this question is not an evasion but rather an intrinsic part of answering it. Nobody has to answer this question seriously, because they are *already* answering it seriously—with their bodies and their willpower and their pain. The body submits itself in utter earnest, in degradation and commitment, to what words can speak of only lightly. Maybe this is why so many ultra-runners are former addicts: they want to redeem the bodies they once punished, master the physical selves whose cravings they once served.

41   There is a gracefully frustrating tautology[5] to this embodied testimony: Why do I do it? I do it because it hurts so much and I'm still willing to do it. The **sheer** ferocity of the effort implies that the effort is somehow worth it. This is purpose by implication rather than direct articulation. Laz says, "No one has to ask them why they're out here; they all know."

42   It would be easy to fix upon any number of possible purposes—conquering the body, fellowship in pain—but it *feels* more like significance dwells in concentric circles of labor around an empty center: commitment to an impetus that resists fixity or labels. The persistence of "why" is the point: the elusive horizon of an unanswerable question, the conceptual equivalent of an un-runnable race.

...

XI.

43   One of the most compelling inquiries into the question of why—to my mind, at least—is really an inquiry *around* the question, and it lies in a tale of temporary madness: A.T.'s frightening account of his fifth-loop "crisis of purpose" back in 2004.

44   By "crisis of purpose," he means "losing my mind in the full definition of the phrase," a relatively unsurprising condition, given the circumstances. He's not alone in this experience. Another ultra-runner named Brett Maune describes hallucinating a band of helpful Indians at the end of his three-day run of the John Muir trail:

45   They watched over me while I slept and I would chat with them briefly every time I awoke. They were very considerate and even helped me pack everything when I was ready to resume hiking. I hope this does not count as aid!

46   A.T. describes wandering without any clear sense of how he'd gotten to the trail or what he was meant to be doing there: "The Barkley would be forgotten for minutes on end although the premise lingered. I had to get to the Garden

---

5. **tautology** something that expresses the same thing twice

Spot, for . . . *why?* Was there someone there?" His amnesia captures the endeavor in its starkest terms: premise without motivation, hardship without context. But his account offers flashes of wonder:

47 I stood in a shin-deep puddle for about an hour—squishing the mud in and out of my shoes. . . . I walked down to Coffin Springs (the first water drop). I sat and poured gallon after gallon of fresh water into my shoes. . . . I inspected the painted trees, marking the park boundary; sometimes walking well into the woods just to look at some paint on a tree.

48 In a sense, Barkley does precisely this: forces its runners into an appreciation of what they might not otherwise have known or noticed—the ache in their quads when they have been punished beyond all reasonable measure, fatigue pulling the body's puppet strings inexorably downward, the mind gone numb and glassy from pain.

49 By the end of A.T.'s account, the facet of Barkley deemed most brutally taxing, that sinister and sacred "self-sufficiency," has become an inexplicable miracle: "When it cooled off, I had a long-sleeve shirt. When I got hungry, I had food. When it got dark, I had a light. I thought: *Wow, isn't it strange that I have all this perfect stuff, just when I need it?*"

50 This is **benevolence** as surprise, evidence of a grace beyond the self that has, of course, come *from* the self—the same self that loaded the fanny pack hours before, whose role has been obscured by bone-weary delusion, turned other by the sheer fact of the body losing its own mind. So it goes. One morning a man blows a conch shell, and two days later—still answering the call of that conch—another man finds all he needs strapped to his own body, where he can neither expect nor explain it.

Leslie Jamison, "The Immortal Horizon" from *The Empathy Exams: Essays.* Copyright © 2014 by Leslie Jamison. Used with the permission of The Permissions Company, Inc., on behalf of Graywolf Press, www.graywolfpress.org

✎ WRITE

CORRESPONDENCE: This text details the blunt hardships of a race—win or lose. Think about a significant victory or loss in your own life. Then write a letter to a friend, mentor, or confidante relating what you experienced and how it made you feel.

The Four Foods

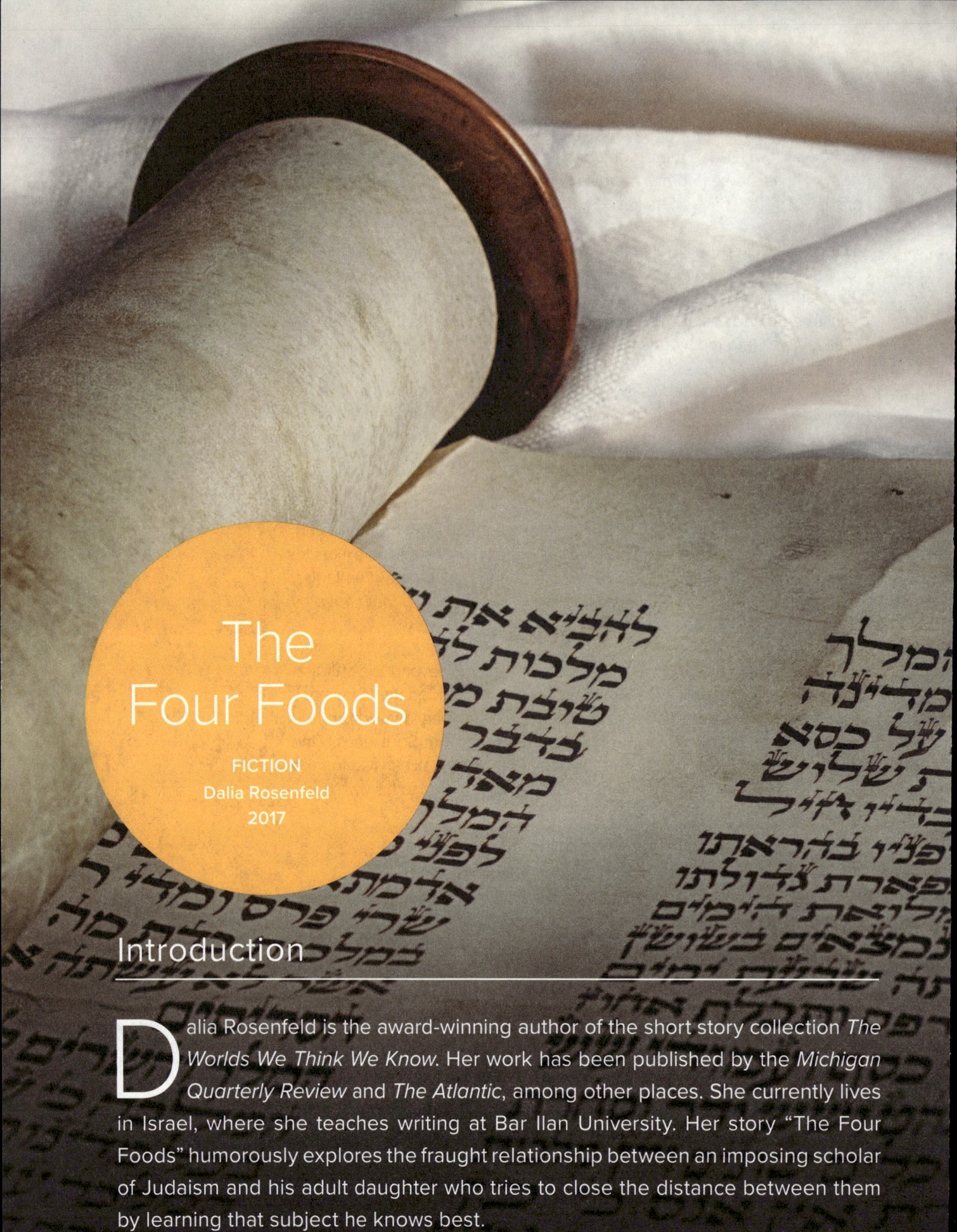

FICTION
Dalia Rosenfeld
2017

Introduction

Dalia Rosenfeld is the award-winning author of the short story collection *The Worlds We Think We Know*. Her work has been published by the *Michigan Quarterly Review* and *The Atlantic*, among other places. She currently lives in Israel, where she teaches writing at Bar Ilan University. Her story "The Four Foods" humorously explores the fraught relationship between an imposing scholar of Judaism and his adult daughter who tries to close the distance between them by learning that subject he knows best.

"Together my father and I chew. We chew and chew and chew."

1. My father is an **imposing** man. Small, with dark, sad eyes and gums that bleed when he brushes them in the morning. I ask my mother why he scares me so much. "It's his knowledge," she says. "He knows things."

2. I go out and buy a dictionary. I go out and buy textual sources for the study of world religions. History. Philosophy. The natural sciences. I craft concepts into sentences, theories into questions best asked over the telephone. I call my father. I say, "Dad?"

3. My mother tells me not to call him so often. "You're distracting him from his writing," she says. "Call me instead."

4. I cry into the phone. "You're so easy, and he's so hard."

5. "Now, honey." My mother tries to comfort me. "Now, pussycat."

6. We meet for lunch, my father and I. We sit across from each other like retirees and squint at the specials written in pink chalk above the counter.

7. Midway through our sandwiches we begin to talk. "Mom says she's allergic to goose feathers," I say. "What are you going to do with all the pillows from Europe?"

8. My father takes a sip of water. "Those pillows belonged to your great-grandmother. The feathers in them came all the way from Lvov."

9. I nod. "It's the **shtetl**. Mom doesn't want to go back."

10. My father sucks up a sesame seed through a gap between his teeth, and I wait for him to acknowledge my analysis. For years, the pillows have reminded my mother that she has not always been an American. Now she is starting to sneeze whenever she gets near them.

11. "There is no shtetl anymore. There is no going back," my father says.

12 "But **figuratively**, the Old World—" That evening, my mother scolds me over the phone. "There is no figuratively," she says. "Why do you always have to blab about what you don't know?"

13 "I thought we could talk about Europe or something—what it means to us."

14 "To us?"

15 "As Jews."

16 My mother thinks for a moment, then says, "Some Jews have allergies to feathers. I happen to be one of them. Burden your father with something else."

17 I sit in my apartment and stare at the wall. Through it I hear a brief hammering, then a silence, and then someone knocking at my door. I cannot pretend that it is anyone but Jake.

18 "Can you help me out a minute?" he says, pointing in the direction of his door, two pairs of bunny ears hanging from the toes of his house slippers.

19 While he nails a poster of Christie Brinkley to the wall, I lend Jake my eye. "Left," I say. "Left—OK, now right." "Like this?" "If it has to be." I try to take the encounter at face value. I try to subtract the hammer and the house slippers and the bikini behind the glass, and see Jake for the ordinary man he is. "The picture looks good," I say.

20 Jake opens the refrigerator and pulls out a carton of milk. He drinks. "What do you have on your walls?" I stare at the ring of milk above his mouth. "I'm waiting for just the right thing. A family picture, perhaps. Or maybe a picture of just my father, sitting at his typewriter. I would blow it up really big, and hang it in my living room." Jake puts down the milk carton. "Are you serious?"

21 I imagine my father sitting at his typewriter, whacking at the keys with **agitated** fingers. I have never actually seen him do this; the door to his study is always closed. "Maybe I would put it in the bathroom," I say, reconsidering.

22 "My father can only work in complete solitude." My parents have me over for dinner. We sit around the kitchen table like a family and pass things: the salad, the bread, the soup bowls to be filled and then refilled. My father pours himself a glass of wine for his heart and asks, "Leah, have you been jogging lately?"

23 "I made a few rounds this morning," I say. "And I was thinking, if Leonard Bernstein was Jewish, why did he write a Mass?"

24 My father stares at his reflection in the soup. "I really don't know, honey."

25 I wait for more, but nothing comes. "Of course you know," I say. "You just don't feel like thinking when I'm around." My mother deflects a frown by raising a napkin to her lips. "Leonard Bernstein is dead," she says firmly. "There's nothing to think about." She lowers the napkin and frowns anyway. I turn to my father. He looks tired. A nerve twitches at his neck whenever he swallows, as though keeping time to some silent music. My father sees me looking and says, "You think a lot about Jews, don't you?"

26 I shrug. "I guess it runs in the family." My father has written many books, all of them about Jews.

27 "How about thinking about the family instead?" my mother suggests.

28 I want to explain to my father that I am trying to do just that, but he is already immersed in other, more intimate concerns, his eyes looking right at me but without registering a thing. Mahler's conversion to Catholicism? The expulsion from Spain? 1933? I am losing him. Again. Still. I call my mother. I say, "It's not his knowledge. It's something else."

29 "It's *your* knowledge," my mother agrees. "It gets in the way."

30 "My knowledge? What do I know?"

31 "Nothing," my mother agrees. "That's the problem."

32 I go out and attend lectures, study forms and functions, foundations and first principles. I take notes while watching television. It is not a joke, I don't laugh. Usually I cry.

33 My mother calls me in the midst of it all. "Your father is in the hospital," she says. "He's got a hernia."

34 "Was it me?" I ask.

35 "It wasn't me," my mother says. I visit my father in the hospital. He is lying in a small white bed in a small white room divided by a curtain. The nurse has parted his hair on the wrong side. My mother tells me to leave the curtain drawn; a very sick man is lying on the other side, and the separation will do my father good.

36 I look at my father, open my mouth, then close it again. My mother takes over. "How are you feeling, Howard?" My father sticks out his tongue. "Ugh," he says. I have never heard my father say ugh before. I repeat it. "Ugh?" My

The Four Foods

37 mother pretends to smooth out a wrinkle in my father's sheet, and pinches me. "Ow!" I squeal.

37 My father opens his eyes a little wider. "Ow?" Soon the nurse comes in to serve lunch. She places a plastic tray wrapped in aluminum foil on my father's lap, then disappears behind the curtain. I sit at the edge of my father's bed and remove the foil. Together we study the four **compartments**: chicken, broccoli, pears, water.

38 There is so much I want to say to my father at this moment, but I'm not sure where to begin, especially with my mother standing over me, at the ready. At the very least I want to tell him how good he looks in his hospital gown, like one of the high priests of the Temple in Jerusalem, before it was destroyed.

39 "You look good, Dad," I say, blinking away everything in the room but the robe. I am close enough to feel that it is cotton. "Like one of the *kohanim*[1] in the *Beit Hamikdash*."[2]

40 I give my father a few seconds to answer, and when he doesn't, pick up the fork on his tray and slide it under a piece of chicken.

41 "What are you doing, Leah?" My mother tries to stop me, but I push her away. During visiting hours he is as much mine as anyone else's. Carefully I reach over and place the chicken into my father's mouth.

42 My father takes the food between his lips. He chews and chews and chews. "How is the food, Howard?" my mother asks, still thinking I am flubbing it all up. "Is it too salty?" Before he can answer, I break off two more pieces of chicken with my fingers. One piece I gently push into my father's mouth; the second piece I put into my own.

43 Together my father and I chew. We chew and chew and chew.

44 When we can chew no more, I look at my father and wait for a signal.

45 "*Nu*, how's the food, you pigs?" my mother asks again.

46 We swallow; my father belches. The stripes of his gown ripple under his raised belly.

47 Together we say, "Mmm."

---

1. **kohanim** hereditary Jewish priests of the first temple on Jerusalem's Temple Mount
2. **Beit Hamikdash** the first temple on Jerusalem's Temple Mount

Dalia Rosenfeld, "The Four Foods" from *The Worlds We Think We Know*. Originally in *The Los Angeles Review*. Copyright © 2015, 2017 by Dalia Rosenfeld. Reprinted with the permission of The Permissions Company, Inc. on behalf of Milkweed Editions, www.milkweed.org.

✏ WRITE

PERSONAL RESPONSE: Can you relate to the narrator's misunderstandings with her father? How much has your awareness of cultural or familial traditions been shaped, either actively or passively, by an older generation? Do you differ in the way you interpret those traditions? Are there particular traditions that bring you and your family together? Write a personal response in which you compare and contrast your experiences with those of the narrator and her father in "The Four Foods." Use personal anecdotes as well as evidence from the text in your response.

Gaman

POETRY
Christine Kitano
2016

Introduction

Christine Kitano is a celebrated Japanese and Korean American poet, as well as a professor of creative writing, poetry, and Asian American literature. Her works include the poetry collections *Sky Country* and *Birds of Paradise*. The title of her poem "Gaman" means "to endure, persist, or persevere" in Japanese. In this poem, the speaker explores her family history through the eyes of her grandmother, who immigrated to the United States from Japan only to have her family's life torn apart when her son, Kitano's father, was sent to an internment camp in Utah during World War II.

"For the sake of the children, / we'll teach them to forgive the fears of others"

1 It was night when the buses stopped.
2 It was too dark to see the road,

3 or if there was a road. So we waited.
4 We watched. We thought of back home,

5 how the orchards would swell with fruit,
6 how the trees would strain, then give way

7 under their **ripe** weight. The pockmarked
8 moon the face of an apple, pitted

9 with rot. But of course not. Someone
10 would **intervene**, would make of our absence

11 a profit. When we came, the boat, anchored
12 at San Francisco Bay, swayed for hours . . .

13 the gauntlet of uniformed men so intent
14 on finding cause to turn us away. And now

15 again, we wait. We watch. Our American children
16 press against us with their small backs.

17 Which gives us pause. For the sake of the children,
18 we'll teach them to forgive the fears of others,

19 the offenses. But what we don't **anticipate**
20 is how the dust of the desert will clot our throats,

21 how much fear will conspire to keep us silent.
22 And how our children will read this silence

23 as shame. However much we tried, we thought,
24 to **demonstrate grace**. When the buses stopped,

25 it was too dark to see the road. Or if there was a road.
26 It was night. And instead of speaking, we waited.

27 Instead of speaking, we watched.

Christine Kitano, "Gaman" from *Sky Country*. Copyright © 2017 by Christine Kitano. Reprinted with the permission of The Permissions Company, Inc., on behalf of BOA Editions Ltd., www.boaeditions.org

✏ WRITE

LITERARY ANALYSIS: Analyze how the characteristics of poetry are used to communicate the author's purpose and lend structure to "Gaman." Are the stanzas constructed similarly, or do they vary? Who is the speaker? What kinds of sound devices are used? Be sure to cite evidence from the text and specifically address stanzas, line breaks, speaker, and sound devices in your analysis.

Demeter's Prayer to Hades

POETRY
Rita Dove
1995

Introduction

Rita Dove (b. 1952) is an American poet, the second African American ever to receive the Pulitzer Prize for Poetry, and a former poet laureate to the Library of Congress. Her poem "Demeter's Prayer to Hades" is from Dove's collection of poems *Mother Love*. The collection is an exploration of the mother-daughter relationship set in Dove's retelling of the Greek myth of Demeter and Persephone. Demeter, the Greek goddess of agriculture, mourns the loss of her daughter, Persephone, who was kidnapped by Hades, the Greek god of the Underworld. In this poem, imagined as a prayer from Demeter to Hades, Demeter expresses her feelings towards Hades and warns him of the consequences of his actions.

Demeter's Prayer to Hades

"Believe in yourself, / go ahead—see where it gets you."

NOTES

**Skill:
Poetic Elements and Structure**

This poem does not have a regular rhyme scheme, but the poet does rhyme the first two lines, which draws attention to the message. She also uses anaphora in lines 2 and 3 to emphasize Demeter's message in the opening of the poem.

1 This alone is what I wish for you: **knowledge**.
2 To **understand** each desire has an edge,
3 to know we are responsible for the lives
4 we change. No **faith** comes without cost,
5 no one believes without dying.
6 Now for the first time
7 I see clearly the trail you planted,
8 what ground opened to waste,
9 though you dreamed a wealth
10 of flowers.

11 There are no curses—only mirrors
12 held up to the souls of gods and **mortals**.
13 And so I give up this fate, too.
14 Believe in yourself,
15 go ahead—see where it gets you.

Persephone Returns, by Leighton, Frederic, 1891

From *Collected Poems 1974–2004*, by Rita Dove (W.W. Norton, 2016). Reprinted by permission of the author.

First Read

DEMETER'S PRAYER TO HADES

Read "Demeter's Prayer to Hades." After you read, complete the Think Questions below.

THINK QUESTIONS

1. What is the speaker's tone in the first five lines of the first stanza? Use evidence from the poem to explain your answer.

2. What do you think the speaker means when she says, "There are no curses—only mirrors / held up to the souls of gods and mortals"? Use evidence from the text to support your answer.

3. What can the reader infer about the relationship between the "I" and the "You" in this poem? Use evidence from the text to support your answer.

4. What is the meaning of the word **faith** as it is used in the text? Write your best definition here, along with a brief explanation of how you arrived at its meaning.

5. Use context clues to determine the meaning of the word **mortals** as it is used in "Demeter's Prayer to Hades." Write your definition of *mortals* here, along with those words or phrases from the text that informed your definition. Check a dictionary to verify your understanding.

Demeter's Prayer to Hades

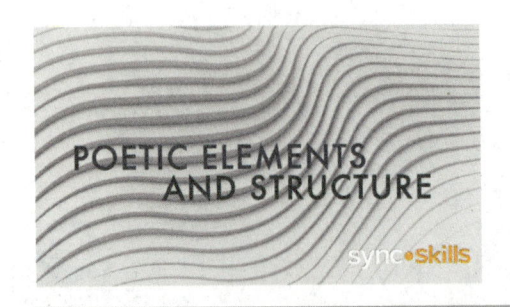

Skill:
Poetic Elements and Structure

Use the Checklist to analyze Poetic Elements and Structure in "Demeter's Prayer to Hades." Refer to the sample student annotations about Poetic Elements and Structure in the text.

••• CHECKLIST FOR POETIC ELEMENTS AND STRUCTURE

In order to identify a poet's choices concerning how to structure specific parts of a poem, note the following:

- ✓ the forms and overall structure of the poem
- ✓ the rhyme, rhythm, and meter and the sound or feeling they create
- ✓ use of devices such as anaphora (repetition of a word at the beginning of succeeding lines or clauses), assonance (repetition of a sound, usually a vowel, in nearby stressed syllables), or alliteration (repetition of a sound at the beginning of nearby words)
- ✓ lines and stanzas in the poem that suggest its meanings and aesthetic impact
- ✓ how the poet began or ended the poem
- ✓ if the poet provided a comedic or tragic resolution

To analyze how a poet's choices concerning how to structure specific parts of a poem contribute to its overall structure and meaning, as well as its aesthetic impact, consider the following questions:

- ✓ How does the poet structure the poem itself and its specific parts?
- ✓ How do the poet's choices contribute to the poem's overall structure and meaning, as well as to its aesthetic impact?
- ✓ How do individual elements contribute to the sense of the poem and to its message?

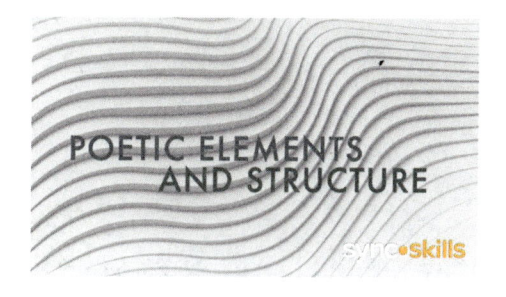

Skill: Poetic Elements and Structure

Reread lines 11–15 of "Demeter's Prayer to Hades." Then, using the Checklist on the previous page, answer the multiple-choice questions below.

YOUR TURN

1. Lines 11 and 12 contain an example of—

   - A. anaphora.
   - B. end rhyme.
   - C. alliteration.
   - D. metaphor.

2. Based on lines 13–15, the speaker's perspective, or view, is that—

   - A. Hades must look in the mirror to understand what it is like to be mortal.
   - B. if Hades continues to be selfish, he will learn it leads him nowhere.
   - C. Hades must look in the mirror to understand what he should do in the future.
   - D. if Hades has faith in himself, his fate will be to one day rule the gods.

Demeter's Prayer to Hades

Close Read

Reread "Demeter's Prayer to Hades." As you reread, complete the Skills Focus questions below. Then use your answers and annotations from the questions to help you complete the Write activity.

SKILLS FOCUS

1. Recall lines 3 and 4 of "Gaman": ". . . So we waited. / We watched. We thought of back home." Compare the alliteration used in these lines with that used in lines 1–4 of "Demeter's Prayer to Hades."

2. In "Gaman," some lines do not have end punctuation, may divide clauses, and use enjambment, creating a flow of words from line to line. Analyze how line breaks are used in "Demeter's Prayer to Hades," and suggest why the author made these decisions.

3. The speaker reveals a realization near the end of "Gaman" that begins with the words "But what we don't anticipate . . ." Where does Demeter reveal a new self-knowledge in "Demeter's Prayer to Hades"? Compare and contrast the realizations, considering the impact each has on the speaker's understanding.

4. Recall in "The Four Foods" when Leah breaks off two pieces of chicken, taking one piece for herself and feeding the other to her father. Then locate the passage in "Demeter's Prayer to Hades" that discusses mirrors. Analyze the context in each text to draw a conclusion about the meaning of the imagery and how it relates to a theme concerning self-knowledge.

5. Identify the role that justice plays in "Demeter's Prayer to Hades." To what extent does Demeter seek to bring about justice? Cite textual evidence to support your response.

WRITE

LITERARY ANALYSIS: "Demeter's Prayer to Hades," "The Four Foods," and "Gaman" all implicitly address the subject of self-knowledge. Analyze how each text addresses this topic. What is each author's message about self-knowledge? How does the poetic or narrative structure help shape the author's message? Are the messages in the three texts similar or different? How so? Cite evidence from each text in your analysis.

Extended Oral Project and Grammar

Extended Oral Project and Grammar

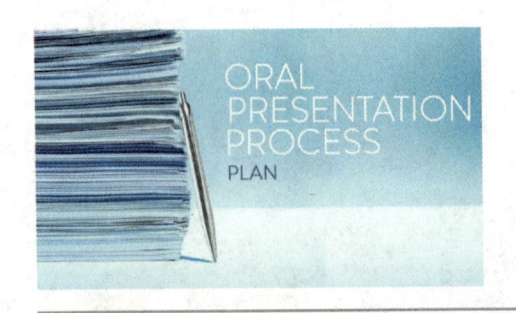

Oral Presentation Process: Plan

| PLAN | DRAFT | REVISE | EDIT AND PRESENT |

Members of a society are connected in many ways. Consequently, the actions of one person may, with or without intention, harm someone else. When we feel we have been wronged, we often have the right to pursue a fairer outcome, though the path to justice is rarely an easy one.

WRITING PROMPT

How can we seek justice?

"American Horse," *Fences*, and *Hunger: A Memoir of (My) Body* all explore themes of justice and injustice on different levels, ranging from individual to national. In each of these texts, individuals and groups advocate or yearn for a more just world. Think of a change, whether in your school or society, that you believe would result in greater equity. Then, craft a thesis to argue why this change should be made, how it should be implemented, and why it would be beneficial. Be sure to include specific evidence from the texts or outside research to support your argument. Then, consider how you might include visual aids to enhance your audience's comprehension or engagement. Additionally, use rhetorical devices in your presentation in order to persuade your audience. In order to prepare for your presentation, consider how best to meet the needs of the audience, purpose, and occasion by employing the following:

- a logical structure, including smooth transitions
- accurate evidence, well-chosen details, and rhetorical devices
- speaking techniques such as eye contact, an appropriate speaking rate and volume, enunciation, pauses for effect, purposeful gestures, and a confident and relaxed posture
- visual aids that support the information presented, including citations and a works cited list for any information obtained from outside sources

Introduction to Oral Presentation

Compelling oral presentations use both effective speaking techniques and engaging writing to express ideas or opinions. Oral presentations can have a variety of purposes, including persuasion.

The characteristics of an effective argumentative oral presentation can be organized into four major categories: Context, Structure, Style & Language, and Elements of Effective Communication. See the chart below, which you can use to help you plan, draft, revise, and edit your oral presentation.

Oral Presentation Guide

Context	Structure	Style & Language	Elements of Effective Communication
Audience Who will be listening to my presentation, and what information will they need to follow my argument?	**Thesis** What is the main claim in my argument?	**Formal** When I'm stating and proving my thesis, what formal language would be best?	**Verbal** How can I use rhetoric, speaking rate, volume, enunciation, and conventions of language to communicate effectively?
Purpose What do I hope to accomplish by giving this presentation?	**Reasons/Evidence** What reasons and evidence support my thesis?	**Informal** Is there anywhere in my oral presentation where informal language would be appropriate and effective?	**Nonverbal** How can I use eye contact, facial expressions, and purposeful gestures to communicate effectively?
Occasion Why, where, and when am I giving this presentation?	**Organization** How can I organize my ideas to exhibit a clear, logical structure with smooth transitions?	**Technical** When I explain a process, what technical language would be best?	**Media** How can I use slides, images, and videos to communicate effectively? Where are the best places to use graphic elements, any video or audio, or charts to enhance understanding and add interest?

As you continue with this extended oral project, you'll receive more detailed instruction and practice at crafting each of the characteristics of argumentative writing and speaking to create your own oral presentation.

Extended Oral Project and Grammar

Before you get started on your own argumentative oral presentation, read this oral presentation that one student, Susie, wrote in response to the writing prompt. As you read the Model, highlight and annotate the features of oral presentation writing that Susie included in her presentation.

NOTES

STUDENT MODEL

A Girl's Right to Learn

By Susie Anthony

Introduction

On mornings when frost covers our windows, the hot sun begs us outside, or we're exhausted from a restless night, going to school is the last thing we want to do. It's easy to take school for granted when its doors are wide open to us.

Introduction continued

But for one out of every five children globally, life is different. One-hundred thirty million girls worldwide are not in school ("Girls' education"). Imagine if you never had the choice to step foot into a classroom. Where would you be today? What kind of opportunities and future could you look forward to?

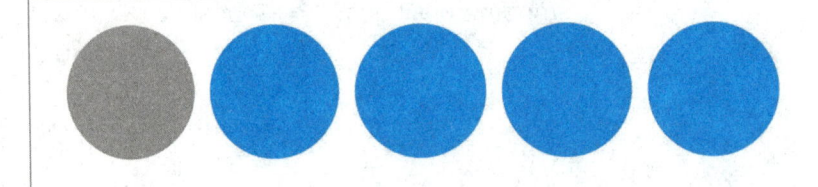

1 OUT OF EVERY 5 CHILDREN WORLDWIDE DO NOT ATTEND SCHOOL.
ONE HUNDRED THIRTY MILLION GIRLS WORLDWIDE ARE NOT IN SCHOOL.

"Girls' education," Malala Fund

Claim

Ensuring that all citizens of the world can fully exercise their human right to an education should matter to everyone. Access to school for girls and women is particularly crucial because they have been disproportionately affected by inequalities in education.

- Educating women provides a wider range of employment options and enables women of all ages to lead healthier and more prosperous lives.

- In order to enact change, it is key to understand how gender stereotypes negatively affect women's access to education. The Right to Education Initiative emphasizes the status of education as a "multiplier right," meaning that ensuring a woman's right to education dramatically increases her chances of improving her socioeconomic status by safeguarding "key rights, such as those related to work, property, political participation, access to justice, freedom from violence and health."

Education Makes a Difference

- Educating women enables women of all ages to lead healthier and more prosperous lives.
- Education dramatically increases a woman's chances of improving her socioeconomic status by safeguarding her "key rights."

Evidence and Analysis #1

Historical gender disparities in education have had a dramatic impact on women. For instance, over two-thirds of the nearly 800 million illiterate people in the world are women ("Facts & Figures").

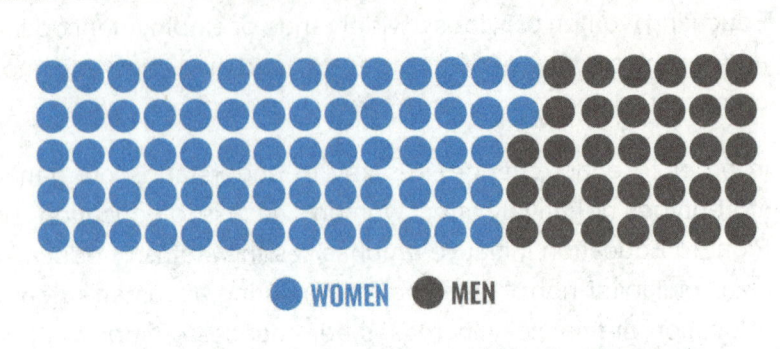

GLOBAL ILLITERACY RATES BY GENDER

● WOMEN ● MEN

"Facts & Figures," UN Women

Evidence and Analysis #2

Women's access to quality education in locations across the globe is blocked by a variety of factors.

- Many girls are pressured into the labor market at a young age in order to support their families. Instead of getting an education and learning the skills they need for professional employment, girls work in low-skilled jobs for low wages, which is detrimental to their health and development.

- A lack of education funding in some countries means families are required to pay for any education their child receives. For many families, especially those living in poor countries, the fees are prohibitive.

- Some schools even lack basic resources. Many students have to make long journeys to and from school (UNICEF).

Education Is Withheld for a Variety of Reasons

- Many girls are pressured into the labor market at a young age in order to support their families.
- Lack of education funding in some countries means families are required to pay for any education that their child receives.
- Some schools lack even basic resources and require students to make long journeys to and from school (UNICEF).

Evidence and Analysis #3

Educating women is beneficial on an individual and global scale because it is a multiplier right.

- Women with a secondary school education earn more money and are better able to support themselves and their families.

- The World Bank also found that not educating women "costs countries between $15 trillion and $30 trillion in lost lifetime productivity and earnings."

- Increased access to education means more women in the workforce and more people contributing to the world's economy.

- Investing in education for women, therefore, initiates a chain reaction that positively benefits women *and* society as a whole.

Educating Women Helps Everyone

- Women earn more money and are able to support themselves.
- Lack of education "costs countries between $15 trillion and $30 trillion in lost lifetime productivity and earnings" (The World Bank).
- More women in the workforce means more people contributing to the world's economy.

Evidence and Analysis #4

Organizations like the Malala Fund are working to increase girls' access to education.

- This non-profit organization supports women's education and gives young girls a platform to share their experiences.

Evidence and Analysis #5

The successful achievement of providing worldwide access to K–12 education for girls requires people to evaluate their own stereotypes about gender.

- In order to enact change, it is key to understand how gender stereotypes negatively affect women's access to education. Organizations like the Right to Education Initiative address gender stereotypes as a key factor in educational reform. They do not seek to change people's beliefs. Rather, they aim to point out that "gender stereotyping is considered *wrongful* when it results in a violation or violations of human rights and fundamental freedoms" ("Women and girls").

Gender Stereotypes

- Education for girls requires people to evaluate their own stereotypes about gender.
- Gender stereotypes negatively affect women's access to education.

Counterargument

You might be familiar with the stereotype that women's cognitive abilities are better suited for the arts and humanities. Such gender stereotypes discourage girls and women from pursuing STEM-related degrees or careers, producing inequality in education and employment.

- For example, gender stereotypes produce inequality in employment. Women represent 47% of the workforce, but only 12% of engineers ("Women in Computer Science"). A disproportionate percentage of men reap the monetary benefits of careers in engineering. Additionally, gender stereotypes lead to unequal political participation and representation. Consequently, women have limited access to or are barred from positions of power, which they could use to advocate for women's rights.

Gender Stereotypes

- A disproportionate percentage of men reap the monetary benefits of careers in engineering.
- Women have limited access to or are barred from positions of power, which they can use to advocate for women's rights.

Counterargument continued

The gender stereotype of domesticity is considered harmful when girls are forced to marry and bear children before the age of 18.

- According to the Global Partnership for Education, "Child marriage leads girls to have children earlier and more children over their lifetime. This in turn reduces the ability of households to meet their basic needs, and thereby contributes to poverty" (Wodon).

- Jessica Chastain sums up the issues with this practice in an interview with NBC (watch the interview in the Plan lesson on the StudySync site).

- The knowledge women gain in school prepares them to make better healthcare decisions for themselves and their families. Furthermore, non-adolescent mothers and their children have lower rates of health complications and mortality ("Missed Opportunities").

Conclusion

The ways in which girls and women worldwide are subjected to discrimination cannot be encapsulated by a single narrative. If we are to create justice, we must keep in mind that women all over the world face inequality in different ways. This may seem like a tall order, but the first step is to pay attention to experiences outside of our own. Denying a woman's right to equal education is also a denial of her rights to freedom and representation.

> Thank you for your attention! I hope you've gained a better understanding of the benefits of providing education to girls worldwide.
>
> "When girls are educated, their countries become stronger and are more prosperous."
>
> - Michelle Obama, FLOTUS Travel Journal: An Example to Follow

Conclusion continued

Elevating the status of women worldwide through equal access to education will improve the lives of deserving individuals and help cultivate future generations of enlightened leaders.

Works Cited

"About Us." Girls Who Code, Girls Who Code, girlswhocode.com/about-us/?nabe=6554069360181248:0.

Cook, Rebecca J., and Simone Cusack. Gender Stereotyping: Transnational Legal Perspectives. University of Pennsylvania Press, 2010.

"The Current State of Women in Computer Science." ComputerScience.Org, ComputerScience.Org, www.computerscience.org/resources/women-in-computer-science/.

"Facts & Figures." UN Women, www.unwomen.org/en/news/in-focus/commission-on-the-status-of-women-2012/facts-and-figures.

"Girls' education." Malala Fund, Malala Fund, www.malala.org/girls-education.

Global Partnership for Education, Global Partnership for Education, 29 June 2017, www.globalpartnership.org/blog/child-marriage-and-education-impacts-costs-and-benefit.

"Jessica Chastain talks about gender inequality around the globe." NBC News Archives Express, featuring Jessica Chastain, NBCUniversal Media, LLC, 2 June 2013, www.nbcnewsarchivesxpress.com/contentdetails/195331.

"Missed Opportunities: The High Cost of Not Educating Girls." The World Bank, World Bank Group, 11 July 2018, www.worldbank.org/en/topic/education/publication/missed-opportunities-the-high-cost-of-not-educating-girls.

Obama, Michelle. "FLOTUS Travel Journal: An Example to Follow." The White House Archives, National Archives and Records Administration, 27 June 2013, obamawhitehouse.archives.gov/blog/2013/06/27/flotus-travel-journal-example-follow.

"One in every five children, adolescents, and youth is out of school worldwide." UNESCO, UNESCO, en.unesco.org/news/one-every-five-children-adolescents-and-youth-out-school-worldwide.

"Supplies and Logistics: Education." UNICEF, UNICEF, www.unicef.org/supply/index_education.html.

Wodon, Quentin. "Child marriage and education: impacts, costs, and benefits."

"Women and girls." Right to Education, Right to Education Initiative, www.right-to-education.org/girlswomen.

Works Cited

"About Us." *Girls Who Code*, Girls Who Code, girlswhocode.com/about-us/?nabe=6554069360181248:0.

Cook, Rebecca J., and Simone Cusack. *Gender Stereotyping: Transnational Legal Perspectives*. University of Pennsylvania Press, 2010.

"The Current State of Women in Computer Science." *ComputerScience.Org*, ComputerScience.Org, www.computerscience.org/resources/women-in-computer-science/.

"Facts & Figures." *UN Women*, UN Women, www.unwomen.org/en/news/in-focus/commission-on-the-status-of-women-2012/facts-and-figures.

"Girls' education." *Malala Fund*, Malala Fund, www.malala.org/girls-education.

"Jessica Chastain talks about gender inequality around the globe." *NBC News Archives Express*, featuring Jessica Chastain, NBCUniversal Media, LLC, 2 June 2013, https://www.nbcnewsarchivesxpress.com/contentdetails/195331.

"Missed Opportunities: The High Cost of Not Educating Girls." *The World Bank*, World Bank Group, 11 July 2018, www.worldbank.org/en/topic/education/publication/missed-opportunities-the-high-cost-of-not-educating-girls.

Obama, Michelle. "FLOTUS Travel Journal: An Example to Follow." *The White House Archives*, National Archives and Records Administration, 27 June 2013, obamawhitehouse.archives.gov/blog/2013/06/27/flotus-travel-journal-example-follow.

"One in every five children, adolescents, and youth is out of school worldwide." *UNESCO*, UNESCO, 28 Feb. 2018, en.unesco.org/news/one-every-five-children-adolescents-and-youth-out-school-worldwide.

"Supplies and Logistics: Education." *UNICEF*, UNICEF, 23 June 2016, www.unicef.org/supply/index_education.html.

Wodon, Quentin. "Child marriage and education: impacts, costs, and benefits." *Global Partnership for Education*, Global Partnership for Education, 29 June 2017, www.globalpartnership.org/blog/child-marriage-and-education-impacts-costs-and-benefits.

"Women and girls." *Right to Education*, Right to Education Initiative, www.right-to-education.org/girlswomen.

Extended Oral Project and Grammar

WRITE

When you write, it is important to consider your audience and purpose so you can write appropriately for them. Your purpose is implied in the writing prompt. Reread the prompt to determine your purpose for writing.

To begin, review the questions below and then select a strategy, such as brainstorming, journaling, reading, or discussing, to generate ideas.

- **Purpose:** What will be the focus of your presentation, and what important ideas do you want to convey?
- **Audience:** Who is your audience, and what message do you want to express to your audience?
- **Thesis:** What claim will you argue about a change that will create a more just world?
- **Evidence:** What facts, evidence, and details might you include? Which texts will help you support your ideas? What other research might you need to do? What anecdotes from your personal life or what background knowledge is relevant to the topic of your presentation?
- **Organization:** How can you organize your presentation so that it is clear and easy to follow?
- **Clear Communication:** How will you make sure that your audience can hear and understand what you are saying?
- **Gestures and Visual Aids:** What illustrations or other visual aids could you use during your presentation? What effect will they have on your audience? What physical gestures and body language will help you communicate your ideas?

Response Instructions

Use the questions in the bulleted list and the questions you generated to write a one-paragraph summary. Your summary should describe what you will discuss in your oral presentation.

Don't worry about including all of the details now; focus only on the most essential and important elements. You will refer to this short summary as you continue through the steps of the writing process.

Extended Oral Project and Grammar

Skill: Organizing an Oral Presentation

••• CHECKLIST FOR ORGANIZING AN ORAL PRESENTATION

In order to present information, findings, and supporting evidence conveying a clear and distinct perspective, do the following:

- choose a style for your oral presentation, either formal or informal
- determine whether the development and organization of your presentation, as well as its substance and style, are appropriate for your purpose, audience, and task
- determine whether your presentation conveys a clear and distinct perspective so that listeners can follow your line of reasoning
- make sure you address alternative perspectives that oppose your own in your presentation
- make strategic, or deliberate, use of digital media, such as textual, graphical, audio, visual, and interactive elements, to add interest and enhance your audience's understanding of the findings, reasoning, and evidence in your presentation

To present information, findings, and supporting evidence conveying a clear and distinct perspective, consider the following questions:

- Did I make sure that the information in my presentation conveys a clear and distinct perspective, so that listeners can follow my line of reasoning?
- Have I presented opposing or alternative viewpoints in my presentation?
- Did I make sure that the information in my presentation follows a logical order, so my listeners can follow my line of reasoning?
- Are the organization, development, substance, and style appropriate for my purpose and audience?
- Have I made strategic use of media to add interest and enhance my audience's understanding of my presentation?

Extended Oral Project and Grammar

YOUR TURN

Read the sentences below. Then, complete the chart on the next page by determining where each sentence belongs in the outline. Write the corresponding letter for each sentence in the appropriate row.

	Sentences
A	I will provide examples of regions in need of resilient farming practices like Central America's Dry Corridor where agricultural production is affected by years of drought. I will also discuss successful initiatives such as how the Food and Agriculture Organization installed fisheries and coconut-based farming systems in the Philippines after Typhoon Haiyan.
B	I can use words like *next*, *since*, and *additionally* to improve the logical progression of my ideas.
C	Many people in the world rely on farming, livestock, fishing, etc., to feed their families and make a living. Every year, people become hungry or food insecure after natural disasters eliminate their source of food or income. People need to be educated about sustainable farming practices to eliminate hunger and reduce the risk of a world food crisis. We need to support farmers and build resilience against the challenges of climate change, malnutrition, and poverty.
D	In the end, I will reiterate the importance of taking action now to prevent a world food crisis. I will rephrase my thesis and summarize my main points.
E	I can include photos of locations devastated by violent weather and drought.
F	I want to convince people why it is important to collaborate and protect communities that depend heavily on farming from devastation due to natural disasters.
G	Some people might think that it is more important to invest in more secure food sources like genetically modified crops. I will explain the shortcomings of such an approach.

Extended Oral Project and Grammar

Purpose	
Introduction / Thesis Statement	
Body / Evidence	
Alternative/Opposing Viewpoints	
Visual Aids and Digital Media	
Logical Progression	
Conclusion / Rephrasing of Thesis	

✎ WRITE

Use the questions in the checklist to outline your formal oral presentation. Be sure to include a clear thesis and a logical progression of valid evidence from reliable sources.

Extended Oral Project and Grammar

Skill: Evaluating Sources

••• CHECKLIST FOR EVALUATING SOURCES

First, reread the sources you gathered and identify the following:

- where information seems inaccurate, biased, or outdated
- where information strongly relates to your task, purpose, and audience
- where information helps you make an informed decision or solve a problem

In order to conduct advanced searches to gather relevant, credible, and accurate print and digital sources, use the following questions as a guide:

- Is the material published by a well-established source or expert author?
- Is the source material written by a recognized expert on the topic or a well-respected author or organization?
- Is the material up-to-date or based on the most current information?
- Is the source based on factual information that can be verified by another source?
- Are there discrepancies between the information presented in different sources?
- Is the source material objective and unbiased?
- Does the source contain omissions of important information that supports other viewpoints?
- Does the source contain faulty reasoning?

In order to refine your search process, consider the following questions:

- Are there specific terms or phrases that I can use to adjust my search?
- Can I use *and, or,* or *not* to expand or limit my search?
- Can I use quotation marks to search for exact phrases?

YOUR TURN

Read the factors below. Then, complete the chart by sorting the factors into two categories: those that are credible and reliable and those that are not. Write the corresponding letter for each factor in the appropriate column.

	Factors
A	The author holds an advanced degree in a subject related to your topic of research.
B	The text is objective and includes perspectives that are properly cited.
C	The article states only the author's personal opinions.
D	The text makes uncited claims to persuade readers.
E	The article includes clear arguments that are supported by factual information.
F	The article is not peer reviewed or published anywhere of note.

Credible and Reliable	Not Credible or Reliable

Extended Oral Project and Grammar

🔄 YOUR TURN

Complete the chart below by filling in the title and author of a source for your presentation and answering the questions about it.

Questions	Answers
Source Title and Author:	
Reliability: Has the source material been published in a well-established book or periodical or on a well-established website? Is the source material up-to-date or based on the most current information?	
Accuracy: Is the source based on factual information that can be verified by another source?	
Credibility: Is the source material written by a recognized expert on the topic? Is the source material published by a well-respected author or organization?	
Bias: Is the source material objective and unbiased?	
Omission: Does the source contain omissions of important information that supports other viewpoints?	
Faulty Reasoning: Does the source contain faulty reasoning?	
Should I use this source in my presentation?	

Skill: Considering Audience and Purpose

••• CHECKLIST FOR CONSIDERING AUDIENCE AND PURPOSE

In order to present information, findings, and supporting evidence so that listeners can follow the line of reasoning and to ensure that the organization, development, substance, and style of your presentation are appropriate for the purpose, audience, and task, note the following:

- when writing your presentation, convey and maintain a clear and distinct perspective or viewpoint
- check the development and organization of the information in your presentation to see that they are appropriate for your purpose, audience, and task
- determine whether the substance, or basis of your presentation, is also appropriate for your purpose, audience, and task
- remember to adapt your presentation to your task, and if it is appropriate, use formal English and not language you would use in ordinary conversation

To better understand how to present information, findings, and supporting evidence so that listeners can follow the line of reasoning and to ensure that the organization, development, substance, and style of your presentation are appropriate for the purpose, audience, and task, consider the following questions:

- Have I organized the information in my presentation so that my perspective is clear?
- Have I developed and organized the information so that it is appropriate for my purpose, audience, and task?
- Are the substance and style suitable?

Extended Oral Project and Grammar

YOUR TURN

Read each statement below. Then, complete the chart by identifying whether the statements are appropriate for a formal presentation. Write the corresponding letter for each statement in the appropriate column.

	Statements
A	She was definitely the best NCAA soccer player that year.
B	Knowing basic first aid could help save lives.
C	According to its spokesperson, the labor union demands fair compensation for its members' work.
D	Some people seem to think that drinking green tea is the key to health, but I'm not sure if I can get on board with that.
E	I can't believe you don't know about Frank Lloyd Wright.
F	The majority of teachers reported an increase in student participation following the implementation of electronic tablets in the classroom.

Appropriate	Inappropriate

YOUR TURN

Complete the chart by answering each question about your presentation.

Question	My Response
What is my purpose, and who is my audience?	
Do I plan to use formal or informal language?	
What sort of tone, or attitude, do I want to convey?	
How would I describe the voice I would like to use in my presentation?	
How will I use vocabulary and language to create that particular voice?	

Extended Oral Project and Grammar

Skill: Persuasive Techniques

••• CHECKLIST FOR PERSUASIVE TECHNIQUES

In order to draft argumentative oral presentations, use the following steps:

- First, consider your audience and purpose by asking:
    > Who is my primary audience? What is my audience's primary motivation?
    > What is my purpose? What do I hope to achieve?
- Next, think about the following persuasive techniques and the ways you might use one or more:
    > Appeals to Logic
        o What facts or statistics will persuade my audience to agree with my argument?
        o What is the most effective way to present factual information to persuade my audience that my argument is logically sound and reasonable?
    > Appeals to Emotion
        o What emotions do I want my audience to feel about my topic?
        o What words or phrases should I include to bring about those feelings in my audience?
    > Appeals to Ethics
        o Which experts could I use to establish the credibility of my claims?
        o What words or phrases should I include to remind my audience of our shared values?
    > Rhetorical Devices
        o How can I use language in artful and persuasive ways to convince my audience?
        o What specific rhetorical devices, such as rhetorical questions, repetition, or parallelism, do I want to use to make my argument more persuasive?
    > Counterclaim
        o What is an opposing opinion that my audience might have?
        o How can I rebut that opposing opinion in a way that respects my audience and strengthens my argument?

YOUR TURN

Read the appeals below. Then, complete the chart by placing each appeal in the appropriate category. Write the corresponding letter for each appeal in the appropriate column.

	Appeals
A	Decorating your home with plants will have a positive influence on your mood.
B	The president of the local food bank has worked on issues of food security for over 25 years.
C	You should stay away from isolated tall trees during a thunderstorm because lightning tends to strike the tallest objects in an area.
D	Having worked as a counselor, teacher, and advocate for youth for many years, the new Youth Services director had a reputation for fairness, being a good listener, and taking the concerns of young people seriously.
E	There is no greater satisfaction than watching your child succeed.
F	You can save money on groceries by using coupons.

Appeal to Logic	Appeal to Emotion	Appeal to Ethics

WRITE

Use the questions in the checklist to brainstorm persuasive techniques you will use in your presentation. When you have finished brainstorming persuasive techniques, write out your notes.

Extended Oral Project and Grammar

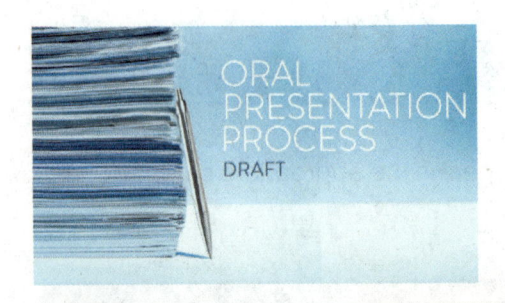

Oral Presentation Process: Draft

| PLAN | **DRAFT** | REVISE | EDIT AND PRESENT |

You have already made progress toward writing your argumentative oral presentation. Now it is time to draft your argumentative oral presentation.

✏ WRITE

Use your plan and other responses in your Binder to draft your argumentative oral presentation. You may also have new ideas as you begin drafting. Feel free to explore those new ideas as you have them. You can also ask yourself these questions to ensure that your writing is focused, organized, and developed:

Draft Checklist:

- **Focused:** Is the topic of my presentation clear to my audience? Have I included only relevant information and details about my topic? Have I avoided extraneous details that might confuse or distract my audience?

- **Organized:** Is the organization of ideas and events in my presentation logical? Have I reinforced this logical structure with transitional words and phrases to help my audience follow the order of ideas?

- **Developed:** Do all of my details support my thesis about why this change would promote justice in the world? Do I have enough evidence from different sources to support my thesis?

Before you submit your draft, read it over carefully. You want to be sure that you've responded to all aspects of the prompt.

Extended Oral Project and Grammar

Here is Susie's argumentative oral presentation draft. As you read, notice how Susie develops her draft to be focused, organized, and developed. As she continues to revise and edit her argumentative oral presentation, she will find and improve weak spots in her writing, as well as correct any language or punctuation mistakes.

☰ STUDENT MODEL: FIRST DRAFT

A Girl's Right to Learn

Sometimes going to school is a bummer. It's easy to take school for granted when its doors are wide open to us. But for one out of every five children globaly, life is different. One-hundred thirty million girls worldwide are not in school (Malala Fund). Imagine if you never had the choice to step foot into a classroom.

~~Enshering that all citizens of the world can fully exercise their human right to an education should matter to everyone, especially to students like you and me. Access to school for girls and women is particularly crushal when they are disproportionately affected by inequalities in education. For instance, over two thirds of the nearly 800 million illiterit people in the world are women (UN Women). Educating women provides a wider range of employment options. The Right to Education Initiative emphasizes the status of education as a "multiplier right."~~

Claim

Ensuring that all citizens of the world can fully exercise their human right to an education should matter to everyone. Access to school for girls and women is particularly crucial because they have been disproportionately affected by inequalities in education.

- Educating women provides a wider range of employment options and enables women of all ages to lead healthier and more prosperous lives.

- In order to enact change, it is key to understand how gender stereotypes negatively affect women's access to education. The Right to Education Initiative emphasizes the status of education as a "multiplier right," meaning that ensuring a woman's right to education dramatically increases her chances of improving her

Skill: Communicating Ideas

Susie decides to show slides highlighting her key ideas throughout her presentation. As she discusses the ideas, she'll point to them on the slides. She'll use these gestures to focus the audience's attention on the information and help keep her listeners engaged.

Extended Oral Project and Grammar

socioeconomic status by safeguarding "key rights, such as those related to work, property, political participation, access to justice, freedom from violence and health."

[Show slide with a bulleted list of ideas, titled "Education Makes a Difference."]

Women's access to quality education in locations across the globe is impeded or blocked by a variety of economic, geographical, and political factors. Many girls are pressured into the labor market at a young age in order to support their families. Girls work in low-skilled jobs for low wages. A lack of education funding in some countries means families are required to pay for any education their child receives. The fees are prohibitive for many families, especially those living in poor countries. There are countries that do provide free access to education. But even in such countries, budget limitations lead to a shortage of trained educators, overcrowding, and no support for students with additional learning needs. Some schools even lack basic resources such as suffishent shelter, desks, chairs, school supplies, books, and bathroom facilities (UNICEF). Many students across the world long journeys to and from school everyday. Some places have violent conflicts that make commuting to and attending school dangerous.

~~Educating women is beneficial on an individual and global scale because it is a multiplier right. Women with secondary school education earn more money. According to The World Bank in July 2018, "women with secondary school education earn almost twice as much as those with no education at all." The World Bank also found that not educating women "costs countries between $15 trillion and $30 trillion in lost lifetime productivity and earnings." Increased access to education means more women in the workforce. Investing in education for women, therefore, has a chane reaction that positively benefits women *and* society as whole.~~

Evidence and Analysis #3

Educating women is beneficial on an individual and global scale because it is a multiplier right.

- Women with a secondary school education earn more money and are better able to support themselves and their families.

Skill: Engaging in Discourse

Susie's partner points out that Susie hasn't explained how educating women benefits "society as a whole." So Susie expands on the significance of her evidence, adding details that improve the coherence of this section of her presentation.

- The World Bank also found that not educating women "costs countries between $15 trillion and $30 trillion in lost lifetime productivity and earnings."

- Increased access to education means more women in the workforce and more people contributing to the world's economy.

- Investing in education for women, therefore, initiates a chain reaction that positively benefits women *and* society as a whole.

[Show slide with bullet points.]

Organizations like the Malala Fund are working to increase girls' access to education. The Malala Fund was founded by Pakistani activist and Nobel Prize laureate Malala Yousafzai and her father Ziauddin Yousafzai. The Malala Fund advocates for twelve years of free, safe, and quality education for all girls worldwide. This non-profit organization supports women's education through an international network of dedicated educational activists. The goal of the network is to give girls a secondary education so they are "more able and likely to contribute fully in their families, communities and societies, as earners, informed mothers, and agents of change" (Malala Fund). The work of the Malala Fund includes filanthropy, recruiting teachers, developing student outreach programs, and giving young girls a platform to share their experiences. Anyone can contribute on a smaller scale through donations or by speaking about this issue to raise awareness.

The goal of providing worldwide access to K–12 education for girls and women is not impeded solely by economic factors, however. The successful achievement of this goal also requires people to be less lazy when thinking about gender. *Gender Stereotyping: Transnational Legal Perspectives* says a gender stereotype is "a generalised view or preconception about attributes or characteristics that are or ought to be possessed by, or the roles that are or should be performed by women and men." It is key to understand how gender stereotypes work. Organizations like the Right to Education Initiative address gender stereotypes as a key factor in educational reform. They do not seek change people's beliefs rather they aim to point out that "gender stereotyping is considered *wrongful* when it

Extended Oral Project and Grammar

results in a violation or violations of human rights and fundamental freedoms" ("Women and girls").

~~You might be familiar with the stereotype that women's cognitive abilities are better suited for the arts and humanities than math and sciences. Such gender stereotypes discourage girls and women from pursuing STEM-related degrees or careers, producing inequality in education and employment. Women represent 47% of the workforce, but only 12% of engineers ("Women in Computer Science"). A disproportionate percentage of men reap the monetary benefits of careers in engineering. Programs are working to close the gender gap in technology by offering learning opportunities and career pathways for female engineers. Also lead to unequal political participation and representation. Women have limited access to, or are barred from, positions of power that they could use to advocate for women's rights. This is unjust because this denies women their right to equal education, employment, and representation.~~

Counterargument

You might be familiar with the stereotype that women's cognitive abilities are better suited for the arts and humanities. Such gender stereotypes discourage girls and women from pursuing STEM-related degrees or careers, producing inequality in education and employment.

- For example, gender stereotypes produce inequality in employment. Women represent 47% of the workforce, but only 12% of engineers ("Women in Computer Science"). A disproportionate percentage of men reap the monetary benefits of careers in engineering. Additionally, gender stereotypes lead to unequal political participation and representation. Consequently, women have limited access to or are barred from positions of power, which they could use to advocate for women's rights.

[Show slide with bullet points.]

~~Another stereotype is the belief that a young women's education should prepare them for domestic duties as a wife and mother, rendering a formal education unnecessary. This gender stereotype considered harmful when girls are forced to marry and bear children before the age of 18. Advocating for all women's right to an education~~

Skill: Transitions

Susie realizes that she should clarify the connections between her sentences. She adds the transitions *for example* and *consequently* to help her audience follow the sequence of her ideas.

~~nessessitates enforcing laws to protect children from underaged marriages. Education creates more opportunities in life for women beyond marriage and motherhood.~~

Counterargument continued

The gender stereotype of domesticity is considered harmful when girls are forced to marry and bear children before the age of 18.

- According to the Global Partnership for Education, "Child marriage leads girls to have children earlier and more children over their lifetime. This in turn reduces the ability of households to meet their basic needs, and thereby contributes to poverty" (Wodon).

- Jessica Chastain sums up the issues with this practice in an interview with NBC. [Show video of Jessica Chastain interview.]

- The knowledge women gain in school prepares them to make better healthcare decisions for themselves and their families. Furthermore, non-adolescent mothers and their children have lower rates of health complications and mortality ("Missed Opportunities").

The ways in which girls and women worldwide are subjected to discrimination varies widely. If we are to create justice, we must keep in mind that women all over the world face inequality in different ways. This may seem like a tall order. The first step is to pay attention to experiences outside of our own. Denying a woman's right to equal education prevents her from living a healthy and fruitful life. Denying a woman's right to equal education is also a denial of her rights to freedom and representation. Therefore, we must give the girls and women of the world a voice by sharing their stories and looking for justice. Consider the words of Former First Lady Michelle Obama, "When girls are educated, their countries become stronger and more prosperous," thus elevating the status of women worldwide through equal access to education will improve the lives of deserving individuals and help cultivate future generations of enlightened leaders.

NOTES

Skill: Reasons and Evidence

Susie wants to strengthen her point about the gender stereotype of domesticity. She includes support to show why the stereotype is harmful and why education is beneficial.

Skill: Sources and Citations

Susie provides citations for the quotation and paraphrased information that she adds to this section of her presentation. She includes the author's last name in the first citation. In the second citation, she lists the title of the work since the author is not known.

Sources

- Video interview to provide an ethical appeal.

- Statistics about access to education and the consequences of education inequality Potential options:

    - "Women and girls." *Right to Education*, HYPERLINK "http://www.right-to-education.org/girlswomen"www.right-to-education.org/girlswomen. Accessed 17 Dec. 2018.

    - "Girls' education." *Malala Fund*, HYPERLINK "https://www.malala.org/girls-education"www.malala.org/girls-education. Accessed 17 Dec. 2018.

    - "Missed Opportunities: The High Cost of Not Educating Girls." *The World Bank*, HYPERLINK "https://www.worldbank.org/en/topic/education/publication/missed-opportunities-the-high-cost-of-not-educating-girls"www.worldbank.org/en/topic/education/publication/missed-opportunities-the-high-cost-of-not-educating-girls. Accessed 17 Dec. 2018.

    - "One in every five children, adolescents, and youth is out of school worldwide." *UNESCO*, HYPERLINK "https://en.unesco.org/news/one-every-five-children-adolescents-and-youth-out-school-worldwide"en.unesco.org/news/one-every-five-children-adolescents-and-youth-out-school-worldwide. Accessed 18 Dec. 2018.

- Visualizations of statistics, such as graphs, infographics, orcharts.

- Persuasive quotations about the importance of women's access to education.

Extended Oral Project and Grammar

Skill: Transitions

••• CHECKLIST FOR TRANSITIONS

Before you revise your current draft to include transitions, think about:

- the key ideas you discuss
- the major sections of your oral presentation
- the organizational structure of your oral presentation
- the relationships between complex ideas and concepts

Next, reread your current draft and note places in your oral presentation where:

- the organizational structure is not yet apparent
  > For example, if you are comparing and contrasting ideas, your explanations about how these ideas are similar and different should be clearly stated
- the relationship between ideas from one paragraph to the next is unclear
  > For example, when you describe a process in sequential order, you should clarify the order of the steps by using transitional words like *first, then, next,* and *finally*
- your ideas do not create cohesion, or a unified whole
- your transitions and/or syntax is inappropriate

Revise your draft to use appropriate and varied transitions and syntax to link the major sections of your oral presentation, create cohesion, and clarify the relationships between complex ideas and concepts, using the following questions as a guide:

- What kind of transitions should I use to make the organizational structure clear to readers?
- Are my transitions linking the major sections of my oral presentation?
- What transitions create cohesion between complex ideas and concepts?
- Are my transitions and syntax varied and appropriate?
- Have my transitions clarified the relationships between complex ideas and concepts?

Extended Oral Project and Grammar

YOUR TURN

Choose the best answer to each question.

1. Below is a passage from a previous draft of Susie's oral presentation. The connection between the two sentences is unclear. What transition should Susie add to the beginning of the second sentence to make her writing more coherent and fluid?

   > United States federal law requires equity in education as well as in athletics. Girls across the nation are discouraged from playing sports due to gender inequalities in their school athletic programs.

   - A. Although this may be true,
   - B. Eventually,
   - C. Particularly,
   - D. As a result,

2. Below is a passage from a previous draft of Susie's argumentative oral presentation. Susie did not use an appropriate transition to show the relationship between the paragraphs. Which of the following transitions is the best replacement for the word *Unless*? Choose the transition that makes her writing more fluid and is the most appropriate for the purpose, topic, and context of her presentation, as well as her audience.

   > Due to overcrowding, many students do not get the individualized attention they need to thrive in school.
   >
   > Unless, the National Center for Education Statistics found that a high student-to-teacher ratio has a negative effect on standardized testing scores.

   - A. Initially,
   - B. Although,
   - C. On the other hand,
   - D. As a matter of fact,

WRITE

Use the questions in the checklist to revise your argumentative oral presentation so that it exhibits fluid and coherent transitions.

Skill: Reasons and Evidence

••• CHECKLIST FOR REASONS AND EVIDENCE

In order to identify a speaker's point of view, reasoning, and use of evidence and rhetoric, note the following:

- the stance, or position, the speaker takes on a topic
- whether the premise, or the basis of the speech or talk, is based on logical reasoning
- whether the ideas follow one another in a way that shows clear, sound thinking
- whether the speaker employs the use of exaggeration, especially when citing facts or statistics
- the speaker's choice of words, the points he or she chooses to emphasize, and the tone, or general attitude

In order to evaluate a speaker's point of view, reasoning, and use of evidence and rhetoric, consider the following questions:

- What stance, or position, does the speaker take? Is the premise based on sound, logical reasoning? Why or why not?
- Does the speaker use facts and statistics to make a point? Are they exaggerated?
- What points does the speaker choose to emphasize?
- How does the speaker's choice of words affect his or her tone?

Extended Oral Project and Grammar

YOUR TURN

Read the examples of reasoning from a draft of Susie's oral presentation below. Then, complete the chart by sorting the examples into two categories: those that are logical and those that are illogical. Write the corresponding letter for each example in the appropriate column.

	Examples
A	Organizations like the Malala Fund are working to increase girls' access to education, thus providing an important service.
B	The Malala Fund is a really cool organization that will eliminate all inequalities in education.
C	These gender stereotypes discourage girls and women from pursuing STEM-related degrees or careers, producing equality in education and employment.
D	Such gender stereotypes discourage girls and women from pursuing STEM-related degrees or careers, producing inequality in education and employment.
E	All women face inequality, and we have to come up with a single solution that works for everyone to make it better.
F	If we are to create justice, we must keep in mind that women all over the world face inequality in different ways.

Logical Reasoning	Illogical Reasoning

Extended Oral Project and Grammar

YOUR TURN

Below are three examples of an ineffective use of evidence from a previous draft of Susie's oral presentation. In the second column, rewrite the sentences to use the evidence effectively, without exaggeration or faulty reasoning. The first row has been completed for you as an example.

Ineffective Use of Evidence	Effective Use of Evidence
But for one out of every five children in the world, life is different. This means that billions of children have lived differently since the dawn of time.	But for one out of every five children in the world, life is different. Access to quality education is an issue whose impact should not be ignored.
For instance, over two-thirds of the nearly 800 million illiterate people in the world are women. Therefore, nearly all people in the world who are illiterate are women.	
When gender stereotypes are enforced or allowed in education, they limit girls' access to potentially "lucrative and influential" fields of employment. Women who are subjected to strict gender stereotypes are extremely poor, and all wish they could have careers in STEM fields.	

Reading & Writing Companion

Skill: Sources and Citations

••• CHECKLIST FOR SOURCES AND CITATIONS

In your oral presentation, provide citations for any information that you obtained from an outside source. This includes the following:

- direct quotations
- paraphrased information
- tables and data
- images
- videos
- audio files

The citations in your presentation should be as brief and unobtrusive as possible. Follow these general guidelines:

- The citation should indicate the author's last name and the page number(s) on which the information appears (if the source has numbered pages), enclosed in parentheses.
- If the author is not known, the citation should list the title of the work and, if helpful, the publisher.

At the end of your presentation, include your works cited list. These are the elements and the order in which they should be listed in works cited entries, according to the MLA style:

- author
- title of source
- container, or the title of the larger work in which the source is located
- other contributors
- version
- number
- publisher
- publication date
- location
- URL, without the "http://"

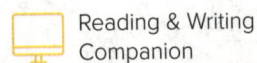

Not all of these elements will apply to each citation. Include only the elements that are relevant for the source.

To check that you have gathered and cited sources correctly, consider the following questions:

- Did I cite the information I found using a standard format to avoid plagiarism?
- Did I include all my sources in my works cited list?

Extended Oral Project and Grammar

YOUR TURN

Read the elements and examples below. Then, complete the chart by placing them in the correct order, according to the MLA style for a works cited list. Write the corresponding letter for each element and example in the appropriate column.

	Elements and Examples
A	publisher
B	"Child marriage and education: impacts, costs, and benefits"
C	URL
D	29 June 2017
E	author
F	publication date
G	www.globalpartnership.org/blog/child-marriage-and-education-impacts-costs-and-benefits
H	Global Partnership for Education
I	Wodon, Quentin
J	title of source

Elements	Examples

✏️ WRITE

Use the information in the checklist to create or revise your citations and works cited list. Make sure that each slide with researched information briefly identifies the source of the information. This will let your audience know that the information you are presenting is trustworthy. When you have completed your citations, compile a list of all your sources and write out your works cited list. Refer to the *MLA Handbook* as needed.

Extended Oral Project and Grammar

Skill: Communicating Ideas

••• CHECKLIST FOR COMMUNICATING IDEAS

Follow these steps as you rehearse your presentation:

- **Eye Contact:** Practice looking up and making eye contact while you speak. Rehearse your presentation in front of a mirror, making eye contact with yourself. Consider choosing a few audience members to look at during your presentation, but scan the audience from time to time so it doesn't seem as if you're speaking directly to only two or three people.

- **Speaking Rate:** Record yourself so you can judge your speaking rate. If you find yourself speaking too fast, time your presentation and work on slowing down your speech. In addition, you might want to plan pauses in your presentation to achieve a specific effect.

- **Volume:** Be aware of your volume. Make sure that you are speaking at a volume that will be loud enough for everyone to hear you, but not so loud that it will be uncomfortable for your audience.

- **Enunciation:** Decide which words you want to emphasize, and then enunciate them with particular clarity. Emphasizing certain words or terms can help you communicate more effectively and drive home your message.

- **Purposeful Gestures:** Rehearse your presentation with your arms relaxed at your sides. If you want to include a specific gesture, decide where in your presentation it will be most effective, and practice making that gesture until it feels natural.

- **Conventions of Language:** Make sure that you are using appropriate conventions of language for your audience and purpose.

Extended Oral Project and Grammar

YOUR TURN

Read the examples of students who are communicating their ideas below. Then, complete the chart by first identifying the appropriate category for each example and then deciding whether the example illustrates effective or ineffective communication. Write the corresponding letter for each example in the appropriate place in the chart.

	Examples
A	A student ends his formal presentation by saying, "And that's all I've got for you today, folks!"
B	A student projects his or her voice, but does not shout. He or she pronounces words carefully and speaks at a slightly slower rate than used in normal conversation.
C	A student speaks very softly and rushes through the presentation, using a monotone voice.
D	A student makes eye contact with various members of the audience as well as his or her co-presenters.
E	A student does not look up from his or her notecards.
F	A student uses his or her hands to emphasize a particularly important idea and point to visual aids.
G	A student allows his or her arms to hang limply and does not move at all.
H	A student stands up straight in clear view of his or her audience.
I	A student ends his formal presentation by saying, "Thank you for listening."
J	A student faces a board or screen and stands with his or her arms crossed.

Category	Example of Effective Communication	Example of Ineffective Communication
Posture		
Eye Contact		
Rate/Volume/Enunciation		
Gestures		
Conventions of Language		

Extended Oral Project and Grammar

✏️ WRITE

Take turns delivering your oral presentation in front of a partner.

As you present, do the following:

- Employ steady eye contact with your partner.
- Use an appropriate speaking rate and volume, pauses, and enunciation to clearly communicate with your partner.
- Use natural gestures to add interest and meaning as you speak.
- Maintain a comfortable, confident posture to engage your audience.
- Use language conventions appropriate for a formal presentation, and avoid slang or inappropriate speech.

As you watch your partner's presentation, use the checklist to evaluate his or her communication of ideas.

When you finish giving your presentation, write a brief but honest reflection about your experience of communicating your ideas. Did you make eye contact? Did you speak too quickly or too softly? Did you maintain a comfortable, confident posture? Did you use appropriate language? Did you struggle to incorporate gestures that looked and felt natural? How can you better communicate your ideas in the future?

Skill: Engaging in Discourse

••• CHECKLIST FOR ENGAGING IN DISCOURSE

You and a partner will take turns practicing your oral presentations and giving feedback. The feedback you provide should be meaningful and respectful. That is, you should offer an honest assessment as well as specific tips for improvement, while using kind and considerate language.

In your feedback, make sure to evaluate and critique the speaker using these categories. Remember to always start by telling the speaker what he or she did particularly well.

Positive Points:

- What is most effective about the oral presentation?
- What strong points does the speaker make?
- Which particular phrases are well written and memorable?

Clarity:

- Does the speaker express his or her ideas in a clear, understandable way?
- What changes can the speaker make to improve the clarity of his or her message?

Coherence:

- Does the speaker use transitions and explanations effectively to show the relationship between ideas?
- Where can the speaker add transitions or explanations to improve the coherence of his or her message?

Diction:

- Does the speaker's choice of words have an impact, or a strong effect?
- Where can the speaker improve his or her word choice to create a stronger impact?

Syntax:

- Does the speaker vary sentence length and complexity to create a strong impact?
- Where can the speaker build techniques, such as parallelism or ending a sentence with the most important idea, into his or her syntax to improve the clarity and impact of the presentation?

Persuasive Techniques:

- Does the speaker use language persuasively?
- Where can the speaker employ specific rhetorical strategies, such as appeals to logic, emotion, and ethics, to more effectively persuade his or her audience?

Extended Oral Project and Grammar

YOUR TURN

Read the examples of feedback below. Then, complete the chart by placing the examples in the appropriate category. Write the corresponding letter for each example of feedback in the appropriate row. Some examples may belong in more than one category.

	Feedback
A	The transition word *likewise* shows a strong connection between your ideas in this paragraph.
B	I think this sentence would be stronger if you moved the most important phrase to the end.
C	I like how you posed a rhetorical question to engage your audience.
D	I like how you inserted an anecdote to make your presentation more personal and relatable.
E	The wording of this sentence is a little vague. You might consider revising passive sentence constructions.
F	I'm not sure what you were referencing when you said, "as previously discussed." Can you please elaborate?

Category	Feedback
Positive Points	
Clarity	
Coherence	
Diction	
Syntax	
Persuasive Techniques	

WRITE

Take turns reading your presentation aloud to a partner. When you finish, write a reflection about your experience of engaging in discourse by giving feedback. How did you ensure that your feedback was both meaningful and respectful? What did you do well? How can you improve in the future?

Extended Oral Project and Grammar

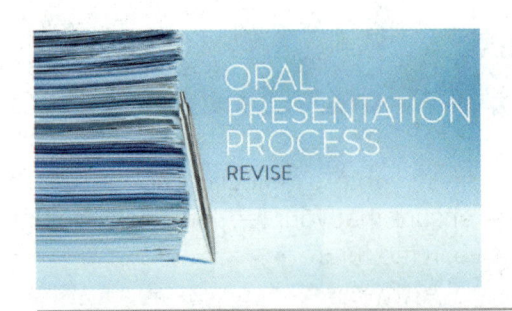

Oral Presentation Process: Revise

| PLAN | DRAFT | REVISE | EDIT AND PRESENT |

You have written a draft of your argumentative oral presentation. You have also received input from your peers about how to improve it. Now you are going to revise your draft.

REVISION GUIDE

Examine your draft to find areas for revision. Keep in mind your purpose and audience as you revise for clarity, development, organization, and style. Use the guide below to help you review:

Review	Revise	Example
Clarity		
Identify concepts that may need defining or explaining.	Make sure you define or explain key terms that may not be familiar to your audience. Add headings to your presentation slides to clarify your ideas and claims for your audience, and simplify your ideas by turning them into brief bullet points.	The Right to Education Initiative emphasizes the status of education as a "multiplier right:," meaning that ensuring a woman's right to education dramatically increases her chances of improving her socioeconomic status by safeguarding "key rights, such as those related to work, property, political participation, access to justice, freedom from violence and health."

Review	Revise	Example
\multicolumn{3}{c}{**Development**}		
Identify and annotate places in your presentation where your thesis is not supported by details or evidence.	Make sure you have a strong main idea in each paragraph, and add accurate evidence, examples, well-chosen details, or other supporting information to develop your ideas. Include images, graphs, videos, and other visual elements that support your argument in your presentation.	Many girls are pressured into the labor market at a young age in order to support their families. Instead of getting an education and learning the skills they need for professional employment, ~~Girls~~ girls work in low-skilled jobs for low wages~~.~~, which is detrimental to their health and development. [Project slide with key points listed in bulleted form.]
\multicolumn{3}{c}{**Organization**}		
Syntax can help you emphasize ideas. Identify strong words and phrases that show your main ideas.	Revise sentences so that the most important word or phrase comes at the end. Think about places where a visual aid might enhance a section of the presentation.	A lack of education funding in some countries means families are required to pay for any education their child receives. ~~The fees are prohibitive for~~ For many families, especially those living in poor countries~~.~~, the fees are prohibitive.
\multicolumn{3}{c}{**Style: Word Choice**}		
Identify key words and phrases that connect ideas across sentences. Annotate places where more precise language would strengthen the connection.	Replace vague or repetitive words and phrases with precise language that emphasizes the connections between your ideas.	The ways in which girls and women worldwide are subjected to discrimination ~~varies widely.~~ cannot be encapsulated by a single narrative. If we are to create justice, we must keep in mind that women all over the world face inequality in different ways.

Review	Revise	Example
Style: Sentence Fluency		
Read your presentation aloud, and listen to the way the text sounds. Does it sound choppy? Or does it flow smoothly with rhythm, movement, and emphasis on important details and events?	Shorten a section of long sentences, or join shorter sentences together using conjunctions or dependent clauses.	This may seem like a tall order. The, but the first step is to pay attention to experiences outside of our own. Denying a woman's right to equal education prevents her from living a healthy and fruitful life. Denying a woman's right to equal education is also a denial of her rights to freedom and representation.

✎ WRITE

Another helpful step in the revision process is shortening your draft by trimming and bulleting your draft paragraphs to create more succinct, scannable notes. For example, you might cut information that is overly complex and place it in a list or diagram instead. Make each main idea or point a separate bullet. When delivering your presentation, you can use these notes to remind yourself of the key ideas you want to deliver to your audience.

Use the revision guide and the step described above, as well as your peer reviews, to help you evaluate your oral presentation to determine places that should be revised.

Once you have finished revising your draft, write out your revised oral presentation.

Extended Oral Project and Grammar

Grammar: Commonly Misspelled Words

By following a few simple steps, you can learn to spell new words—even words that are unfamiliar or difficult. As you write, keep a list of words you have trouble spelling. Refer to online or print resources for pronunciation, Latin or Greek roots, and other information that may help you. Then, use the steps below to learn to spell those words.

Say it. Look at the word again and say it aloud. Say it again, pronouncing each syllable clearly.

See it. Close your eyes. Picture the word. Visualize it letter by letter.

Write it. Look at the word again and write it two or three times. Then, write the word without looking at the printed version.

Check it. Check your spelling. Did you spell it correctly? If not, repeat each step until you can spell it easily.

Here are some words that can sometimes confuse even strong spellers.

Commonly Misspelled Words		
absence	apologetically	answer
accessible	caricature	connoisseur
cruelty	detrimental	devastation
division	exhilaration	exist
exuberant	fascism	fundamentally
genius	humorous	hypocrite
ideally	intellectual	leisurely
malicious	maneuver	negotiable
neighborhood	newsstand	possessed
salable	restaurant	synonymous

Extended Oral Project and Grammar

YOUR TURN

1. How should this sentence be changed?

   > Each morning Mr. Fritts takes a liesurely walk to his favorite newsstand and buys a paper.

   - A. Change **liesurely** to **leisurly** and **newsstand** to **newstand**.
   - B. Change **liesurely** to **leisurely**.
   - C. Change **liesurely** to **leisiurely**.
   - D. No change needs to be made to this sentence.

2. How should this sentence be changed?

   > Ideally, the florist for the wedding will be a true conoiseur of color, scent, and space.

   - A. Change **Ideally** to **Idealy**.
   - B. Change **conoiseur** to **connoisure**.
   - C. Change **conoiseur** to **connoisseur**.
   - D. No change needs to be made to this sentence.

3. How should this sentence be changed?

   > Some people think Eddie is malicous, but I know he is just exhuberant.

   - A. Change **malicous** to **malicious** and **exhuberant** to **exuberant**.
   - B. Change **exhuberant** to **exuberent**.
   - C. Change **malicous** to **malischious**.
   - D. No change needs to be made to this sentence.

4. How should this sentence be changed?

   > Ms. Peabody's fourth-grade class loves that particular book because it is both humorous and accessible.

   - A. Change **humorous** to **humerous**.
   - B. Change **humorous** to **humurus** and **accessible** to **accesible**.
   - C. Change **accessible** to **acessible**.
   - D. No change needs to be made to this sentence.

Grammar: Sentence Variety—Openings

Sentence Openers

Sentence openers introduce and connect ideas. Openers can be single words or phrases and can function as different parts of speech that describe or indicate time or show similarity, contrast, cause or effect, and other connections with surrounding sentences. Using a variety of sentence openers throughout your writing keeps the reader engaged and helps the flow of ideas from sentence to sentence. Avoid the repetition of syntax and diction as that encourages the repetition of common sentence openers. Combine the use of these additional strategies when beginning sentences:

Strategies	Text
Use a prepositional phrase to begin a sentence.	With blasphemous oaths, he called me a black liar, a runaway from Georgia, and every other profane and vulgar **epithet** that the most indecent fancy could conceive. 12 Years a Slave
Use an adverb to begin a sentence.	Implicitly, it accepted the position of Northern Ireland within the United Kingdom. A Brief History of Ireland
Use a very short sentence, which can help emphasize an important point or create excitement.	We can do that. A More Perfect Union
Use transitional words to begin a sentence.	By the same token, a just law is a code that a majority compels a minority to follow and that it is willing to follow itself. Letter from Birmingham Jail
Use words that correspond to time or a sequence of events to begin a sentence.	Soon after nine o'clock of a Saturday morning, kids began spraying out of all the side streets on to Manhattan Avenue, the main thoroughfare. A Tree Grows in Brooklyn

Extended Oral Project and Grammar

YOUR TURN

1. How should this sentence be changed to use a causal transition as a sentence opener?

   > Many people were left without power for 48 hours.

   - A. Frighteningly, many people were left without power for 48 hours.
   - B. As a result, many people were left without power for 48 hours.
   - C. In rural areas, many people were left without power for 48 hours.
   - D. No change needs to be made to this sentence.

2. How should this sentence be changed to use an adverb as a sentence opener?

   > Thankfully, my hard work paid off.

   - A. My hard work paid off, thankfully.
   - B. I am thankful that my hard work paid off.
   - C. My hard work thankfully paid off.
   - D. No change needs to be made to this sentence.

3. How should this sentence be changed to make the sentence opener clearer?

   > Bats live in cities.

   - A. Cities are places that bats live.
   - B. The bats live in cities.
   - C. Many bats live in cities.
   - D. No change needs to be made to this sentence.

4. How should this sentence be changed to use a time transition as a sentence opener?

   > Clemens began using the pen name Mark Twain and started writing for the *Enterprise* in Virginia City.

   - A. Mark Twain started writing for the *Enterprise* soon after.
   - B. Surprisingly, Samuel Clemens started writing for the *Enterprise* in Virginia City.
   - C. Soon Clemens, who had begun using the pen name Mark Twain, was writing for the *Enterprise* in Virginia City.
   - D. No change needs to be made to this sentence.

Grammar: Sentence Variety—Length

Like an interesting conversation, writing should engage the reader. Using varied and rhythmic sentence length and syntax injects more interest into your writing. Varying your syntax and sentence length will help emphasize important pieces of information, enhance descriptions and narratives, and reduce repetition. The strategies in this lesson are useful in any type of writing.

Strategy	Text
Vary the rhythm by alternating short and long sentences.	Anyway, Ashley finishes her story and then goes around the room and asks everyone else why they're supporting the campaign. They all have different stories and reasons. Many bring up a specific issue. And finally they come to this elderly black man who's been sitting there quietly the entire time. And Ashley asks him why he's there. And he does not bring up a specific issue. A More Perfect Union
Use simple, compound, complex, and compound-complex sentences to vary syntax and sentence length.	It was no use trying the lift. Even at the best of times it was seldom working, and at present the electric current was cut off during daylight hours. It was part of the economy drive in preparation for Hate Week. The flat was seven flights up, and Winston, who was thirty-nine and had a varicose ulcer above his right ankle, went slowly, resting several times on the way. 1984
Use different sentence openers to encourage sentence variety.	And I love Havana, its noise and decay and painted ladyness. I could happily sit on one of those wrought-iron balconies for days, or keep my grandmother company on her porch, with its ringside view of the sea. I'm afraid to lose all this. To lose Abuela Celia again. But I know that sooner or later I'd have to return to New York. Dreaming in Cuban
Use different sentence types, including imperative, interrogative, and exclamatory sentences, to help vary length.	And today, I want just to take a moment once again to look around this beautiful auditorium at the people who helped you on your journey—your families and friends, everyone in your school and your communities—all the people who pushed you and poured their love into you and believed in you even when you didn't believe in yourselves sometimes. Today is their day, too, right? So let's, graduates, give them a big, old, loud shout-out and love to our families. Thank you all. Yes! Commencement Address to the Santa Fe Indian School

Extended Oral Project and Grammar

↻ YOUR TURN

1. How was this sentence edited to become longer?

   > Sample Sentence: The kitten caught the butterfly.
   >
   > Edited Sentence: Leaping into the air, the kitten caught the butterfly.

   - A. The sample sentence was changed to a compound sentence.
   - B. The sample sentence was changed to a compound-complex sentence.
   - C. The sample sentence was changed to use a participial phrase as a sentence opener.
   - D. The sample sentence was changed to use an adverb as a sentence opener.

2. How was the sample sentence edited to become longer?

   > Sample Sentence: Jason stared at his feet.
   >
   > Edited Sentence: While thinking of an answer, Jason stared at his feet.

   - A. The sample sentence was changed to a phrase as a sentence opener.
   - B. The sample sentence was changed to an imperative sentence.
   - C. The sample sentence was changed to a compound-complex sentence.
   - D. The sample sentence was changed to have a verb as a sentence opener.

3. How can this sentence be shortened and correctly edited to create a complex sentence?

   > If this snow continues, school will be canceled, and we'll have to stay home.

   - A. Remove **If this snow continues,** and capitalize **school.**
   - B. Replace the second comma with a period and remove **and we'll have to stay home.**
   - C. Replace the second comma and conjunction **and** with a semicolon.
   - D. Replace the first comma with a semicolon and remove **school will be canceled, and.**

4. How can this sentence be changed into a compound-complex sentence, effectively making it longer?

   > When small children are really tired, they are short-tempered.

   - A. Add *until they fall asleep* after **short-tempered.**
   - B. Replace the comma with a semicolon.
   - C. Add a semicolon and *some will cry and fuss until they fall asleep* after **short-tempered.**
   - D. Remove the comma.

Extended Oral Project and Grammar

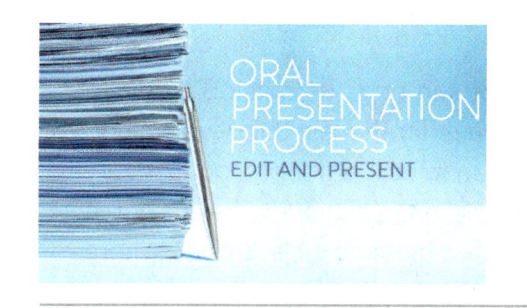

Oral Presentation Process: Edit and Present

| PLAN | DRAFT | REVISE | **EDIT AND PRESENT** |

You have revised your oral presentation based on your peer feedback and your own examination.

Now, it is time to edit your argumentative oral presentation. When you revised, you focused on the content of your oral presentation. You practiced strategies for communicating your ideas and engaging in discourse. When you edit, you focus on the mechanics of your oral presentation, paying close attention to standard English conventions that can be heard by your audience while you are talking.

Use the checklist below to guide you as you edit:

☐ Are there sentences that are too long and hard to follow? Can I use different sentence types to vary the length of sentences?

☐ Have I used punctuation such as periods, commas, colons, and semicolons correctly to indicate pauses for effect?

☐ Have I included a variety of sentence openers in my presentation?

☐ Have I correctly spelled all words?

☐ Have I used any language that is too informal for my presentation?

☐ Have I added visual aids and digital media strategically to enhance my presentation?

Notice some edits Susie has made:

- Changed a sentence opener to better engage her audience
- Replaced slang or informal language with formal language
- Corrected a commonly misspelled word
- Added rhetorical questions to vary sentence types

Extended Oral Project and Grammar

[Title slide.] On mornings when frost covers our windows, the hot sun begs us outside, or we're exhausted from a restless night, ~~Sometimes~~ going to school is ~~a bummer~~ the last thing we want to do. It's easy to take school for granted when its doors are wide open to us. But for one out of every five children ~~globaly~~ globally, life is different. One-hundred thirty million girls worldwide are not in school ("Girls' education"). Imagine if you never had the choice to step foot into a classroom. Where would you be today? What kind of opportunities and future could you look forward to?

✏️ WRITE

After Susie rehearses her presentation, she decides to edit her introduction further by dividing up her points. In addition, she decides to help her audience visualize some of the information in her introduction by including a slide with a graphic.

Use the checklist, as well as your peer reviews, to help you evaluate your oral presentation to determine places that need editing. Then, edit your presentation to correct those errors. Finally, rehearse your presentation, including both the delivery of your written work and the strategic use of the visual aids and digital media you plan to incorporate.

Once you have made all your corrections and rehearsed with your digital media selections, you are ready to present your work. You may present to your class or to a group of your peers. You can record your presentation to share with family and friends or post it on your blog. If you publish online, share the link with your family, friends, and classmates.

PHOTO/IMAGE CREDITS:

cover, iStock.com/agaliza
p. iii, iStock.com/Alex Potemkin, istock.com, istock.com
p. v, iStock.com/DNY59
p. xii, iStock.com/Alex Potemkin, iStock.com/eyewave
p. xiii, iStock.com/Alex Potemkin
p. xiv, Chimamanda Ngozi Adichie - Taylor Hill/Contributor/FilmMagic/Getty Images
p. xiv, John F. Carter, Jr - Public Domain
p. xiv, Kate Chopin - Public Domain
p. xiv, Paul Laurence Dunbar - Anthony Barboza/Contributor/Archive Photos/Getty Images
p. xiv, Alice Dunbar Nelson - Interim Archives/Contributor/Archive Photos/Getty Images
p. xiv, Ralph Waldo Ellison - Everett Collection Historical/Alamy Stock Photo
p. xv, William Faulkner - Eric Schaal/Contributor/The LIFE Images Collection/Getty Images
p. xv, F. Scott Fitzgerald - American Stock Archive/Contributor/Archive Photos/Getty Images
p. xv, Charlotte Perkins Gilman - Public Domain
p. xv, Ernest Hemingway - World History Archive/Alamy Stock Photo
p. xv, Langston Hughes - Underwood Archives/Contributor/Archive Photos/Getty Images
p. xv, Zora Neale Hurston - Archive Photos/Fotosearch/Stringer: Getty Images
p. 0, iStock.com/LordRunar
p. 1, Topical Press Agency/Hulton Archive/Getty Images
p. 2, Bettmann/Bettmann/Getty Images
p. 5, iStock.com/LordRunar
p. 6, LoraLiu/iStock.com
p. 7, Fotosearch/Archive Photos/Getty Images
p. 25, LoraLiu/iStock.com
p. 26, iStock.com/Orla
p. 27, iStock.com/Orla
p. 28, LoraLiu/iStock.com
p. 29, iStock.com/Blackbeck
p. 30, Public Domain Image
p. 33, iStock.com/Blackbeck
p. 34, iStock.com/urbancow
p. 35, iStock.com/urbancow
p. 36, iStock.com/LdF
p. 37, iStock.com/LdF
p. 38, iStock.com/Blackbeck
p. 39, iStock.com/Yuri_Arcurs
p. 43, Mondadori Portfolio/Mondadori Portfolio/Getty Images
p. 46, iStock.com/cristianl
p. 51, iStock.com/cristianl
p. 52, iStock.com/LdF
p. 53, iStock.com/LdF
p. 54, iStock.com/cristianl
p. 55, iStock.com/wragg
p. 60, iStock.com/SondraP
p. 70, iStock.com/Boogich
p. 72, Anthony Barboza/Archive Photos/Getty Images
p. 74, Library of Congress/Corbis Historical/Getty Images
p. 77, iStock.com/Boogich
p. 78, Alfred Eisenstaedt/Contributor/The LIFE Picture Collection/Getty Images
p. 79, Alfred Eisenstaedt/Contributor/The LIFE Picture Collection/Getty Images
p. 81, Peter Horree/Alamy Stock Photo
p. 83, Alfred Eisenstaedt/Contributor/The LIFE Picture Collection/Getty Images
p. 84, iStock.com/S. Greg Panosian
p. 92, ©iStock.com/DanBrandenburg
p. 93, Public Domain Image
p. 94, Public Domain Image
p. 95, Public Domain Image
p. 96, iStock.com/Gregory_DUBUS
p. 97, Hulton Archive/Archive Photos/Getty Images
p. 99, istock.com/LeoPatrizi
p. 103, iStock.com/margotpics
p. 108, iStock.com/margotpics
p. 109, iStock.com/ThomasVogel
p. 110, iStock.com/ThomasVogel
p. 111, iStock.com/fotogaby
p. 112, iStock.com/fotogaby
p. 113, iStock.com/Brostock
p. 114, iStock.com/Brostock
p. 115, iStock.com/margotpics
p. 116, iStock.com/Peeter Viisimaa
p. 120, iStock.com/Peeter Viisimaa
p. 121, iStock.com/urbancow
p. 122, iStock.com/urbancow
p. 123, iStock.com/Peeter Viisimaa
p. 124, iStock.com/hanibaram, iStock.com/seb_ra, iStock.com/Martin Barraud
p. 125, iStock.com/Martin Barraud
p. 129, Michael Ochs Archives/Michael Ochs Archives/Getty Images
p. 130, StudySync Graphic
p. 134, iStock.com/koya79
p. 137, iStock.com/Mutlu Kurtbas
p. 140, iStock.com/DNY59
p. 143, iStock.com/Martin Barraud
p. 150, iStock.com/SKrow
p. 152, iStock.com/horiyan
p. 154, iStock.com/tofumax
p. 156, iStock.com/me4o
p. 158, iStock.com/Martin Barraud
p. 160, iStock.com/Customdesigner
p. 162, ©iStock.com/wingmar
p. 164, ©iStock.com/Thomas Shanahan
p. 166, iStock.com/Martin Barraud

Please note that excerpts and passages in the StudySync® library and this workbook are intended as touchstones to generate interest in an author's work. The excerpts and passages do not substitute for the reading of entire texts, and StudySync® strongly recommends that students seek out and purchase the whole literary or informational work in order to experience it as the author intended. Links to online resellers are available in our digital library. In addition, complete works may be ordered through an authorized reseller by filling out and returning to StudySync® the order form enclosed in this workbook.

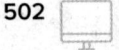

PHOTO/IMAGE CREDITS.

p. 169, iStock.com/scanrail, iStock.com/eyewave
p. 171, iStock.com/scanrail
p. 172, Lorraine Hansberry - BTJP1G, Everett Collection Inc/Alamy Stock Photo
p. 172, John Hersey - Everett Collection Historical/Alamy Stock Photo
p. 172, Langston Hughes - Underwood Archives/Contributor/Archive Photos/Getty Images
p. 172, Lyndon B. Johnson - Bettmann/Contributor/Bettmann/Getty
p. 172, Jack Kerouac -Bettmann/Contributor/Getty
p. 173, Martin Luther King Jr. - Bettmann/Contributor/Bettmann/Getty Images
p. 173, George Marshall - Culture Club/Contributor/Hulton Archive/Getty
p. 173, Arthur Miller - Bettmann/Contributor/Bettmann/Getty
p. 173, Aimee Nezhukumatahil - Used by permission of Aimee Nezhukumatathil.
p. 173, Flannery O'Connor - Apic/RETIRED/Contributor/Hulton Archive/Getty
p. 174, iStock.com/Pgiam
p. 176, Hulton Deutsch/Corbis Historical/Getty Images
p. 177, George Skadding/The LIFE Picture Collection/Getty Images
p. 178, Bettman/Bettman/Getty Images
p. 181, iStock.com/Pgiam
p. 182, iSock.com/RichLegg
p. 186, iStock.com/Anton_Sokolov
p. 202, iStock.com/Anton_Sokolov
p. 203, iStock.com/ValentinaPhotos
p. 205, iStock.com/ValentinaPhotos
p. 206, iStock.com/Orla
p. 207, iStock.com/Orla
p. 208, iStock.com/Anton_Sokolov
p. 209, ©iStock.com/kieferpix
p. 210, TASS/TASS/Getty Images
p. 211, Hulton Deutsch/Corbis Historical/Getty Images
p. 211, Fred Ramage/Hulton Archive/Getty Images
p. 215, ©iStock.com/kieferpix
p. 216, iStock.com/Brostock
p. 217, iStock.com/Brostock
p. 218, iStock.com/Caval
p. 220, iStock.com/Caval
p. 221, iStock.com/Murat Göçmen
p. 222, iStock.com/Murat Göçmen
p. 223, iStock.com/kieferpix
p. 224, iStock.com/Marius_Kempf
p. 228, iStock.com/alexeys
p. 231, iStock.com/poco_bw

p. 235, iStock.com/poco_bw
p. 236, iStock/Spanishalex
p. 237, iStock/Spanishalex
p. 239, iStock.com/Dominique_Lavoie
p. 239, iStock.com/Dominique_Lavoie
p. 240, iStock.com/poco_bw
p. 241, Matthew Abbott/Contributor/Moment/GettyImages
p. 242, Everett Collection Inc/Alamy Stock Photo
p. 245, UtCon Collection/Alamy Stock Photo
p. 247, Matthew Abbott/Contributor/Moment/GettyImages
p. 248, iStock.com/
p. 251, iStock.com/PeopleImages
p. 254, iStock.com/franny-anne
p. 255, Bettmann/Bettmann/Getty Images
p. 257, iStock.com/franny-anne
p. 258, iStock.com/peepo
p. 259, iStock.com/peepo
p. 260, iStock.com/Orla
p. 261, iStock.com/Orla
p. 262, iStock.com/janrysavy
p. 263, iStock.com/janrysavy
p. 264, iStock.com/franny-anne
p. 265, iStock.com/SonerCdem
p. 266, Boston Globe/Boston Globe/Getty Images
p. 269, iStock.com/Michael Warren
p. 279, iStock.com/Michael Warren
p. 280, iStock.com/ThomasVogel
p. 281, iStock.com/ThomasVogel
p. 282, iStock.com/pixhook
p. 283, iStock.com/pixhook
p. 284, iStock.com/antoni_halim
p. 285, iStock.com/antoni_halim
p. 286, iStock.com/Michael Warren
p. 287, iStock.com/hanibaram, iStock.com/seb_ra, iStock.com/Martin Barraud
p. 288, iStock.com/Martin Barraud
p. 296, iStock.com/gopixa
p. 298, iStock.com/fstop123
p. 301, iStock.com/Domin_domin
p. 303, iStock.com/Martin Barraud
p. 309, iStock.com/bo1982
p. 311, iStock.com/Jeff_Hu
p. 313, iStock.com/stevedangers
p. 315, iStock.com/Martin Barraud
p. 318, iStock.com/Fodor90
p. 320, ©iStock.com/wildpixel
p. 322, ©iStock.com/wildpixel
p. 324, iStock.com/
p. 326, iStock.com/Martin Barraud

PHOTO/IMAGE CREDITS:

p. 328, iStock.com/Nikada, iStock.com/eyewave
p. 330, iStock.com/DNY59
p. 331, iStock.com/Nikada
p. 332, Michael Arndt - Kevin Winter/Staff/Getty Images Entertainment
p. 332, Rita Dove - Getty Images Europe: Barbara Zanon/Contributor
p. 332, Louise Erdrich - Ulf Andersen/Contributor/Getty Images Entertainment
p. 332, Roxane Gay - Brandon Williams/Contributor/Getty
p. 332, Leslie Jamison - Photo credit: Adam Golfer
p. 332, Christine Kitano - Author Picture
p. 333, Rixhard Linklater - Vittorio Zunino Celotto/Staff
p. 333, Toni Morrison - Timothy Fadek/Contributor/Getty
p. 333, Naomi Shabib Nye - Roberto Ricciuti/Contributor/Getty Images Entertainment
p. 333, Dalia Rosenfeld - Used by permission of Dalia Rosenfeld
p. 333, Isabel Wilkerson - Boston Globe/Contributor/Boston Globe Collection/Getty
p. 333, August Wilson - Boston Globe/Contributor/Boston Globe/Getty Images
p. 334, iStock.com/andieymi
p. 337, AFP/AFP/Getty Images
p. 339, 20th Century Fox/Moviepix/Getty Images
p. 340, Matt Cardy/Getty Images News/Getty Images
p. 341, iStock.com/andieymi
p. 342, iStock.com/sudok1
p. 348, iStock.com/MoreISO
p. 352, iStock.com/ZargonDesign
p. 357, iStock.com/ZargonDesign
p. 358, iStock.com/Spanishalex
p. 359, iStock.com/Spanishalex
p. 360, iStock.com/
p. 361, iStock.com/
p. 363, iStock.com/ZargonDesign
p. 364, iStock.com/ortlemma
p. 376, iStock.com/ortlemma
p. 377, iStock.com/ValentinaPhotos
p. 378, iStock.com/ValentinaPhotos
p. 379, iStock.com/Bill Oxford
p. 380, iStock.com/Bill Oxford
p. 381, iStock.com/ortlemma
p. 382, iStock.com/diane39
p. 385, iStock.com/Poravute
p. 386, iStock/narvikk
p. 387, Jared Siskin/Patrick McMullan/Getty Images
p. 388, Michael Kovac/Getty Images Entertainment/Getty Images

p. 390, iStock.com/Poravute
p. 391, iStock.com/GaryAlvis
p. 397, iStock.com/BongkarnThanyakij
p. 398-402, From HYPERBOLE AND A HALF: Unfortunate Situations, Flawed Coping Mechanisms, Mayhem, and other Things that Happened by Allie Brosh. Copyright © 2013 by Alexandra Brosh. Reprinted with the permission of Touchstone, a division of Simon & Schuster, Inc. All rights reserved.
p. 403, iStock.com/Imagesrouges
p. 406, iStock.com/Imagesrouges
p. 407, iStock.com/Orla
p. 408, iStock.com/Orla
p. 409, iStock.com/Imagesrouges
p. 410, iStock.com/Jcomp
p. 415, iStock.com/Jcomp
p. 416, iStock.com/Hohenhaus
p. 417, iStock.com/Hohenhaus
p. 418, iStock.com/Jcomp
p. 419, iStock.com/kool99
p. 428, istock.com/Coquinho
p. 434, istock.com/_creativedot_
p. 437, iStock.com/221A
p. 438, Picturenow/Universal Images Group/Getty Images
p. 439, iStock.com/221A
p. 440, iStock.com/Andrey_A
p. 441, iStock.com/Andrey_A
p. 442, iStock.com/221A
p. 443, iStock.com/hanibaram, iStock.com/seb_ra, iStock.com/Martin Barraud
p. 444, iStock.com/Martin Barraud
p. 446, StudySync Image
p. 448, StudySync Image
p. 450, James D. Morgan/Getty Images News/Getty Images
p. 452, NBC Universal Archives
p. 457, iStock.com/BilevichOlga
p. 460, iStock.com/Mutlu Kurtbas
p. 463, iStock.com/
p. 466, iStock.com/DNY59
p. 468, iStock.com/Martin Barraud
p. 475, iStock.com/Jeff_Hu
p. 477, iStock.com/peepo
p. 480, iStock.com/tofumax
p. 484, iStock.com/polesnoy
p. 487, iStock.com/SasinParaksa
p. 490, iStock.com/Martin Barraud
p. 493, iStock.com/efks
p. 495, iStock.com/mooltfilm
p. 497, iStock.com/mooltfilm
p. 499, iStock.com/Martin Barraud

Please note that excerpts and passages in the StudySync® library and this workbook are intended as touchstones to generate interest in an author's work. The excerpts and passages do not substitute for the reading of entire texts, and StudySync® strongly recommends that students seek out and purchase the whole literary or informational work in order to experience it as the author intended. Links to online resellers are available in our digital library. In addition, complete works may be ordered through an authorized reseller by filling out and returning to StudySync® the order form enclosed in this workbook.

studysync

Text Fulfillment Through StudySync

If you are interested in specific titles, please fill out the form below and we will check availability through our partners.

ORDER DETAILS

Date:

TITLE	AUTHOR	Paperback/ Hardcover	Specific Edition *If Applicable*	Quantity

SHIPPING INFORMATION

Contact:
Title:
School/District:
Address Line 1:
Address Line 2:
Zip or Postal Code:
Phone:
Mobile:
Email:

BILLING INFORMATION ☐ SAME AS SHIPPING

Contact:
Title:
School/District:
Address Line 1:
Address Line 2:
Zip or Postal Code:
Phone:
Mobile:
Email:

PAYMENT INFORMATION

☐ **CREDIT CARD**

Name on Card:

Card Number: Expiration Date: Security Code:

☐ **PO**

Purchase Order Number:

StudySync Text Fulfillment, BookheadEd Learning, LLC
610 Daniel Young Drive | Sonoma, CA 95476